Lecture Notes in Computer Science 15401

Founding Editors

Gerhard Goos
Juris Hartmanis

Editorial Board Members

Elisa Bertino, *Purdue University, West Lafayette, IN, USA*
Wen Gao, *Peking University, Beijing, China*
Bernhard Steffen, *TU Dortmund University, Dortmund, Germany*
Moti Yung, *Columbia University, New York, NY, USA*

The series Lecture Notes in Computer Science (LNCS), including its subseries Lecture Notes in Artificial Intelligence (LNAI) and Lecture Notes in Bioinformatics (LNBI), has established itself as a medium for the publication of new developments in computer science and information technology research, teaching, and education.

LNCS enjoys close cooperation with the computer science R & D community, the series counts many renowned academics among its volume editors and paper authors, and collaborates with prestigious societies. Its mission is to serve this international community by providing an invaluable service, mainly focused on the publication of conference and workshop proceedings and postproceedings. LNCS commenced publication in 1973.

Anna Schroder · Xiang Li ·
Tanveer Syeda-Mahmood · Neil P. Oxtoby ·
Alexandra Young · Alessa Hering ·
Tejas S. Mathai · Pritam Mukherjee ·
Sven Kuckertz · Tiantian He ·
Isaac Llorente-Saguer · Andreas Maier ·
Satyananda Kashyap · Hayit Greenspan ·
Anant Madabhushi
Editors

Medical Image Computing and Computer Assisted Intervention – MICCAI 2024 Workshops

LDTM 2024, MMMI/ML4MHD 2024, ML-CDS 2024
Held in Conjunction with MICCAI 2024
Marrakesh, Morocco, October 6–10, 2024
Proceedings

Editors
Anna Schroder
University College London
London, UK

Tanveer Syeda-Mahmood
IBM Almaden Research Center
San Jose, CA, USA

Alexandra Young
University College London
London, UK

Tejas S. Mathai
National Institutes of Health
Bethesda, MD, USA

Sven Kuckertz
Fraunhofer MEVIS
Lübeck, Germany

Isaac Llorente-Saguer
University College London
London, UK

Satyananda Kashyap
IBM Research
San Jose, CA, USA

Anant Madabhushi
Emory University
Atlanta, GA, USA

Xiang Li
Massachusetts General Hospital
Somerville, MA, USA

Neil P. Oxtoby
University College London
London, UK

Alessa Hering
Radboud University Medical Center
Nijmegen, The Netherlands

Pritam Mukherjee
National Institutes of Health
Bethesda, MD, USA

Tiantian He
University College London
London, UK

Andreas Maier
Friedrich-Alexander-Universität
Erlangen-Nuremberg
Erlangen, Germany

Hayit Greenspan
Mount Sinai Hospital
New York, NY, USA

ISSN 0302-9743   ISSN 1611-3349 (electronic)
Lecture Notes in Computer Science
ISBN 978-3-031-84524-6   ISBN 978-3-031-84525-3 (eBook)
https://doi.org/10.1007/978-3-031-84525-3

© The Editor(s) (if applicable) and The Author(s), under exclusive license
to Springer Nature Switzerland AG 2025

This work is subject to copyright. All rights are solely and exclusively licensed by the Publisher, whether the whole or part of the material is concerned, specifically the rights of translation, reprinting, reuse of illustrations, recitation, broadcasting, reproduction on microfilms or in any other physical way, and transmission or information storage and retrieval, electronic adaptation, computer software, or by similar or dissimilar methodology now known or hereafter developed.
The use of general descriptive names, registered names, trademarks, service marks, etc. in this publication does not imply, even in the absence of a specific statement, that such names are exempt from the relevant protective laws and regulations and therefore free for general use.
The publisher, the authors and the editors are safe to assume that the advice and information in this book are believed to be true and accurate at the date of publication. Neither the publisher nor the authors or the editors give a warranty, expressed or implied, with respect to the material contained herein or for any errors or omissions that may have been made. The publisher remains neutral with regard to jurisdictional claims in published maps and institutional affiliations.

This Springer imprint is published by the registered company Springer Nature Switzerland AG
The registered company address is: Gewerbestrasse 11, 6330 Cham, Switzerland

If disposing of this product, please recycle the paper.

Preface of LDTM 2024

Our workshop on Longitudinal Disease Tracking and Modelling with Medical Images and Data (LDTM) was held in conjunction with the 27th International Conference on Medical Image Computing and Computer Assisted Intervention (MICCAI) in Marrakesh, Morocco on 10th October, 2024.

Clinical workflows are increasing data-driven. Medical data, including imaging, is routinely employed to track the progression of disease or to assess response to treatment. For example, patients with cancer are often followed up longitudinally using radiological imaging (e.g., CT/MR/PET) to identify and track lesions, and assess treatment response. Recent developments in AI and machine learning have shown promise in automating or improving parts of the clinical workflow, from being able to find lesions in various organs, to classification and diagnosis of diseases. Unfortunately, despite the key role of serial imaging in the clinical workflow, developing AI systems that can track or model disease progression by learning from and exploiting longitudinal imaging has not received much attention until recently. Besides their role in the everyday clinical workflow, such models can enhance biological understanding of diseases to shape prevention and intervention strategies, inform clinical trial design, and support clinical decision making, such as patient diagnosis and prognosis.

Submissions for the LDTM workshop were solicited on the theme of tracking and modeling disease progression with imaging and/or multimodal data. This volume contains papers that address several topics, such as longitudinal modeling and assessment of multiple sclerosis, co-registration of longitudinal liver exams for tumor assessment, growth predictions of lesions in longitudinal studies, modeling the trajectory of Alzheimer's disease, and tracking sub-trajectories in pathologies, among others.

The 9 full papers presented in this volume were reviewed and selected from 11 submissions using a double-blind review process. A total of 23 reviewers were involved in reviewing the papers, with an average of two reviews per paper.

December 2024

Anna Schroder
Neil P. Oxtoby
Alexandra Young
Tiantian He
Isaac Llorente-Saguer
Alessa Hering
Tejas S. Mathai
Pritam Mukherjee
Sven Kuckertz

Organization

Proceedings Chair

Anna Schroder — University College London, UK

Workshop Chairs

Tiantian He — University College London, UK
Alessa Hering — Radboudumc, The Netherlands
Sven Kuckertz — Fraunhofer MEVIS, Germany
Isaac Llorente-Saguer — University College London, UK
Tejas S. Mathai — National Institutes of Health, USA
Pritam Mukherjee — National Institutes of Health, USA
Neil P. Oxtoby — University College London, UK
Alexandra Young — University College London, UK

Preface of MMMI/ML4MHD 2024

On behalf of the organizing committee, we welcome you to the 5th International Workshop on Multiscale Multimodal Medical Imaging (MMMI 2024) and the 1st Workshop on Machine Learning for Multimodal/-sensor Healthcare Data (ML4MHD 2024), held in conjunction with the International Conference on Medical Image Computing and Computer-Assisted Intervention (MICCAI 2024) in Marrakech, Morocco. The workshop was organized by the combined efforts of the Friedrich-Alexander University Erlangen-Nuremberg and Massachusetts General Hospital.

The combined MMMI/ML4MHD workshop focused on advancing the rapidly growing field of multiscale multimodal medical imaging, where multiple imaging techniques or scales are used together to provide complementary information about medical conditions. With the recent developments in foundation models enabling integrated frameworks for multiple imaging modalities, the workshop aimed to advance both algorithmic development and methodological implementation while fostering collaboration between medical image analysis and machine learning experts. The workshop covered an array of diverse topics, including image segmentation, reconstruction techniques, registration methods, disease diagnosis, and novel radiomics methods, with particular emphasis on data fusion, multi-fidelity methods, and multi-source learning approaches.

The MMMI/ML4MHD workshop attracted 14 submissions this year, with each paper undergoing rigorous evaluation through a double-blind peer review process involving two independent reviewers and one Program Committee member. Based on review scores and committee feedback, 8 high-quality papers were selected for presentation and inclusion in the workshop proceedings. We extend our sincere gratitude to all Program Committee members and reviewers whose dedicated efforts helped maintain the workshop's high academic standards.

We are confident that this combined effort served as a valuable platform for researchers to share their latest findings, exchange innovative ideas, and forge new collaborations in the field of multimodal medical imaging and healthcare data analysis. The diverse range of accepted papers sparked engaging discussions and inspired future research directions in this rapidly evolving domain. The presentations and interactive sessions at Marrakech contributed to advancing our understanding of multiscale multimodal approaches in medical imaging and healthcare applications.

September 2024   MMMI/ML4MHD 2024 Workshop Chairs

Organization

General Chairs

Andreas Maier   Friedrich-Alexander University Erlangen-Nuremberg, Germany
Xiang Li   Massachusetts General Hospital, USA

Workshop Chairs

Bin Dong	Peking University, China
Daniel Rueckert	Technical University of Munich, Germany
Hao Chen	Hong Kong University of Science and Technology, China
Hui Ren	Massachusetts General Hospital, USA
Jinglei Lv	University of Sydney, Australia
Paula Andrea Perez-Toro	Friedrich-Alexander University Erlangen-Nuremberg, Germany
Quanzheng Li	Massachusetts General Hospital, USA
Richard M. Leahy	University of Southern California, USA
Tomas Arias-Vergara	Friedrich-Alexander University Erlangen-Nuremberg, Germany
Xiaoxiao Li	University of British Columbia, Canada
Yuankai Huo	Vanderbilt University, USA

Reviewers

Chang Liu	Friedrich-Alexander University Erlangen-Nuremberg, Germany
Cheng Chen	Massachusetts General Hospital, USA
Cheng Chen	Massachusetts General Hospital, USA
Fei Wu	Friedrich-Alexander University Erlangen-Nuremberg, Germany
Frauke Wilm	Friedrich-Alexander University Erlangen-Nuremberg, Germany
Hanqi Jiang	University of Georgia, Athens, USA

Jin Cheng	The Hong Kong University of Science and Technology, China
Laura Pfaff	Friedrich-Alexander University Erlangen-Nuremberg, Germany
Lina Felsner	Technical University of Munich, Germany
Luis Rivera Monroy	Friedrich-Alexander University Erlangen-Nuremberg, Germany
Mareike Thies	Friedrich-Alexander University Erlangen-Nuremberg, Germany
Maria A. Zuluaga	EURECOM, France
Mathias Öttl	Friedrich-Alexander University Erlangen-Nuremberg, Germany
Matthew Tivnan	Massachusetts General Hospital, USA
Noah Maul	Friedrich-Alexander University Erlangen-Nuremberg, Germany
Peng Shu	University of Georgia, USA
Saahil Islam	Siemens Healthineers, Germany
Sekeun Kim	Massachusetts General Hospital, USA
Stefan Ploner	Friedrich-Alexander University Erlangen-Nuremberg, Germany
Yiwei Li	University of Georgia, USA
Yixing Huang	Friedrich-Alexander University Erlangen-Nuremberg, Germany
Yiyang Zhang	South China University of Technology, China
Yongsheng Mei	George Washington University, USA
Yucheng Shi	University of Georgia, USA

Preface for ML-CDS 2024

On behalf of the organizing committee, we welcome you to the Workshop on Multimodal Learning and Fusion Across Scales for Clinical Decision Support (ML-CDS 2024) being held in person at MICCAI 2024 in Marrakesh, Morocco. This was the 13th edition of our workshop since 2009. Overall, the goal of this series of workshops has been to bring together medical image analysis and machine learning researchers with clinicians to tackle the important challenges of acquiring and interpreting multimodal medical data at multiple scales for clinical decision support and treatment planning, and to present and discuss the latest developments in the field.

The previous workshops on this topic have been well-received at MICCAI, specifically, Singapore (2022), Strasbourg (2021), Lima (2020), Shenzhen (2019), Granada (2018), Quebec City (2017), Athens (2016), Munich (2015), Nagoya (2013), Nice (2012), Toronto (2011), and London (2009). Continuing the momentum built by these workshops, this year's edition focused on integrating diagnostic imaging, pathology imaging, and genomic datasets for diagnosis and treatment planning and clinical decision support on a holistic basis.

All submissions underwent a double-blinded peer-review process, with each submission being reviewed by at least 2 independent reviewers. Based on the review scores and comments, 4 papers were accepted for presentation at the workshop, and they are included in this Springer LNCS volume. We would like to thank the authors for their submissions and all the Program Committee members for handling the submissions with professional judgements and constructive comments.

With fewer than 5% of medical image analysis techniques translating to clinical practice, workshops on this topic have helped raise the awareness of our field among clinical practitioners. The approach taken in the workshop was to scale it to large collections of patient data exposing interesting issues of multimodal learning and its specific use in clinical decision support by practicing physicians. The ultimate impact of these methods can be judged when they begin to affect treatment planning in clinical practice.

With the introduction of a clinical program at MICCAI 2024 as part of the main conference, and the appointment of clinical chairs, the goals of the workshop on spreading awareness of this topic within the MICCAI community have effectively been reached. We thank MICCAI for supporting the workshop through the years and look forward to another successful edition of the workshop in 2025.

November 2024

Tanveer Syeda Mahmood
Satyananda Kashyap
Hayit Greenspan
Annant Madabhushi

Organization

Program Chairs

Tanveer Syeda Mahmood	IBM Research, USA
Satyananda Kashyap	IBM Research, USA
Hayit Greenspan	Icahn School of Medicine at Mount Sinai, USA
Anant Madabhushi	Emory University, USA

Program Committee

Srinath Vanga	o9 Solutions, Inc, USA
Alexandros Karargyris	ML Commons, USA
Niharika S. D'Souza	IBM Research, USA
Yiming Chen	Massachusetts Institute of Technology, USA
Ken C. L. Wong	IBM Research, USA
Amarachi Blessing Madu	Virginia Tech, USA
Ehsan Degan	IBM Research, USA

Contents

LDTM Workshop

Disease Progression Modelling and Stratification for Detecting Sub-trajectories in the Natural History of Pathologies: Application to Parkinson's Disease Trajectory Modelling 3
  Alessandro Viani, Boris A. Gutman, Emile d'Angremont, and Marco Lorenzi

Back to the Future: Challenges of Sparse and Irregular Medical Image Time Series 15
  Nico Albert Disch, Robin Peretzke, Saikat Roy, Constantin Ulrich, David Zimmerer, Rainer Stiefelhagen, Jens Kleesiek, and Klaus Maier-Hein

Individualized Multi-horizon MRI Trajectory Prediction for Alzheimer's Disease 26
  Rosemary He, Gabriella Ang, and Daniel Tward

Towards Longitudinal Characterization of Multiple Sclerosis Atrophy Employing SynthSeg Framework and Normative Modeling 38
  Pedro M. Gordaliza, Nataliia Molchanova, Maxence Wynen, Pietro Maggi, Alessandro Cagol, Cristina Granziera, and Meritxell Bach Cuadra

SegHeD: Segmentation of Heterogeneous Data for Multiple Sclerosis Lesions with Anatomical Constraints 52
  Berke Doga Basaran, Xinru Zhang, Paul M. Matthews, and Wenjia Bai

Longitudinal Segmentation of MS Lesions via Temporal Difference Weighting 64
  Maximilian R. Rokuss, Yannick Kirchhoff, Saikat Roy, Balint Kovacs, Constantin Ulrich, Tassilo Wald, Maximilian Zenk, Stefan Denner, Fabian Isensee, Philipp Vollmuth, Jens Kleesiek, and Klaus Maier-Hein

Registration of Longitudinal Liver Examinations for Tumor Progress Assessment 75
  Walid Yassine, Martin Charachon, Céline Hudelot, and Roberto Ardon

Tracking Lesion Evolution Using a Boundary Enhanced Approach for MS
Change Segmentation (BEAMS) 88
  Prateek Mathur, Brendan S. Kelly, Ronan P Killeen, and Aonghus Lawlor

A Radiological-Based Coordinate System for the Human Body:
A Proof-of-Concept 101
  *Teresa M. T. Bucho, Thierry N. Boellaard, Mateus Taveira,
  Zuhir Bodalal, Thi D. L. Nguyen-Kim, Regina Beets-Tan,
  and Stefano Trebeschi*

MMMI-ML4MHD Workshop

Language Models Meet Anomaly Detection for Better Interpretability
and Generalizability 113
  *Jun Li, Su Hwan Kim, Philip Müller, Lina Felsner, Daniel Rueckert,
  Benedikt Wiestler, Julia A. Schnabel, and Cosmin I. Bercea*

A Diffusion Model Embedded WCSAU-Net for 3D MRI Brain Tumor
Segmentation 124
  Zizhen Ji, Rui Chen, Pinyu Qiu, Xiaoyong Fu, Sheng Li, and Jun Tan

Predicting Human Brain States with Transformer 136
  *Yifei Sun, Mariano Cabezas, Jiah Lee, Chenyu Wang, Wei Zhang,
  Fernando Calamante, and Jinglei Lv*

Cross-Modality Image Quality Prediction for Time-Resolved CT
from Breathing Signals 147
  *Annette Schwarz, Jannis Dickmann, Christian Hofmann,
  Juliane Szkitsak, Christoph Bert, Andreas Maier,
  and Tomás Arias-Vergara*

RATNUS: Rapid, Automatic Thalamic Nuclei Segmentation Using
Multimodal MRI Inputs 157
  *Anqi Feng, Zhangxing Bian, Blake E. Dewey, Alexa Gail Colinco,
  Jiachen Zhuo, and Jerry L. Prince*

HyperMM: Robust Multimodal Learning with Varying-Sized Inputs 170
  *Hava Chaptoukaev, Vincenzo Marcianó, Francesco Galati,
  and Maria A. Zuluaga*

HEMIT: H&E to Multiplex-Immunohistochemistry Image Translation
with Dual-Branch Pix2pix Generator 184
  Chang Bian, Beth Phillips, Tim Cootes, and Martin Fergie

Physics-Informed Latent Diffusion for Multimodal Brain MRI Synthesis 198
   Sven Lüpke, Yousef Yeganeh, Ehsan Adeli, Nassir Navab,
   and Azade Farshad

ML-CDS Workshop

MedPromptX: Grounded Multimodal Prompting for Chest X-Ray
Diagnosis 211
   Mai A. Shaaban, Adnan Khan, and Mohammad Yaqub

Predicting Stroke Through Retinal Graphs and Multimodal Self-supervised
Learning 223
   Yuqing Huang, Bastian Wittmann, Olga Demler, Bjoern Menze,
   and Neda Davoudi

Multimodality for Diagnosis of Asian Choroidal Vasculopathy: Results
from a Novel Dataset and Deep-Learning Experiments 235
   Daehyun Cho, Young Ho Kim, Somin Ahn, Jaeryung Oh,
   and Christian Wallraven

Multimodality Frequency Feature Customized Learning for Pediatric
Ventricular Septal Defects Identification 248
   Feifei Jin, Cheng Zhao, Peng Yang, Zhuo Xiang, Xunyi Chen, Yu Zhang,
   Shumin Fan, Luyao Zhou, Weiling Chen, Tianfu Wang, and Baiying Lei

Author Index 261

LDTM Workshop

LTM Workshop

Disease Progression Modelling and Stratification for Detecting Sub-trajectories in the Natural History of Pathologies: Application to Parkinson's Disease Trajectory Modelling

Alessandro Viani[1]($\boxtimes$), Boris A. Gutman[2], Emile d'Angremont[3], and Marco Lorenzi[1]

[1] Epione Research Team, Inria Center of Université Côte d'Azur, Sophia Antipolis, France
`alessandro.viani@inria.fr`
[2] Department of Biomedical Engineering, Illinois Institute of Technology, Chicago, USA
[3] Department of Anatomy and Neurosciences, Amsterdam University Medical Center, Amsterdam, The Netherlands

Abstract. Modelling the progression of Degenerative Diseases (DD) is essential for detection, prevention, and treatment, yet it remains challenging due to the heterogeneity in disease trajectories among individuals. Factors such as demographics, genetic conditions, and lifestyle contribute to diverse phenotypical manifestations, necessitating patient stratification based on these variations. Recent methods like Subtype and Stage Inference (SuStaIn) have advanced unsupervised stratification of disease trajectories, but they face potential limitations in robustness, interpretability, and temporal granularity. To address these challenges, we introduce Disease Progression Modelling and Stratification (DP-MoSt), a novel probabilistic method that optimises clusters of continuous trajectories over a long-term disease time-axis while estimating the confidence of trajectory sub-types for each biomarker. We validate DP-MoSt using both synthetic and real-world data from the Parkinson's Progression Markers Initiative (PPMI). Our results demonstrate that DP-MoSt effectively identifies both sub-trajectories and sub-populations, and is a promising alternative to current state-of-the-art models.

Keywords: Disease Progression Modelling · Expectation Maximisation · Parkinson Disease

1 Introduction

Modelling the progression of Degenerative Diseases (DD) is crucial for detection, prevention, and treatment purposes [9]. This task is challenging due the generally large heterogeneity of disease trajectories observed across subjects. Despite a common degenerative process, the manifestation of symptoms and the configuration of biomarkers may vary widely among individuals, due for example to demographics, genetics conditions and life-style [17]. For this reason researchers are steering their attention towards the problem of *patients stratification* based on phenotypical manifestations of the disorder [4].

Typical disease progression modelling approaches generally focus on estimating long-term biomarkers evolution from short-term patients observation. For instance, the Gaussian Process Progression Model (GPPM) [8] and the Personalized Input-Output Hidden Markov Model [14] characterise the transition of biomarkers over time from normal to pathological stages, based on the assumption of an underlying disease trajectory defined by an absolute time axis. On the other hand, other approaches focus on the detection of sub-populations, for example biomarkers values [21] or genetic observations [16].

In the last decade, innovative methodologies have attempted to automatically stratify sub-types of disease trajectories. SuStaIn is a popular unsupervised method detecting sub-populations and their respective trajectories within a given dataset of patients and control population [18–20]. SuStaIn has been demonstrated in a variety of applications, showing its ability to identify sub-populations exhibiting common patterns of biomarkers changes [1,22]. Nevertheless, from an analytical perspective, SuStaIn presents some relevant limitations in terms of robustness and interpretability. First, disease progression is described as a discrete series of events, which limits the interpretability and temporal granularity of the estimated trajectories. Second, SuStaIn assumes the existence of cutoff values optimising separation between disease stages across biomarkers; the assumptions behind this statistical construct (e.g. Gaussian) are non-necessarily realistic about the biomarkers distribution across stages, and may negatively affect the robustness of the clustering task. Third, SuStaIn does not directly quantify the uncertainty in whether each biomarker exhibits a distinct trajectory between subtypes. For example, although certain biomarkers may not be discriminating between sub-types, SuStaIn will attempt at estimating group-specific cutoff values which may lead to poor interpretability and generalisation of the results. Finally, SuStain is designed to model cross-sectional information, without accounting for the temporally correlated nature of patients' time-series. Recent extensions of SuStain (t-SuStaIn) [18], attempt to overcome this latter limitation by accounting for multiple measures per subjects. However, this approach still presents the above mentioned limitations, as it relies on the estimation of sequences of events occurring in a discrete space.

Disease Course Mapping (DCM) [12] is an orthogonal approach to SuStain, in which continuous parametric disease trajectories are optimized by accounting for patient's random effects represented by time-warp functions. DCM was recently extended to account for mixture of trajectories (MM-DCM) [11]. However, the mixture model there proposed assumes that all biomarkers' trajectories should be split into sub-progressions. This approach thus does not allow uncertainty quantification of the split across biomarkers, and ultimately does not account for the specificity of certain biomarkers in characterising disease sub-types.

To address these limitations, in this paper we present Disease Progression Modelling and Stratification (DP-MoSt), a novel probabilistic method to identify differential disease progression trajectories in heterogeneous cohorts. DP-MoSt relies on the optimisation of clusters of continuous trajectories across a long-term disease time-axis, while also estimating the confidence for the existence of trajectories sub-types for each biomarker.

We validate our model on both synthetic and real-world data from the Parkinson's Progression Markers Initiative (PPMI) [2]. Our results show that our model is a promising alternative to the state-of-the-art, effectively identifying sub-trajectories and sub-populations, while providing interpretable and clinically meaningful solutions.

The manuscript is structured as follows: in Sect. 2.1 we introduce DP-MoSt, and in Sect. 2.2 we describe the optimisation procedure and the statistical assumptions. In Sect. 3.1 we present results on a panel of synthetic benchmarks, and in Sect. 3.2 we provide a comparison between DP-MoSt and SuStaIn on clinical data from the PPMI database.

2 Disease Progression Modelling and Stratification Model

In this section, we provide the mathematical details of DP-MoSt, by describing the underlying statistical assumptions along with the associated optimization procedure.

2.1 Model Definition

DP-MoSt is based on the optimization of two complementary problems: (i) estimating an absolute long-term disease time axis from short-term observations, and (ii) identifying along this disease time axis the existence of sub-populations with respective sub-trajectories.

Considering problem (i), for each individual j we define the observations across all biomarkers as $\boldsymbol{x}^j = (\boldsymbol{x}_b^j)_{b=1}^{B}$; where $\boldsymbol{x}_b^j = (\boldsymbol{x}_b^j(\tilde{t}_1), \dots, x_1^j(\tilde{t}_{k_j}))$ and B is the number of biomarkers. Without loss of generality, for notational convenience, we assume that the sampling times are common among all subjects and biomarkers. To map the individual observations to a common disease time scale, we parameterize the individual time axis via a translation by a time-shift $\delta \tilde{t}_j$, i.e. $\boldsymbol{t}_j = \tilde{t}_{1:k_j} + \delta \tilde{t}_j$. In this work, we evaluate the time shifts relying on the Gaussian process theory of GPPM [8], which is based on the monotonic description of biomarkers trajectories from normal to pathological stages.

Considering problem (ii), given the measured observations $\boldsymbol{x} = \boldsymbol{x}^{1:J}$, where J is the number of subjects, and the estimated absolute time $\boldsymbol{t} = \boldsymbol{t}_{1:J}$, we define a trajectory mixture model to identify the existence of sub-populations.

To achieve our goal, we assume that the evolution of each biomarker b can be split into multiple sub-trajectories with probability ξ_b ($b = 1, \ldots, B$). Once a sub-trajectory is considered, we assume that each subject j is issued from this trajectory with probability π_j ($j = 1, \ldots, J$). We observe that both $\xi = (\xi_b)_1^B$ and $\pi = (\pi_j)_1^J$ are independent with respect to time. This allows our model to link information deriving from longitudinal data; we also note that the probability for a subject belonging to one sub-trajectory must be consistent across all the biomarkers.

To simplify the inference process, compatibly with the monotonic assumption of GPPM, we adopt a parametric approach for the disease trajectories assuming that biomarkers follow increasing sigmoidal functions over time. We furthermore assume that the given measures are perturbed by additive Gaussian noise with standard deviation $\sigma = (\sigma_b)_{b=1}^B$. Given the assumptions above, the posterior distribution for our model can be written as:

$$p(\theta, \sigma, \xi, \pi \mid x) \propto p(\theta, \sigma, \xi, \pi) \prod_{j,b} p(x_b^j \mid \theta_b, \sigma_b, \xi_b, \pi_j) \tag{1}$$

where for simplicity we omitted the conditioning on the time points. We observe that Eq. (1) implicitly assumes independence between the unknown parameters as well as independence between different subjects and biomarkers.

We can rewrite the equation by expanding the likelihood function in order to highlight the two-level mixture model formulation. In this setting, a first level deals with the sub-trajectory discovery task, while a second one determines the probability of a subject to belong to the sub-trajectory:

$$p(x \mid \theta, \sigma, \xi, \pi) = \prod_{j,b} \Big[p(x_b^j \mid \theta_b^0, \sigma_b)\xi_b + \Big(\pi_j p(x_b^j \mid \theta_b^1, \sigma_b) + (1 - \pi_j) p(x_b^j \mid \theta_b^2, \sigma_b) \Big)(1 - \xi_b) \Big], \tag{2}$$

where $p(x_b^j \mid \theta_b^i, \sigma_b) = \prod_{\ell=1}^{k_j} \text{NormPDF}\left(x_b^j(t_\ell), f(t_\ell \mid \theta_b^i), \sigma_b\right)$ due to the assumption of additive Gaussian noise, and $f(t_\ell \mid \theta_b^i)$ is a Sigmoid function with parameters θ_b^i evaluated at t_ℓ.

2.2 Two-Levels Expectation-Maximization

Model (1) accounts for a substantial number of parameters. For each biomarker it includes: three parameters for each of the three Sigmoid functions $\theta_b^{0:2}$; the noise parameters σ_b; the probability for the existence of sub-trajectories ξ_b; and the membership probabilities for each subject π. To limit the computational cost, we focus on Maximum a Posteriori (MAP) estimation through Expectation Maximisation (EM), exploiting the two-levels mixture nature of the model:

$$\hat{\theta}, \hat{\xi}, \hat{\pi}, \hat{\sigma} = \arg\max \ \ln(p(\theta, \sigma, \xi, \pi \mid \boldsymbol{x}))$$
$$= \arg\max \ \ln(p(\boldsymbol{x} \mid \theta, \sigma, \xi, \pi)) + \beta \sum_b \xi_b - \beta_N \sum_b \left(\ln(\sigma_b) + \frac{1}{\sigma_b}\right). \tag{3}$$

We rely on the following prior assumptions:

- $p(\theta) \propto 1$ and $p(\pi) \propto 1$ as improper uniform prior for the Sigmoid parameters and sub-population subdivision in order to encode lack of information;
- $p(\sigma) = \prod_b p(\sigma_b)$, where $p(\sigma_b)$ is an Inv-Gamma distribution of shape parameter $\beta_N - 1$ and scale parameter $\beta_N > 1$ as classical prior distribution for the noise standard deviation [3] in order to penalise small values;
- $p(\xi) = \prod_b p(\xi_b)$, where $p(\xi_b)$ is a Laplace distribution [7] of location 1 and scale parameter $1/\beta$ restricted to the interval $[0, 1]$, as regularisation term for penalising the introduction of a sub-trajectory to prevent overfitting.

DP-MoSt is designed to provide interpretable progression dynamics: first, we estimate the parameters for the continuous biomarkers trajectories; second, we estimate the probability for each biomarker to present sub-trajectories; finally, we estimate for each subject its probability to belong to each sub-population.

3 Results

In this section, we validate the model on two different experimental scenarios[1]: first, we demonstrate the effectiveness of the method in identifying sub-trajectories and sub-populations on an extensive synthetic benchmark; second, we apply the model to the real data from the PPMI dataset, comparing the solution to state-of-the-art solutions as provided by SuStaIn. The decision to validate only the clustering component of the model stems from the fact that the time-shift is assessed using GPPM, whose effectiveness has already been proven.

3.1 Experiment on Synthetic Data

Data Generation. We analyze the performance of DP-MoSt on the task of sub-trajectories and sub-populations identification by evaluating its performances across increasing levels of data complexity. This involves altering both the number of biomarkers and the Signal to Noise Ratio (SNR) [5] between sub-trajectories. Specifically, we consider three different sets of biomarkers with $B = 2, 5, 10$ and assess performance under three distinct SNR conditions: low, normal, and high. This systematic variation allows us to test the robustness and accuracy of our model across a range of realistic scenarios of increasing difficulty.

For each configuration, we generate 100 datasets with the following parameters:

---

[1] The code for DP-MoSt can be found at https://github.com/alessandro-viani/DP-MoSt.git.

- $J = 100$ subjects
- $k_{1:J} = 1$, i.e. one time point for each subject, randomly sampled in $[0, 20]$.
- $\sigma_b = 0.5$ to ensure a reasonable amount of noise in the data.
- Three fixed thresholds (low = 0.1, normal = 0.5, and high = 1) for the Mean Squared Error (MSE) between sub-trajectories to achieve a controlled SNR.
- Half of the biomarkers exhibit sub-trajectories (in the case of 5 biomarkers, 3 of them show the split).
- Equal partitioning of subjects between sub-populations.
- Parameters for the Sigmoid function describing the biomarker trajectories are randomly sampled from Gaussian distributions with parameters ensuring a positive supremum and rate of growth.

Model Setup. For each simulated dataset, we evaluate the parameters of the model described by Eq. (1) using the EM method described in Sect. 2.2.

We initialize the model as follows to avoid local maxima for the posterior distribution:

- set $\xi_b = 0.5$ and $\pi_j = 0.5$, assuming a complete lack of information on the sub-trajectories and sub-population probabilities;
- Initialize the noise standard deviation as the standard deviation of the data;
- randomly select the parameters for the Sigmoid functions from Gaussian distributions ensuring to provide a positive rate of growth and supremum;
- Set the prior parameters β and β_N as the 15% of the number of subjects; this choice ensures effective regularisation while maintaining the values within a reasonable range.

Performance Metrics. To validate the proposed method, we use different metrics to evaluate the error in parameter approximations. For evaluating the error on the biomarker trajectories, we employ the Optimal Subpattern Assignment (OSPA) metric [13,15]; this metric is particularly suitable because it accounts for potential differences in the number of true and estimated configurations. The OSPA metric measures the minimum MSE between the actual configuration of Sigmoids and the estimated one:

$$\text{OSPA}(\theta, \hat{\theta}) = \min_{\phi} \sum_{i=1}^{\min\{\hat{d},d\}} \frac{1}{N} \sum_{j}^{N} \left\| f(t_j \mid \hat{\theta}_i) - f(t_j \mid \theta_{\phi(i)}) \right\|_2^2 \quad (4)$$

where $\hat{\theta}$ and $\hat{d}$ represent the estimated parameters and number of sub-trajectories, respectively; θ and d denote the true values of the parameters; and the symbol ϕ represents all possible permutations.

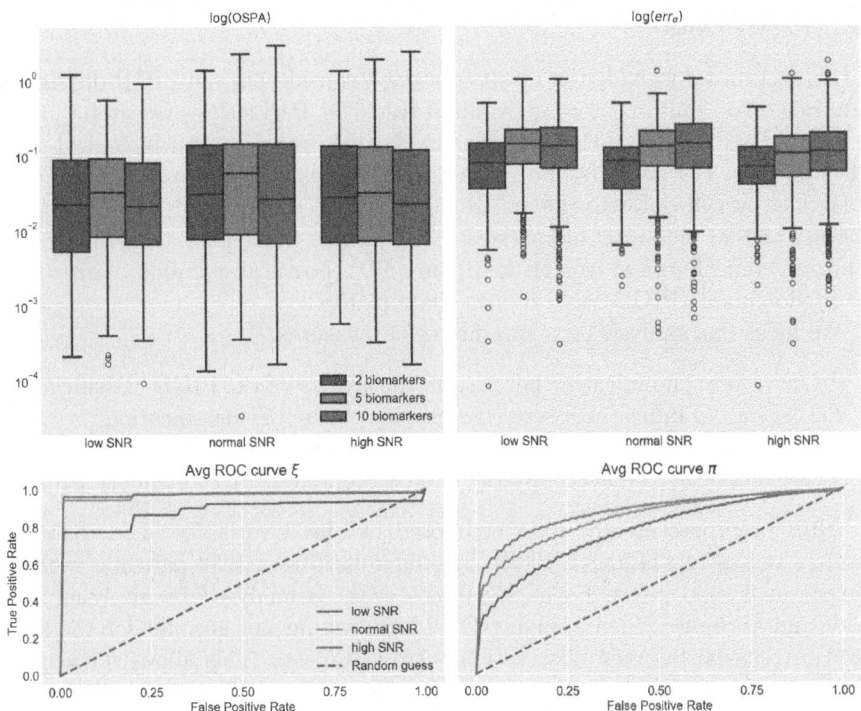

Fig. 1. The figure shows performance metrics obtained on synthetic data. In the first row we show the OSPA error for the trajectories approximation and the error on the noise standard deviation; in the second row we show the ROC curves respectively for trajectory and individual clustering, as identified by parameters ξ and π.

Results. The obtained results are summarised in Fig. 1, where we show:

- First Panel, First Row: the logarithm of the OSPA error subdivided by the number of features considered and SNR levels. We observe that variations in data complexity do not significantly impact the trajectory approximation; indeed the error remains roughly constant over different data configurations.
- Second Panel, First Row: the logarithm of the relative error on the noise standard deviation subdivided by the number of features considered and SNR levels. We can observe that the approximation error for the noise std increases with the data complexity.
- First/Second Panel, Second Row: the ROC curve for the parameters ξ and π. We observe that the method performs better in estimating the number of sub-trajectories compared to the estimation of sub-populations, probably due to the fewer number of parameters to be estimated.

3.2 PPMI Data

In this section we provide the results obtained considering the PPMI dataset, a comprehensive, multi-center longitudinal study for Parkinson's research.

The PPMI dataset includes extensive clinical, imaging, and biological data collected from PD patients, individuals with PD risk factors, and healthy controls. The overall data considered in this work is composed of a total of 3559 patients and 93 measured biomarkers. Each patient is labelled according to the following clinical scores: tremor-dominant (TD), postural instability gait disorder predominant (PIGD), and intermediate [2,10].

We focus our analysis on a specific set of measures:

– *PIGD_score*: an indicator that asserts the gravity of the PIGD classification;
– *TD_score*: an indicator asserts the gravity of the TD classification;
– *MCATOT*: the total amount of Montreal Cognitive Assessment scores [6];
– *NP2PTOT* & *NP3PTOT*: are the total score of MDS-UPDRS part 2 and 3.

After preprocessing the data composed by the 5 variables of interest, we obtain a dataset including 10198 longitudinal data from 1954 patients, with an average of 5 time points for each subject. Data is analysed by applying DP-MoSt and SuStain. When applying DP-MoSt, we did not account for the temporal correlation between observations across subjects. This allows for a more fair comparison with SuStAin, where data are treated disregarding temporal dependency.

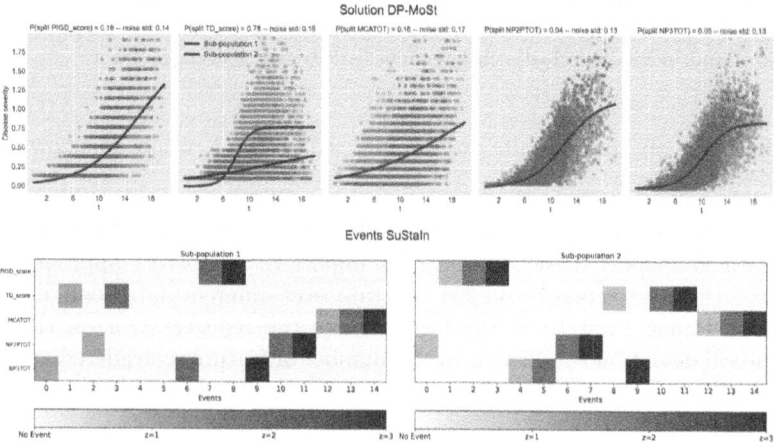

Fig. 2. The figure shows the results obtained on the PPMI dataset. The first row shows the results obtained with DP-MoSt: (sub-)trajectories are represented as solid coloured lines, and subjects are colour-coded based on their estimated subgroups. The second row shows the event progression estimated by SuStaIn as two coloured matrices, one for each sub-population.

SuStaIn Setup. SuStaIn estimates the maximum likelihood (ML) solution for the number of sub-types in the dataset as well as the associated sequence of events (i.e., stages of severity increase). Based on previous works, we decided to implement the z-score SuStaIn with three different progression stages associated to the quartiles (z_1, z_2, z_3) and 100000 MCMC steps.

DP-MoSt Setup. We assess DP-MoSt by considering the same parameter values as for the experiment on synthetic data (Sect. 3.1). However, differently from the synthetic experiment in which we evaluated solely the clustering step of our method, we also optimise individual time-shift parameters, establishing an absolute time axis for the disease progression.

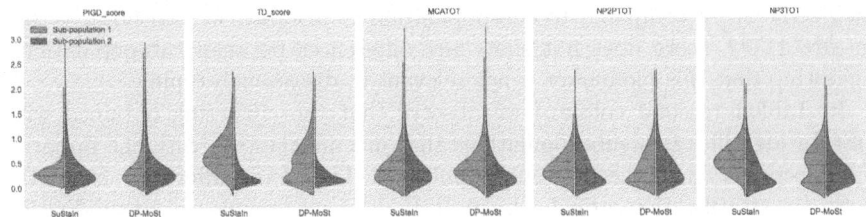

Fig. 3. The figure shows the distribution for the biomarker values across the two different sub-populations detected by SuStaIn and DP-MoSt, where we highlight the quartiles of the distributions as dotted lines.

Results. In Fig. 2 (first row) we show the solution for DP-MoSt, representing biomarker trajectories as solid lines with respect to the absolute time axis for disease progression (in years), and subjects as dots colour-coded based on their estimated sub-group. We observe that there is one clinical score that primarily governs the split into two sub-groups ($\xi_b > 0.5$): the *TD_score*. The two sub-groups that result from this split show a clear subdivision with respect to *TD_score* values: sub-population 1 is associated with higher values for this biomarker compared to sub-population 2, with a clear differentiation of trajectories after t = 6 years on the reparameterized time axis. We also observe that, in spite of the split identified for the *TD_score* trajectory, the progressions of the other clinical scores do not exhibit clear partitioning in sub-trajectories ($\xi_b < 0.5$). This aspect is illustrated in Fig. 3 where, besides the *TD_score*, the clinical scores' distributions between sub-populations show a substantial overlap. We finally note that, due to the continuous nature of DP-MoSt trajectories, the resulting clinical scores' distributions can be multi-modal, as they describe the entire disease history across pathological stages (e.g. *TD_score* in Sub-population 1). This is less evident for SuStAin (Fig. 3, left panels), which enforces a stronger separation between distributions across sub-groups, probably due to the discrete assumption for the events ordering.

In Table 1 (first column), we show the distribution of subjects into different sub-populations based on their label available at the last visit (Intermediate, PIGD, TD). We can observe that the sub-trajectories identified by DP-MoSt are respectively associated to subjects labeled as TD and PIGD, providing a clinically meaningful partitioning of the subjects. More specifically, DP-MoSt associates to sub-population 1 the majority of TD subjects (76%) and to sub-population 2 the majority of PIGD subjects (62%). The subjects labelled as Intermediate are not clearly assigned into any specific sub-population, probably because of their mixed composition.

In Fig. 2 (second row) we show the solution identified by SuStaIn as two coloured matrices, one for each sub-population, indicating the event ordering for each biomarker. SuStaIn identifies 2 sub-populations, with sub-population 1 characterised by a faster increase of the *TD_score* and a slower change of the *PIGD_score* compared to sub-population 2. Notably, we can observe that the *MCATOT* score does not show any differences between sub-populations, suggesting that this biomarker is not relevant to disease sub-typing.

In Table 1 (second column) we observe that the clustering obtained with SuStaIn identifies two sub-populations that are unbalanced, with the majority of subjects (72%) in the first sub-population. Therefore, differently from DP-MoSt, the stratification provided by SuStaIn does not provide a clear subdivision between clinical groups, substantially including the majority of subjects into the first sub-population.

Table 1. The Table shows the subdivision between different sub-populations considering solution provided by DP-MoSt and SuStaIn.

Condition	DP-MoSt		SuStaIn	
	Sub-pop 1	Sub-pop 2	Sub-pop 1	Sub-pop 2
Intermediate	0.56	0.44	0.84	0.16
PIGD	0.38	**0.62**	0.78	0.22
TD	**0.76**	0.24	0.48	0.52
N°% data	56%	44%	72%	28%

4 Conclusions

In this paper, we introduced DP-MoSt, an innovative probabilistic method for identifying continuous biomarker trajectories and stratifying sub-populations in the context of DPMs. DP-MoSt addresses key limitations of current state-of-the-art methods by ensuring interpretability and robustness through a two-level mixture model that captures sub-population clusters while incorporating temporal information from longitudinal data. Additionally, DP-MoSt provides uncertainty quantification for both sub-trajectories and sub-population composition, enabling the characterization of pathological trajectory patterns.

We validated the model's performance with synthetic data, demonstrating its effectiveness. Furthermore, its application to the PPMI dataset yielded interpretable and clinically relevant results; this feature can be due to the continuous formulation of DP-MoSt, improving the model's reliability and interpretability.

It is important to observe that SuStaIn provides an estimation of the number of sub-populations, a feature currently not included in DP-MoSt. However, we note that the introduction of multiple sub-populations with their respective sub-trajectories may also be obtained with DP-MoSt: this primarily involves more complex notation and higher computational costs, and is one of the improvements that will be implemented in future work.

Overall, DP-MoSt's ability to capture detailed sub-population characteristics makes it a promising tool for analysing heterogeneous disease progression patterns in longitudinal studies.

Acknowledgments. This work has been supported by the Michael J. Fox Foundation for Parkinson's Research (MJFF), and to the French government, through the 3IA Côte d'Azur Investments in the Future project managed by the National Research Agency (ANR) with the reference number ANR-19-P3IA- 0002, by the TRAIN project ANR-22-FAI1-0003-02, and by the ANR JCJC project Fed-BioMed 19-CE45-0006-01. Data used in the preparation of this article were obtained on 05/01/2024 from the Parkinson's Progression Markers Initiative (PPMI) database.

Disclosure of Interests. The authors have no competing interests to declare that are relevant to the content of this article.

References

1. Aksman, L.M., et al.: pysustain: a python implementation of the subtype and stage inference algorithm. SoftwareX **16**, 100811 (2021)
2. Aleksovski, D., Miljkovic, D., Bravi, D., Antonini, A.: Disease progression in Parkinson subtypes: the PPMI dataset. Neurol. Sci. **39**, 1971–1976 (2018). https://link.springer.com/article/10.1007/s10072-018-3522-z
3. Calvetti, D., Hakula, H., Pursiainen, S., Somersalo, E.: Conditionally gaussian hypermodels for cerebral source localization. SIAM J. Imag. Sci. **2**(3), 879–909 (2009)
4. Greenland, J.C., Williams-Gray, C.H., Barker, R.A.: The clinical heterogeneity of Parkinson's disease and its therapeutic implications. Eur. J. Neurosci. **49**(3), 328–338 (2019)
5. Johnson, D.H.: Signal-to-noise ratio. Scholarpedia **1**(12), 2088 (2006)
6. Julayanont, P., Nasreddine, Z.S.: Montreal cognitive assessment (MOCA): concept and clinical review. In: Larner, A.J. (ed.) Cognitive Screening Instruments, pp. 139–195. Springer, Cham (2017). https://doi.org/10.1007/978-3-319-44775-9_7
7. Kaban, A.: On Bayesian classification with Laplace priors. Pattern Recogn. Lett. **28**(10), 1271–1282 (2007)
8. Lorenzi, M., Filippone, M., Frisoni, G.B., Alexander, D.C., Ourselin, S., Initiative, A.D.N., et al.: Probabilistic disease progression modeling to characterize diagnostic uncertainty: application to staging and prediction in alzheimer's disease. Neuroimage **190**, 56–68 (2019)

9. Mould, D.: Models for disease progression: new approaches and uses. Clin. Pharmacol. Ther. **92**(1), 125–131 (2012)
10. Pötter-Nerger, M., et al.: Serum neurofilament light chain and postural instability/gait difficulty (PIGD) subtypes of Parkinson's disease in the mark-PD study. J. Neural Transm. **129**(3), 295–300 (2022)
11. Poulet, P.-E., Durrleman, S.: Mixture modeling for identifying subtypes in disease course mapping. In: Feragen, A., Sommer, S., Schnabel, J., Nielsen, M. (eds.) IPMI 2021. LNCS, vol. 12729, pp. 571–582. Springer, Cham (2021). https://doi.org/10.1007/978-3-030-78191-0_44
12. Schiratti, J.B., Allassonnière, S., Colliot, O., Durrleman, S.: A Bayesian mixed-effects model to learn trajectories of changes from repeated manifold-valued observations. J. Mach. Learn. Res. **18**(133), 1–33 (2017)
13. Schuhmacher, D., Vo, B.T., Vo, B.N.: A consistent metric for performance evaluation of multi-object filters. IEEE Trans. Signal Process. **56**(8), 3447–3457 (2008). https://doi.org/10.1109/TSP.2008.920469
14. Severson, K.A., Chahine, L.M., Smolensky, L., Ng, K., Hu, J., Ghosh, S.: Personalized input-output hidden Markov models for disease progression modeling, pp. 309–330 (2020)
15. Viani, A., Luria, G., Bornfleth, H., Sorrentino, A.: Where Bayes tweaks gauss: conditionally gaussian priors for stable multi-dipole estimation. arXiv preprint arXiv:2006.04141 (2020)
16. Whitwell, J.L., et al.: Neuroimaging signatures of frontotemporal dementia genetics: C9orf72, tau, progranulin and sporadics. Brain **135**(3), 794–806 (2012)
17. Yang, E., et al.: Quantifying the pathophysiological timeline of Alzheimer's disease. J. Alzheimers Dis. **26**(4), 745–753 (2011)
18. Young, A.L., Aksman, L.M., Alexander, D.C., Wijeratne, P.A., Initiative, A.D.N.: Subtype and stage inference with timescales. In: Frangi, A., de Bruijne, M., Wassermann, D., Navab, N. (eds.) Information Processing in Medical Imaging. IPMI 2023. LNCS, vol. 13939, pp. 15–26. Springer, Cham (2023). https://doi.org/10.1007/978-3-031-34048-2_2
19. Young, A.L., et al.: Uncovering the heterogeneity and temporal complexity of neurodegenerative diseases with subtype and stage inference. Nat. Commun. **9**(1), 4273 (2018)
20. Young, A.L., et al.: Ordinal sustain: subtype and stage inference for clinical scores, visual ratings, and other ordinal data. Front. Artif. Intell. **4**, 613261 (2021)
21. Zhang, X., Mormino, E.C., Sun, N., Sperling, R.A., Sabuncu, M.R., Yeo, B.T., Initiative, A.D.N.: Bayesian model reveals latent atrophy factors with dissociable cognitive trajectories in Alzheimer's disease. Proc. Natl. Acad. Sci. **113**(42), E6535–E6544 (2016)
22. Zhou, C., et al.: Two distinct trajectories of clinical and neurodegeneration events in Parkinson's disease. NPJ Parkinson's Dis. **9**(1), 111 (2023)

Back to the Future: Challenges of Sparse and Irregular Medical Image Time Series

Nico Albert Disch[1,2,3]( )[iD], Robin Peretzke[1,8][iD], Saikat Roy[1,3][iD], Constantin Ulrich[1,8][iD], David Zimmerer[1,2][iD], Rainer Stiefelhagen[5], Jens Kleesiek[6,7][iD], and Klaus Maier-Hein[1,4][iD]

[1] Division of Medical Image Computing, German Cancer Research Center, Heidelberg, Germany
[2] HIDSS4Health - Helmholtz Information and Data Science School for Health, Karlsruhe, Heidelberg, Germany
[3] Faculty of Mathematics and Computer Science, University of Heidelberg, Heidelberg, Germany
nico.disch@dkfz-heidelberg.de
[4] Pattern Analysis and Learning Group, Department of Radiation Oncology, Heidelberg University Hospital, Heidelberg, Germany
[5] Karlsruhe Institute of Technology, Karlsruhe, Germany
[6] Institute for Artificial Intelligence in Medicine (IKIM), University Hospital Essen, Essen, Germany
[7] Cancer Research Center Cologne Essen (CCCE), University Hospital Essen, West German Cancer Center Essen, Essen, Germany
[8] Medical Faculty Heidelberg, University of Heidelberg, Heidelberg, Germany

Abstract. In longitudinal medical image analysis, most work focuses on regularly sampled images, or on tasks like regression or classification. However, in the clinical context, images are frequently generated irregularly due to factors such as cost constraints. This work tackles the problem of irregularly sampled longitudinal medical imaging by evaluating methods in segmentation and reconstruction tasks. We examine the reconstruction for real-life MRI from patients with Alzheimer's Disease (AD), where the model predicts future MRI scans from an arbitrary number of input images sampled at irregular intervals. However, experiments show that most models cannot surpass the performance of using an image from the same patient at a different time point as a baseline. Therefore, we conducted experiments on a synthetic dataset to better isolate effects in temporal learning. These experiments offer insights into model behavior and serve as a benchmark for validating models' longitudinal learning capability, thus providing a straightforward method to assess temporal understanding in a controlled environment.

Keywords: Irregular Longitudinal Medical Imaging · State Space Models · Attention · Neural Processes · Benchmarks · Metrics

1 Introduction

The integration of AI has led to significant changes in the medical field, as discussed in Anaya et al. [1]. However, these advances still do not match human analysis in many medical contexts. For example, tumor boards require expert evaluation of patient histories and across various modalities, as discussed in [14,15]. In particular, longitudinal medical images suffer from *temporal sparseness and irregularity*, because patients receive scans on demand, and acquisition periods can span months or even years. This challenge hinders the development of automatic disease forecasting, limiting the potential to emulate the human expertise in critical settings like tumor boards. Although significant progress has been made in related tasks, as discussed in Cascarano et al. [3], several approaches address only specific aspects of this challenge. Rubanova et al. [18] use NeuralODEs, introduced by Chen et al. [4], to model irregularly sampled time series and classification on electronic health records, while Li et al. [12] focuses on multimodal longitudinal nodule classification. Other methods simplify the problem by treating irregular sequences as regular, or by ignoring temporal differences (Zhang et al. [19], Elazab et al. [5]). Using NeuralODEs, Lachinov et al. [11] proposed a model to predict longitudinal segmentation masks. Their focus is on atrophy growth prediction, but only from a single image. Despite their relative success, such simplifications limit their applicability, given the prevalence of irregularities in medical image time series. One study that can handle sparse and irregular images is from Sauty et al. [2], where longitudinal Variational Autoencoders (l-VAEs) were used for image reconstruction for MRI and PET of AD patients. In addition to image reconstruction, they predict age and disease onset from these images. Gaussian Processes, classically used to model irregular time series, have been generalized as Neural Processes (NPs) by Garnelo et al. [7] in order to also model higher dimensional distributions, such as images. Inspired by the use of skip connections in the successful U-Net by Ronneberger et al. [17], these NPs were extended by Petersen et al. [16], where they developed continuous-time models for predicting glioblastoma segmentations. They achieved this using attention as skip connections.

Our main contributions are as follows; We show that current approaches struggle to accurately model patient trajectories under conditions such as time irregularity, and highly varying growth parameters, although these models show great performance on their respective tasks and datasets. Our findings reveal the poor performance of these models or the inadequacy of basic metrics, since simple random image is not credibly surpassed. We show models can significantly decrease losses and respective metrics, but comparisons with simple heuristics makes their efficacy appear worse. Furthermore, due to the limitations of experiments with real-life data, we have employed a simple synthetic benchmark to systematically test for these failures. Albeit simple and not novel in themselves, these experiments allow us to control the experimental parameters and identify which characteristics are challenging for each method. We note that similar synthetic experiments should be used as a simple baseline. While the synthetic experiments have shown some promise, their results are highly dependent on

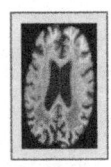 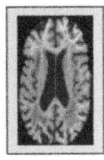 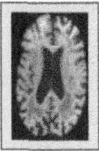 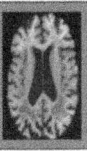

Fig. 1. Conceptual problem statement, predicting a target image given variable amount of input images at various times. The arrow signifies the progression of time. Yellow circles are context time points with their respective image. Red point is the query time, i.e. the time we would like the model to generate the image or segmentation, and the respective image is the target image. So for all models the input consists of context times and images, as well as an query time. In practice this query time is arbitrary. (Color figure online)

particular experimental conditions. In addition, there are still performance differences between models designed specifically for longitudinal imaging even in dense prediction tasks. Finally, we emphasize the critical need to establish more comprehensive longitudinal medical benchmarks and metrics that are specifically tailored to detect changes in longitudinal imaging in order to lay the groundwork for the development of new models for this task.

2 Methods

In this work we compare four different methods. In Fig. 2, a summary of the networks in use is shown. We note that for all models, the encoder, decoder and the bottleneck are the same, except for the l-VAE, where instead of a summation, a pre-defined geodesic function is implemented in the bottleneck.

Longitudinal VAE The two simpler models are Neural Processes and longitudinal VAE. The l-VAE is a VAE, where the bottleneck function consists of a geodesic function (see [2]). By using a predefined geodesic, the l-VAE has a strong inductive bias towards the disease trajectory. We use the l-VAE for the AD experiments. **Neural Processes** In general, NPs can generally have multiple architectural designs, but as is commonly done [7]. For this work, we define an NP as an encoder decoder architecture with a summation of input representations at the bottleneck (at S_4). Since the NP is flexible enough to learn the underlying distribution, in the case of time series a trajectory, we chose it for the synthetic experiments, rather than the l-VAE where the trajectory is chosen beforehand and not learned. **Attentive Segmentation Process (ASP)** We adapt the approach of Petersen et al. [16], and keep the same configuration, where S_0, S_1 are temporal attention blocks, and S_2, S_3 are temporal-spatial attention blocks, and S_4 involves the summation of representations, followed by a concatenation of the context and target time point. Thus, the upper two layers compute the attention over input representations and time. The lower two layers compute

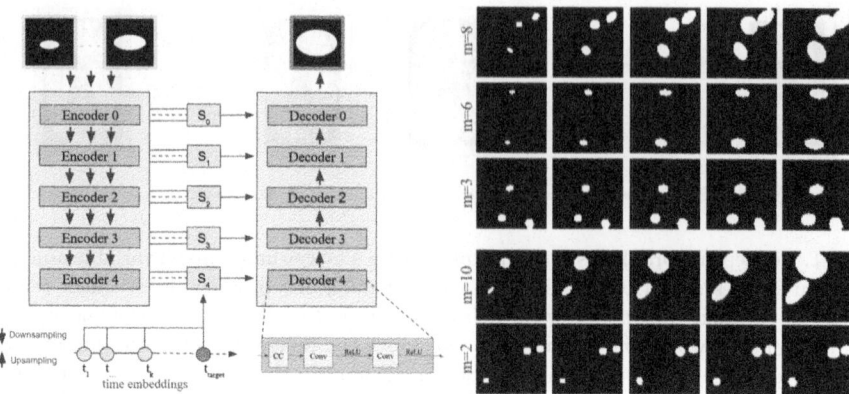

Fig. 2. Left: Basic network architecture overview: Squares with yellow borders are input images. The square with the red border is the target image. t_i with $i \in \{1,\ldots,k\}$ are the input times, and t_{target} is the target, i.e. query, time. Green boxes are the skip links of the respective model. The gray boxes are encoder and decoder, with the blue boxes being the building boxes. These building blocks are described on the lower right. The orange box (S_4) is the bottleneck function, for Mamba and ASP it is a summation, for l-VAE it is a sigmoidal geodesic. CC stands for concatenation of coordinates. The blue box on the bottom right shows the operations within the decoder and encoder blocks. Right: example images from the synthetic experiments. The upper three rows correspond to experiments 0-4. The last two rows show minimum and maximum growth examples of experiment 5. (Color figure online)

the attention over spatial and temporal dimensions, providing more expressiveness. The bottom layer contains a summation of input representations. Further implementation details are given in [16]. We note, however, that due to the use of the attention mechanism, this model struggles with scalability when extended to $3D + t$ data. **Mamba Blocks on Skip Connections:** Due to the scaling problem of ASP in the attention skip layers, and the recent success of Mamba, first introduced by Gu et al. [8], we adapt ASP using Mamba for the skip connections. In medical image segmentation, U-Mamba by Ma et al. [13] has had recent success. They employ the Mamba block within the nnU-Net framework [6]. We follow a similar approach to convert the image into a sequence. Before applying the Mamba block, we sum up all input representations to make the input representations into the same shape as the output representations. We use this summation from S_0 to S_3 and keep S_4 the same as the NP. The notable difference to the ASP is, that our adaption only uses the image representations, whereas the ASP combines image representations context time representations and target time representations using attention.

3 Experiments

3.1 Data

Alzheimer Data. For the real-life MRI reconstruction task, the Alzheimer's Disease Neuroimaging Initiative (ADNI) dataset is used, accessible at https://adni.loni.usc.edu/. This dataset includes patients with AD, and its longitudinal nature makes it ideal for modeling longitudinal trajectories in medical imaging. It is important to note that we use the ADNI data for methodological validation and *do not aim to specifically or exclusively* model AD. Our preprocessing pipeline involves converting DICOM images using plastimatch, followed by registration to the MNI space using flirt [10], and brain extraction using HD-BET [9]. We select patients with a confirmed diagnosis of AD, resulting in a cohort of 270 patients with a total of 870 T1-weighted images. We normalize the images and the time offsets per patient.

Synthetic Data. In this dataset we artificially generate objects to test the limitations of the different methods. A closer explanation of the data generation can be found in 1. The objects within these images are intentionally kept simple to better isolate and analyze the causal effects. This approach simplifies detecting failures in trajectory prediction. This predefined setting also allows us to adjust the difficulty of experiments. For example, we can change the number of context time points, determine whether our context time is regular, and alter the apparent shape of the object to be segmented or the number of shapes. As we will see in the results, these experiments range from being almost solved, to being outperformed by using the last available previous image as a predictor. For simplicity, we consider only segmentations as targets. For these experiments, we have a batch size of 32 and $1k$ iterations per epoch. We train for 100 epochs.

3.2 Experimental Setting

Experimental Notation. We define $k \geq 2$ as the context times of the same patient or object. We denote the context times t as $t_1, \ldots t_k$ with each corresponding image $I_1, \ldots I_k$, and an arbitrary target time t_{target}. The model receives context time and context image, as well as query time. For the AD experiments, I_i are T1 images, and in the synthetic experiments, binary ellipses. We denote experiments, or more precisely time series, as regular if the difference between time points constant; otherwise they are *irregular*. In experiments where the network is prevented from using time information, we refer to these as *masked time points*.

Reconstruction. For the AD dataset, we focus on image reconstruction. In the experiments, we choose 2 context times and one target time, removing the need to bootstrap timepoints for most patients. Due to constraints of ASP, we choose a single 2D slice of each patient, with the same view, the offset of the slice is randomly varying. For completion we note here that using randomly all three views randomly decreases performance but does not change the overall picture.

Segmentation. For the synthetic experiments, the focus is exclusively on predicting masks, not on image generation. For most experiments we have $k = 4$ and a single target time. Our study considers *normalized time*, where $t_0 = 0$ and $t \in [0, 1]$. More details can be found in the appendix.

4 Results and Discussion

4.1 Reconstruction Experiments

First, we consider experiments on MRI reconstruction. To estimate the extent to which these models explicitly use temporal information, we train each model twice; once with explicit time, and once with a masked input time, i.e., where no time information available during training and inference. For this experiment, we consider arbitrary time points for reconstruction, i.e., the target time can be any of the possible input times, and the input times are then two other time points of the recorded patient. This is slightly different from the clinical task of disease forecasting from real images. These experiments serve to establish a preliminary performance baseline for the methods.

Table 1. Quantitative results with all of the models. With time means that the models receive the relative time input, as opposed to *masked time*. We compare the three models, as well as inserting a random input image I_i, for $i \in [k]$, and compare all metrics between I_i and the target image I_{target}.

Model	Time	$MSE(10^{-2})\downarrow$	$LPIPS\downarrow$	$PSNR\uparrow$	$SSIM(10^{-2})\uparrow$
ASP	✓	**3.199** (0.126)	**5.74** (1.66)	**34.50** (0.38)	**47.40** (3.62)
	x	**3.221** (0.143)	6.32 (3.04)	**34.44** (0.42)	46.98 (5.43)
l-VAE	✓	4.955 (0.005)	14.65 (0.05)	30.06 (0.01)	27.78 (0.03)
	x	4.982 (0.024)	14.91 (0.05)	29.99 (0.03)	27.50 (0.10)
Mamba skip	✓	3.435 (0.016)	5.82 (0.22)	33.78 (0.04)	45.95 (0.29)
	x	3.436 (0.024)	5.87 (0.19)	33.80 (0.05)	45.77 (0.36)
Random I_i	x	3.839	**3.43**	32.69	**47.41**

To better understand model performance, we compare the results to a random input image from the respective time series as a basic benchmark (Random I_i). As shown in 1 for each model the performance with and without explicit time input to the model is compared. We see that **including explicit temporal information does not improve the models' ability to predict changes over time** in patient MRI scans. This suggests that the models themselves either *capture the necessary temporal details from the images* or that the changes over time for the specific diseases being studied are *too subtle for the models to learn effectively*. For this task, these models, as currently designed, cannot explicitly use temporal information for medical image inputs. Furthermore, insufficient data pre-processing, particularly in registration, may have prevented the models from capturing the changes effectively. Additionally, the constraint of low input size and the reduction to two dimensions could have further impacted their efficacy. These results, therefore, raise questions about the optimal methods for evaluating model performance and the most appropriate metrics to use. Metrics such as MSE and PSNR are heavily biased towards pixel-wise similarities, while LPIPS and SSIM focus on higher-level information. The failure of the models to significantly outperform a random image I_i underscores the importance of thoroughly investigating model behavior. Consequently, we will investigate synthetic experiments to further analyze model behavior with respect to experimental settings.

4.2 Synthetic Object Segmentation

The generation of the object is described in Algorithm 1, with the parameters given in Table 2. For all the following experiments, we use 4 context times. Table 3 shows experiments, roughly ordered by difficulty, to facilitate visual comparison. We highlight a number of compelling results.

Table 2. Parameters for the synthetic experiments. The results are shown in Table 3. The nomenclature is the same as in Algorithm 1. N is the number of objects, *growth* is the growth rate, *shear* is the shear of the ellipses, *start* is the minimum size of the object, *time* indicates whether the time points are irregular and whether they are masked. *Var* means that the growth is uniformly sampled from the interval, *Fixed* means the objects have a fixed growth rate.

ID	Shape	N	Growth (m)	start	shear (s)	time
0	Ellipse	[1,4]	Var ($m \in [3,8]$)	[4,6]	[0,3,1.0]	regular
1	Circle	[1,4]	Var ($m \in [3,8]$)	[4,6]	1	irregular
2	Ellipse	[1,4]	Fixed ($m = 6$)	[4,6]	[0,3,1.0]	irregular
3	Ellipse	[1,4]	Var ($m \in [3,8]$)	[4,6]	[0,3,1.0]	regular & masked
4	Ellipse	[1,4]	Var ($m \in [3,8]$)	[4,6]	[0,3,1.0]	irregular
5	Ellipse	[1,3]	Var ($m \in [2,10]$)	[3,8]	[0.3,1.3]	irregular

Irregular Time Series Pose a Bigger Challenge. Given that ASP performs significantly better than I_k for experiments 0-4, we conclude that ASP can generally learn this task. Mamba does not perform as well, suggesting that we may need temporal information within the skip connections rather than just using image representations. However, the comparison of experiment 0 and 2 suggests that irregular time is more challenging than regular time with various growth patterns. We want to mention that for increasing amounts of context time points, the task becomes *easier*, because the difference between target and

Table 3. Dice score values (%) of synthetic experiments. I_k represents the dice score between the previous input image and the target image, averaged over more than 2k random object generation runs for comparison. The rounded brackets are the standard deviation for the models over 3 runs. The resolution is 64 × 64. The exact values for each parameter can be found in Table 2. For shorthand, we will denote each experiment by an *ID*, which can be interpreted as a *relative difficulty*. * time is *masked*. ** See Table 2 for differences.

ID	Shape	Growth	Time	NP	Mamba	ASP	I_k
0	Ellipse	Var ($m \in [3,8]$)	reg	76.66 (0.75)	81.47 (0.76)	**94.32 (0.57)**	84.98
1	Circle	Var ($m \in [3,8]$)	irreg	84.81 (0.83)	84.87 (1.12)	**90.36 (0.08)**	85.33
2	Ellipse	Fixed ($m = 6$)	irreg	83.42 (2.92)	86.41 (0.51)	**89.29 (0.31)**	83.38
3*	Ellipse	Var ($m \in [3,8]$)	reg * 0	76.89 (0.88)	80.67 (2.46)	**90.27 (0.14)**	84.98
4**	Ellipse	Var ($m \in [3,8]$)	irreg	84.90 (0.84)	84.50 (0.97)	**89.87 (0.30)**	84.98
5**	Ellipse	Var ($m \in [2,10]$)	irreg	73.84 (1.99)	76.42 (1.62)	83.62 (0.34)	**86.26**

last context time decreases. For example, in experiment 5, the dice score of I_k is [41.25, 71.09, 81.41, 86.28, 89.26], for 1 to 5 context time points respectively.

Even Simple Experiments are Challenging Enough for Models in their Current State. Experiment 5 shows that for some parameters, the experiments are too challenging for the models. This indicates that these synthetic experiments are useful for assessing how well models perform in the longitudinal setting. Compare this to experiment 4, where some settings are the same, but only the parameters are different. Furthermore, while the experiments seem simple, they are not *solved*. And for experiments 0-4, Mamba and NP can only solve one task beyond the dice score of I_k. The performance of the two models is poor in experiments 0 and 3.

The Previous Segmentation or Image is a Strong Baseline. In Table 1, the random image baseline achieves competitive results in most metrics. Table 3 shows that the segmentation of the previous time point has a high dice score. In experiment 5 I_k surpasses even all of the networks. This has two implications: First, the similarity *between I_k and I_{target} should serve as a simple baseline*. Interestingly, none of the models learn the shortcut of I_k for every experiment, cf. experiment 5. Second, evaluating the *dice score based on the difference between I_k and I_{target}* could provide insights into the amount of change between time points. Alternatively, this difference could indicate how much models are able to learn beyond just the last image.

5 Conclusion and Further Work

While existing methods address some challenges of longitudinal medical imaging, our work highlights opportunities for improvement. Both the real-world and simple synthetic experiments, reveal limitations of current models and metrics.

The latter offer a simple benchmark for evaluating future approaches. We hope our benchmark insights will contribute to advancements in the field addressing this problem. Furthermore, we address the need to develop metrics tailored to longitudinal imaging.

Declarations. The authors have no conflicts of interest to declare that are relevant to the content of this article.

Acknowledgements. The present contribution is supported by the Helmholtz Association under the joint research school "HIDSS4Health - Helmholtz Information and Data Science School for Health.

A Qualitative Images

Here we show some qualitative images from the synthetic experiments. The figures show the growth overlaid, between minimal and maximal examples. I.e., the maximal growth and minimal growth. The generation of the synthetic data is described in 1, the parameters for the ellipses in 2.

Algorithm 1 Syntehtic Object generation

1: $m \leftarrow$ UniformRNG(range) ▷ growth rate
2: $N \leftarrow$ RandomInteger(range) ▷ Number of objects
3: Obj $\leftarrow$ Empty array
4: **for** $j \leftarrow 0$ to N **do**
5: $\quad x, y \leftarrow$ RandomInteger(range) ▷ x and y offset
6: $\quad start \leftarrow$ UniformRNG(range) ▷ start size
7: $\quad s \leftarrow$ UniformRNG(0.3, 1.0) ▷ shear for ellipse
8: $\quad \phi \leftarrow$ UniformRNG($-\pi$, π) ▷ random rotation
9: $\quad$ **for** t in $t_0, \ldots, t_k$ **do**
10: $\quad\quad$ Obj $\leftarrow$ Obj $\cup$ DrawEllipse(x, y, $start + t \cdot m \cdot s$, $start + t \cdot m$, ϕ)

B Further Experimental Details

Here we note further additional experimental results. We use the popular deep learning library of Pytorch. The code itself is adapted from the ASP model from [16]. We train for 100 epochs, with 1000 iterations per epoch. Learning rate is $1e-4$ with a cosine learning rate scheduler. We note that higher learning rates lead to higher probability of model collapse during training, especially with ASP. We use data augmentation for the image domain. We use commonly used augmentations such as spatial, elastic, mirror, brightness, gamma, gaussian noise and blurring with a probability of 0.15.

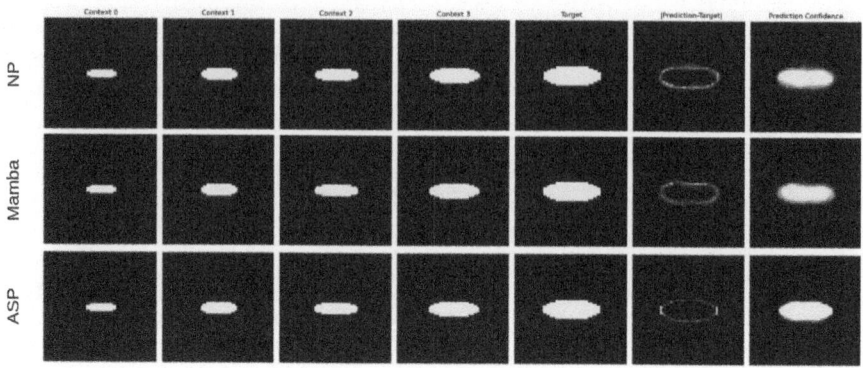

Fig. 3. Simple target sequence, with the three models [$ASP, Mamba, NP$]. The left 4 images are the context images, the fifth image is the target. The sixth is the difference between target and model prediction, and the last image in the column is the model prediction. Despite being simple, all of the models show non perfect prediction. The image is centered and without rotation, with a growth of 9.

References

1. Anaya-Isaza, A., Mera-Jiménez, L., Zequera-Diaz, M.: An overview of deep learning in medical imaging. Inform. Med. Unlocked **26**, 100723 (2021). https://doi.org/10.1016/j.imu.2021.100723
2. Sauty, B., Durrleman, S.: Progression models for imaging data with longitudinal variational auto encoders. In: Wang, L., Dou, Q., Fletcher, P.T., Speidel, S., Li, S. (eds.) Medical Image Computing and Computer Assisted Intervention – MICCAI 2022: 25th International Conference, Singapore, September 18–22, 2022, Proceedings, Part I, pp. 3–13. Springer Nature Switzerland, Cham (2022). https://doi.org/10.1007/978-3-031-16431-6_1
3. Cascarano, A., Mur-Petit, J., Hernández-González, J., Camacho, M., de Toro Eadie, N., Gkontra, P., Chadeau-Hyam, M., Vitrià, J., Lekadir, K.: Machine and deep learning for longitudinal biomedical data: a review of methods and applications. Artif. Intell. Rev. **56**(S2), 1711–1771 (2023). https://doi.org/10.1007/s10462-023-10561-w
4. Chen, R.T., Rubanova, Y., Bettencourt, J., Duvenaud, D.K.: Neural ordinary differential equations. **6** (2018). http://arxiv.org/abs/1806.07366
5. Elazeb, A., et al.: GP-GAN: brain tumor growth prediction using stacked 3D generative adversarial networks from longitudinal MR Images. Neural Netw. **132**, 321–332 (2020). https://doi.org/10.1016/j.neunet.2020.09.004
6. Isensee, F., Jaeger, P.F., Kohl, S.A.A., Petersen, J., Maier-Hein, K.H.: nnU-Net: a self-configuring method for deep learning-based biomedical image segmentation. Nature Methods **18**(2), 203–211 (2021). https://doi.org/10.1038/s41592-020-01008-z
7. Garnelo, M., et al.: Neural Processes **7** (2018). http://arxiv.org/abs/1807.01622
8. Gu, A., Dao, T.: Mamba: Linear-Time Sequence Modeling with Selective State Spaces. Technical report. https://github.com/state-spaces/mamba

9. Isensee, F., et al.: Automated brain extraction of multisequence MRI using artificial neural networks. (2019). https://doi.org/10.1002/hbm.24750, https://onlinelibrary.wiley.com/doi/10.1002/hbm.24750
10. Jenkinson, M., Bannister, P., Brady, M., Smith, S.: Improved optimization for the robust and accurate linear registration and motion correction of brain images. NeuroImage **17**(2), 825–841 (2002). https://doi.org/10.1006/nimg.2002.1132
11. Lachinov, D., Chakravarty, A., Grechenig, C., Schmidt-Erfurth, U., Bogunovic, H.: Learning spatio-temporal model of disease progression with neuralodes from longitudinal volumetric data. IEEE Trans. Med. Imag. XX (1), 2023. https://doi.org/10.1109/TMI.2023.3330576. http://adni.loni.usc.edu/
12. Li, T.Z., et al.: Longitudinal multimodal transformer integrating imaging and latent clinical signatures from routine ehrs for pulmonary nodule classification. LNCS (including subseries Lecture Notes in Artificial Intelligence and Lecture Notes in Bioinformatics), pp. 649–659 ISSN: 16113349. https://doi.org/10.1007/978-3-031-43895-0_61, https://link.springer.com/chapter/10.1007/978-3-031-43895-0_61
13. Ma, J., Li, F., Wang, B.: U-Mamba: Enhancing Long-range Dependency for Biomedical Image Segmentation. Technical report. https://wanglab.ai/u-mamba.html
14. Mano, M.S., çitaku, F.T., Barach, P.: Implementing multidisciplinary tumor boards in oncology: a narrative review. Future Oncol. **18**(3), 375–384 (2022). https://doi.org/10.2217/fon-2021-0471
15. Okasako, MSN, FNP-BC, RN, AOCNP, J., Bernstein, MSN, FNP-BC, RN, C.: Multidisciplinary tumor boards and guiding patient care: the AP role. J. Adv. Practitioner Oncol. **13**(3), 227–230 (2022). https://doi.org/10.6004/jadpro.2022.13.3.9
16. Petersen, J., et al.: Continuous-time deep glioma growth models. In: de Bruijne, M., Cattin, P.C., Cotin, S., Padoy, N., Speidel, S., Zheng, Y., Essert, C. (eds.) Medical Image Computing and Computer Assisted Intervention – MICCAI 2021: 24th International Conference, Strasbourg, France, September 27–October 1, 2021, Proceedings, Part III, pp. 83–92. Springer International Publishing, Cham (2021). https://doi.org/10.1007/978-3-030-87199-4_8
17. Ronneberger, O., Fischer, P., Brox, T.: U-net: Convolutional networks for biomedical image segmentation. Lecture Notes in Computer Science (including subseries Lecture Notes in Artificial Intelligence and Lecture Notes in Bioinformatics), 9351: 234–241, 2015. ISSN 16113349https://doi.org/10.1007/978-3-319-24574-4_28/COVER
18. Rubanova, Y., Chen, R.T., Duvenaud, D.K.: Latent ODEs for Irregularly-Sampled Time Series. 7 2019. http://arxiv.org/abs/1907.03907
19. Zhang, L., et al.: Spatio-temporal convolutional LSTMs for tumor growth prediction by learning 4D longitudinal patient data. IEEE Trans. Med. Imag. **39**(4), 1114–1126 (2020). https://doi.org/10.1109/TMI.2019.2943841

Individualized Multi-horizon MRI Trajectory Prediction for Alzheimer's Disease

Rosemary He[1,2]⬤, Gabriella Ang[1]⬤, Daniel Tward[2,3(✉)]⬤, and for the Alzheimer's Disease Neuroimaging Initiative

[1] Departments of Computer Science, University of California, Los Angeles, USA
[2] Departments of Computational Medicine, University of California, Los Angeles, USA
[3] Departments of Neurology, University of California, Los Angeles, USA
DTward@mednet.ucla.edu

Abstract. Neurodegeneration as measured through magnetic resonance imaging (MRI) is recognized as a potential biomarker for diagnosing Alzheimer's disease (AD), but is generally considered less specific than amyloid or tau based biomarkers. Due to a large amount of variability in brain anatomy between different individuals, we hypothesize that leveraging MRI time series can help improve specificity, by treating each patient as their own baseline. Here we turn to conditional variational autoencoders to generate individualized MRI predictions given the subject's age, disease status and one previous scan. Using serial imaging data from the Alzheimer's Disease Neuroimaging Initiative*, we train a novel architecture to build a latent space distribution which can be sampled from to generate future predictions of changing anatomy. This enables us to extrapolate beyond the dataset and predict MRIs up to 10 years. We evaluated the model on a held-out set from ADNI and an independent dataset (from Open Access Series of Imaging Studies). By comparing to several alternatives, we show that our model produces more individualized images with higher resolution. Further, if an individual already has a follow-up MRI, we demonstrate a usage of our model to compute a likelihood ratio classifier for disease status. In practice, the model may be able to assist in early diagnosis of AD and provide a counterfactual baseline trajectory for treatment effect estimation. Furthermore, it generates a synthetic dataset that can potentially be used for downstream tasks such as anomaly detection and classification.

Keywords: Conditional VAE · Disease progression · Alzheimer's Disease

---

Data used in preparation of this article were obtained from the Alzheimer's Disease Neuroimaging Initiative(ADNI) database https://adni.loni.usc.edu/. As such, the investigators within the ADNI contributed to the design and implementation of ADNI or provided data but did not participate in analysis or writing of this report. A complete listing of ADNI investigators can be found at: https://adni.loni.usc.edu/wp-content/uploads/how/_to/_apply/ADNI/_Acknowledgement/_List.pdf.

1 Introduction

1.1 Background

Neurodegeneration as observed in magnetic resonance imaging (MRI) is recognized as a potential biomarker for diagnosing Alzheimer's disease (AD) [13]. While MRI has the advantage of being noninvasive, it is generally considered not specific enough, unlike biomarkers of amyloid or tau [14]. The potential for using machine learning approaches ("data-driven statistical approaches in which many different brain regions are evaluated simultaneously" [2]) has been recognized. However, an important challenge in making diagnoses from brain images is the large amount of interpersonal variability, compared to minor structural changes in the earliest stages of the disease such as the transentorhinal stage (Braak stage I and II) [5]. We hypothesize that this issue can be overcome by carefully modeling timeseries of imaging data, allowing each person to be compared to their own baseline, rather than to a population average.

1.2 Related Work

One strategy for timeseries analysis in brain imaging is to quantify structural changes using the diffeomorphism group [4]. After defining an appropriate metric, geodesics can be computed to study changes over time [7,27,29]. More recently, deep learning has been applied to model disease progression via changing pixel values, with models including deep structural causal models [1], variational autoencoders (VAE) [24,33], generative adversarial networks (GAN) [21,31], and diffusion models [19,32]. Among these works, we highlight two that train on timeseries MRIs to predict the aging brain, conditioned on age and diagnosis. The first [24] combines a variational autoencoder with a mixed-effect model imposed on the latent space to simulate the aging process. By explicitly modeling age in the latent space, this model synthesizes images across 30+ years with atrophy patterns consistent with expectation. However, the model focuses on providing a population trajectory and is not specific enough for individual predictions, and images produced tend to be lower resolution as is typical of VAEs. In the second, 4D-DANI-Net, a GAN model with specified loss functions and a weight profile function, is proposed to simulate the aging process both globally and locally [22]. Additional techniques are used to synthesize images that are high resolution, more individualized, and consistent with atrophy patterns associated to AD. Unlike VAEs which typically impose a Gaussian distribution on the latent space through their encoder, GAN models typically offer a uniform distribution where no point is more likely than any other, and cannot be directly used for statistical modeling to classify trajectories as normal or abnormal.

1.3 Our Contribution

In this work, we aim to develop an approach that combines the complementary strengths of the two highlighted previous methods. We maintain an interpretable latent space in the VAE framework, but introduce a new architecture to condition on past images leading to more realistic and higher resolution outputs. This is achieved by a novel double-encoder CVAE architecture to model changing pixel values. Our model takes in conditional inputs of two data types: a previous image and other demographic information (age, elapsed time and disease status), leading to a novel network architecture where the encoder and decoder don't exhibit the symmetry typical in VAE work. This approach allows prediction for an arbitrary elapsed time, i.e. multi-horizon prediction. Compared to previous VAE-based methods [24], we increase output resolution and subject specificity by incorporating a prior MRI. Compared to previous GAN-based approaches [22], our method produces a latent space, in which we can estimate a posterior probability of disease status for disease classification.

Second, we introduce a novel training strategy to reduce computational requirement per sample and augment the dataset, where the network is trained on all possible pairs of images in a timeseries. The model we develop can predict future brain images with good accuracy, and we validate it in terms of mean square error (MSE) on the held out test and independent external dataset, while comparing to other baseline methods. Lastly, if a pair of scans has already been obtained, we show how our encoder can be used to build a likelihood ratio classifier. By focusing on individual trajectories in timeseries of MRI rather than population averages, our work has the potential to improve neurodegeneration biomarkers for AD.

We list our contribution as follows: i) we design a novel architecture that directly takes in both conditional images and demographic variables, ii) we propose a novel training strategy for computational cost reduction and data augmentation, iii) we propose a novel utilization of the latent space produced by our encoder for disease classification.

2 Method

2.1 Data Preparation

We obtain our dataset from the Alzheimer's Disease Neuroimaging Initiative (ADNI) database (https://adni.loni.usc.edu/), led by Principal Investigator Michael W. Weiner, MD. The primary goal of ADNI is to measure the progression of mild cognitive impairment (MCI) and early Alzheimer's disease. We include subjects from ADNI 1, 2 and 3 studies as of July 11, 2023, by searching for all MPRAGE scans. Here, we introduce a novel data preparation strategy to solve two problems we face in medical imaging datasets: data scarcity and computational limits. We structure our dataset so that each sample contains two images from the same patient, age and disease status when the first image was taken, and the time difference between the two images. For subjects with only one image, a pair of the same image is included, and the time difference is 0. For subjects with more than 2 images, we include all combinations of pairs both forward (positive time difference) and backward (negative time difference) in time. Including a negative time difference may or may not have direct clinical utility, but doubles our sample size. For example, if a person has 3 images we take the pairs {(1,1),(1,2),(1,3),(2,1),(2,2),(2,3),(3,1),(3,2),(3,3)}. This training strategy converts serial inputs into pairs of images, effectively augmenting our dataset and reducing computational costs per sample during training. We note this may introduce a bias where patients with more scans are overrepresented, and alternative sampling schemes will be the subject of future research. To simulate real data, often lower quality than carefully curated public datasets, we performed minimal quality check and did not discard any images.

For scalar conditional variables, we standardize age and time difference to mean 0 and variance 1. ADNI groups patients into 6 categories: cognitive normal, subjective memory complaint, early mild cognitive impairment, mild cognitive impairment, late mild cognitive impairment and AD. We follow the same grouping and assign a number from 0 to 5, noting this is a reasonable approximation of slightly different disease categories across ADNI studies. We assume that this progression is ordered, so we use a single number rather than a one hot encoded representation. We take only the diagnosis for the first scan of the pair, assuming future diagnostic labels are unknown. For the training set, we constructed 15,579 pairs from 907 subjects. For the test set, we held out 4 subjects at random from each category, for a total of 24 subjects, 180 images and 430 pairs. Characteristics of our ADNI cohort are shown in Table 1. In addition to ADNI, we obtain an independent set from OASIS3 [18] with 1085 subjects for external validation. We follow the same preprocessing procedure as above. Since OASIS and ADNI have different conventions for disease status, we keep consistency by grouping OASIS subjects into cognitive normal, cognitive impairment and AD, and assign them a number of 0, 3 and 5.

Each image was rigidly aligned to the 2020 MNI extended nonlinear symmetric average template [10]. First, the template was aligned to each brain image using an affine transformation, accounting for contrast differences using code from [28] (https://github.com/twardlab/emlddmm). Second, a Procrustes method was used to project this transform onto the closest rigid transform [6] by minimizing sum of square error in voxel locations. This ensured that size and shape differences would be modeled by our network, and not "normalized away" by registration. We found through visual inspection that an *accurate* affine transformation followed by projection led to less variability, relative to an *inaccurate* rigid transformation directly. Finally, we cropped and downsampled all images to $80 \times 80 \times 80$, $2mm^3$ voxels due to computational limitations.

2.2 Autoencoders, VAE and CVAE

First, we give an overview of autoencoder models and their extensions. Autoencoders are a class of neural network methods that learn a low-dimensional representation of high-dimensional structured data [8]. They consist of two parts: an encoder that projects high dimensional data into a latent space with lower dimensions, and a decoder that learns to map a point in the latent space back to its high dimensional representation. The latent distribution of an autoencoder is unknown, making inference difficult and prompting the need for VAEs [16].

Table 1. ADNI cohort characteristics stratified by disease status.

	Normal (n=219)	SMC (n=73)	EMCI (n=253)	MCI (n=86)	LMCI (n=140)	AD (n=136)
Male	104(47.5%)	34(46.6%)	133(52.6%)	53(61.6%)	71(50.7%)	71(52.2%)
Age*	75.51 [6.91]	71.87 [5.6]	70.84 [7.23]	76.27 [8.37]	72.02 [7.92]	74.92 [7.98]
50–70	49(22.4%)	35(47.9%)	123(48.6%)	21(24.4%)	54(38.6%)	29(21.3%)
70–80	112(51.1%)	33(45.2%)	99(39.1%)	33(38.4%)	63(45%)	75(55.1%)
80–90	56(25.6%)	4(5.5%)	31(12.3%)	32(37.2%)	22(15.7%)	31(22.8%)
90+	2(0.9%)	1(1.4%)	0	0	1(0.7%)	1(0.7%)
Scans per subject	4.74 [2.76]	2.44 [1.14]	4.7 [1.87]	6.53 [4.71]	4.49 [1.68]	3.53 [2.09]
Length (years)	2.48 [1.83]	1.61 [0.95]	2.48 [1.6]	1.98 [1.44]	2.24 [1.53]	0.88 [0.69]

*mean and [standard deviation] of age at first visit

VAE models assume the samples x are generated from a distribution conditioned on the latent space z, where $z \sim p_\theta(z)$ and $x \sim p_\theta(x|z)$ [16]. In practice, posterior inference may be intractable and estimating the posterior distribution is challenging [16]. To address this problem, a more tractable distribution, $q_\phi(z|x)$, is used to approximate the true posterior [16]. Therefore, VAEs can be trained to efficiently sample from unknown distributions using the variational lower bound of the log-likelihood, which can be written as follows [16]:

$$\mathcal{L}(\theta, \phi, x) = -D_{KL}(q_\phi(z|x) \| p_\theta(z)) + E_{q_\phi(z|x)}[\log p_\theta(x|z)], \quad (1)$$

where D_{KL} is the Kullback-Leibler divergence [17] that measures how similar two distributions are, and $E_{q_\phi(z|x^i)}$ measures the sum of squared reconstruction error where we assume $p_\theta(x|z)$ is Gaussian with mean predicted by our decoder and fixed variance 1. We use the common choice that $p_\theta(z)$ is multivariate standard normal, with no learnable parameters.

As with many medical applications, conditional variables offer additional information and can improve parameter estimation. A natural extension to the VAE is CVAE [26], which includes an additional variable y as the conditional variable. The variational lower bound for CVAE to optimize is as follows [26]:

$$\mathcal{L}_{\text{CVAE}}(\theta, \phi, x, y) = -D_{KL}(q_\phi(z|x, y) \| p_\theta(z)) + E_{q_\phi(z|x,y)}[\log p_\theta(y|x, z)]. \quad (2)$$

2.3 Our Double Encoder CVAE

We present our novel model architecture, inspired by CVAE [26], to generate 3D MR images. While previous methods have conditioned on a learned representation of an image, our architecture allows for a direct conditional image input. In our model, the encoder and decoder are not "symmetric", but rather the encoder takes the form of a standard CNN with two image inputs, and the decoder takes the form of a U-net [23]. The latter allows the prior MR image and conditional variables, as well as the latent space representation to be used for decoding. A point in the latent space does not represent an image, but a transformation between images, linking VAE modeling and classical work with diffeomorphisms.

Objective Function. We follow the same underlying assumptions of the distribution process as CVAE [26], where MR images are generated from the distribution $p_\theta(x|z)$ conditioned on 4 variables: the base image, age, disease status and elapsed time between two images. Though we have multi-modality conditional variables, the generation inference remains the same. Therefore, our empirical objective function follows closely to that of CVAE [26] in Equation (2).

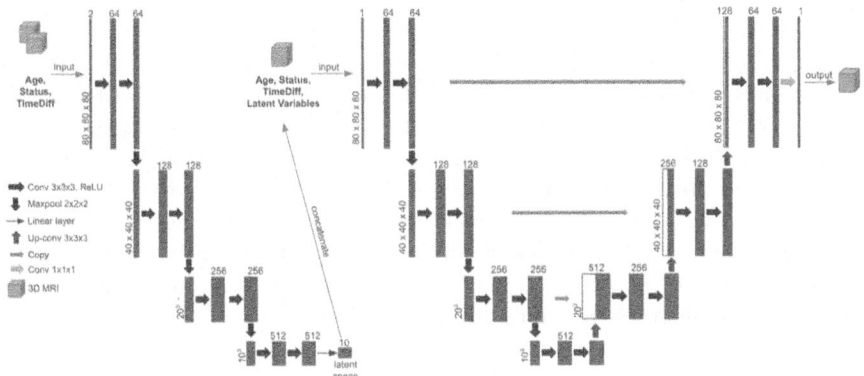

Fig. 1. Model architecture.

Model Architecture. Due to our conditional variables' multi-modality nature, we implement a novel architecture to incorporate scalar variables (age, elapsed time, disease status) and a conditional 3D image. The overall architecture consists of an encoder and a U-net [23] shaped decoder. The encoder consists of 4 blocks, where each block contains 2 convolutional layers and 1 max pooling layer. We choose a kernel size of 3 and stride of 1 for all convolutional layers except the last, and a kernel size of 2 and stride of 2 for max pooling layers. Each convolution is followed by a group normalization layer [30] with group size of 4 and a ReLU layer. During training, we take in an input of 2 stacked images and conditional variables, and project it down to a latent space of dimension 10 (i.e. we output 10 means and 10 log-variances). The decoder takes in the conditional image, latent space sample and scalar variables as inputs, and outputs the predicted image. Since the downsampling branch of the U-Net can be thought of as an encoder, we call this architecture a "double encoder CVAE". All non-image inputs are linearly transformed and added to each layer before the nonlinearity, following a strategy similar to "timestep embedding" common in modern diffusion models [11]. We show a visualization of our model in Fig. 1 and make our code available on GitHub at https://github.com/rosie068/Double_Encoder_CVAE_AD.

Training Procedure. We used the Adam optimizer [15] with learning rate 1e-5 and batch size of 4. We trained our model for 1000 epochs with early stopping on a single NVIDIA GeForce RTX 4090 GPU with a training time of 5 d.

2.4 Comparison to Alternative Methods

We attempted a comparison of our method to those described in Sect. 1.2, but were unable to produce satisfactory results using publicly available code and documentation. We omit the comparisons, rather than casting these methods in a negative light. We suggest that a challenge style comparison, where authors can optimize parameter selection for their own methods and have them run automatically on a hidden test set, would be more appropriate for head to head comparisons. In this work we compare to several simpler models to put our method into context and understand typical values of our figures of merit. Our goal is to provide insight into the challenge of longitudinal image prediction by developing a new approach, not claim superiority or inferiority. For a simple baseline, we use the conditional image as a prediction of the future image, and the other methods we compare to are described below.

Low Rank Linear Prediction. For N individuals, we take the first and last images in their trajectories and form two matrices X and Y, both of size 80^3 (number of pixels) by N. We include demographic variables by appending additional rows to X for age, status, elapsed time and 1 (for mean). We perform singular value decomposition: $X = USV^T$, and take the first 10 (the same dimension as our CVAE latent space) or 100 (for better results) singular vectors as the latent space representation. To estimate the future MRI $\hat{Y}$ for individual i, we use the first few singular values (indicated by $\tilde{\ }$) and calculate as: $\hat{Y}_i = Y\tilde{V}\tilde{S}^{-1}\tilde{U}^T X_i$

VAE with Linear Mixed Effect Estimation. We train an autoencoder using the architecture described in [24], and fit a linear mixed effects (LME) model in the latent space using the statsmodels package in python [25]. While other authors [33] have noted that this approach should be improved upon, it provides a simple model based on standard VAEs for comparison. Images are predicted using the following procedure. First a baseline image is passed through the encoder. Second, its latent space representation is shifted based on our LME model parameters, in a manner depending on time difference and disease status. Third, the resulting vector is passed through the decoder.

3 Results

3.1 Trajectory Prediction

First, we compare results for trajectory reconstruction in the held-out test set. In Fig. 2, we visualize sample reconstructions for randomly selected healthy and AD individuals in the test set. As a healthy brain does not change much over 1 year, the ground truth does not have much variation and both the 100 dim. SVD method and our method perform well. In the diseased trajectory, we observe a noticeable enlargement in the ventricles, which is predicted well by our method but not the linear methods. The 10 dimensional SVD and VAE+ LME model did not produce satisfactory images, and we do not show their outputs.

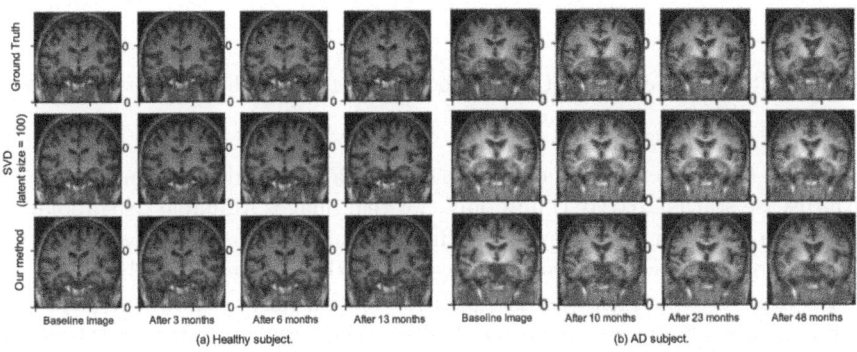

Fig. 2. Sample prediction in the held-out test set.

For a quantitative comparison, we calculate mean squared error (MSE) in test and external validation datasets for 5 methods: our double encoder CVAE, VAE+ LME model, SVD with both latent space sizes, and baseline. We conduct comparisons in three regions of interest (ROIs) to reflect global and local performance: the entire image, a region surrounding the hippocampus and a region surrounding the ventricles (both associated with AD progression [3,9]). ROIs were identified during image registration, using an affine transform of the MNI atlas and dilating annotations by several pixels. Out of 230 pairs, our model achieves the best performance in 202 pairs (88%) in the whole brain and 218 pairs in both the hippocampus and ventricles (95%). In the OASIS validation set, our model achieves the lowest MSE across all three regions, but the distribution has longer tails. Out of 1085 pairs of images, our model achieves the best performance in 855 pairs (79%) in the whole brain, 889 pairs (82%) in the hippocampus, and 922 pairs (85%) in the ventricles. In Fig. 3, we visualize the distribution of MSE on a log scale and show our proposed model reconstructs trajectories with more accuracy globally and locally. While still performing best, our method seems to follow a bimodal distribution with long tails in OASIS data, an observation which warrants further investigation.

In addition, we demonstrate our model's ability to interpolate between images and extrapolate beyond the last image in the timeseries. We generate images by sampling a standard multivariate normal in the latent space, and pass it through the decoder with the original image and scalar variables. The random latent sample is fixed across all panels, and only the elapsed time is changed. In Fig. 4,

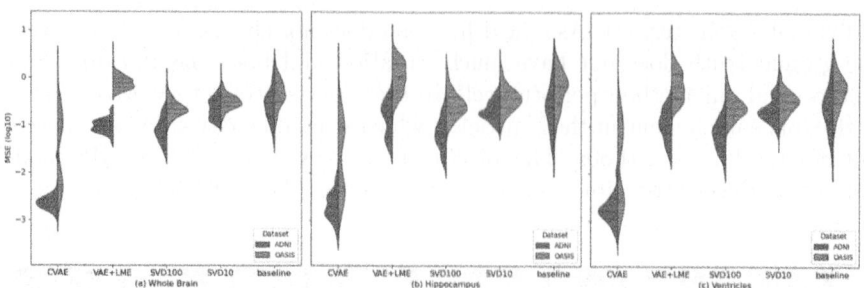

Fig. 3. MSE (log scale) in test (left) and external (right) validation set in 3 ROIs.

we predict the trajectory annually over 10 years for one individual in the test set with disease status 4 (LMCI) and only two real images available (extrapolation beyond the 4th year). We visualize structural changes over time by calculating a smooth optical flow estimate, and overlaying the divergence of the flow field. Values close to 0 are transparent, positive (expansion) is shown in blue, and negative (contraction) is shown in red. We observe expansion in the ventricular space over time including its inferior horn in the temporal lobe, and contraction of nearby brain structures, in accordance with the AD aging process.

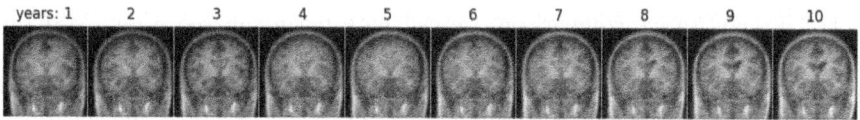

Fig. 4. Ten year prediction from one base image. Incremental changes (non-cumulative) shown via optical flow divergence, blue: expansion, red: contraction. (Color figure online)

3.2 Latent Space Disease Status Probability Estimation

In addition to trajectory estimation, we propose a practical use of the latent space to estimate a posterior probability of a subject's disease status given a pair of images. For subjects in the test set, we set the disease status to both normal and AD to obtain two sets of latent space representations. Let $\mu_{i,j}$ be the jth dimension of the encoder output when disease status is i (0 for healthy and 5 for AD), and define $f_i = \prod_{j=1}^{10}(2\pi)^{-1/2}\exp(-\mu_{ij}^2/2)$ (taking a product over the 10 dimensional outputs, reflecting our standard normal latent space distribution). Our posterior probability of disease status 0 is defined as $p_0 = f_0/(f_0 + f_5)$. We show two examples of disease classification analysis in Fig. 5, one healthy and one AD (same subjects as Fig. 2), where the posterior probability significantly favors the hypothesis corresponding to their true disease status.

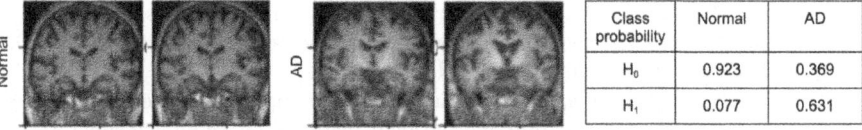

Fig. 5. Hypothesis testing for disease status, H_0: null, H_1: AD.

4 Discussion

In this work, we present our double encoder CVAE, a novel architecture that predicts 3D MRI at an arbitrary time given a conditional prior image, age, disease status, and the future time. We compared our model on two datasets against other simpler methods, and showed our model is better at tracking both global and local changes during the aging process associated with AD. Our goal is to design a predictive model that operates on images and demographics only. While ADNI provides other biomarker information such as amyloid and tau pathology, we do not include them in this work but will consider in the future. One strength of our work is that our model learns aging patterns from populations without losing specificity when making individualized predictions. Given a baseline image, it could be used to understand potential trajectories of healthy aging or disease. Another strength is that our model produces a latent space for downstream inference, as demonstrated by our likelihood ratio classifier example. Our model has characteristics similar to "image translation" like the popular pix2pix model [12]. However, pix2pix is deterministic [20], whereas our model allows users to explore uncertainty in future trajectories. Lastly, model predictions could be used for downstream analysis, including treatment effect comparison (where our model predicts the trajectory with no intervention).

One limitation of this work is that we were unable to perform head-to-head comparisons with state-of-the-art methods, and we suggest this could be addressed in the future in a challenge framework, where each author can run their own code. Another is that it is not straightforward to incorporate more than one previous scan when making predictions, unlike in [24]. Future work will incorporate serial conditional images to increase predictive performance. Lastly, our test set size was relatively small due to a smaller cohort size compared to some computer vision datasets. With potential treatments for AD now approved, early diagnosis has become critical. Our model can generate synthetic datasets that can potentially be used for downstream tasks such as anomaly detection and classification. This work, which seeks to improve measures of neurodegeneration as a biomarker of AD by leveraging timeseries analysis, has the potential to impact treatment decisions.

Disclosure of Interests. The authors have no competing interests.

References

1. Abdulaal, A., Castro, D.C., Alexander, D.C.: Deep structural causal modelling of the clinical and radiological phenotype of alzheimer's disease. In: NeurIPS 2022 Workshop on Causality for Real-world Impact (2022)
2. Albert, M.S., et al.: The diagnosis of mild cognitive impairment due to alzheimer's disease: recommendations from the national institute on aging-alzheimer's association workgroups on diagnostic guidelines for alzheimer's disease. Alzheimer's Dementia **7**(3), 270–279 (2011)
3. Apostolova, L.G., et al.: Hippocampal atrophy and ventricular enlargement in normal aging, mild cognitive impairment (mci), and alzheimer disease. Alzheimer Disease Assoc. Disorders **26**(1), 17–27 (2012)
4. Beg, M.F., Miller, M.I., Trouvé, A., Younes, L.: Computing large deformation metric mappings via geodesic flows of diffeomorphisms. Int. J. Comput. Vision **61**, 139–157 (2005)
5. Braak, H., Braak, E.: Neuropathological stageing of alzheimer-related changes. Acta Neuropathol. **82**(4), 239–259 (1991)
6. Challis, J.H.: A procedure for determining rigid body transformation parameters. J. Biomech. **28**(6), 733–737 (1995)
7. Durrleman, S., Pennec, X., Trouvé, A., Braga, J., Gerig, G., Ayache, N.: Toward a comprehensive framework for the spatiotemporal statistical analysis of longitudinal shape data. Int. J. Comput. Vision **103**, 22–59 (2013)
8. Ehrhardt, J., Wilms, M.: Autoencoders and variational autoencoders in medical image analysis. In: Biomedical Image Synthesis and Simulation, pp. 129–162. Elsevier (2022)
9. Evans, M.C., et al.: Volume changes in alzheimer's disease and mild cognitive impairment: cognitive associations. Eur. Radiol. **20**, 674–682 (2010)
10. Fonov, V., et al.: Unbiased average age-appropriate atlases for pediatric studies. Neuroimage **54**(1), 313–327 (2011)
11. Ho, J., Jain, A., Abbeel, P.: Denoising diffusion probabilistic models. Adv. Neural. Inf. Process. Syst. **33**, 6840–6851 (2020)
12. Isola, P., Zhu, J.Y., Zhou, T., Efros, A.A.: Image-to-image translation with conditional adversarial networks. In: Proceedings of the IEEE Conference on Computer Vision and Pattern Recognition, pp. 1125–1134 (2017)
13. Jack, C.R., Jr., et al.: Introduction to the recommendations from the national institute on aging-alzheimer's association workgroups on diagnostic guidelines for alzheimer's disease. Alzheimer's Dementia **7**(3), 257–262 (2011)
14. Jack, C.R., Jr., et al.: Nia-aa research framework: toward a biological definition of Alzheimer's disease. Alzheimer's Dementia **14**(4), 535–562 (2018)
15. Kingma, D.P., Ba, J.: Adam: A method for stochastic optimization. arXiv preprint arXiv:1412.6980 (2014)
16. Kingma, D.P., Welling, M.: Auto-encoding variational bayes. arXiv preprint arXiv:1312.6114 (2013)
17. Kullback, S.: Kullback-leibler divergence (1951)
18. LaMontagne, P.J., et al.: Oasis-3: longitudinal neuroimaging, clinical, and cognitive dataset for normal aging and alzheimer disease. MedRxiv, pp. 2019–12 (2019)
19. Puglisi, L., Alexander, D.C., Ravì, D.: Enhancing spatiotemporal disease progression models via latent diffusion and prior knowledge. arXiv preprint arXiv:2405.03328 (2024)
20. Raad, R., et al.: Conditional generative learning for medical image imputation. Sci. Rep. **14**(1), 171 (2024)

21. Ravi, D., Alexander, D.C., Oxtoby, N.P., Initiative, A.D.N.: Degenerative adversarial neuroimage nets: generating images that mimic disease progression. In: International Conference on Medical Image Computing and Computer-Assisted Intervention, pp. 164–172. Springer (2019)
22. Ravi, D., et al.: Degenerative adversarial neuroimage nets for brain scan simulations: Application in ageing and dementia. Med. Image Anal. **75**, 102257 (2022)
23. Ronneberger, O., Fischer, P., Brox, T.: U-net: Convolutional networks for biomedical image segmentation. In: Medical Image Computing and Computer-Assisted Intervention–MICCAI 2015: 18th International Conference, Munich, Germany, October 5-9, 2015, Proceedings, Part III 18, pp. 234–241. Springer (2015)
24. Sauty, B., Durrleman, S.: Progression models for imaging data with longitudinal variational auto encoders. In: International Conference on Medical Image Computing and Computer-Assisted Intervention, pp. 3–13. Springer (2022)
25. Seabold, S., Perktold, J.: statsmodels: Econometric and statistical modeling with python. In: 9th Python in Science Conference (2010)
26. Sohn, K., Lee, H., Yan, X.: Learning structured output representation using deep conditional generative models. In: Advances in Neural Information Processing Systems **28** (2015)
27. Thomas Fletcher, P.: Geodesic regression and the theory of least squares on riemannian manifolds. Int. J. Comput. Vision **105**, 171–185 (2013)
28. Tward, D., et al.: Diffeomorphic registration with intensity transformation and missing data: application to 3d digital pathology of alzheimer's disease. Front. Neurosci. **14**, 52 (2020)
29. Tward, D., et al.: Entorhinal and transentorhinal atrophy in mild cognitive impairment using longitudinal diffeomorphometry. Alzheimer's Dementia: Diagnosis, Assess. Disease Monitor. **9**(1), 41–50 (2017)
30. Wu, Y., He, K.: Group Normalization. In: Ferrari, V., Hebert, M., Sminchisescu, C., Weiss, Y. (eds.) Computer Vision – ECCV 2018: 15th European Conference, Munich, Germany, September 8-14, 2018, Proceedings, Part XIII, pp. 3–19. Springer International Publishing, Cham (2018). https://doi.org/10.1007/978-3-030-01261-8_1
31. Xia, T., Chartsias, A., Tsaftaris, S.A., Initiative, A.D.N.: Consistent brain ageing synthesis. In: Medical Image Computing and Computer Assisted Intervention–MICCAI 2019: 22nd International Conference, Shenzhen, China, October 13–17, 2019, Proceedings, Part IV 22, pp. 750–758. Springer (2019). DOI:https://doi.org/10.1007/978-3-030-32251-9_82
32. Yoon, J.S., Zhang, C., Suk, H.-I., Guo, J., Li, X.: SADM: sequence-aware diffusion model for longitudinal medical image generation. In: Frangi, A., de Bruijne, M., Wassermann, D., Navab, N. (eds.) Information Processing in Medical Imaging: 28th International Conference, IPMI 2023, San Carlos de Bariloche, Argentina, June 18–23, 2023, Proceedings, pp. 388–400. Springer Nature Switzerland, Cham (2023). https://doi.org/10.1007/978-3-031-34048-2_30
33. Zhao, Q., Adeli, E., Honnorat, N., Leng, T., Pohl, K.M.: Variational autoencoder for regression: Application to brain aging analysis. In: Medical Image Computing and Computer Assisted Intervention–MICCAI 2019: 22nd International Conference, Shenzhen, China, October 13–17, 2019, Proceedings, Part II 22, pp. 823–831. Springer (2019)

Towards Longitudinal Characterization of Multiple Sclerosis Atrophy Employing SynthSeg Framework and Normative Modeling

Pedro M. Gordaliza[1,2(✉)], Nataliia Molchanova[1,2,3], Maxence Wynen[4,5], Pietro Maggi[5,6], Alessandro Cagol[7], Cristina Granziera[7], and Meritxell Bach Cuadra[1,2]

[1] CIBM Center for Biomedical Imaging, Vaud, Switzerland
Pedro.macias.gordaliza@gmail.com
[2] Department of Radiology, Lausanne University Hospital (CHUV), University of Lausanne (UNIL), Lausanne, Switzerland
[3] University of Applied Sciences Western Switzerland (HES-SO), Delémont, Switzerland
[4] ICTEAM, Universite catholique de Louvain, Louvain-la-Neuve, Belgium
[5] Neuroinflammation Imaging Lab (NIL), Universite catholique de Louvain, Ottignies-Louvain-la-Neuve, Belgium
[6] Cliniques Universitaires Saint-Luc, Universite catholique de Louvain, Ottignies-Louvain-la-Neuve, Belgium
[7] Department of Medicine and Biomedical Engineering, Translational Imaging in Neurology (ThINk), Basel Hospital and University of Basel (USB), Basel, Switzerland

Abstract. Multiple Sclerosis (MS) is a complex neurodegenerative disease characterized by heterogeneous progression patterns. Traditional clinical measures like the Expanded Disability Status Scale (EDSS) inadequately capture the full spectrum of disease progression, highlighting the need for advanced Disease Progression Modeling (DPM) approaches. This study harnesses cutting-edge neuroimaging and deep learning techniques to investigate deviations in subcortical volumes in MS patients. We analyze T1-weighted and Fluid-attenuated inversion recovery (FLAIR) Magnetic Resonance Imaging (MRI) data using advanced DL segmentation models, *SynthSeg$^+$* and *SynthSeg-WMH*, which address the challenges of conventional methods in the presence of white matter lesions. By comparing subcortical volumes of 326 MS patients to a normative model from 37,407 healthy individuals, we identify significant deviations that enhance our understanding of MS progression. This study highlights the potential of integrating DL with normative modeling to refine MS progression characterization, automate informative MRI contrasts, and contribute to data-driven DPM in neurodegenerative diseases.

1 Introduction

Multiple Sclerosis (MS) is a chronic autoimmune neurodegenerative disease affecting approximately 2.3 million people globally [14]. MS presents significant challenges due to its heterogeneous manifestations and unclear etiology [21]. Traditionally, MS is clinically characterized by the pseudo-quantitative Expanded Disability Status Scale (EDSS), which pseudo-quantitatively measures the level of disability [42] and, to a limited extent, tracks cognitive impairment over time [4,41]. However, this approach represents an insufficient proxy for essential Disease Progression Modeling (DPM), unable to characterize the set of underlying mechanisms such as neuroinflammation and degenerative processes recently known as Smouldering MS [19,34].

Magnetic Resonance Imaging (MRI) plays a crucial role in the clinical assessment of MS patients, for diagnosis, prognosis, and Disease Modifying Therapies (DMT) assessment [42]. Structural MRI provides information on focal lesion dissemination in the brain and spinal cord, as well as brain structure characterization [43]. While cross-sectional analysis of Fluid-Attenuated Inversion Recovery (FLAIR) and T1-weighted (T1w) contrasts are routinely acquired in clinical settings for lesion identification [28], lesion-derived biomarkers have shown controversial or limited relationships with disease phenotypes and progression. This highlights the need for more robust approaches to capture disease progression over time, particularly for DPM.

In contrast, brain structure evolution assessment provides atrophy-related imaging biomarkers of well-proven neurodegeneration, which is more acute in MS patients [17,22]. Studies employing global and regional atrophy imaging biomarkers have associated deviations from control measures for MS patients with cognitive impairment [5,13], depression [3], and physical disability [23,32].

The literature shows how subcortical structures are implicated in the pathophysiology of MS due to their involvement in key neurological functions often compromised in the disease, compared with cortical regions, which are more difficult to analyze in conventional MRI sequences [33]. Findings across several studies have revealed that gray matter atrophy in MS is more pronounced, particularly in subcortical regions such as the thalamus [2] and the putamen [27], compared to the rates of atrophy in healthy controls [43]. This regional Grey Matter (GM) analysis enables deeper studies about MS mechanisms and allows further disease progression modeling [5]. Recent models to characterize the longitudinal trajectory of brain region volumes for MS patients have been published [10,26], emphasizing the importance of longitudinal data projection in understanding disease progression.

However, these approaches face several challenges: they are difficult to implement in clinical practice, may be limited by small sample sizes, and struggle to account for the heterogeneity of MS evolution. Furthermore, they do not provide a direct comparison to healthy population norms. To address these limitations, we propose to measure the deviance of each patient at each time-point concerning a longitudinal trajectory model based on thousands of healthy subjects. This approach has been successfully applied to other neurological diseases through the normative modeling framework [25,39], allowing for a more robust and clinically applicable method of characterizing individual disease trajectories.

Practically, manual segmentation of main brain structures for thousands of subjects is unfeasible. Models often rely on automatic segmentation provided by tools such as FreeSurfer [15] or more recently DL approaches [9], which provide acceptable segmentations for quality T1w images of healthy subjects. However, these tools tend to be more uncertain on volume estimations for MS patients who present white matter lesions (WML), where more reliable information is usually contained within the FLAIR contrast (see Fig. 1) [35]. Recent advancements in DL-based segmentation algorithms have improved on this issue. SynthSeg [7] allows for obtaining reliable volumetric measures when employing FLAIR [36], and its new version, *SynthSeg-WMH* [29], can handle the presence of WML. These developments could accelerate the use of regional atrophy-related imaging biomarkers leveraging normative modeling fed by regions segmented through DL models, empowering speed and reliability.

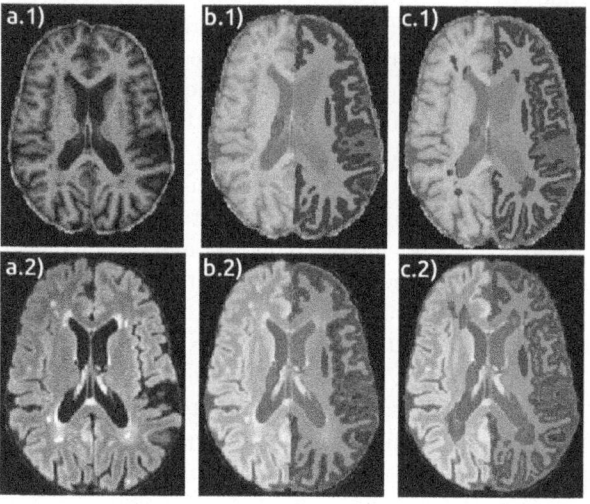

Fig. 1. The a) column shows an axial slice of a T1-weighted (T1) image and a Fluid-Attenuated Inversion Recovery (FLAIR) image, respectively. The b) column contains the corresponding $SynthSeg^+$ [7] segmentation, while the c) column depicts the *SynthSeg-WMH* [29] segmentation. Note the White Matter Lesions (WML) in violet.

To explore this potential and address the limitations of previous approaches, we present a pilot study investigating deviations in brain morphometry with three key innovations: 1) utilizing a normative *healthy* brain model rather than MS-specific models [26], 2) comparing segmentations based on both T1w and FLAIR images, which is rarely done in MS studies [36], and 3) employing a tissue segmentation algorithm that jointly segment subcortical structures and white matter lesions (WML) rather than first finding lesions and lesion-filling the input images. Our approach leverages the most advanced deep learning (DL) tools for domain agnostic segmentation of subcortical volumes from MR images (FLAIR and T1w) and utilizes the CentileBrain normative model, based on 37,407 healthy individuals [18]. This methodological combination allows for a more comprehensive and potentially more accurate assessment of brain morphometry in MS patients compared to traditional T1w-only approaches that do not account for WML or utilize normative modeling.

2 Materials and Methods

2.1 Materials

We analyzed a heterogeneous dataset comprising 326 MS patients from five sources: three in-house datasets (Lausanne University Hospital (CHUV), Louvain Neuroinflammation Imaging Lab (NIL), and Imaging Axonal Damage & Repair in Multiple Sclerosis (INsIDER) [20]) and two public datasets (MICCAI-MSSEG2016 challenge [8] and OpenMSLong [30]). All patients underwent Fluid Attenuated Inversion Recovery (FLAIR) MRI scanning and T1w contrasts (i.e., Magnetization Prepared RApid Gradient Echo - MPRAGE- or MP2RAGE). Imaging protocols varied across datasets, with magnetic field strengths ranging from 1.5T to 3T. For OpenMSLong, Anonymous Dataset 1, and Anonymous Dataset3, two time points were available for some subjects, resulting in a total of 460 3D-FLAIR and T1w MRI scans (Table 1).

Table 1. Summary of available datasets

Dataset	N (Female)	Age Avg. (Min.-Max.)	Long. (N)	Sequence (FLAIR/T1w)	Voxel Size(mm)
MSSEG2016	53 (38)	45.15 (24–66)	No	3D FLAIR	$0.47-1 \times 0.47-1 x 0.9-1.25$
				3D T1	$0.47-1.08x0.47-1.08x0.6-1.25$
OpenMSLong	20 (15)	34.1 (19–50)	Yes (20)	3D FLAIR	$0.47x0.47x0.8$
				2D T1	$0.42x0.42x3.3$
CHUV	41 (25)	34.51 (20–60)	Yes (36)	3D FLAIR	$1x1x1$
				MP2RAGE	$1x1x1.2$
NIL	47 (26)	40.64 (22.58–72.03)	No	3D FLAIR	$0.69x0.66x0.66$
				MPRAGE	$0.71x0.66x0.66$
INsIDER	165 (98)	46.44 (18.27–76.51)	Yes (78)	3D FLAIR	$1x1x1$
				MP2RAGE	$1x1x1$

2.2 Methods

In this study, we developed a processing framework for the automatic segmentation of subcortical regions in MS patients using T1w and FLAIR contrasts and the evaluation of deviations from the expected volumes from a large-scale healthy brain model. As depicted in Fig. 2, each MRI contrast independently feeds into two different $SynthSeg$ models. These models are used to obtain the surrogate ground truth for each patient (i), contrast (c), subcortical region (r), algorithm (a), and sex (s) denoted as y_{icras}. The $CentileBrain$ model [18] employs patient-specific age and sex covariates to estimate the subcortical volume of a healthy subject of such age and sex, represented as $\hat{y}_{irs}$. Finally, y_{icra} and $\hat{y}_{irs}$ are used to extract evaluation metrics to assess the deviation from normative values.

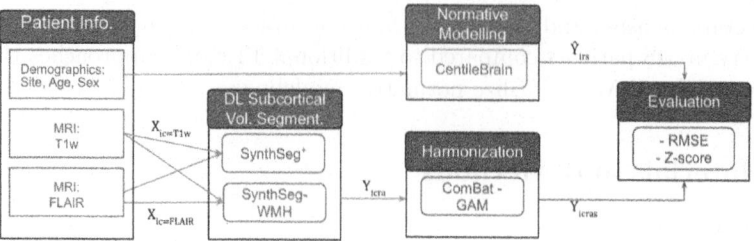

Fig. 2. Pipeline: Each available MRI contrast, X_{ic} (where i represents an MS patient and c the contrast, either T1w or FLAIR), independently feeds both *SynthSeg* models (a): $SynthSeg^+$ [7] and *SynthSeg-WMH* [29]. These models provide the surrogate ground truth per patient, contrast, subcortical region, algorithm and sex (s) Y_{icras}. In parallel, the *CentileBrain* model [18] estimates the subcortical volume for a healthy subject depending on age and sex, $\hat{Y}_{irs}$, using per-patient age and sex covariates.

Subcortical Volumes Segmentation - Automatic segmentation of subcortical structures is particularly challenging in MS patients due to the presence of focal and sparse MS lesions. Tools such as the FreeSurfer suite [15] tend to be less reliable as they depend more on T1w images, which are less informative than FLAIR sequences for depicting MS lesions [35,36]. In this work, we employ segmentation methods designed with a resolution and contrast-agnostic approach [7]. We perform the segmentation of all subcortical regions using both T1w images and FLAIR sequences, as well as the DL algorithms $SynthSeg^+$ [7] and *SynthSeg-WMH* [29], referred to as y_{icra}. $SynthSeg^+$ is a more robust version of the previously released *SynthSeg* [6], which accounts for image quality beyond resolution and contrast agnosticism. *SynthSeg-WMH* is a branch of the former, intended for more reliable segmentation in the presence of WML. Note that the most robust version of $SynthSeg^+$ is optional and was enabled for this study; no extra parameter setting is needed for any of the DL segmentation algorithms.

Subcortical Volumes Site Harmonization - Beyond the mentioned confounders, age and sex, multi-site MRI studies face the challenge of variability in imaging protocols, which can introduce site-related biases in the data. To address this, we used ComBat-GAM harmonization [16], an advanced technique that combines the ComBat method with Generalized Additive Models (GAMs). ComBat-GAM effectively harmonizes neuroimaging data by accounting for age and sex, in addition to mitigating site effects, making it suitable for studies involving large, heterogeneous datasets. By applying ComBat-GAM, we ensure that the subcortical volume estimates, y_{icras}, derived from our segmentation methods are comparable across different sites, thereby enhancing the reliability of our normative models and subsequent analyses.

Normative Modeling - A brain normative model is a statistical framework that characterizes the healthy range of brain structure across a large population by leveraging longitudinal data [31,39], allowing for the disentanglement of normal changes from deviations linked to neurological diseases. The power of a normative model resides in the sample size used for training, which helps to characterize biological variability across the lifespan better, accounting for confounders of brain changes beyond age, such as sex, and robust model selection. Recently, the *CentileBrain* [18] model trained with 37,407 healthy individuals (53.3% females, age range 3–90) from 81 datasets has been released. The *CentileBrain* employs Multivariate Factorial Polynomial Regression (MFPR) [38] algorithm which performs robustly on healthy subjects, generating sex-specific normative models for the volume estimation of subcortical regions in both right and left brain hemispheres: Thalamus, Caudate, Putamen, Pallidum, Hippocampus, Amygdala, and Accumbens. The same regions are given by both DL segmentation models, making *CentileBrain* ideal for our purposes since subcortical degeneration has been found to be more significant in MS patients [5,43].

Evaluation - Our evaluation process consisted of several steps first to assess which surrogate truths y_{icras} coincide with expected findings as well as those given from the normative deviation, and to quantify the deviation of MS patients from the normative brain volume trajectories. Notably, while *SynthSeg-WMH* is theoretically more suitable for MS lesion-rich environments, its recent development necessitates comparison with its more validated counterpart, $SynthSeg^+$, to rigorously assess performance and reliability in this specific context.

1. **Preliminary comparison with literature values:** To ensure our volume estimations are within a reasonable range, we conducted a preliminary comparison with values reported in the literature. We compared our average subcortical volume estimations from both T1w and FLAIR-based segmentations (using both SynthSeg models) against values from studies that performed a brief review of automatic segmentation on T1w images from several classic segmentation software tools, as described in [37]. This comparison serves as an initial validation step, acknowledging that exact matches are not expected due to methodological differences, particularly with our novel FLAIR-based approach. Potential biases and implications of this comparison will be addressed in the discussion section. For each subcortical region, hemisphere, contrast, and algorithm, the Kolmogorov-Smirnov (K-S) test was used to compute p-values that quantify the similarity between our segmented volume distributions and the reference values provided in the literature for MS patients. A higher p-value indicates a closer match to the literature-reported mean values. These p-values were then used to identify and highlight the best matching segmentation approaches, ensuring the accuracy and reliability of our methods.
2. **Subcortical Volume Longitudinal Trajectory Analysis**: MFPR was applied to analyze the age-related trajectories of the harmonized subcortical volumes, y_{icras}, stratified by sex and the tissue segmentation model employed. For a more comprehensive understanding of these trajectories, the Root Mean Square Error (RMSE) between the real volumes (y_{icras}) and the

estimated healthy volumes ($\hat{y}_{irs}$) was calculated across all patients for each region: $RMSE_{cras} = \sqrt{\frac{1}{n}\sum_{i=1}^{n}(y_{icras} - \hat{y}_{irs})^2}$, where n is the number of scans. This $RMSE_{cras}$ provides an estimation of the average deviation of the MS cohort from the normative model predictions, stratified by sex, contrast, DL model, and subcortical region.
3. **Individual Deviation Scores and Longitudinal Deviation**: For each patient and each region, we computed a Z-score to quantify the individual deviation from the normative value: Z-score$_{icras} = \frac{y_{icras} - \hat{y}_{irs}}{\sqrt{\sigma_{rs}^2 + \sigma_{icras}^2}}$. Note that the uncertainty normalization term, σ_{rs}^2, which assumes normality, is approximated using the reported RMSE model (see supplement in [18]) as in [11,12,24]. Finally, from the set of individual scores, we approximated the *longitudinal deviation trajectory*. We plotted the Z-scores against age for each region and hemisphere to visualize the longitudinal trajectories of deviations. Regression lines were fitted to these plots to identify trends in deviations across the lifespan.

3 Results

On the Robustness and Reliability of Subcortical Segmentations: Figure 3 shows the average volume per region and hemisphere for each of the contrast (FLAIR and T1w) and segmentation model ($SynthSeg^+$ and $SyntheSeg$-WMH) combinations, along with comparisons to reference values for each subcortical volume in the literature [37] (depicted as horizontal lines in Fig. 3). Comparing the four combinations, we found that for both hemispheres of the caudate, pallidum, and putamen, the four options for volume extraction did not present significant differences (ANOVA, p ¿ 0.05). In contrast, for the amygdala, accumbens, hippocampus, and thalamus, differences were primarily due to the DL model used, except for the thalamus, where differences were also observed between using FLAIR or T1w (e.g. average left-thalamus volume employing FLAIR and $SynthSeg^+$ is 7492.2 ± 112.1 vs 6248 ± 101.4 when employing T1w and $SynthSeh$-WMH). Regarding the comparison with reference values extracted from the literature using the K-S test, it was observed that in regions where significant differences existed between the segmentation pipelines, the extraction model was consistent between hemispheres. Segmentations using $SynthSeg$-WMH were closer to the reference values (e.g., 600 ± 100 for left accumbens), with no significant differences between the contrasts used, except for the thalamus volume. The thalamus volume showed greater similarity to the reference value when segmented using the FLAIR sequence and $SynthSeg^+$ ($p - val = 0.548$).

Subcortical Volume Longitudinal Trajectory - In Fig. 4, for the sake of clarity and conciseness, we present only the results for the FLAIR contrast, as there were no significant differences for most regions except the thalamus.

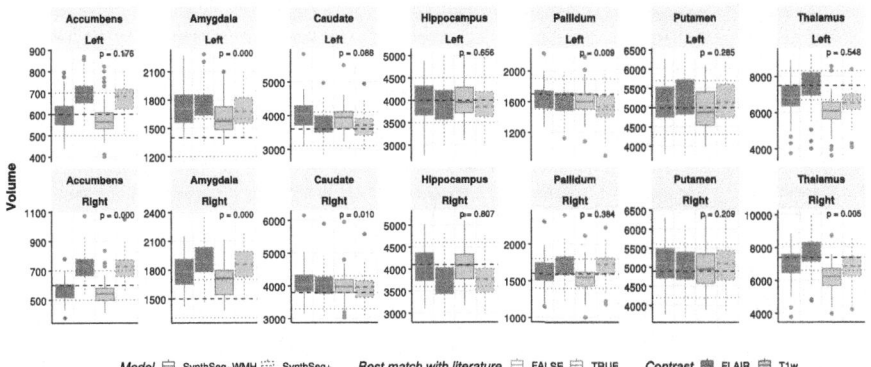

Fig. 3. Average Estimation and Comparison with Literature-Reported Subcortical Volumes: Boxplots show the distribution of the subcortical volumes given by each model and contrast. Horizontal lines represent the literature average values for each subcortical region along with their corresponding confidence intervals [37]. Red-bordered boxplots highlight the distributions that are closest to the reference values, distinguished by the highest p-value (shown in the upper-right corners) of the four comparisons from the univariate Kolmogorov-Smirnov test. (Color figure online)

All regions exhibit the expected atrophy trend, independent of sex and the segmentation model used, except for the pallidum region in males. For both hemispheres of the accumbens, amygdala, and thalamus, $SynthSeg^+$ produced significantly larger volumes ($p < 0.05$, paired t-test) compared to $SynthSeg$-WMH, as well as for the right hemisphere of the pallidum, which contrasts with its trend in the left hemisphere. Conversely, the RMSE with respect to the normative model estimation for these regions behaves differently: for the left thalamus, with similar tendency in the right thalamus, it reaches 2038.95 ± 112.1 for males when using $SynthSeg$-WMH with T1w, compared to just 1304 ± 109.2 for $SynthSeg^+$. Meanwhile, the accumbens shows an RMSE of 166.96 ± 10.1 for FLAIR in males when using $SynthSeg^+$, which is almost fifty percent less than its counterpart using T1w and $SynthSeg$-WMH, similarly to the amygdala.

Volumetric Deviations from Normative Trajectories - Figure 5 illustrates the longitudinal trajectories of subcortical volumes for MS patients compared to the expected trajectories for healthy subjects. We observed a consistent trend across sexes, showing an increasing deviation with age in the thalamus of both hemispheres independently of the segmentation algorithm used. Although not significant, a similar trend was found for the putamen. Overall, $SynthSeg^+$ and $SynthSeg$-WMH show significant differences in deviation when stratified by sex. In general, and consistent with the trends for subcortical volume segmentation, $SynthSeg^+$ shows more extreme values.

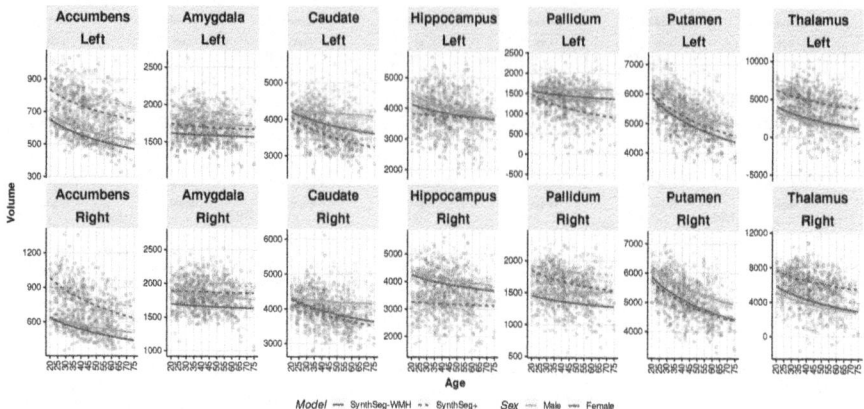

Fig. 4. Multivariate Factorial Polynomial Regression (MFPR) [38] of each subcortical volume against the age in 326 MS patients, stratified by sex and the DL model used for segmentation employing FLAIR contrast.

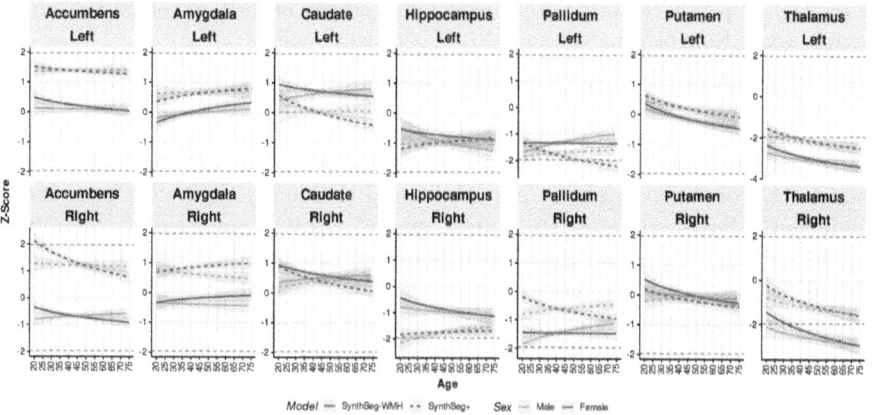

Fig. 5. Deviation, Z-score, of each MS patient's subcortical volume from the normative value for their age and sex employing the FLAIR contrast. The Z-score trajectory is shown as its regression against age. Red dashed lines at ± 1.96 identify the 95% confidence interval. $|Z\text{-score}| > 1.96$ are considered extreme deviants. (Color figure online)

4 Conclusions

This pilot study explores the feasibility of normative models in identifying and quantifying brain atrophy in MS patients using state-of-the-art DL algorithms for subcortical structure segmentation, offering initial insights into disease progression. Preliminary results demonstrate that DL models can estimate subcortical volumes for MS patients. While these results are not equally relevant for all structures, it's important to note that reference values are based on corrected automatic segmentations, often derived from T1w sequences. This could potentially bias results in favor of T1w-based methods [37], although our findings suggest this bias varies by region. The DL algorithms, in conjunction with harmonization techniques, provide results within credible ranges for all regions, as well as expectable rates of change [5,10] as shown in Figs. 4 and 5. Although direct comparisons are challenging, our findings align with literature on comparative studies for hippocampus [23], putamen [27], pallidum, and thalamus [2]. Limitations were observed in regions like the amygdala, known for its segmentation difficulties [40]. Notably, the amygdala is the only region not presenting a typical atrophy pattern (see Fig. 4). Future work will incorporate lesion load analysis at specific localizations to assess its impact on volumetric measures. This will involve comparing manual lesion segmentations (not yet available for all datasets) with automatic segmentations to explore full process automation. This study confirms that FLAIR sequences can be highly relevant for adequate characterization of certain subcortical structures, such as caudate, hippocampus, and accumbens [1], paving the way for future inclusion of additional subcortical regions (currently only available through $SynthSeg^+$). Automatic segmentation, even in the presence of WML, proves reliable, especially when using $SynthSeg$-WMH. This is evidenced by the RMSE with respect to the normative model, where $SynthSeg$-WMH provides estimates of expected deviations in MS patients with age, as well as their deviation from normativity.

In conclusion, while substantial work remains to confirm these initial findings and establish their clinical relevance, our preliminary study suggests potential subcortical volume deviations in MS patients. It primarily serves to highlight the need for further research and methodological validation. By addressing the limitations of current segmentation techniques and expanding upon this normative modeling approach, future studies can work towards more accurate DPM, improved patient stratification, and ultimately, more personalized and effective treatments for individuals with MS.

Acknowledgments. The authors acknowledge access to facilities and expertise of the CIBM, a Swiss research center of excellence founded and supported by CHUV, UNIL, EPFL, UNIGE, HUG.

Disclosure of Interests. PMG and MBC have no competing interests to declare relevant to the content of this article. NM: Funded by Hasler Foundation Responsible AI program. MW: funded by TRAIL and the Walloon Region. PM: Received consulting honoraria from Sanofi, Biogen, and Merck. AC: Supported by EUROSTAR E!113682 HORIZON2020, speaker honoraria from Novartis. CG: The USB and the RC2NB, as the employers of CG, have received the following fees for research support from Siemens, GeNeuro, Sanofi, Biogen, Roche. Consultancy fees from Actelion, Sanofi, Novartis, GeNeuro, Merck, Biogen and Roche; and speaker fees from Sanofi, Novartis, GeNeuro, Merck, Biogen and Roche.

References

1. Abuaf, A.F., et al.: Analysis of the extent of limbic system changes in multiple sclerosis using FreeSurfer and voxel-based morphometry approaches. PLoS ONE **17**(9), e0274778 (Sep2022). https://doi.org/10.1371/journal.pone.0274778, https://www.ncbi.nlm.nih.gov/pmc/articles/PMC9499213/
2. Azevedo, C.J., et al.: Thalamic Atrophy in Multiple Sclerosis: A Magnetic Resonance Imaging Marker of Neurodegeneration throughout Disease. Ann. Neurol. **83**(2), 223–234 (Feb2018). https://doi.org/10.1002/ana.25150, https://www.ncbi.nlm.nih.gov/pmc/articles/PMC6317847/
3. Baller, E.B., et al.: Mapping the relationship of white matter lesions to depression in multiple sclerosis. Biol. Psych. **95**(12), 1072–1080 (2024). https://doi.org/10.1016/j.biopsych.2023.11.010
4. Benedict, R.H.B., Amato, M.P., DeLuca, J., Geurts, J.J.G.: Cognitive impairment in multiple sclerosis: clinical management, MRI, and therapeutic avenues. The Lancet Neurol. **19**(10), 860–871 (2020). https://doi.org/10.1016/S1474-4422(20)30277-5
5. Bermel, R.A., Bakshi, R.: The measurement and clinical relevance of brain atrophy in multiple sclerosis. Lancet Neurol. **5**(2), 158–170 (2006). https://doi.org/10.1016/S1474-4422(06)70349-0
6. Billot, B., et al.: SynthSeg: Domain Randomisation for Segmentation of Brain Scans of any Contrast and Resolution (Dec 2021), http://arxiv.org/abs/2107.09559, arXiv:2107.09559 [cs, eess]
7. Billot, B., Magdamo, C., Cheng, Y., Arnold, S.E., Das, S., Iglesias, J.E.: Robust machine learning segmentation for large-scale analysis of heterogeneous clinical brain MRI datasets. Proc.Nat. Acad. Sci. **120**(9) (2023). https://doi.org/10.1073/pnas.2216399120
8. Commowick, O., et al.: Multiple sclerosis lesions segmentation from multiple experts: the MICCAI 2016 challenge dataset. Neuroimage **244**, 118589 (2021). https://doi.org/10.1016/j.neuroimage.2021.118589
9. Coupé, P., et al.: AssemblyNet: a large ensemble of CNNs for 3D whole brain MRI segmentation. Neuroimage **219**, 117026 (2020). https://doi.org/10.1016/j.neuroimage.2020.117026
10. Coupé, P., et al.: Lifespan neurodegeneration of the human brain in multiple sclerosis. Hum. Brain Mapp. **44**(17), 5602–5611 (Aug 2023). https://doi.org/10.1002/hbm.26464, https://www.ncbi.nlm.nih.gov/pmc/articles/PMC10619394/
11. Dima, D., et al.: Subcortical volumes across the lifespan: Data from 18,605 healthy individuals aged 3-90years. Human Brain Mapp. **43**(1), 452–469 (Feb 2021). https://doi.org/10.1002/hbm.25320, https://www.ncbi.nlm.nih.gov/pmc/articles/PMC8675429/
12. ENIGMA Clinical High Risk for Psychosis Working Group: Normative Modeling of Brain Morphometry in Clinical High Risk for Psychosis. JAMA Psychiat. **81**(1), 77–88 (Jan 2024). https://doi.org/10.1001/jamapsychiatry.2023.3850, https://doi.org/10.1001/jamapsychiatry.2023.3850
13. Eshaghi, A., et al.: Deep gray matter volume loss drives disability worsening in multiple sclerosis. Ann. Neurol. **83**(2), 210–222 (2018). https://doi.org/10.1002/ana.25145, https://onlinelibrary.wiley.com/doi/abs/10.1002/ana.25145, _eprint: https://onlinelibrary.wiley.com/doi/pdf/10.1002/ana.25145
14. Filippi, M., et al.: Assessment of lesions on magnetic resonance imaging in multiple sclerosis: practical guidelines. Brain **142**(7), 1858–1875 (Jul 2019). https://doi.org/10.1093/brain/awz144, https://doi.org/10.1093/brain/awz144

15. Fischl, B.: FreeSurfer. NeuroImage **62**(2), 774–781 (Aug 2012). https://doi.org/10.1016/J.NEUROIMAGE.2012.01.021, https://www.sciencedirect.com/science/article/pii/S1053811912000389, publisher: Academic Press
16. Fortin, J.P., et al.: Harmonization of cortical thickness measurements across scanners and sites. Neuroimage **167**, 104–120 (Feb 2018). https://doi.org/10.1016/j.neuroimage.2017.11.024, https://www.sciencedirect.com/science/article/pii/S105381191730931X
17. Friese, M.A., Schattling, B., Fugger, L.: Mechanisms of neurodegeneration and axonal dysfunction in multiple sclerosis. Nat. Rev. Neurol. **10**(4), 225–238 (Apr 2014). https://doi.org/10.1038/nrneurol.2014.37, https://www.nature.com/articles/nrneurol.2014.37, publisher: Nature Publishing Group
18. Ge, R., et al.: Normative modelling of brain morphometry across the lifespan with CentileBrain: algorithm benchmarking and model optimisation. Lancet Digital Health **6**(3), e211–e221 (Mar 2024). https://doi.org/10.1016/S2589-7500(23)00250-9, https://www.thelancet.com/journals/landig/article/PIIS2589-7500(23)00250-9/fulltext, publisher: Elsevier
19. Giovannoni, G., et al.: Smouldering multiple sclerosis: the 'real MS'. Ther. Adv. Neurol. Disord. **15**, 17562864211066752 (Jan 2022). https://doi.org/10.1177/17562864211066751, https://doi.org/10.1177/17562864211066751, publisher: SAGE Publications Ltd STM
20. Granziera, C.: INsIDER: ImagiNg the Interplay between Axonal DamagE and Repair in Multiple Sclerosis (Jun 2018). https://app.dimensions.ai/details/grant/grant.7548493
21. Granziera, C., et al.: The MAGNIMS Study Group: Quantitative magnetic resonance imaging towards clinical application in multiple sclerosis. Brain **144**(5), 1296–1311 (May 2021). https://doi.org/10.1093/brain/awab029, https://doi.org/10.1093/brain/awab029
22. Graves, J.S., Krysko, K.M., Hua, L.H., Absinta, M., Franklin, R.J.M., Segal, B.M.: Ageing and multiple sclerosis. The Lancet Neurology **22**(1), 66–77 (Jan 2023). https://doi.org/10.1016/S1474-4422(22)00184-3, https://www.thelancet.com/journals/laneur/article/PIIS1474-4422(22)00184-3/fulltext, publisher: Elsevier
23. Hänninen, K., et al.: Thalamic Atrophy Predicts 5-Year Disability Progression in Multiple Sclerosis. Frontiers in Neurology **11** (Jul 2020). https://doi.org/10.3389/fneur.2020.00606, https://www.frontiersin.org/journals/neurology/articles/10.3389/fneur.2020.00606/full, publisher: Frontiers
24. Janssen, J., et al.: Longitudinal allometry of sulcal morphology in health and schizophrenia. Journal of Neuroscience ((In press)) (2022)
25. Janssen, J., et al.: Dissimilarity in sulcal width patterns in the cortex can be used to identify patients with schizophrenia with extreme deficits in cognitive performance. Schizophrenia Bulletin p. 2020.02.04.932210 (2020). https://academic.oup.com/schizophreniabulletin/advance-article/doi/10.1093/schbul/sbaa131/5910387
26. Keshavan, A., Peterson, D., Alexander-Bloch, A., Leyden, K.M.: Brain Charts for People Living with. Mult. Scler. (Nov 2023). https://doi.org/10.1101/2023.11.02.565251, https://www.biorxiv.org/content/10.1101/2023.11.02.565251v1, pages: 2023.11.02.565251 Section: New Results
27. Krämer, J., Meuth, S.G., Tenberge, J.G., Schiffler, P., Wiendl, H., Deppe, M.: Early and degressive putamen atrophy in multiple sclerosis. Int. J. Mol. Sci. **16**(10), 23195–23209 (Sep 2015). https://doi.org/10.3390/ijms161023195, https://www.ncbi.nlm.nih.gov/pmc/articles/PMC4632693/

28. La Rosa, F., et al.: Cortical lesions, central vein sign, and paramagnetic rim lesions in multiple sclerosis: Emerging machine learning techniques and future avenues. NeuroImage: Clinical **36**, 103205 (Jan 2022). https://doi.org/10.1016/J.NICL.2022.103205,publisher: Elsevier
29. Laso, P., et al.: Quantifying white matter hyperintensity and brain volumes in heterogeneous clinical and low-field portable MRI (Feb 2024). https://doi.org/10.48550/arXiv.2312.05119,http://arxiv.org/abs/2312.05119, arXiv:2312.05119 [cs, eess]
30. Lesjak, Ž, Pernuš, F., Likar, B., Špiclin, Ž: Validation of white-matter lesion change detection methods on a novel publicly available mri image database. Neuroinformatics **14**(4), 403–420 (2016). https://doi.org/10.1007/s12021-016-9301-1
31. Marquand, A.F., Rezek, I., Buitelaar, J., Beckmann, C.F.: Understanding heterogeneity in clinical cohorts using normative models: beyond case-control studies. Biol. Psychiat. **80**(7), 552–561 (Oct 2016). https://doi.org/10.1016/J.BIOPSYCH.2015.12.023, https://www.sciencedirect.com/science/article/pii/S0006322316000020, publisher: Elsevier
32. Matthew, P.M., et al.: The association between brain volume loss and disability in multiple sclerosis: a systematic review. Multiple sclerosis and related disorders **74**, 104714 (2023). https://doi.org/10.1016/j.msard.2023.104714
33. Matías-Guiu, J.A., et al.: Identification of cortical and subcortical correlates of cognitive performance in multiple sclerosis using voxel-based morphometry. Front. Neurol. **9** (2018). https://doi.org/10.3389/fneur.2018.00920
34. Müller, J., et al.: Harmonizing definitions for progression independent of relapse activity in multiple sclerosis: a systematic review. JAMA Neurol. **80**(11), 1232 (2023). https://doi.org/10.1001/jamaneurol.2023.3331
35. van Nederpelt, D.R., et al.: Reliability of brain atrophy measurements in multiple sclerosis using MRI: an assessment of six freely available software packages for cross-sectional analyses. Neuroradiology **65**(10), 1459–1472 (2023). https://doi.org/10.1007/s00234-023-03189-8, https://www.ncbi.nlm.nih.gov/pmc/articles/PMC10497452/
36. Noteboom, S., et al.: Feasibility of detecting atrophy relevant for disability and cognition in multiple sclerosis using 3D-FLAIR. J. Neurol. **270**(11), 5201–5210 (2023). https://doi.org/10.1007/s00415-023-11870-4
37. Popescu, V., et al.: Grey matter atrophy in multiple sclerosis: clinical interpretation depends on choice of analysis method. PLoS ONE **11**(1), e0143942 (2016). https://doi.org/10.1371/journal.pone.0143942
38. Royston, P., Altman, D.G.: Regression using fractional polynomials of continuous covariates: parsimonious parametric modelling. J. Royal Stat. Society. Series C (Applied Statistics) **43**(3), 429–467 (1994). https://doi.org/10.2307/2986270, https://www.jstor.org/stable/2986270, publisher: [Wiley, Royal Statistical Society]
39. Rutherford, S., et al.: The normative modeling framework for computational psychiatry. Nat. Protoc. **17**(7), 1711–1734 (Jul 2022). https://doi.org/10.1038/s41596-022-00696-5, https://www.nature.com/articles/s41596-022-00696-5, publisher: Nature Publishing Group
40. Sadil, P., Lindquist, M.A.: Comparing Automated Subcortical Volume Estimation Methods; Amygdala Volumes Estimated by FSL and FreeSurfer Have Poor Consistency (Mar 2024). https://doi.org/10.1101/2024.03.07.583900, https://www.biorxiv.org/content/10.1101/2024.03.07.583900v1, pages: 2024.03.07.583900 Section: New Results

41. Sumowski, J.F., et al.: Cognition in multiple sclerosis. Neurology **90**(6), 278–288 (Feb 2018). https://doi.org/10.1212/WNL.0000000000004977, https://www.ncbi.nlm.nih.gov/pmc/articles/PMC5818015/
42. Thompson, A.J., et al.: Diagnosis of multiple sclerosis: 2017 revisions of the McDonald criteria. Lancet Neurol. **17**(2), 162–173 (Feb2018). https://doi.org/10.1016/S1474-4422(17)30470-2, publisher: Elsevier
43. Tokarska, N., Tottenham, I., Baaklini, C., Gawryluk, J.R.: How does the brain age in individuals with multiple sclerosis? a systematic review. Front. Neurol. **14**, 1207626 (Jun 2023). https://doi.org/10.3389/fneur.2023.1207626, https://www.ncbi.nlm.nih.gov/pmc/articles/PMC10349663/

SegHeD: Segmentation of Heterogeneous Data for Multiple Sclerosis Lesions with Anatomical Constraints

Berke Doga Basaran[1,2(✉)], Xinru Zhang[3,4], Paul M. Matthews[3,5,6], and Wenjia Bai[1,2,3]

[1] Department of Computing, Imperial College London, London, UK
[2] Data Science Institute, Imperial College London, London, UK
bdb19@imperial.ac.uk
[3] Department of Brain Sciences, Imperial College London, London, UK
[4] School of Integrated Circuits and Electronics, Beijing Institute of Technology, Beijing, CN, China
[5] UK Dementia Research Institute, Imperial College London, London, UK
[6] Rosalind Franklin Institute, Didcot, UK

Abstract. Assessment of lesions and their longitudinal progression from brain magnetic resonance (MR) images plays a crucial role in diagnosing and monitoring multiple sclerosis (MS). Machine learning models have demonstrated a great potential for automated MS lesion segmentation. Training such models typically requires large-scale high-quality datasets that are consistently annotated. However, MS imaging datasets are often small, segregated across multiple sites, with different formats (cross-sectional or longitudinal), and diverse annotation styles. This poses a significant challenge to train a unified MS lesion segmentation model. To tackle this challenge, we present SegHeD, a novel multi-dataset multi-task segmentation model that can incorporate heterogeneous data as input and perform all-lesion, new-lesion, as well as vanishing-lesion segmentation. Furthermore, we account for domain knowledge about MS lesions, incorporating longitudinal, spatial, and volumetric constraints into the segmentation model. SegHeD is assessed on five MS datasets and achieves a high performance in all, new, and vanishing-lesion segmentation, outperforming several state-of-the-art methods in this field.

Keywords: Lesion segmentation · Multi-task segmentation · Heterogeneous data · Longitudinal data

1 Introduction

Multiple sclerosis (MS) is an inflammatory and demyelinating neurological disorder affecting the central nervous system. Segmenting and quantifying MS lesions

---

Supplementary Information The online version contains supplementary material available at https://doi.org/10.1007/978-3-031-84525-3_5.

from brain MR images plays a crucial role in clinical diagnosis and research. While many lesion segmentation methods, such as those based on machine learning, have been proposed in recent years, they are often trained on well-curated datasets with a consistent format [5–7,10]. Clinical MS studies involve collection of heterogeneous imaging data from multiple sites that come in diverse data and annotation formats, which are incompatible for training off-the-shelf segmentation models [15,18]. There is a scarcity of approaches tailored to address lesion segmentation in the presence of heterogeneous data and annotation formats. Efforts to bridge this gap are crucial for advancing the accuracy and applicability of lesion segmentation models in MS research and clinical practice. In this work, we propose SegHeD, a novel multi-dataset multi-task brain lesion segmentation model that utilises heterogeneous data for training. SegHeD allows learning from both cross-sectional (a single timepoint) and longitudinal (multiple timepoints) images, and learning from diverse annotations for all lesions, new lesions, and less explored vanishing lesions [25]. We incorporate temporal and volume consistency, and anatomical plausibility for the segmented lesions. Experiments show competitive results against state-of-the-art methods.

1.1 Related Works

Longitudinal Lesion Segmentation. There have been numerous contributions to machine learning methods for cross-sectional brain lesion segmentation [2,20,32]. Longitudinal lesion segmentation, which takes advantage of the temporal information within longitudinal imaging data, is relatively less explored. Elliott et al. utilises the difference map between the two timepoints to detect new lesions in the second timepoint [11]. Jain et al. also utilises the difference map and formulates an expectation-maximisation framework to perform joint segmentation for both timepoints [19]. Denner et al. incorporates a displacement field to learn spatio-temporal changes between timepoints [9]. Basaran et al. employs an nnU-Net [18] along with lesion-aware data augmentation to detect new lesions at the second timepoint [1].

Learning from Heterogeneous Data. Publicly available datasets for brain lesion segmentation vary in format and annotation protocols. Some are cross-sectional with a single timepoint scan, where others are longitudinal with two or more timepoints. It creates a formidable challenge in developing a universal machine learning model that is inclusive of different formats of data. Wu et al. proposes to learn from heterogenous data for all and new-lesion segmentation by imposing relation regularisation onto all-lesion prediction [30]. Liu et al. trains a multi-organ segmentation model using 13 different organ datasets and incorporating CLIP-inspired label encoding [22]. Shi et al. proposes a marginal loss and an exclusion loss to learn a single multi-organ segmentation model from partially annotated datasets [27].

Enforcing Anatomical Plausibility. The incorporation of anatomical plausibility within machine learning models enhances the reliability and trustworthiness of models for clinical use. Dalca et al. proposes a model with a variational auto-encoder to learn location-specific priors for brain structure segmentation [8]. Strumia et al. constrains the lesion segmentation to be within the white matter using a geometric brain model [28]. Finally, Hirsh et al. employs a multi-prior network with tissue probability maps for MRI head anatomy segmentation [16].

1.2 Contributions

The contributions of the proposed method, SegHeD, are three-fold: (1) It is a general framework that accounts for heterogeneous data of different data formats and annotation protocols. (2) It simultaneously performs multiple tasks, including vanishing-lesion segmentation, a task rarely accounted for in previous research. (3) It incorporates domain knowledge about MS lesion segmentation, including temporal consistency and anatomical plausibility.

2 Method

2.1 Overall Architecture

SegHeD is a universal model that can learn from heterogeneous MS imaging data. In terms of data heterogeneity, we account for two data formats: cross-sectional and longitudinal. In terms of label heterogeneity, we account for three annotations protocols: all-lesion annotation, new-lesion annotation which only annotates new lesions in the second timepoint scan, and vanishing-lesion annotation which only annotates lesions that vanish in the second timepoint. The latter two protocols focus on the longitudinal evolution of lesions and avoid annotating all lesions to save time in practice. SegHeD aims to learn and perform all three annotation tasks. Figure 1 illustrates the overall framework of the method.

We assume that the imaging data has two timepoints. SegHeD takes 4 input channels: a first timepoint scan (baseline), x^{t1}, a second timepoint scan (follow-up), x^{t2}, an all-lesion label map for the first timepoint scan, y_a^{t1}, and a white matter mask for the second timepoint scan, x_{wm}^{t2}. For heterogeneous datasets, not all the above inputs are available. Where a second timepoint is not available, the first timepoint is passed as the second, $x^{t2} = x^{t1}$. Where a first timepoint all-lesion label map is not available, y_a^{t1} is replaced with a zero matrix of the same size as x^{t1}. The second timepoint white matter mask, x_{wm}^{t2}, can be obtained using the pretrained SynthSeg brain parcellation tool, which is robust in white matter segmentation even when lesions exist [4]. SegHeD learns to generate 4 outputs: first timepoint all-lesion segmentation, p_a^{t1}, second timepoint all-lesion segmentation, p_a^{t2}, second timepoint new-lesion segmentation, p_n^{t2}, and second timepoint vanishing-lesions, p_v^{t2}. It is formulated as Eq. (1),

$$p_a^{t1}, p_a^{t2}, p_n^{t2}, p_v^{t2} = F(x^{t1}, x^{t2}, y_a^{t1}, x_{wm}^{t2}), \qquad (1)$$

where F denotes the SegHeD model. The all-lesion map, y_a^{t1}, is only input for second timepoint lesion predictions to provide temporal context, and not used for predicting p_a^{t1}. The model allows for a maximum of two timepoints as inputs

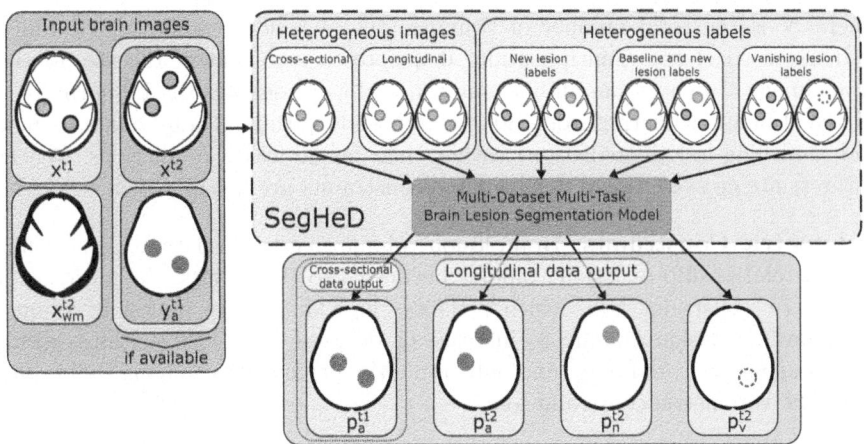

Fig. 1. Visualisation of the proposed framework. SegHeD learns from heterogeneous datasets varying in image and label formats. It can analyse cross-sectional and longitudinal data, and segment all (red), new (green), and vanishing (dashed blue) lesions. (Color figure online)

due to computational limitations. For datasets where a subject has more than two timepoint scans [5], we implement a sliding window approach across the multiple timepoints to perform training and inference. We implement SegHeD with a 3D V-Net architecture [23], with a composite training loss function which includes the Dice loss, longitudinal, spatial, and volumetric constraint losses.

2.2 Anatomical Constraints

SegHeD is trained using a novel combination of losses we term *anatomical constraints*. We take inspiration from how radiologists analyse longitudinal images for identifying lesions [17]. Anatomical constraints formulate the longitudinal, spatial, and volumetric relations for lesion segmentations at the two timepoints.

Longitudinal Constraints. We take advantage of the prior knowledge encoded within the lesion annotation protocol: (1) Predicted new-lesions at the second timepoint, p_n^{t2}, can not be present in the all-lesion label at the first timepoint, y_a^{t1}, but must be present in the second timepoint all-lesion label, y_a^{t2}. (2) Predicted vanishing-lesions at the second timepoint, p_v^{t2}, must be present in the first timepoint all-lesion label, y_a^{t1}, but can not be present in the second timepoint all-lesion label, y_a^{t2}. We formulate these longitudinal constraints using a mean square error loss,

$$\mathcal{L}_{Long} = \frac{1}{N}\sum_{i=1}^{N}\|y_{a_i}^{t1} \odot p_{n_i}^{t2} - \mathbf{0}\|^2 + \frac{1}{N}\sum_{i=1}^{N}\|y_{a_i}^{t2} \odot p_{n_i}^{t2} - \mathbf{1}\|^2 + \\ \frac{1}{N}\sum_{i=1}^{N}\|y_{a_i}^{t1} \odot p_{v_i}^{t2} - \mathbf{1}\|^2 + \frac{1}{N}\sum_{i=1}^{N}\|y_{a_i}^{t2} \odot p_{v_i}^{t2} - \mathbf{0}\|^2, \quad (2)$$

where N is the total number of training images, i denotes the image index, $\odot$ denotes voxel-wise multiplication, $\mathbf{0}$ denotes a zero matrix the size of the input image, $\mathbf{1}$ denotes an all-ones matrix, and $\|\cdot\|^2$ denotes the L2-norm for a flattened image. Differing from [30], we impose longitudinal constraints on new and vanishing-lesion predictions rather than on all-lesion predictions. Where datasets are cross-sectional, longitudinal constraints are not imposed.

Volumetric Constraints. Brain lesion volume changes over time. To account for the relationship of lesion volumes between two timepoints, we construct a volumetric constraint loss, which penalises high differences in lesion volume. We allow the lesion volume to increase or decrease [12,14,26] within certain percentages, α_{high} and α_{low}, and only apply the penalty if any change is beyond this. The volumetric constraint loss is

$$\mathcal{L}_{Vol} = \begin{cases} \frac{1}{N}\sum_{i=1}^{N}(V_{a_i}^{t2} - \alpha_{high} \cdot V_{a_i}^{t1})^2 & \text{if } V_{a_i}^{t2} \geq \alpha_{high} \cdot V_{a_i}^{t1} \\ \frac{1}{N}\sum_{i=1}^{N}(V_{a_i}^{t2} - \alpha_{low} \cdot V_{a_i}^{t1})^2 & \text{if } V_{a_i}^{t2} \leq \alpha_{low} \cdot V_{a_i}^{t1} \\ 0 & \text{otherwise,} \end{cases} \quad (3)$$

where $V_{a_i}^{t1}$ and $V_{a_i}^{t2}$ denote the total lesion volume at timepoint 1 and timepoint 2 for the i-th image, respectively. To our knowledge, there is no study on the proportion by how much lesion volume may *decrease* with respect to time. We empirically set α_{low} to 0.8, after analysing the largest lesion volume decrease in a longitudinal MS dataset [5]. Similarly, we set α_{high} to 1.2, which conforms with medical literature [24]. α_{high} and α_{low} are set for annual percentage change. When a cross-sectional dataset is used, this penalty does not take effect.

Spatial Constraint. MS primarily affects the white region of the brain, with lesions appearing hyperintense on FLAIR images [21,28,29]. We incorporate this prior in two ways: using the white matter mask, x_{wm}^{t2}, as an input channel to leverage the anatomical information; and also by constructing a spatial relation loss function, formulated as the mean square error between the predicted lesions, p, outside of the white matter, x_{wm}^{t2}, and a zero matrix the size of the image,

$$\mathcal{L}_{Spat} = \frac{1}{N}\sum_{i=1}^{N}\|p \odot (\mathbf{1} - x_{wm_i}^{t2}) - \mathbf{0}\|^2. \quad (4)$$

We employ a curriculum learning strategy [3] and introduce the constraint losses after certain number of epochs. The total training loss function is

$$\mathcal{L} = \begin{cases} \mathcal{L}_{DSC} & \text{if } n < \frac{n_{epoch}}{2}, \\ \mathcal{L}_{DSC} + \lambda_L \cdot \mathcal{L}_{Long} + \lambda_V \cdot \mathcal{L}_{Vol} + \lambda_S \cdot \mathcal{L}_{Spat} & \text{if } n \geq \frac{n_{epoch}}{2}, \end{cases} \quad (5)$$

where $\mathcal{L}_{DSC}$ denotes the Dice loss, n is the epoch, n_{epoch} denotes the total number of epochs for training, and λ_L, λ_V and λ_S are weighting parameters.

3 Experiments

3.1 Data

We curate five MS brain lesion datasets with data format or annotation heterogeneities. The first three are public datasets, including the ISBI 2015 MS lesion dataset (MS2015) [5], MICCAI 2016 MS lesion dataset (MS2016) [6], and MICCAI 2021 MS new-lesion segmentation challenge dataset (MSSEG-2) [7]. MS2015 and MS2016 contain all-lesion annotations. MSSEG-2 only contains new-lesion annotations at the second timepoint. A fourth dataset (MSSEG-2+) is constructed based on MSSEG-2, which includes all-lesion annotations at the first timepoint, conducted by an experienced expert in-house using ITK-SNAP [31], along with new-lesion annotations at the second timepoint. Due to the lack of public datasets for vanishing lesions, a fifth dataset, (VAN), is constructed to simulate vanishing lesions by inverting the timepoints in MSSEG-2. Thus new lesions at the second timepoint become the lesions which will vanish from the first timepoint. These five datasets contain lesion images acquired from various MR scanners, patient cohorts, and with different annotation protocols. Further details of the datasets, including the training-test splits, are provided in Supple. Table 1. For all datasets, FLAIR images are used for lesion segmentation, which are resampled to $1 \times 1 \times 1$ mm^3 voxel spacing, followed by brain extraction using SynthSeg [4] and rigid registration into the MNI template space [13].

3.2 Implementation Details

SegHeD is built on a 3D V-Net [23] with four heads at the last layer for four lesion segmentation tasks. We utilise the V-Net architecture with five downsampling layers and an image patch size of $96 \times 96 \times 96$. The method is developed using PyTorch and NVIDIA Tesla T4 GPUs. We use the Adam optimizer with an initial learning rate of 0.001 and train for 20,000 epochs. λ_L, λ_V, and λ_S are empirically set to 5, 1, and 1, respectively. Data augmentations include flipping, rotating, elastic deformation, additive and multiplicative brightness alterations, and additive Gaussian noise. Five-fold cross validation is conducted over a total of 144 training images, which results in an ensemble of five models. We report the performance of the ensemble on the test set.

3.3 Results

SegHeD is a unified model that can perform all-lesion, new-lesion, and vanishing-lesion segmentation tasks. We evaluate its multi-task performance and compare it against state-of-the-art (SOTA) task-specific segmentation methods, nnUnet [18], nnFormer [34], UNETR [15], a recent heterogeneous data learning method, CoactSeg [30], and specifically designed new-lesion segmentation methods [1,33], shown in Table 1. Task-specific SOTA methods are trained twice, once for all-lesion segmentation task (using MS2015 and MS2016) and once for new-lesion segmentation task (using MSSEG-2). It is not possible to include the MSSEG-2+dataset into SOTA training, as these methods do not allow for the heterogeneous annotations which MSSEG-2+ possess. CoactSeg [30] is only trained once. For new lesion segmentation on MSSEG-2, we report Dice scores of MedICL [33], Basaran [1], and the average score of 4 human experts, *Avg. of Experts*, officially released by the challenge organisers [7], and include the lesion-wise $F1$ scores in Supple. Table 2, in accordance with the MSSEG-2 challenge. Exemplar segmentations are compared in Fig. 2, and further provided in Supple. Figure 1.

Table 1. Mean and standard deviations of lesion segmentation Dice scores (%). Best results are in bold. N/A: output not available for the given method. †: Methods where two models need to be trained, one for all-lesion and one for new-lesion segmentation. ‡: Not trained on MSSEG-2+. Asterisks indicate statistical significance (*: $p \leq 0.05$, **: $p \leq 0.01$, ***: $p \leq 0.005$) when using a paired Student's t-test comparing SegHeD's performance to benchmarked methods.

Type	Method	Segmentation task (lesion type)				
		All		New	All&New	Vanishing
		MS2015	MS2016	MSSEG-2	MSSEG-2+	VAN
New-lesion methods	MedICL [33]	N/A	N/A	$50.67_{29.38}$	N/A	N/A
	Basaran et al. [1]	N/A	N/A	$51.06_{28.92}$	N/A	N/A
	Avg. of Experts [7]	N/A	N/A	$55.52_{34.43}$	N/A	N/A
Task-specific SOTA	nnU-Net [18] †	$73.01^{***}_{4.91}$	$74.87^{***}_{7.54}$	$48.89_{31.20}$	N/A	N/A
	nnFormer [34] †	$72.56^{***}_{7.15}$	$74.12^{***}_{8.52}$	$47.01^{*}_{33.39}$	N/A	N/A
	UNETR [15] †	$72.79^{***}_{6.13}$	$73.78^{***}_{7.98}$	$45.51^{**}_{30.84}$	N/A	N/A
Hetero. methods	CoactSeg [30] ‡	$71.28^{***}_{8.24}$	$71.31^{***}_{9.15}$	$47.35_{38.12}$	$58.54^{***}_{18.54}$	N/A
	SegHeD	**$78.10_{6.96}$**	**$84.73_{7.12}$**	$48.64_{33.81}$	**$65.51_{19.67}$**	$35.23_{20.62}$

All-Lesion Segmentation. Table 1 shows that SegHeD significantly outperforms both task-specific SOTA methods and heterogeneous learning method CoactSeg in all-lesion segmentation task. For example, on MS2016 test set, SegHeD improves the Dice score by over 10%. This can be attributed to several factors. SegHeD allows heterogeneous data input and thus can include more images for model training (Table 3). The domain knowledge encoded via anatomical constraints also helps reduce false positives, as shown in Fig. 2.

New-Lesion Segmentation. SegHeD performs competitively against task-specific SOTA methods and CoactSeg in new-lesion segmentation, achieving similar or slightly higher Dice scores. Although it slightly underperforms MedICL [33] and Basaran [1], two top methods in MSSEG-2 challenge specifically designed for this dataset, SegHeD is capable of performing multiple tasks with a single model.

Vanishing-Lesion Segmentation. There are no existing methods dedicated for this objective. In this new yet challenging task, we achieve a Dice score of 35.23%. The difficulty of this task is the joint modelling of vanishing lesions with all and new lesions. While task-specific methods need to learn either hyperintense region features for new and all-lesion segmentation, *or* hypointense region features for vanishing lesion segmentation, SegHeD learns both features with respect to previous timepoints and surrounding tissues. We hope the results here provide useful insights for future dataset curation efforts and benchmarking work.

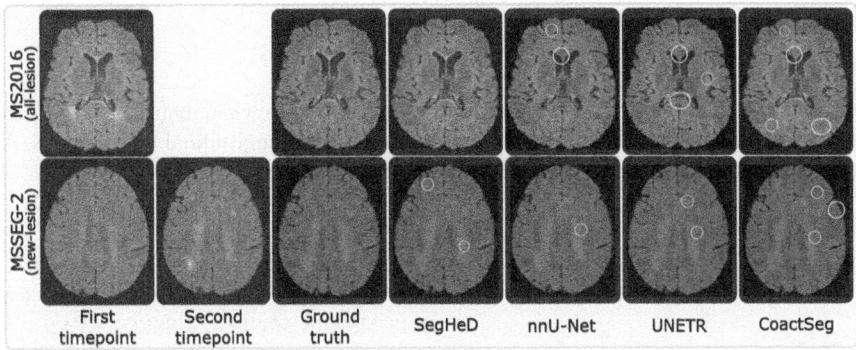

Fig. 2. Qualitative comparison of all-lesion (top row) and new-lesion (bottom row) segmentation performance. Yellow regions denote false positive segmentations, whereas cyan regions denote false negative segmentations. (Color figure online)

Ablation Studies. We perform two ablation studies for the different loss terms and the white matter mask input channel and the effect of incorporating heterogeneous data input. Table 2 shows that each component contributes to different tasks, while also increasing overall Dice scores when all incorporated. Notably, new and vanishing-lesion segmentation performance increases when $\mathcal{L}_{Long}$ is introduced, all-lesion segmentation performance increases when $\mathcal{L}_{Vol}$ is introduced, and an overall increase occurs when $\mathcal{L}_{Spat}$ and x_{wm}^{t2} are presented. We also provide ablation results on SegHeD performance with varying amounts of heterogeneous data input in Table 3. In particular, we observe a performance boost when datasets containing overlapping tasks are included. For instance, adding the MSSEG-2+ dataset, which specifically encompasses both the all-lesion and new-lesion segmentation tasks, leads to improvements in both all-lesion and new-lesion segmentation.

Improved Temporal Consistency. Figure 3 displays predicted lesion volumes across multiple timepoints for two test subjects from MS2015. SegHeD predictions (blue) show higher temporal consistency with the ground truth (black) due to the proposed constraints, obtaining the highest Pearson's correlation coefficient with the ground truth. Improved temporal consistency facilitates downstream analysis tasks, such as evaluating annual lesion atrophy or growth rate.

Table 2. Ablation study of proposed losses and white matter mask input channel. Asterisks indicate statistical significance (*: p≤ 0.05, **: p ≤ 0.01, ***: p ≤ 0.005) when using a paired Student's t-test comparing SegHeD's performance to ablated methods.

Ablation Settings				Dice score (%)				
$\mathcal{L}_{Long}$	$\mathcal{L}_{Vol}$	$\mathcal{L}_{Spat}$	x_{wm}^{t2}	MS2015	MS2016	MSSEG-2	MSSEG-2+	VAN
-	-	-	-	$73.19^{***}_{7.20}$	$76.93^{***}_{9.01}$	$45.28^{***}_{38.54}$	$60.25^{***}_{20.04}$	$30.97^{***}_{27.34}$
-	-	-	✓	$73.59^{***}_{8.03}$	$77.40^{***}_{9.05}$	$46.15^{***}_{37.06}$	$61.80^{***}_{20.90}$	$31.50^{***}_{26.60}$
✓	-	-	-	$73.40^{***}_{6.88}$	$77.38^{***}_{8.99}$	$48.55_{34.80}$	$64.86^{*}_{21.12}$	$33.88^{**}_{28.97}$
✓	✓	-	-	$75.91^{**}_{7.59}$	$81.99^{**}_{8.03}$	$48.49_{35.00}$	$65.01^{*}_{20.21}$	$34.52^{*}_{30.63}$
✓	✓	✓	-	$77.93_{6.72}$	$82.71^{**}_{7.42}$	$48.56_{34.04}$	$65.20^{*}_{19.79}$	$34.90^{*}_{28.57}$
✓	✓	✓	✓	$78.10_{6.96}$	$84.73_{7.12}$	$48.64_{33.81}$	$65.51_{19.07}$	$35.23_{20.62}$

Table 3. Ablation study to show the improved performance when including additional heterogeneous datasets. All studies are implemented with longitudinal reasoning. N/A: output not available for the given dataset.

Datasets included					Dice score (%)			
MS2015	MS2016	MSSEG-2	MSSEG-2+	VAN	Segmentation task (lesion type)			
					All	New	All&New	Vanishing
					MS2015	MS2016	MSSEG-2	MSSEG-2+	VAN
✓	✓	-	-	-	$74.97_{5.35}$	$77.92_{7.40}$	N/A	N/A	N/A
-	-	✓	-	-	N/A	N/A	$49.00_{32.32}$	N/A	N/A
✓	✓	✓	-	-	$75.30_{6.51}$	$78.11_{8.42}$	$46.73_{34.17}$	$61.16_{21.50}$	N/A
✓	✓	✓	✓	-	$77.93_{7.39}$	$84.76_{7.19}$	$48.02_{35.27}$	$65.88_{19.20}$	N/A
✓	✓	✓	✓	✓	$78.10_{6.96}$	$84.73_{7.12}$	$48.64_{33.81}$	$65.51_{19.67}$	$35.23_{20.62}$

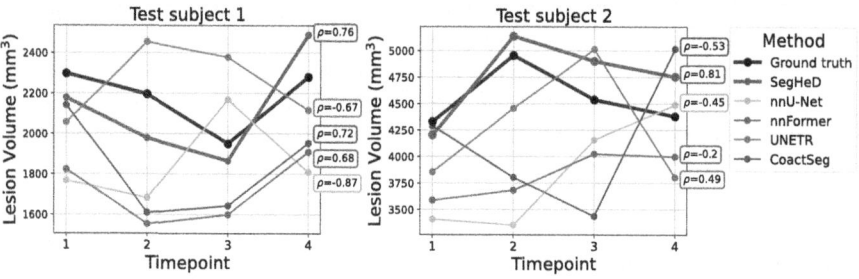

Fig. 3. Predicted lesion volumes across four timepoints for two test subjects. SegHeD (blue) predictions are temporally more consistent with the ground truth (black), compared to competing methods. The ρ value for each method indicates its Pearson's correlation coefficient with the ground truth, the higher the better. (Color figure online)

4 Conclusion

We present SegHeD, a novel multi-task MS lesion segmentation method for learning from heterogeneous and longitudinal data. It is capable of segmenting all, new, and vanishing lesions for both cross-sectional and longitudinal datasets. Experiments on five MS lesion datasets show that SegHeD outperforms other competing segmentation methods for all-lesion segmentation, and performs competitively for new-lesion segmentation. Notably, its capability of leveraging heterogeneous data will greatly advance existing MS imaging studies and facilitate large-scale multi-site data analyses with diverse data formats and annotations.

Acknowledgments. This work is supported by the UKRI CDT in AI for Healthcare http://ai4health.io (Grant No. EP/S023283/1). W. Bai is co-funded by EPSRC DeepGeM Grant (EP/W01842X/1) and NIHR Imperial Biomedical Research Centre (BRC). The views expressed are those of the authors and not necessarily those of the NIHR or the Department of Health and Social Care.

References

1. Basaran, B.D., Matthews, P.M., Bai, W.: New lesion segmentation for multiple sclerosis brain images with imaging and lesion-aware augmentation. Front. Neurosci. **16** (2022)
2. Basaran, B.D., Zhang, W., Qiao, M., et al.: LesionMix: A lesion-level data augmentation method for medical image segmentation. In: MICCAI DALI Workshop (2023)
3. Bengio, Y., Louradour, J., Collobert, R., Weston, J.: Curriculum learning. In: International Conference on Machine Learning (2009)
4. Billot, B., et al.: SynthSeg: segmentation of brain MRI scans of any contrast and resolution without retraining. Medical Image Anal. **86**, 102789 (2023). https://doi.org/10.1016/j.media.2023.102789
5. Carass, A., Roy, S., Jog, A., et al.: Longitudinal multiple sclerosis lesion segmentation: Resource and challenge. NeuroImage (2017)
6. Commowick, O., et al.: Objective evaluation of multiple sclerosis lesion segmentation using a data management and processing infrastructure. Sci. Reports **8**(1) (2018). https://doi.org/10.1038/s41598-018-31911-7
7. Commowick, O., Masson, A., Combes, B., et al.: MICCAI 2021 MSSEG-2 challenge quantitative results (2021). https://zenodo.org/records/5775523
8. Dalca, A.V., Guttag, J., Sabuncu, M.R.: Anatomical priors in convolutional networks for unsupervised biomedical segmentation. In: Computer Vision and Pattern Recognition (CVPR) (2018)
9. Denner, S., Khakzar, A., Sajid, M., et al.: Spatio-temporal learning from longitudinal data for multiple sclerosis lesion segmentation. In: Crimi, A., Bakas, S. (eds.) Brainlesion: Glioma, Multiple Sclerosis, Stroke and Traumatic Brain Injuries (2021)
10. Eisenmann, M., Reinke, A., Weru, V., et al.: Biomedical image analysis competitions: The state of current participation practice. arXiv preprint arXiv:2212.08568 (2022)

11. Elliott, C., Arnold, D.L., Collins, D.L., Arbel, T.: Temporally consistent probabilistic detection of new multiple sclerosis lesions in brain MRI. IEEE Trans. Med. Imag. **32**(8), 1490–1503 (2013). https://doi.org/10.1109/TMI.2013.2258403
12. Filippi, M., Horsfield, M.A., Tofts, P.S., et al.: Quantitative assessment of MRI lesion load in monitoring the evolution of multiple sclerosis. Brain **118**(6), 1601–1612 (1995)
13. Fonov, V., Evans, A., McKinstry, R., et al.: Unbiased nonlinear average age-appropriate brain templates from birth to adulthood. In: NeuroImage (2009)
14. Genovese, D., et al.: Atrophied brain T2 lesion volume at MRI Is associated with disability progression and conversion to secondary progressive multiple sclerosis. Radiology **293**(2), 424–433 (2019). https://doi.org/10.1148/radiol.2019190306
15. Hatamizadeh, A., Tang, Y., Nath, V., et al.: UNETR: Transformers for 3D medical image segmentation. In: Proceedings of the IEEE/CVF Winter Conference on Applications of Computer Vision (2022)
16. Hirsch, L., Huang, Yu., Parra, L.C.: Segmentation of MRI head anatomy using deep volumetric networks and multiple spatial priors. J. Med. Imag. **8**(03) (2021). https://doi.org/10.1117/1.JMI.8.3.034001
17. Homssi, M., Sweeney, E., Demmon, E., et al.: Evaluation of the statistical detection of change algorithm for screening patients with MS with new lesion activity on longitudinal brain MRI. Am. J. Neuroradiol. **44**(6) (2023)
18. Isensee, F., Jaeger, P.F., Kohl, S.A.A., et al.: nnU-Net: a self-configuring method for deep learning-based biomedical image segmentation. Nature Methods (2021)
19. Jain, S., Ribbens, A., Sima, D.M., et al.: Two time point MS lesion segmentation in brain MRI: An expectation-maximization framework. Front. Neurosci. **10** (2016)
20. Kamnitsas, K., et al.: Efficient multi-scale 3D CNN with fully connected CRF for accurate brain lesion segmentation. Med. Image Anal. **36**, 61–78 (2017). https://doi.org/10.1016/j.media.2016.10.004
21. Lassmann, H.: Multiple sclerosis pathology. Cold Spring Harbor Perspectives in Medicine **8**(3) (2018)
22. Liu, J., Zhang, Y., Chen, J., et al.: CLIP-driven universal model for organ segmentation and tumor detection. In: International Conference on Computer Vision (2023)
23. Milletari, F., Navab, N., Ahmadi, S.A.: V-net: Fully convolutional neural networks for volumetric medical image segmentation. In: International Conference on 3D Vision (3DV) (2016)
24. Molyneux, P.D., et al.: Correlations between monthly enhanced MRI Lesion rate and changes in T2 Lesion volume in multiple sclerosis. Ann. Neurol. **43**(3), 332–339 (1998). https://doi.org/10.1002/ana.410430311
25. Prineas, J.W., Barnard, R.O., Revesz, T., et al.: Multiple sclerosis: pathology of recurrent lesions. Brain **116**(3) (1993)
26. Sethi, V., et al.: Slowly eroding lesions in multiple sclerosis. Multiple Sclerosis J. **23**(3), 464–472 (2017). https://doi.org/10.1177/1352458516655403
27. Shi, G., Xiao, L., Chen, Y., Zhou, S.K.: Marginal loss and exclusion loss for partially supervised multi-organ segmentation. Med. Image Anal. **70**, 101979 (2021). https://doi.org/10.1016/j.media.2021.101979
28. Strumia, M., Schmidt, F.R., Anastasopoulos, C., Granziera, C., Krueger, G., Brox, T.: White matter MS-lesion segmentation using a geometric brain model. IEEE Trans. Med. Imag. **35**(7), 1636–1646 (2016). https://doi.org/10.1109/TMI.2016.2522178

29. Van Leemput, K., Maes, F., Vandermeulen, D., Colchester, A., Suetens, P.: Automated segmentation of multiple sclerosis lesions by model outlier detection. IEEE Trans. Med. Imag. **20**(8), 677–688 (2001). https://doi.org/10.1109/42.938237
30. Wu, Y., Wu, Z., Shi, H., et al.: CoactSeg: Learning from heterogeneous data for new multiple sclerosis lesion segmentation. In: Medical Image Computing and Computer Assisted Intervention (2023)
31. Yushkevich, P.A., Gao, Y., Gerig, G.: Itk-snap: An interactive tool for semi-automatic segmentation of multi-modality biomedical images. In: 2016 38th Annual International Conference of the IEEE Engineering in Medicine and Biology Society (EMBC) (2016)
32. Zeng, C., Gu, L., Liu, Z., Zhao, S.: Review of deep learning approaches for the segmentation of multiple sclerosis lesions on brain MRI. Front. Neuroinform. **14** (2020). https://doi.org/10.3389/fninf.2020.610967
33. Zhang, H., Li, H., Oguz, I.: Segmentation of new MS lesions with tiramisu and 2.5D stacked slices. MSSEG-2 challenge proceedings: Multiple sclerosis new lesions segmentation challenge using a data management and processing infrastructure **61** (2021)
34. Zhou, H.-Y., et al.: nnFormer: volumetric medical image segmentation via a 3D transformer. IEEE Trans. Image Process. **32**, 4036–4045 (2023). https://doi.org/10.1109/TIP.2023.3293771

Longitudinal Segmentation of MS Lesions via Temporal Difference Weighting

Maximilian R. Rokuss[1,2(✉)], Yannick Kirchhoff[1,2,3], Saikat Roy[1,2],
Balint Kovacs[1,4], Constantin Ulrich[1,4], Tassilo Wald[1,2,5],
Maximilian Zenk[1,4], Stefan Denner[1,4], Fabian Isensee[1,5],
Philipp Vollmuth[1,6,7], Jens Kleesiek[8,9], and Klaus Maier-Hein[1,10]

[1] German Cancer Research Center (DKFZ), Division of Medical Image Computing, Heidelberg, Germany
{yannick.kirchhoff,maximilian.rokuss}@dkfz-heidelberg.de
[2] Faculty of Mathematics and Computer Science, Heidelberg University, Heidelberg, Germany
[3] HIDSS4Health - Helmholtz Information and Data Science School for Health, Karlsruhe, Heidelberg, Germany
[4] Medical Faculty Heidelberg, Heidelberg University, Heidelberg, Germany
[5] Helmholtz Imaging, German Cancer Research Center, Heidelberg, Germany
[6] Department of Neuroradiology, Heidelberg University Hospital, Heidelberg, Germany
[7] Division for Computational Neuroimaging, Department of Neuroradiology, Heidelberg University Hospital, Heidelberg, Germany
[8] Institute for Artificial Intelligence in Medicine (IKIM), University Hospital Essen, Essen, Germany
[9] Cancer Research Center Cologne Essen (CCCE), University Hospital Essen, West German Cancer Center Essen, Essen, Germany
[10] Pattern Analysis and Learning Group, Department of Radiation Oncology, Heidelberg University Hospital, Heidelberg, Germany

Abstract. Accurate segmentation of Multiple Sclerosis (MS) lesions in longitudinal MRI scans is crucial for monitoring disease progression and treatment efficacy. Although changes across time are taken into account when assessing images in clinical practice, most existing deep learning methods treat scans from different timepoints separately. Among studies utilizing longitudinal images, a simple channel-wise concatenation is the primary albeit suboptimal method employed to integrate timepoints. We introduce a novel approach that explicitly incorporates temporal differences between baseline and follow-up scans through a unique architectural inductive bias called Difference Weighting Block. It merges features from two timepoints, emphasizing changes between scans. We achieve

---

M. R. Rokuss, and Y. Kirchhoff—Contributed equally. Each co-first author may list themselves as lead author on their CV.

Supplementary Information The online version contains supplementary material available at https://doi.org/10.1007/978-3-031-84525-3_6.

© The Author(s), under exclusive license to Springer Nature Switzerland AG 2025
A. Schroder et al. (Eds.): MICCAI 2024 Workshops, LNCS 15401, pp. 64–74, 2025.
https://doi.org/10.1007/978-3-031-84525-3_6

superior scores in lesion segmentation (Dice Score, Hausdorff distance) as well as lesion detection (lesion-level F_1 score) as compared to state-of-the-art longitudinal and single timepoint models across two datasets. Our code is made publicly available at: www.github.com/MIC-DKFZ/Longitudinal-Difference-Weighting.

Keywords: Medical Image Segmentation · Longitudinal Imaging · Multiple Sclerosis

1 Introduction

Multiple sclerosis (MS) is an inflammatory disease in the central nervous system (CNS), characterized by the accumulation of demyelinating white-matter lesions in the brain and spinal cord, especially affecting young adults [12]. Magnetic resonance imaging (MRI) has been proven as a valuable diagnostic tool for identifying and monitoring MS. In clinical practice, patients typically undergo routine screenings that involve multiple MRI scans throughout their treatment. For instance, official MS guidelines advocate for regular screenings at intervals ranging from 3 to 12 months [21]. Monitoring the progress of MS lesions is crucial for evaluating the effectiveness of anti-inflammatory disease-modifying drugs [7]. However, analyzing the lesion load of several MS scans at different timepoints is a heavy burden for clinicians, adding to their workload [25]. Thus, automating lesion segmentation is critical for clinical computer-aided diagnosis (CAD) systems, facilitating precise quantification for evaluating treatment response [23].

There has been a multitude of approaches proposed for the automated segmentation of MS lesions in brain MRI sequences, with deep learning being widely utilized [9,26]. However, common methods for white-matter lesion segmentation process images from various timepoints independently [4,22], deviating from the clinical practice of comprehensively assessing patients' progression over time. Current state-of-the-art biomedical image segmentation pipelines like nnUNet [16] or SwinUNETR [15] are cross-sectional methods, meaning they only use information from single timepoints, even when longitudinal (multiple timepoint) data is available. So far, only a few works proposed using the information of prior scans for the segmentation task [11]. Early work from Birenbaum et al. [3] passes 2D slices from multiple timepoints through a single view CNN, which are then concatenated and used to classify the center pixel. Denner et al. [10] proposed a multitask network simultaneously trained on registration and segmentation using a 2.5D approach. Szeskin et al. [24] employed a multi-channel 3D recurrent residual U-Net model (R2UNet [1]) trained on pairs of registered scans, benefiting from the inclusion of additional time steps as inputs. Wu et al. [25] combine heterogeneous dataset annotations using a model that outputs the new-lesion and all-lesion mask given a baseline and follow-up scan. Notably, the non-deep learning-based neuroimage analysis tool *FreeSurfer* [13] was recently extended with a longitudinal whole-brain and white-matter lesion segmentation method, solving an optimization problem across all scans of a given patient [6].

Nevertheless, none of the above methods impose an explicit architectural inductive bias to guide the network to use the additional timepoint. While multiple timepoints can be trivially incorporated into standard UNet-like architectures by channel-wise concatenation [10,24,25], a potential concern is that the network might primarily emphasize one particular scan similar to a single timepoint model. Previous methods lack thorough evaluation against strong benchmarks [10,24], often comparing only to their own method with single timepoint input or basic U-Net architectures, without considering state-of-the-art single timepoint methods like nnUNet [16] or SwinUNETR [15]. Additionally, a recent review revealed that most longitudinal lesion segmentation models lack publicly available datasets or code, negatively impacting reproducibility [11].

Addressing the aforementioned issues, we propose a method for longitudinal MS lesion segmentation, inherently adhering to clinical practice of assessing an image by comparison, i.e. the difference, to the previous scan. Our method introduces explicit inductive bias to leverage the information surplus from the additional baseline scan. Specifically, our model encodes both baseline and follow-up images into a latent space where a novel *Difference Weighting Block* produces a temporally-informed combined representation which the decoder uses to generate the segmentation mask. Extensive experiments on two public MS datasets from different sites demonstrate that our proposed model outperforms all state-of-the-art single timepoint baselines as well as all publicly available longitudinal MS lesion segmentation methods. It achieves superior performance for both the pixel-based Dice score and the clinically more relevant lesion-based F_1 score, thus improving the lesion detection rate.

Overall, our contributions encompass these key aspects:

- **Pitfalls of existing Longitudinal Methods:** We demonstrate that state-of-the-art single timepoint baselines surpass existing longitudinal methods. However, even naively combining longitudinal data with strong single timepoint models yields superior performance.
- **Difference Weighting Block:** Inspired by clinical practice, we incorporate explicit architectural bias to fully leverage the benefits of longitudinal information. We introduce a novel component for merging features from different timepoints in latent space, significantly enhancing generated segmentations.
- **Cross-Dataset Generalization of Longitudinal Benefits:** Our method demonstrates transferability to unseen datasets, indicating that the advantages of longitudinal information can be effectively applied to real world scenarios.

2 Method

2.1 Integrating Prior Images for Enhanced Segmentation

Similar to a single timepoint method, our model F_θ is designed to predict a segmentation mask $\hat{Y}_c$ for a *current* scan X_c. However, it additionally incorporates information from a *prior* scan X_p by co-learning both representations. The method thus leverages the change between X_p and X_c as depicted in Eq. 1. For instance, the *prior* image can correspond to the baseline scan, and the *current* image represents a subsequent follow-up examination. For predicting the baseline scan we use the subsequent follow-up examination as additional information.

$$F_\theta : \mathbb{R}^3 \to \mathbb{R}^3, \hat{Y}_c = F_\theta(X_c, X_p) \text{ where } X_c \neq X_p \tag{1}$$

The aim of a longitudinal approach is to improve the segmentation by utilizing information from multiple timepoints. Instead of the early fusion of longitudinal scans in the form of channel-wise concatenation, we propose a later fusion of features from the two timepoints. We achieve this by passing both the baseline and follow-up images through a shared encoder. Then, we merge the resulting features using a novel *Difference Weighting Block*, which takes into account information from both scans, explicitly putting focus on the prior scan. Our architecture inherently utilizes the feature space difference between the current and prior scans as a weighting factor. This combined representation is then used by the decoder to produce the output segmentation. Figure 1 shows an overview of our pipeline as well as a schematic of the Difference Weighting Block.

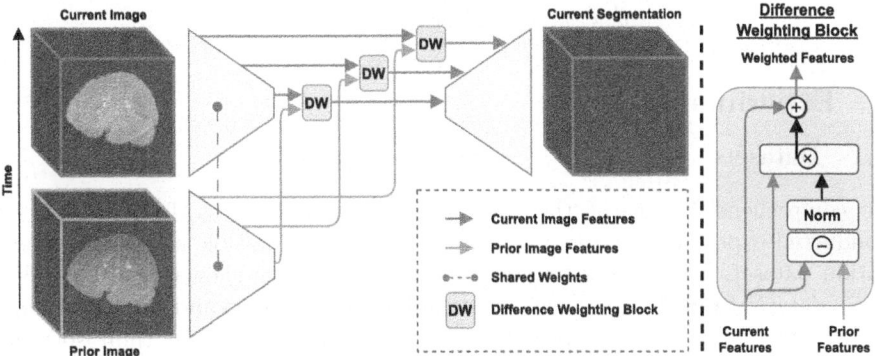

Fig. 1. *Left:* Pipeline of our proposed model. First, the prior image (baseline) and current image (follow-up) are both encoded by a shared encoder. Subsequently, the Difference Weighting Block is applied on all skip connections to merge these encoded representations, emphasizing dissimilarities between the two images. This temporally enhanced representation is then fed to the decoder to produce the segmentation of the current image. *Right:* Architecture of the Difference Weighting Block. Firstly, the difference between the features extracted from the current and prior images is computed, followed by an Instance Norm. This result is then multiplied with the current image features and finally a residual connection is added.

2.2 Difference Weighting Block

The Difference Weighting Block acts as a mechanism to weigh and incorporate the temporal differences between images, enhancing the ability of the network to leverage prior scan information for improved segmentation. The architecture involves a series of steps designed to effectively merge latent representations from both the current and prior images. It operates on all resolutions of the U-Net skip connections. Initially, the block calculates the difference between the features x_c extracted from the current image and features x_p obtained from the prior image. Subsequently, an Instance Normalization is applied to the calculated difference, generating a *normalized attention map highlighting areas of change*. The attention map is then multiplied by the features initially derived from the current image. This multiplication process serves as a weighting to emphasize or de-emphasize specific features based on the differences between the two images. It effectively modulates the importance of each feature in the context of changes over time. In contrast to classical attention our block offers a distinct advantage through its lightweight design, which enables 3D operation at all resolutions, and the inherent focus on the differences between inputs. Finally, to ensure a smooth integration, a residual connection is introduced adding the modified features back to the original features extracted from the current image. The output of the Difference Weighting Block are the temporally informed features x'_c used to predict the mask of the current image as shown in Eq. 2.

$$x'_c = x_c \times \text{InstNorm}(x_c - x_p) + x_c \qquad (2)$$

3 Experiments

3.1 Datasets

To comprehensively assess the efficacy of our model across diverse data, we conducted experiments on two separate longitudinal multiple sclerosis segmentation datasets obtained from distinct medical sites, as shown in Table 1. We use a dataset from the University Medical Center Ljubljana and the Laboratory of Imaging Technologies, University of Ljubljana [19]. It contains 1mm isotropic resolution T1-weighted and FLAIR MR brain images from 162 subjects, each with two to four timepoints, acquired with a 3T Siemens Magnetom Trio MR system. Manual annotations of white-matter lesions were performed through automated segmentation [14], followed by manual corrections by three expert raters [19], with collaborative revisions to achieve consensus. A partial version of the dataset is publicly accessible[1], the rest is available upon request. Additionally, we utilize the publicly accessible training split[2] from the ISBI 2015 Longitudinal MS Lesion Segmentation Challenge [5] for independent model evaluation. It comprises 5 patients, with an average of 4.4 scans per patient, acquired using a 3T MRI scanner from Philips Medical Systems. Manual annotations of white-matter lesions were conducted by two raters. For consistency with the Ljubljana dataset, we exclusively employ the T1-weighted and FLAIR sequences out of the four available sequences (T1w, T2w, PDw, and FLAIR) for evaluation.

---

[1] https://github.com/muschellij2/open_ms_data
[2] https://smart-stats-tools.org/lesion-challenge.

Table 1. Details of the datasets used for training and evaluation. The dataset split is shown in parenthesis (Training, Test). Note that we use the ISBI 2015 dataset solely as an external testset due to the small size.

Origin	Modalities	Patients		Number of scans	
		Train	Test	Train	Test
Ljubljana [19]	T1, FLAIR	129	33	264	67
ISBI 2015 [5]	T1, FLAIR	-	5	-	21

3.2 Evaluation Metrics

In this study, we assess the efficacy of various models using a comprehensive set of metrics, encompassing volumetric, distance-based, and lesion-centered measures. Specifically, we calculate the Dice coefficient for voxel-level accuracy, the 95% Hausdorff distance to evaluate boundary discrepancies, and the lesion-based F_1 score as a clinically relevant lesion detection metric [20]. To align with previous evaluation guidelines [8], lesions smaller than 3 mm^3 are omitted from both the ground truth and predictions prior to metric computation. Results without size filtering are shown in the Appendix. We compute the lesion-based F_1 score as the harmonic mean of separately calculated lesion-based precision and recall. Following best practice guidelines for medical object detection [2,17], we set a threshold of 0.1 for the Intersection over Union of true positive lesions. Crucially, to account for the varying number of scans per patient and to mitigate potential biases, we average all metrics across patients. The patient-wise averaging ensures a fair and balanced evaluation, reflecting the performance in the clinical scenario.

3.3 Implementation Details

First, we perform affine registration utilizing FSL FLIRT [18] to align follow-up examinations with the initial baseline scan. This ensures a consistent image space across all scans for a given patient. Following the methodology of nnUNet [16], we automatically determine the optimal U-Net architecture, normalization scheme, and patch size. Training is conducted with a batch size of 2, utilizing patches of dimensions 128 × 160 × 128 and z-score normalization. It is important to note that during preprocessing, we crop all images of an individual patient to the largest nonzero bounding box encompassing all timepoints. For optimization, we employ the default nnUNet training scheme, that is, SGD optimizer with momentum 0.99, an initial learning rate of 0.01 and polynomial decay.

Table 2. Comparison of state-of-the-art single timepoint and longitudinal methods for MS lesion segmentation on the Ljubljana dataset [19]. *Longitudinal nnUNet* is shown as an ablation. Statistical analysis is given in the Appendix. **Bold**: Best performance, Underlined: best single or multi timepoint baseline.

	Method	5-fold Cross Val			Test Set		
		DSC ↑	HD95 ↓	F_1 ↑	DSC ↑	HD95 ↓	F_1 ↑
Single Timepoint	nnUNet [16]	<u>73.37</u>	<u>4.51</u>	<u>69.83</u>	<u>74.16</u>	<u>4.95</u>	<u>71.27</u>
	SwinUNETR [15]	73.12	4.72	69.34	74.05	4.96	70.67
Longitudinal	FreeSurfer Samseg (2023) [6]	62.47	12.77	37.08	45.54	15.84	33.05
	Denner et.al. (2020) [10]	67.42	5.69	61.56	69.57	5.43	65.59
	Szeskin et.al.[3] (2022) [24]	73.24	4.87	68.45	73.44	5.11	69.08
	Wu et.al. (2023) [25]	71.61	6.16	64.42	72.53	6.57	66.17
	Longitudinal nnUNet *(Ours)*	74.37	4.12	71.32	75.29	**4.59**	72.92
	+ Diff. Weighting *(Ours)*	**75.05**	**3.99**	**72.72**	**75.61**	4.61	**73.28**

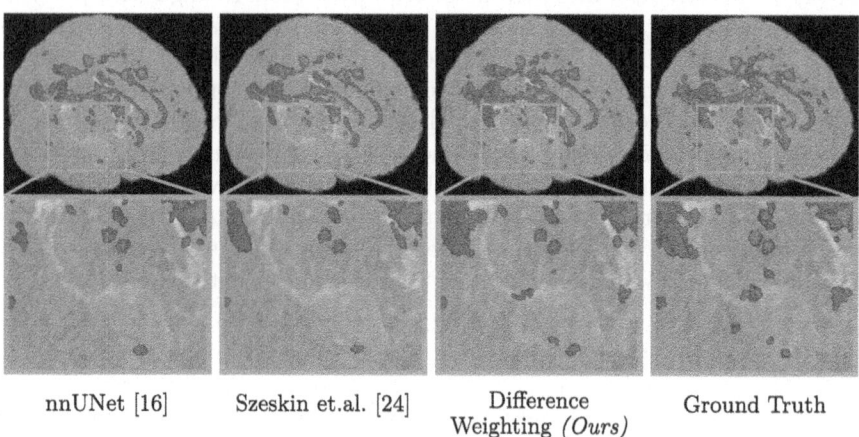

nnUNet [16]　　Szeskin et.al. [24]　　Difference Weighting *(Ours)*　　Ground Truth

Fig. 2. Qualitative results on the Ljubljana dataset. Compared to related work, our proposed method demonstrates superior performance in volumetric delineation of MS lesions and successfully identifies lesions missed by other methods.

4 Results and Discussion

Table 2 illustrates SOTA performance against several established single and multi timepoint baselines on the Ljubljana dataset. We also show the generalizability of our best models on the ISBI 2015 dataset in Table 3 respectively. Figure 2 shows additional qualitative results on the Ljubljana dataset. Overall, we demonstrate the following findings:

Powerful Single Timepoint Networks Outperform Existing Longitudinal Approaches: nnUNet [16], as the best single timepoint model, achieves a

Dice score of 74.16%, a 95% Hausdorff Distance of 4.95mm and a lesion-based F_1 score of 71.27% on the test set of the Ljubljana dataset. The results clearly show that current *longitudinal* approaches consistently struggle to surpass or even reach this performance. The most competitive longitudinal baseline, a reimplementation of Szeskin et.al.'s method [24] within the nnUNet framework, still performs worse than nnUNet on all metrics, especially falling short 2.19% in lesion-based F_1 score. The other two deep learning based baselines from Denner et al. [10] and Wu el.al. [25] demonstrate even lower performances with large decreases in all metrics. The non deep learning based FreeSurfer Samseg tool [6] achieves the worst results with a Dice score of 45.54%, a 95% Hausdorff distance of 15.84mm and a lesion-based F_1 score of 33.05%.

Pairing Powerful Single Timepoint Methods with Longitudinal Data Enables Efficient use of Additional Information: While nnUNet on single timepoints outperforms inefficient longitudinal methods, the ablation of naively integrating longitudinal data into nnUNet through color channel concatenation (*Longitudinal nnUNet*) delivers enhancements across all investigated metrics when compared to previous longitudinal methods and SOTA single timepoint approaches. This underlines the potential gain longitudinal data can have even just as an additional channel input of a powerful single timepoint network.

Employing Inductive Bias via Feature Differences Achieves SOTA Performance: The integration of our novel Difference Weighting method further elevates the model's performance, demonstrating a new state-of-the-art performance. Our proposed method improves upon nnUNet, as the best performing state-of-the-art model, by 1.45% in Dice score and 0.34mm in 95% Hausdorff distance. Notably, we see an increase of 2.01% in lesion-based F_1 score, as the most important clinical metric, indicating that our approach better detects individual lesions. We also surpass the Longitudinal nnUNet indicating that the imposed inductive bias is superior over plain channel-wise concatenation.

Benefits from Longitudinal Data are Transferable Across Datasets: The evaluation on the ISBI 2015 dataset validates the robustness of our method across datasets as shown in Table 3. It is worth noting that this dataset, while used for generalization testing, is too small to properly train longitudinal methods. Although slightly underperforming in the 95% Hausdorff distance, our Difference Weighting approach delivers the best performance in Dice score and lesion-based F_1 score outperforming nnUNet by 1.09% and 2.71% respectively. Surpassing FreeSurfer Samseg it thus demonstrates superior overall performance on the ISBI 2015 dataset which illustrates the effective translation of our findings across multiple MS datasets. This highlights the substantial potential of leveraging longitudinal data for improved disease monitoring and assessment.

Table 3. Generalizability to data from other sites. Independent evaluation of models trained on the Ljubljana dataset [19] and the non-deeplearning tool FreeSurfer [6] on the official ISBI 2015 challenge training dataset.

Method	DSC ↑	HD95 ↓	F_1 ↑
FreeSurfer Samseg (2023) [6]	68.50	12.42	51.97
nnUNet [16]	69.74	**9.95**	59.74
Longitudinal nnUNet *(Ours)*	70.77	12.13	60.64
+ Diff. Weighting *(Ours)*	**70.83**	10.83	**62.45**

5 Conclusion

In this paper, we have presented a novel method for multiple sclerosis lesion segmentation explicitly incorporating temporal information using our Difference Weighting Block. This component fuses baseline and follow-up scan features, emphasizing changes for improved segmentation. Experimental results demonstrated our model's superiority over state-of-the-art single timepoint baselines and existing longitudinal methods. Our findings emphasize that leveraging representational differences outperforms naive channel-wise concatenation, with improvements also transferring to unseen datasets. Further research will focus on utilizing this longitudinal approach in addressing additional diseases.

Acknowledgments. The present contribution is supported by the Helmholtz Association under the joint research school "HIDSS4Health - Helmholtz Information and Data Science School for Health". This work was partly funded by Helmholtz Imaging (HI), a platform of the Helmholtz Incubator on Information and Data Science. PV is funded through an Else Kröner Clinician Scientist Endowed Professorship by the Else Kröner Fresenius Foundation (reference number: 2022_EKCS.17).

Disclosure of Interests. The authors have no competing interests to declare that are relevant to the content of this article.

References

1. Alom, M.Z., Yakopcic, C., Hasan, M., Taha, T.M., Asari, V.K.: Recurrent residual u-net for medical image segmentation. J. Med. Imag. **6**(1), 014006–014006 (2019)
2. Baumgartner, M., Jäger, P.F., Isensee, F., Maier-Hein, K.H.: nndetection: a self-configuring method for medical object detection. In: Medical Image Computing and Computer Assisted Intervention–MICCAI 2021: 24th International Conference, Strasbourg, France, September 27–October 1, 2021, Proceedings, Part V 24, pp. 530–539. Springer (2021)
3. Birenbaum, A., Greenspan, H.: Multi-view longitudinal cnn for multiple sclerosis lesion segmentation. Eng. Appl. Artif. Intell. **65**, 111–118 (2017)

4. Brugnara, G., et al.: Automated volumetric assessment with artificial neural networks might enable a more accurate assessment of disease burden in patients with multiple sclerosis. Eur. Radiol. **30**, 2356–2364 (2020)
5. Carass, A., et al.: Longitudinal multiple sclerosis lesion segmentation: resource and challenge. Neuroimage **148**, 77–102 (2017)
6. Cerri, S., et al.: An open-source tool for longitudinal whole-brain and white matter lesion segmentation. NeuroImage: Clin. **38**, 103354 (2023)
7. Commowick, O., Cervenansky, F., Cotton, F., Dojat, M.: Msseg-2 challenge proceedings: Multiple sclerosis new lesions segmentation challenge using a data management and processing infrastructure. In: MICCAI 2021-24th International Conference on Medical Image Computing and Computer Assisted Intervention, p. 126 (2021)
8. Commowick, O., et al.: Objective evaluation of multiple sclerosis lesion segmentation using a data management and processing infrastructure. Sci. Rep. **8**(1), 13650 (2018)
9. Danelakis, A., Theoharis, T., Verganelakis, D.A.: Survey of automated multiple sclerosis lesion segmentation techniques on magnetic resonance imaging. Comput. Med. Imag. Graph. **70**, 83–100 (2018)
10. Denner, S., et al.: Spatio-temporal learning from longitudinal data for multiple sclerosis lesion segmentation. In: Brainlesion: Glioma, Multiple Sclerosis, Stroke and Traumatic Brain Injuries: 6th International Workshop, BrainLes 2020, Held in Conjunction with MICCAI 2020, Lima, Peru, October 4, 2020, Revised Selected Papers, Part I 6, pp. 111–121. Springer (2021)
11. Diaz-Hurtado, M., et al.: Recent advances in the longitudinal segmentation of multiple sclerosis lesions on magnetic resonance imaging: a review. Neuroradiology **64**(11), 2103–2117 (2022)
12. Filippi, M., et al.: Multiple sclerosis. Nature Rev. Disease Primers **4**(1), 43 (2018). https://doi.org/10.1038/s41572-018-0041-4
13. Fischl, B.: Freesurfer. Neuroimage **62**(2), 774–781 (2012)
14. Galimzianova, A., Pernuš, F., Likar, B., Špiclin, Ž: Stratified mixture modeling for segmentation of white-matter lesions in brain mr images. Neuroimage **124**, 1031–1043 (2016)
15. Hatamizadeh, A., et al.: Swin unetr: Swin transformers for semantic segmentation of brain tumors in MRI images. In: International MICCAI Brainlesion Workshop, pp. 272–284. Springer (2021)
16. Isensee, F., Jaeger, P.F., Kohl, S.A., Petersen, J., Maier-Hein, K.H.: nnu-net: a self-configuring method for deep learning-based biomedical image segmentation. Nat. Methods **18**(2), 203–211 (2021)
17. Jaeger, P.F., et al: Retina u-net: Embarrassingly simple exploitation of segmentation supervision for medical object detection. In: Machine Learning for Health Workshop, pp. 171–183. PMLR (2020)
18. Jenkinson, M., Bannister, P., Brady, M., Smith, S.: Improved optimization for the robust and accurate linear registration and motion correction of brain images. Neuroimage **17**(2), 825–841 (2002)
19. Lesjak, Ž, et al.: A novel public MR image dataset of multiple sclerosis patients with lesion segmentations based on multi-rater consensus. Neuroinformatics **16**, 51–63 (2018)
20. Maier-Hein, L., et al.: Metrics reloaded: recommendations for image analysis validation. Nature methods, pp. 1–18 (2024)
21. Montalban, X., et al.: Ectrims/ean guideline on the pharmacological treatment of people with multiple sclerosis. Mult. Scler. J. **24**(2), 96–120 (2018)

22. Rakić, M., et al.: Icobrain ms 5.1: Combining unsupervised and supervised approaches for improving the detection of multiple sclerosis lesions. NeuroImage: Clin. **31**, 102707 (2021)
23. Stangel, M., Penner, I.K., Kallmann, B.A., Lukas, C., Kieseier, B.C.: Towards the implementation of 'no evidence of disease activity'in multiple sclerosis treatment: the multiple sclerosis decision model. Ther. Adv. Neurol. Disord. **8**(1), 3–13 (2015)
24. Szeskin, A., Rochman, S., Weiss, S., Lederman, R., Sosna, J., Joskowicz, L.: Liver lesion changes analysis in longitudinal cect scans by simultaneous deep learning voxel classification with simu-net. Med. Image Anal. **83**, 102675 (2023)
25. Wu, Y., Wu, Z., Shi, H., Picker, B., Chong, W., Cai, J.: CoactSeg: learning from heterogeneous data for new multiple sclerosis lesion segmentation. In: Greenspan, H., Madabhushi, A., Mousavi, P., Salcudean, S., Duncan, J., Syeda-Mahmood, T., Taylor, R. (eds.) Medical Image Computing and Computer Assisted Intervention – MICCAI 2023: 26th International Conference, Vancouver, BC, Canada, October 8–12, 2023, Proceedings, Part VIII, pp. 3–13. Springer Nature Switzerland, Cham (2023). https://doi.org/10.1007/978-3-031-43993-3_1
26. Zeng, C., Gu, L., Liu, Z., Zhao, S.: Review of deep learning approaches for the segmentation of multiple sclerosis lesions on brain mri. Front. Neuroinform. **14**, 610967 (2020)

Registration of Longitudinal Liver Examinations for Tumor Progress Assessment

Walid Yassine[1,2(✉)], Martin Charachon[2], Céline Hudelot[1], and Roberto Ardon[2]

[1] MICS, CentraleSupélec, Université Paris Saclay, Gif-sur-Yvette, France
{walid.yassine,celine.hudelot}@centralesupelec.fr
[2] Incepto Medical, Paris, France
{martin.charachon,roberto.ardon}@incepto-medical.com

Abstract. Assessing cancer progression in liver CT scans is a clinical challenge, requiring a comparison of scans at different times for the same patient. Practitioners must identify existing tumors, compare them with prior exams, identify new tumors, and evaluate overall disease evolution. This process is particularly complex in liver examinations due to misalignment between exams caused by several factors. Indeed, longitudinal liver examinations can undergo different non-pathological and pathological changes due to non-rigid deformations, the appearance or disappearance of pathologies, and other variations. In such cases, existing registration approaches, mainly based on intrinsic features may distort tumor regions, biasing the tumor progress evaluation step and the corresponding diagnosis. This work proposes a registration method based only on geometrical and anatomical information from liver segmentation, aimed at aligning longitudinal liver images for aided diagnosis. The proposed method is trained and tested on longitudinal liver CT scans, with 317 patients for training and 53 for testing. Our experimental results support our claims by showing that our method is better than other registration techniques by providing a smoother deformation while preserving the tumor burden within the volume. Qualitative results emphasize the importance of smooth deformations in preserving tumor appearance.

Keywords: Longitudinal Data · Liver Cancer · Image Registration · Deep Learning

1 Introduction

Evaluating cancer progression in liver CT scans during patient follow-up poses a significant clinical challenge. In the healthcare workflow, practitioners compare scans taken at different times for the same patient. This process involves identifying new and pre-existing lesions in the latest scans and assessing tumor

---

Supplementary Information The online version contains supplementary material available at https://doi.org/10.1007/978-3-031-84525-3_7.

progression according to the RECIST [11] guidelines. This monitoring demands considerable effort as practitioners must recognize previously detected lesions, compare them to their counterparts in prior exams, identify any newly appearing tumors, and evaluate the overall evolution of the disease. This process gets more complicated in liver examinations due to misalignment and variations caused by temporal factors. In longitudinal studies, variations such as patient movements, positioning, and organ displacement are common. Moreover, being a non-rigid organ, the liver presents additional complexities with recurring changes like large deformations due to stomach pressure, alterations in pathology size (cancerous or not), increased fat content, changes in vessel size, and bile duct dilation. Figure 1 illustrates the complexity of the process by representing a longitudinal exam with multiple lesions. Tools performing automatic alignment of CT scans for precise tumor follow-up may reduce radiologists mental burden.

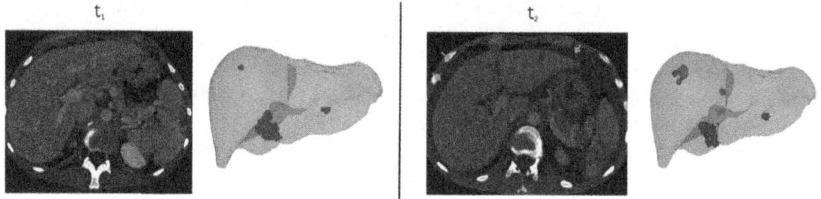

Fig. 1. Liver longitudinal exams: The images show a growing Lesion in red and reveal changes in the liver appearance after two months, e.g., effusion around the liver (orange arrows). The liver segmentation mask is presented in green, existing tumors in blue, and new tumors in red. (Color figure online)

Image Registration for Longitudinal Studies. Registration[1] of medical images has received significant scientific attention. Many deep neural network-based approaches have been developed [1,9,10,15,19,26,29]. These approaches involve feeding pairs of images (the moving and the fixed image) into a neural network. The network predicts a displacement field to align the moving image with the fixed image. In the context of tumor progression monitoring, such registration methods may significantly impact the monitoring process. For instance, non-rigid registration may distort tumor regions when comparing a liver with a tumor at time t to the same liver at $t+1$ with a larger tumor. Intrinsic organ characteristics, like rigidity, also impact the registration process. Existing literature primarily addresses the registration problem by exploiting the image content. In liver exams, many pathological and non-pathological variations can occur. Registration based on intrinsic features (e.g., perceptual content) can impact internal liver structures and, consequently, the tumor burden[2], affecting the tumor progression evaluation. To our knowledge, only a few studies have explored

---

[1] The terms 'alignment' and 'registration' are used interchangeably throughout the document.
[2] Total volume of tissues considered as tumor.

tumor change/evolution detection in longitudinal images. Existing works mainly focus on multiple sclerosis progression in brain MRI [3,6,13,25]. Nevertheless, the brain is not subject to the same factors as the liver. This raises concerns about the applicability of these approaches to liver registration if preserving post-registration tumor integrity is essential. Some methods use the predicted displacement field to identify regions of tumor changes by detecting warping within the brain [23]. Such approaches are unsuitable in liver exams due to the organ's non-rigidity, the diverse pathological/non-pathological changes within the liver, and temporal variations between exams. Alternatively, some use a two-step process: Independent tumor detection, followed by image registration to deduce tumor correspondence in time [5,16,22]. [17] highlighted that independent tumor detection can be less precise and sensitive than considering both exams simultaneously, aligning more closely with real clinical contexts.

Medical Image Registration Background. A recent review [7] evaluates various unsupervised 3D medical image registration methods. The VoxelMorph architecture [1] has been widely employed. It predicts a displacement field coupled with a differentiable spatial transformation layer (STN) [18] to apply transformations. [29] proposes a bidirectional diffeomorphic registration, introducing inverse coherence and anti-folding losses for displacement fields in both forward and backward directions. A diffeomorphic transformation is a smooth, invertible mapping that ensures both the transformation and its inverse are smooth. More recent approaches have introduced transformer-based networks [26], capitalizing on the ability of transformer blocks to capture global image features during registration rather than relying solely on local information. [19] introduced Cyclemorph, a cyclic registration method incorporating cyclic consistency into the network's loss function to enhance performance. Incremental transformations are also discussed in the literature. [27,28] present a network based on neural ordinary differential equations, aiming to perform iterative registration through a neural network. This approach decomposes the displacement field into small steps, each constrained to ensure displacement field regularity. Most of these methods rely on image content (or image + organ segmentation) for registration.

Our main contribution is to propose a registration framework that aligns longitudinal images based only on geometric and anatomical information from liver segmentation, smoothly extrapolating the displacement field within the liver. The rationale behind this is that even though internal structures may not be perfectly aligned, their shape will undergo small deformations while being brought much closer to their counterpart in the reference image. Following the works of [3,6,13,25], we adhere to the strategy where both images should be considered to design a tumor progression/change detector; this paper proposes an adapted registration method to such frameworks.

2 Proposed Methodology

Let A and B represent images of the same patient captured at different time points, denoting the moving and fixed images, respectively. A and B are affinely

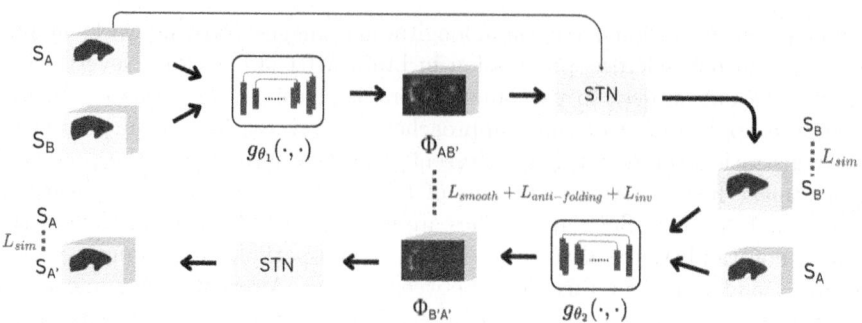

Fig. 2. Cyclic Diffeomorphic Registration: g_{θ_1} takes as input the moving and fixed segmentation masks S_A and S_B and generates a displacement field $\phi_{AB'}$. This field is applied to S_A to obtain $S_{B'}$, the aligned segmentation mask. $S_{B'}$ goes through g_{θ_2} (with S_A) to obtain the cyclically transformed segmentation $S_{A'}$.

aligned during a pre-processing step. We assume that we are equipped with a liver segmentation tool, and we note S_A and S_B as the 3D liver segmentation masks in images A and B, respectively. These entities are defined in a three-dimensional image space $\Omega \in \mathbb{R}^3$. Our objective is to determine a transformation function that aligns the segmentation S_A of the moving image with the segmentation S_B of the fixed image. Inspired by the previously mentioned works, we propose a new registration framework focusing on segmentation maps, illustrated in Fig. 2. The framework trains a model g_{θ_1} to generate a displacement field $\phi_{AB'}$ when provided with a pair of segmentations S_A and S_B. Each component of $\phi_{AB'}$ is a three-dimensional vector indicating the displacement of a specific voxel. Subsequently, we use a differentiable operation based on a spatial transformer network (STN) to apply this displacement field $\phi_{AB'}$ to the segmentation mask S_A, resulting in S'_B: the segmentation mask aligned with S_B. To ensure effective registration, it is necessary to impose a set of constraints:

Displacement Field Regularity. This first classical constraint penalizes the norm of the derivatives of the displacement field to ensure its local smoothness.

$$L_{\text{smooth}}(\phi) = ||\nabla \phi||_2^2 = \Sigma_{i,j} \frac{\partial \phi^i}{\partial x_j}^2 \tag{1}$$

where x_j is the jth coordinate of the spatial domain.

Segmentation Alignment. A second constraint, L_{sim}, ensures alignment between the transformed mask $S_{B'} = S_A + \phi_{AB'}(S_A)$ and the fixed mask S_B.

$$L_{\text{sim}}(S_B, S_{B'}) = 1 - DSC(S_B, S_{B'}) \tag{2}$$

where, DSC refers here and henceforth to the Dice similarity coefficient [8].

Two additional constraints, inspired by [14,20,29], are also incorporated to prevent a trivial solution that excessively stretches the contours of S_A in a non-plausible way to fit S_B.

Anti-folding. The constraint $L_{anti-folding}$, detailed in Eq. 3, prevents displacement field folding, avoiding unrealistic distortions in the image. It maintains local smoothness by ensuring non-overlapping gradient directions around each point p in the image space Ω.

$$L_{\text{anti-folding}}(\phi) = \Sigma_{p \in \Omega} \Sigma_i \delta \left(\frac{\partial \phi^i}{\partial x_i}(p) + 1 \right) \left| \frac{\partial \phi^i}{\partial x_i}(p) \right|^2 \quad (3)$$

where, $\delta(Q)$ is an indexing function that penalizes the gradient ϕ at folding points. Specifically, if $Q \leq 0$, then $\delta(Q) = 1$, otherwise, $\delta(Q) = 0$.

Inverse Consistency. The inverse consistency constraint L_{inv}, detailed in Eq. 4, ensures that the predicted displacement fields are inversely consistent.

$$L_{\text{inv}}(\phi_{AB}, \phi_{BA}) = \|\phi_{AB} + \phi_{BA} \circ (I_d + \phi_{AB})\|^2 \quad (4)$$

where I_d is the d-dimensional identity matrix (d=3). A detailed explanation of how this loss is derived is presented in Appendix. A.

As illustrated in Fig. 2, we employ a cyclic approach inspired by [19]. This involves computing: (i) the transformed moving mask $S_{B'} = S_A + \phi_{AB'}(S_A)$ using the forward displacement field $\phi_{AB'}$, and (ii) the cyclic transformed mask $S_{A'} = S_{B'} + \phi_{B'A'}(S_{B'})$ using the backward displacement field $\phi_{B'A'}$. In a bidirectional approach [29], the computation of displacement fields occurs in two steps: first, the moving mask S_A and the fixed mask S_B are fed into the model to predict the forward displacement field ϕ_{AB}. Then, the masks are fed in reverse order to compute the backward displacement field ϕ_{BA}. In our experiments, the cyclic approach performs better than the bidirectional one (see Sect. 4).

Finally, the total loss function is formulated as follows:

$$\begin{aligned} L(S_A, S_B) =& \alpha\, L_{\text{sim}}(S_{B'}, S_B) + \beta\, (L_{\text{smooth}}(\phi_{AB'}) + L_{\text{smooth}}(\phi_{B'A'})) + \\ & \gamma\, (L_{\text{anti-folding}}(\phi_{AB'}) + L_{\text{anti-folding}}(\phi_{B'A'})) \\ & + \mu\, (L_{\text{inv}}(\phi_{AB'}, \phi_{B'A'}) + L_{\text{inv}}(\phi_{B'A'}, \phi_{AB'})) \end{aligned} \quad (5)$$

Incremental Cyclic Diffeomorphic Registration. We propose to extend our approach by introducing a two-step incremental cyclic diffeomorphic registration process (Fig. 3). The model predicts two displacement fields for each direction. The inverse consistency loss imposes constraints to ensure the displacement fields are inversely consistent. This approach is motivated by the nature of deformations observed in liver examinations, particularly under external pressure from the stomach, which can induce significant deformations. Decomposing

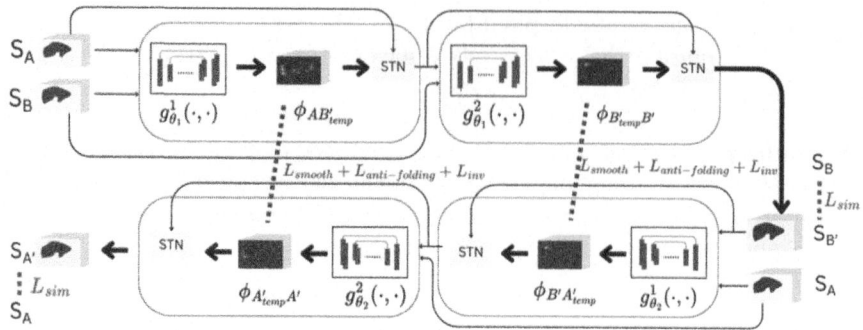

Fig. 3. Incremental Cyclic Diffeomorphic Registration Framework: The model takes as input S_A and S_B and generates two displacement fields, $\phi_{AB'_{temp}}$ and $\phi_{B'_{temp}B'}$, to produce the aligned segmentation $S_{B'}$. $S_{B'}$ then goes through the backward path (with S_A) to obtain the cyclically transformed segmentation $S_{A'}$.

the displacement field into two distinct fields reduces the risk of applying large deformations and minimizes potential irregularities in the transformed image. During inference, the predicted displacement fields (forward direction) are used to compute aligned versions of A and S_A for the moving image and its segmentation.

3 Experiments

Dataset and Implementation Details. Our dataset includes 772 pairs of longitudinal liver examinations from 337 patients. 90% of these patients are allocated for training the registration methods, while a test set of 33 patients is reserved for assessing registration performance. An additional clinical dataset containing 40 exams from 20 liver cancer patients is used to evaluate tumor-wise metrics. A radiologist manually annotated the tumor masks of this dataset. The datasets were collected under the GDPR[3] through a collaboration with a hospital. An initial liver area cropping and an affine registration (similar to [2]) are applied to eliminate global transformations, particularly in cases involving significant changes in patient position between examinations. This aligns with the framework described in Sect. 2, where we assumed that the images are affinely aligned, minimizing deformations of large amplitudes. For affine registration, a fully convolutional network (FCN) is used to predict the transformation matrix applied to the moving images. All Images are resampled to a size of (160, 160, 100), with an average resolution of (1.5, 1.37, 2) mm on the (x, y, z) axes. Segmentation masks are generated by a UNet [24] model trained on 1000 annotated liver masks, with a DSC of 0.96 (internal test dataset) and 0.971 (LiTS dataset [4]). Each CNN network $g_{\theta_j}^i$ for i={1,2} and j={1,2} has a UNet architecture,

---

[3] General Data Protection Regulation.

with four down/up-sampling blocks (the number of filters starts at 8), each containing two convolutional blocks. Convolutional blocks include normalization, leaky ReLU activation, and a convolutional layer. For the incremental framework, we perform two transformation steps, resulting in two fields in each of the forward and backward paths. The $g^i_{\theta_j}$ networks do not share their weights (experiments were less conclusive in a weight-sharing setting). Each network generates a vector field at half the input image resolution, which is then integrated and upsampled to obtain a displacement field at the original resolution. Three-fold cross-validation experiments (on NVIDIA T4 GPUs) were conducted with an Adam optimizer until convergence and with $\alpha=1$, $\beta=0.8$, $\gamma=1$ and $\mu=0.4$.

Evaluation Metrics: i) Alignment between the transformed mask $S_{B'}$ and the fixed mask S_B is assessed using the DSC. ii) Image content-based coherence is evaluated using normalized cross-correlation (NCC) and mutual information (MI). iii) Regularity of the displacement field is evaluated using the Jacobian matrix $J_\phi(p) = \nabla \phi(p) = [\partial \phi^i / \partial x_j]_{i,j}$ through its L_2 norm and by counting the number of voxels within the liver where the determinant $|J_\phi(p)| \leq 0$ (indicating a non-diffeomorphic field). iv) Diffeomorphism is quantified through the L_1 distance between the moving image A and its cyclically reconstructed version A'.

We evaluate our method performance against different registration frameworks: Nifty Reg [21] (cubic B-splines); VoxelMorph under two configurations: 1) trained on images and segmentations with a loss based on image similarity (NCC) and segmentation similarity (DSC), and 2) on segmentations only. Under both configurations, a regularity loss on the displacement field is employed as in Eq. 1. We also evaluate the cyclic diffeomorphic framework with (Fig. 3) and without (Fig. 2) incremental steps (DiffeoCyc_inc-2, DiffeoCyc_inc-1 resp.), and the incremental framework coupled with the diffeomorphic parametrization (Diffeo_inc2); i.e. with a bidirectional path instead of a cyclic one.

To our knowledge, no public dataset exists for longitudinal liver examinations (more details in Appendix. B). The difficulty in acquiring such datasets stems from the temporal link between exams. This limitation prevents benchmarking on public datasets in this specific context.

For tumor-related metrics, evaluation is done on the clinical dataset of 20 patients with 30 annotated tumor masks. We consider only tumors persisting between examinations, whether stable, growing, or shrinking. We evaluate the number of matched lesions, the mean tumor inclusion ratio post-registration (overlap of segmentations over the real tumor volume), and the relative error in tumor burden $= \frac{|V^t_{\text{pre}} - V^t_{\text{post}}|}{|V^t_{\text{pre}}|}$ by comparing the tumor burden V^t (total volume of tissues considered as tumor) within an exam pre/post-registration. A tumor is matched if its inclusion ratio is above 10%. The significance of results was assessed using permutation-based statistical tests [12], with significant results ($p_{\text{value}} < 0.01$) indicated in bold in the tables.

4 Results and Discussion

Results. For field regularity metrics, DiffeoCyc_inc-2 exhibits values of 0.002, 0.008, and 1 for $||\nabla\phi||_2^2$, $||A - A'||_1$, and $|J \leq 0|$ metrics respectively. In contrast, NiftyReg (resp. Voxelmorph (NCC + DSC)), which are content-based methods, report values of 0.09 (resp. 0.04), 0.01 (resp. 0.027), 45145 (resp. 12845). The difference between DiffeoCyc_inc-2 and NiftyReg (resp. Voxelmorph) is significant ($p_{\text{value}} < 0.01$). NCC and MI metrics report comparable values ($p_{\text{value}} > 0.01$) across methods between 0.43 and 0.45, with 0.37 for Voxelmorph (NCC + DSC). For tumor-related metrics, NiftyReg manages to match 1 more tumor than the other methods (tumor inclusion ratio = 0.58). The tumor burden relative error for all methods varies between 0.11 and 0.16. DiffeoCyc_inc-2 reports a displacement field regularity of 0.002 and 0 voxels with non-diffeomorphic deformations.

Discussion. Quantitative results in Table 1 show that our approaches stand out in metrics related to the field smoothness, emphasizing improved regularity in the generated transformations. Figure 4 offers a qualitative analysis of the impact of displacement field regularity. Our method provides smooth displacement fields even for large deformations. In contrast, the transformation induced by Voxel-Morph, applied directly to the segmentation masks, stretches the liver contours (red arrows). Although our approaches operate at the segmentation level rather than the image level, the content-based similarity metrics (NCC and MI) do not show significant differences between all the methods. Cyclic-based approaches (DiffeoCyc_inc-1 and DiffeoCyc_inc-2) perform better than bidirectional-based approaches (Diffeo_inc-2).

Results in Table 2 show that content-based registration methods slightly outperform other methods in matching tumors and achieving higher inclusion ratios for registered tumors. However, these methods exhibit significantly lower regularity in displacement fields and risk warping lesions to better fit tumors at time t + 1. This increases inclusion ratios, but preserving tumor burden alone is insufficient; maintaining tumor shape and appearance is also important for tumor progression evaluation when using both warped and reference images.

Table 1. Quantitative results from longitudinal liver examinations of 33 patients. **inc-i** represents the number of displacement fields in the forward/backward path.

Method	DSC ↑	MI ↑	NCC ↑	$||\nabla\phi||_2^2$ ↓	$||A - A'||_1$ ↓	$|J \leq 0|$ ↓
Nifty Reg	0.96 (0.002)	0.43 (0.003)	0.85 (0.002)	0.09 (0.003)	0.01 (0.001)	45145 (4674)
VoxelMorph (NCC + DSC)	0.98 (0.004)	0.37 (0.005)	0.85 (0.002)	0.04 (0.004)	0.027 (0.003)	12845 (1240)
VoxelMorph (DSC)	0.99 (1e-4)	**0.457** (0.003)	**0.89** (0.001)	0.024 (0.001)	0.017 (0.002)	1462 (770)
Diffeomorphic	0.99 (1e-3)	0.453 (0.004)	0.88 (0.001)	0.006 (0.001)	0.008 (0.001)	10 (7)
Diffeo_inc-2	0.99 (0.001)	0.454 (0.004)	**0.89** (0.002)	0.003 (0.001)	0.009 (0.001)	4 (3)
DiffeoCyc_inc-1	0.989 (0.001)	0.451 (0.003)	0.884 (0.002)	0.004 (0.001)	**0.007** (0.001)	**0 (0)**
DiffeoCyc_inc-2	0.99 (0.001)	0.453 (0.002)	0.885 (0.001)	**0.002** (0.001)	0.008 (0.001)	1 (1)

Table 2. Tumor related quantitative results for 20 liver cancer patients.

	Method Name	Matched tumors	Tumor inclusion ratio ↑	Tumor burden relative error ↓	$\|\|\nabla\phi\|\|_2^2$ ↓	$\|J \leq 0\|$ ↓	MI ↑	NCC ↑
Bbox	-	18/30	0.3	-	-	-	-	-
Bbox + Affine	-	22/30	0.4	-	-	-	-	-
BBox + Affine + Non-Affine	NiftyReg	26/30	**0.58**	0.162	0.08 (0.04)	34553 (22345)	0.481	0.828
	Vxm (NCC+DSC)	25/30	0.47	0.145	0.012 (0.002)	361 (706)	0.506	0.865
	Vxm (DSC)	25/30	0.46	0.268	0.023 (0.003)	1000 (1310)	0.501	0.864
	Difféomorphe	25/30	0.45	0.137	0.005 (0.002)	12 (46)	0.502	0.86
	Difféo_inc-2	25/30	0.45	0.138	0.003 (0.002)	10 (86)	0.504	0.861
	DifféoCyc_inc-1	25/30	0.45	0.115	0.004 (0.002)	3 (8)	0.501	0.858
	DifféoCyc_inc-2	25/30	0.46	0.118	**0.002** (0.001)	**0 (0)**	0.502	0.86

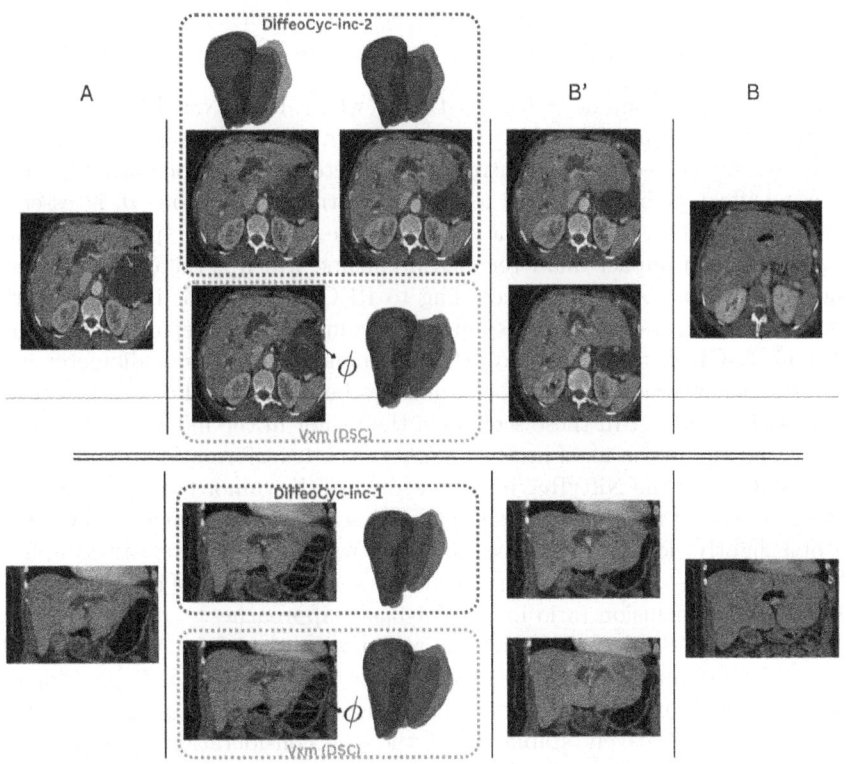

Fig. 4. Left to right: Moving image A, displacement field ϕ (in red), transformed image B', and fixed image B. 3D liver masks are presented in blue for A, red for B', and green for B. Red arrows highlight unrealistically stretched regions. (Color figure online)

Impact on Tumors. We consider three cases highlighting the importance of field regularity. Figure 5 illustrates the case (a) (a detailed illustration of all the cases is in Appendix. C).

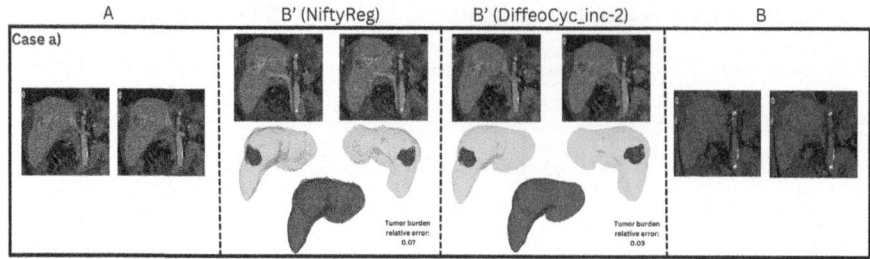

Fig. 5. Left to right: Moving image A (tumor in blue), transformed image B' for *NiftyReg* and our proposed framework *DiffeoCyc_inc-2* (tumor in red), and fixed image B (tumor in orange). The transformed liver masks are represented in green, and the fixed image mask B is represented in red. (Color figure online)

⋆ **Case (a):** We examine a benign tumor where both NiftyReg and Diffeo-Cyc_inc-2 yield comparable relative errors. However, how alterations are applied differs significantly. NiftyReg introduces "stretching" in some tumor areas, whereas DiffeoCyc_inc-2 ensures a more uniform deformation. It is essential to recognize that even when relative errors are similar, the specific deformation strategy can impact diameter measurements, which is the criteria used for tumor progression assessment according to RECIST [11]. For instance, in this case, a relative error of 0.06 corresponds to a volumetric discrepancy of 2.268 mL (2268 mm^3). Given that clinical workflows demand liver tumor diameter measurements accurate up to 5 mm, such nuances become crucial.

⋆ **Cases (b) and c):** In these scenarios, the tumor in the moving image (blue) grows with time in the fixed image (orange). The transformation applied to the tumor (red) using the NiftyReg method stretches the tumor to match the larger tumor in the fixed image, which is larger. Achieving this alignment comes at the cost of a slightly elevated relative error due to warping during registration, highlighting the trade-off between alignment accuracy and error. This also explains the high tumor inclusion ratio in content-based approaches.

The observed results emphasize the role of smooth deformations within the context of registration when the model treats both warped and fixed images. When assessing tumor progression after registration, ensuring that the tumor burden remains relatively stable is not the sole consideration, as tumors can undergo localized deformations while maintaining overall volume. However, such localized deformations may introduce measurement bias, particularly when assessing diameter or other quantitative metrics. Therefore, evaluating registration methods based on a combination of tumor burden conservation and displacement field smoothness provides a more robust metric in this context.

5 Conclusion

In this work, we introduced a registration framework designed to assist tumor progression assessment in longitudinal liver CT scans. Leveraging an automatic segmentation model, our framework aligns liver segmentation masks through smooth displacement fields. This alignment targets tumor alignment with minimal tumor deformation. Even though the internal structures of the liver may not be perfectly aligned after registration, their shape will be nearly preserved while being brought much closer to their counterpart in the reference image. The impact of this registration on a subsequent tumor progress/change detection module is to be addressed in future works.

Disclosure of Interests. The authors have no competing interests to declare that are relevant to the content of this article.

References

1. Balakrishnan, G., Zhao, A., Sabuncu, M.R., Guttag, J., Dalca, A.V.: VoxelMorph: a learning framework for deformable medical image registration. IEEE Trans. Med. Imaging **38**, 1788–1800 (2019)
2. Barbera, G.L., et al.: Automatic size and pose homogenization with spatial transformer network to improve and accelerate pediatric segmentation. In: 2021 IEEE 18th International Symposium on Biomedical Imaging (ISBI), pp. 1773–1776. IEEE (2021)
3. Battaglini, M., et al.: Automated identification of brain new lesions in multiple sclerosis using subtraction images. J. Magn. Reson. Imaging **39**, 1543–1549 (2014)
4. Bilic, P., et al: The liver tumor segmentation benchmark (LiTS) (2022)
5. Cai, J., et al.: Deep lesion tracker: monitoring lesions in 4D longitudinal imaging studies. In: 2021 IEEE/CVF Conference on Computer Vision and Pattern Recognition (CVPR), pp. 15154–15164. IEEE, Nashville, TN, USA (2021). https://doi.org/10.1109/CVPR46437.2021.01491, https://ieeexplore.ieee.org/document/9578122/
6. Carass, A., Roy, S., Jog, A., Cuzzocreo, J.L., Magrath, E., Gherman, A., et al.: Longitudinal multiple sclerosis lesion segmentation. Neuroimage **148**, 77–102 (2017)
7. Chen, J., et al.: A survey on deep learning in medical image registration. Eprint arXiv:2307.15615
8. Crum, W.R., Camara, O., Hill, D.L.G.: Generalized overlap measures for evaluation and validation in medical image analysis. IEEE Trans. Med, Imaging **25**, 1451–1461 (2006)
9. Dalca, A., Rakic, M., Guttag, J., Sabuncu, M.: Learning conditional deformable templates with convolutional networks. In: Wallach, H., Larochelle, H., Beygelzimer, A., d'Alché-Buc, F., Fox, E., Garnett, R. (eds.) Advances in Neural Information Processing Systems, vol. 32. Curran Associates, Inc. (2019). https://proceedings.neurips.cc/paper_files/paper/2019/file/bbcbff5c1f1ded46c25d28119a85c6c2-Paper.pdf
10. van Eijnatten, M., et al.: 3D deformable registration of longitudinal abdominopelvic CT images using unsupervised deep learning. Comput. Methods Programs Biomed. **208**, 106261 (2021)
11. Eisenhauer, E.A., et al.: New response evaluation criteria in solid tumours: revised RECIST guideline (version 1.1). Eur. J. Cancer (Oxford, England: 1990) **45**(2), 228–247 (2009). https://doi.org/10.1016/j.ejca.2008.10.026
12. Ernst, M.D.: Permutation methods: a basis for exact inference. Stat. Sci. **19**(4) (2004). https://doi.org/10.1214/088342304000000396

13. Ganiler, O., et al.: A subtraction pipeline for automatic detection of new appearing multiple sclerosis lesions in longitudinal studies. Neuroradiology **56**, 363–374 (2014)
14. He, J., Christensen, G.E.: Large deformation inverse consistent elastic image registration. In: Taylor, C., Noble, J.A. (eds.) IPMI 2003. LNCS, vol. 2732, pp. 438–449. Springer, Heidelberg (2003). https://doi.org/10.1007/978-3-540-45087-0_37
15. Heinrich, M.P., Hansen, L.: Voxelmorph++ Going beyond the cranial vault with keypoint supervision and multi-channel instance optimisation. Eprint arXiv:2203.00046
16. Hering, A., et al.: Whole-body soft-tissue lesion tracking and segmentation in longitudinal CT imaging studies. In: Proceedings of the Fourth Conference on Medical Imaging with Deep Learning, pp. 312–326. PMLR (2021). https://proceedings.mlr.press/v143/hering21a.html, iSSN: 2640-3498
17. Huang, Y., et al.: Deep learning for brain metastasis detection and segmentation in longitudinal MRI data. Medical Physics **49** (2022). https://doi.org/10.1002/mp.15863
18. Jaderberg, M., Simonyan, K., Zisserman, A., kavukcuoglu, k.: Spatial transformer networks. In: Advances in Neural Information Processing Systems, vol. 28. Curran Associates, Inc. (2015)
19. Kim, B., Kim, D.H., Park, S.H., Kim, J., Lee, J.G., Ye, J.C.: CycleMorph: cycle consistent unsupervised deformable image registration. Med. Image Anal. **71**, 102036 (2021). https://doi.org/10.1016/j.media.2021.102036, https://www.sciencedirect.com/science/article/pii/S1361841521000827
20. Leow, A., Huang, S.C., Geng, A., Becker, J., Davis, S., Toga, A., Thompson, P.: Inverse Consistent Mapping in 3D Deformable Image Registration: Its Construction and Statistical Properties. In: Information Processing in Medical Imaging, pp. 493–503. LNCS, Springer (2005)
21. Modat, M., Taylor, Z.A., Barnes, J., Hawkes, D.J., Ourselin, S.: Fast free-form deformation using the normalised mutual information gradient and graphics processing units (2008)
22. Moltz, J.H., D'Anastasi, M., Kießling, A., Pinto Dos Santos, D., Schülke, C., Peitgen, H.O.: Workflow-centred evaluation of an automatic lesion tracking software for chemotherapy monitoring by CT. European Radiology **22**(12), 2759–2767 (2012). https://doi.org/10.1007/s00330-012-2545-8, http://link.springer.com/10.1007/s00330-012-2545-8
23. Pieperhoff, P., Südmeyer, M., Hömke, L., Zilles, K., Schnitzler, A., Amunts, K.: Detection of structural changes of the human brain in longitudinally acquired MR images by deformation field morphometry: Methodological analysis, validation and application. Neuroimage **43**(2), 269–287 (2008). https://doi.org/10.1016/j.neuroimage.2008.07.031
24. Ronneberger, O., Fischer, P., Brox, T.: U-net: convolutional networks for biomedical image segmentation. In: Navab, N., Hornegger, J., Wells, W.M., Frangi, A.F. (eds.) Medical Image Computing and Computer-Assisted Intervention - MICCAI 2015, pp. 234–241. Springer International Publishing, Cham (2015). https://doi.org/10.1007/978-3-319-24574-4_28
25. Salem, M., et al.: A supervised framework with intensity subtraction and deformation field features for the detection of new T2-w lesions in multiple sclerosis. NeuroImage: Clinical **17**, 607–615 (2018)
26. Wang, Y., Qian, W., Li, M., Zhang, X.: A transformer-based network for deformable medical image registration. In: Fang, L., Povey, D., Zhai, G., Mei, T., Wang, R. (eds.) Artificial Intelligence, pp. 502–513. Springer Nature Switzerland, Cham (2022). https://doi.org/10.1007/978-3-031-20497-5_41

27. Wu, Y., Jiahao, T.Z., Wang, J., Yushkevich, P.A., Hsieh, M., Gee, J.C.: Nodeo: a neural ordinary differential equation based optimization framework for deformable image registration. In: 2022 IEEE/CVF Conference on Computer Vision and Pattern Recognition (CVPR), pp. 20772–20781. IEEE Computer Society (2022). https://doi.org/10.1109/CVPR52688.2022.02014, https://doi.ieeecomputersociety.org/10.1109/CVPR52688.2022.02014
28. Xu, J., Chen, E.Z., Chen, X., Chen, T., Sun, S.: Multi-scale neural odes for 3D medical image registration. In: de Bruijne, M., et al. (eds.) Medical Image Computing and Computer Assisted Intervention - MICCAI 2021, pp. 213–223. Springer International Publishing, Cham (2021). https://doi.org/10.1007/978-3-030-87202-1_21
29. Zhang, J.: Inverse-consistent deep networks for unsupervised deformable image registration. Eprint arXiv:1809.03443 (2018)

Tracking Lesion Evolution Using a Boundary Enhanced Approach for MS Change Segmentation (BEAMS)

Prateek Mathur[1,3]($\boxtimes$), Brendan S. Kelly[2,3,4], Ronan P Killeen[2,4], and Aonghus Lawlor[1,3]

[1] School of Computer Science, University College Dublin, Dublin, Ireland
prateek.mathur@ucdconnect.ie
[2] School of Medicine, University College Dublin, Dublin, Ireland
[3] Insight SFI Research Centre for Data Analytics, Dublin, Ireland
[4] St. Vincent's University Hospital, Dublin, Ireland

Abstract. Multiple sclerosis (MS) is a chronic disease of the Central Nervous System (CNS) primarily characterised on Magnetic Resonance Imaging (MRI) by hyper-intense lesions. Accurate and timely identification of new lesions or growth in existing lesions has a tremendous impact on treatment planning and patient care. Early detection can lead to prompt intervention possibly slowing the disease progression. However, this task is challenging, costly and often prone to observer bias. Our approach consists of three key components (1) redefining the lesion segmentation problem as a change detection challenge focusing only on new and enhancing lesions; (2) adding an additional boundary detection task to an existing Convolutional Neural Network (CNN) to provide detailed context regarding the shape, size, and evolution of enhancing lesions; (3) evaluating the F_β loss objective as an alternative to traditional segmentation loss objectives, aiming to optimise the model's sensitivity and specificity. Furthermore, we employ Gradient-weighted Class Activation Mapping (GradCAM) to visualise the network's attention, aiding in the interpretation and validation of our approach. By providing an objective evaluation, our method aims to streamline clinical decision-making processes for improved patient outcomes.

Keywords: Multiple Sclerosis · Change Detection · Boundary Enhancement

1 Introduction

Multiple sclerosis is a chronic idiopathic disease of the Central Nervous System diagnosed using Magnetic Resonance Imaging [22,23]. More than 2.8 million people worldwide suffer MS with increasing prevalence in young adults [30]. Imaging plays a vital role in the diagnosis and the treatment of MS as hyper-intense lesions can precede the onset of symptoms. However, identifying lesions is a challenging, monotonous and expensive task which is subject to observer bias and can have high inter-rater variability [21]. Coupled with the small target area of new lesions, the variability in the shape and size of the lesions is an outstanding problem [4]. The MSSEG 2016 lesion segmentation challenge and the MSSEG2 new lesion segmentation challenge are representative of the evolution of interest from singular assessment of MS lesions to viewing the challenge from a longitudinal perspective [1,6]. Even though the interest in this area has received a massive boost, new lesion segmentation remains a difficult task as evidenced by the modest performance exhibited by state-of-the-art(SOTA) methods [1]. The small target size of new or enhancing MS lesions is analogous to the challenge of change detection in Remote Sensing(RS), where subtle and minute variations must be accurately identified. Change Detection (CD) challenges in remote sensing are geared at identifying structural alterations in co-registered satellite imaging captured at different times. The objective is to ignore irrelevant features such as seasonal shifts, lighting, atmospheric effects and only segment man-made changes [3]. In medical imaging, prior imaging plays a vital role in the diagnosis and treatment planning, however, the current paradigm of AI in medicine rarely takes image priors into account [2]. U-Net architectures [26] have remained a popular choice in MS lesion segmentation [7]. The nnUNet is an out-of-the-box self-configuring model for segmentation that optimises the basic U-Net for any specific application [9]. Vision Transformers have also been implemented for segmentation tasks in medical imaging [28]. Recently, incorporating boundary of lesions in transformer based methods has been shown to boost segmentation accuracy in skin lesion segmentation tasks [32,33]. In this study, we redefine longitudinal disease tracking in MS as a change detection problem. We propose a novel Boundary Enhanced Approach for MS Segmentation (BEAMS), which builds on existing CNN architectures. Additionally, we investigate the use of the F_β loss, demonstrating its superiority over the commonly used dice loss and its variants. To further our analysis, we use Gradient-weighted Class Activation Mapping [27] to develop interpretations of the model behind the decision making and we examine the impact of the BEAMS enhancement on the underlying architecture. Our goal is to develop methods that assist clinicians to provide objective, robust and intuitive decisions, thereby expediting the clinical decision-making process.

2 Materials and Methods

2.1 Participants and Data

This retrospective study is conducted on an internal cohort of 170 patients diagnosed with MS and additionally validated on an external MS dataset. The participant data has been collected with full IRB approval and the requirement for prospective consent was waived due to the retrospective nature of this work. Our data is hosted on Zenodo and can be made available on request. The publicly available external dataset is from the MSSEG2 challenge proceedings [1].

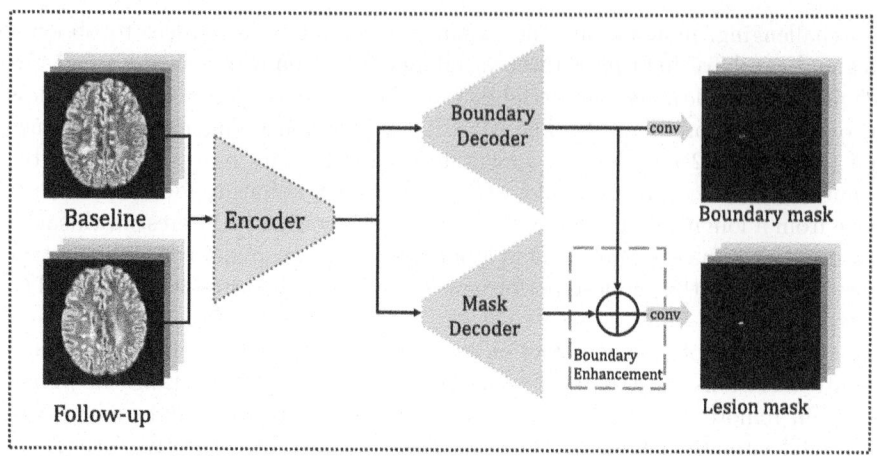

Fig. 1. Schematic for Boundary Enhanced Approach for MS Segmentation

Our internal dataset is comprised of patients who had at least two brain scans (MRI) for MS at St. Vincent's University Hospital, Dublin between January 2019 and December 2022. Images were acquired on a 1.5T SIEMENS MAGNETOM Avanto syngo MRB19 (SIEMENS, Munich, Germany). A three-dimensional T2 Fluid-Attenuated Inversion Recovery(FLAIR) sequence acquired with voxel size 1.1 x 1.1 x 1.1 mm; TR 6000ms; TE 413ms; TI 2030ms; acquisition time 6 min 44 s; sagittal orientation is acquired. The raw acquisition is in the DICOM Standard format. The sequences are converted into 3D NIfTI format using the dcm2niix utility [17].

The FLAIR sequences of all studies for each patient were rigidly registered to the first T1 sequence from the first exam of the patient using the FSL FLIRT utility [11,12]. The sequences were then anonymised by skull stripping using the FSL Brain Extraction tool [29]. The data was split at a patient level to produce 110 patient cases for the training set, 30 for validation set and 30 for the test set. We additionally evaluated our models on the external data to mitigate optimistic performance bias due to this prior split [24]. For each patient case, pairs of studies were chosen where there was a noted change in the radiology report, redefining the new lesion segmentation problem in the Change Detection(CD) paradigm [8]. From these pairs of 3D brain volumes, 2D co-registered brain slices were extracted. A new MS lesion or an enhancement in the MS lesion is rare and sporadic leading to a severe class imbalance at an image level. Thus, we used random selection to limit the number of paired-slices with no-change to match the distribution of paired-slices with observed change for our training set. However, all brain slices were extracted for the validation and test sets.

2.2 Ground Truth Annotation

The ground truth lesion annotation was done semi-automatically. First, we trained a DeepMedic model [13] using only the FLAIR sequences from the publicly available MSSEG2016 lesion segmentation challenge data [6]. The dataset comprises 15 training cases, of which we randomly split the data into 12 cases for training and 3 for validation. The model is trained for 70 epochs and a batch size of 10 using the default network configuration. This pre-trained model was applied to our internal dataset to provide a preliminary segmentation of the lesions. These annotations were manually reviewed and corrected by either one of two radiologists in their first year post board examination using ITK-Snap V3.8.0 [34]. A subset of the annotations were corrected by both radiologists with an inter-reader Dice score of 0.78. The annotations were verified by a third neuro-radiologist with more than 10 years post fellowship experience. A temporal label was also assigned to new/enhanced lesions observed in the respective scan. Ground truth annotations for this study were then extracted by only extracting the temporal change label between the pair of scans.

2.3 Boundary Enhanced Approach for MS Segmentation

MS lesions can appear in the brain slice in varied shapes and sizes. New or enhanced lesions can be even more subtle and hard to identify. We propose a modification to the encoder-decoder architecture by adding another decoder arm for a boundary segmentation task. The encoder is shared by both decoder arms providing relevant context to the encoder during back-propagation. We also enrich the lesion detection path with the spatial boundary features to improve the final lesion segmentation. A schematic of this approach is shown in Fig. 1.

Siamese networks have been extensively applied in CD challenges due to their ability to effectively compare pairs of images and highlight differences [4,8]. Recently, Siamese architectures have been used to assess the severity of disease progression using successive medical images, demonstrating their ability to capture temporal changes in medical conditions [15,16]. Consequently, we employed a Siamese U-Net architecture for the change segmentation task in MS. The variability in size and shape of new/enhancing lesions poses a formidable challenge for accurate detection and segmentation. Feature Pyramid Networks (FPN) are specifically designed for object detection tasks as they are adept at capturing image features across multiple scales [18]. Leveraging the FPN backbone has also proven successful in various applications, including skin lesion segmentation [31]. To tackle the variability in lesion size effectively, we also employ the Panoptic Feature Pyramid Network (PFPN) architecture [14]. The inherent qualities of both the Siamese U-Net and PFPN make them ideal candidates for BEAMS. We modified these architectures as outlined in Fig. 1.

2.4 Preprocessing Pipeline

Each 3D image pair and the corresponding lesion volume is pre-processed and arranged in a data structure commonly used in the change detection challenges.

In most Brain MRI images, a large part of the image is the black background signal. We extracted the largest brain cross-section and identified the area coordinates which minimised background with respect to the brain while maintaining the original aspect ratio. We then applied this dimensional cropping to all image slices containing brain matter as well as the corresponding lesion mask slices to improve the brain to background ratio. Following the dimensional cropping, we reshape the images to 256×256 pixels and apply intensity normalisation to the brain slices. Additionally, we include contrast-limited adaptive histogram equalisation [25] to slightly improve the contrast of the brain slices. Some lesions are considered too small to be considered as progression and were removed following standard procedures [4]. Following this, Boundary Masks were generated by applying a standard canny edge detector [5] to the lesion masks.

2.5 Loss Selection

Dice Loss and Dice Focal loss are popular choices for segmentation, the latter is especially effective in cases of severe class imbalances [19]. In this work we also investigated use of the F_β Loss objective. F_β score (Eq. 1) has been proposed as a promising per-class counting metric [20]. By tuning the value of β the balance of precision and recall can be controlled. For $\beta < 1$, higher weight is given to precision, whereas for $\beta > 1$ a greater emphasis is placed on recall. We conducted a loss ablation study using a baseline Siamese U-Net architecture. Table 1 presents an evaluation of the respective loss trained model on our internal test set following the evaluation method as described in the next section. The F_2 Loss exhibits the highest recall, but the number of false positives renders it unsuitable for clinical applications. We also observed that while Dice and Dice Focal Loss perform well, the $F_{0.5}$ loss strikes a better balance between false positives and false negatives.

$$F_\beta = (1 + \beta^2) \cdot \frac{\text{Precision} \cdot \text{Recall}}{\beta^2 \cdot \text{Precision} + \text{Recall}} \qquad (1)$$

Table 1. Loss study : Evaluating a Siamese-UNet trained with different loss functions.

Loss	Dice	Precision	Recall	Identified Lesions		
				Correct	Incorrect	Missed
Dice Loss	0.373	0.306	0.688	76	451	22
Dice Focal Loss	0.238	0.161	0.723	81	781	17
$F_{\beta=2}$ Loss	0.132	0.076	**0.742**	**85**	1429	**13**
$F_{\beta=0.5}$ Loss	**0.492**	**0.449**	0.653	71	**185**	27

3 Experiments and Results

3.1 Experiment Setup

After the pre-processing pipeline, our data comprises of a total of 20,802 pairs of Brain MRI slices (baseline and follow-up), including training, validation, testing and external validation datasets. We implemented boundary enhancement to two architectures, the Siamese U-Net and the PFPN[1]. We use the performance of the nnUNet, Vision Transformer(ViT) and the XBound-Former as the benchmark for evaluation.

We initially trained the nnUNet using the same CD paradigm as applied to other models. However, this approach yielded unsatisfactory performance. Subsequently, we reverted to the standard method for lesion segmentation and assessed change by computing the difference between successive singular inference [10]. The nnUNet was trained using default configurations except a reduced batch size to accommodate GPU memory capacity. The XBound-Former was adapted to the CD paradigm and trained using the specified Structural loss [32]. The ViT has a ResNet50 backbone pre-trained on ImageNet dataset, and an encoder and decoder depth of 2.

All models were trained on NVIDIA 1080Ti GPUs for 100 epochs using an Adam optimiser and a learning rate of 1e−4, using an empirically selected $F_{0.5}$ loss objective for the new lesion segmentation task and a Binary Cross Entropy loss objective for the boundary segmentation task.

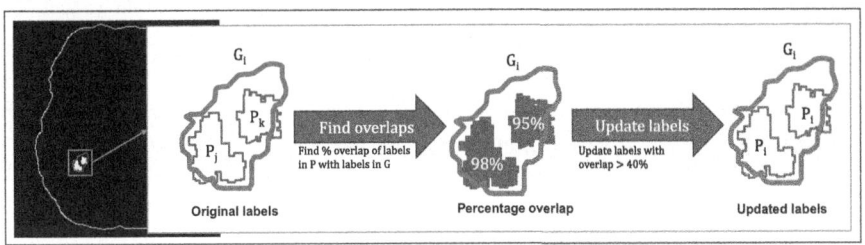

Fig. 2. Illustrating the evaluation strategy projected in 2D. There are two predicted lesions with labels j & k and, both are part of the same ground truth lesion i. The inset demonstrates detailed views of each lesion, the percentage overlap of each predicted lesion P_j & P_k in ground truth lesion G_i and the update applied to predicted labels (j,k) assigning them the same label of the ground truth (i).

3.2 Evaluation

In this study, we train our models with 2D brain image slices. However, we evaluate the model performance in 3D to avoid misleading results which may not

---

[1] https://github.com/insight-ucd/ms_change_detection.

be representative of the number of accurately identified or missed lesions. We reconstruct a 3D volume from 2D predictions. However, predicted lesion volumes can exhibit discontinuities, potentially misrepresenting the number of accurately identified lesions. This requires an additional step to group discontinuous lesions which are part of the same lesion in the ground truth annotation.

We evaluate our models based on their ability to detect lesions using the following methodology: first, identify and assign a label to all lesions using connected component analysis. Subsequently, for each predicted lesion measure the overlap with all lesions in the ground truth. Finally, assign each predicted lesion the label of the corresponding ground truth lesion with the highest volumetric overlap. A 2D projection of this strategy is illustrated in Fig. 2. Using this evaluation strategy, we compute metrics such as precision, recall, and dice score for the identified lesions.

Table 2. Performance comparison for new Lesion detection on our internal test dataset. Our proposed BEAMS Siamese U-Net exhibits the best performance, outperforming their counterparts. *Statistical significance was assessed through a paired t-test (p < 0.05) with bootstrap sampling.

Model	Dice	Precision	Recall	Identified Lesions		
				Correct	Incorrect	Missed
nnUNet	0.055	0.031	**0.680**	80	4522	**18**
XboundFormer	0.097	0.055	0.555	61	1095	37
PFPN	0.451	0.439	0.523	55	153	43
Siamese U-Net	0.492	0.449	0.653	71	185	27
ViT	0.513	0.489	0.649	65	158	33
BEAMS PFPN	0.495	0.529	0.526	52	**93**	46
BEAMS Siam U-Net	**0.593***	**0.585**	0.667	68	114	30

3.3 Results

Table 2 presents the evaluated metrics for the SOTA benchmarks and the BEAMS methods on our internal dataset. Our proposed BEAMS Siamese U-Net outperformed all other models in dice score and precision and achieved a balanced recall. These results indicate the superiority of the method in not only identifying lesions correctly but also in minimising false positives. The nnUNet and the XBound-Former excelled in identifying new or enhancing lesions but produced a high number of false positives. The Vision Transformer performed better than other benchmark methods, indicating the impact of the F_β loss objective. It is worth noting that the BEAMS methods perform better than their non-enhanced counterparts achieving an overall better performance. The ability of the BEAMS methods to identify small lesions is also illustrated in Fig. 3.

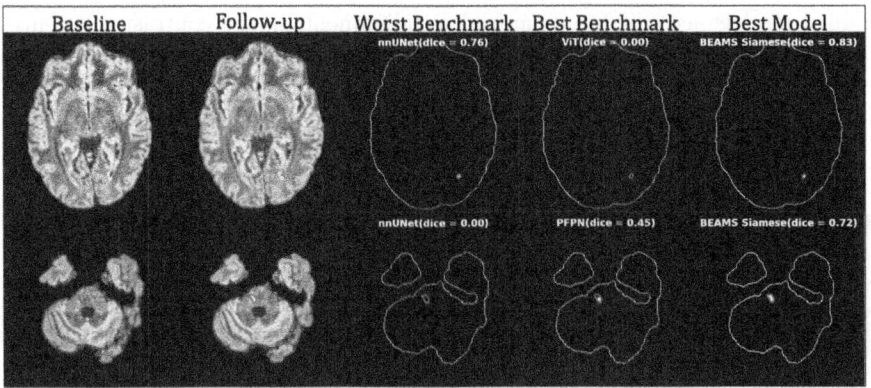

Fig. 3. Qualitative comparison of the worst performing benchmark, the best performing benchmark and the BEAMS Siamese U-Net on internal data (first row) and external data (second row). A correctly identified lesion is marked with a green boundary. While the benchmark methods are inconsistent, the BEAMS method shows its superiority in identifying small new lesions in both cases. (Color figure online)

Table 3 presents an evaluation on the external dataset. Our proposed BEAMS Siamese U-Net had the best dice score, precision and recall, indicating the ability of the method to generalise and also demonstrating its robustness to non-homogeneous data. The nnUNet and the XBound-Former exhibited a similar performance trend to our internal dataset. Surprisingly, the vision transformer method failed to robustly deal with the external data producing sub-optimal results. The sensitivity of the nnUNet and the inferiority of the single inference method for lesion segmentation is illustrated in Fig. 4. In contrast, the CD

Table 3. Performance comparison for new Lesion detection on external dataset. Our proposed BEAMS Siamese U-Net exhibits the best performance striking a balance between correctly identified lesions and minimizing false positives. *Statistical significance was assessed through a paired t-test ($p < 0.05$) with bootstrap sampling.

Model	Dice	Precision	Recall	Identified Lesions		
				Correct	Incorrect	Missed
nnUNet	0.071	0.053	0.329	66	2442	79
XboundFormer	0.108	0.078	0.318	**68**	850	**77**
ViT	0.396	0.519	0.393	50	51	95
Siamese U-Net	0.418	0.546	0.387	53	48	92
PFPN	0.461	0.591	0.455	57	49	88
BEAMS PFPN	0.429	0.600	0.384	43	**28**	102
BEAMS Siam U-Net	**0.537***	**0.665**	**0.507**	53	40	92

trained models account for structural misalignment, image contrast differences and capture new/enhancing lesions effectively both on our internal dataset and external data. The influence of the lesion boundary is also apparent in the prediction by the BEAMS method.

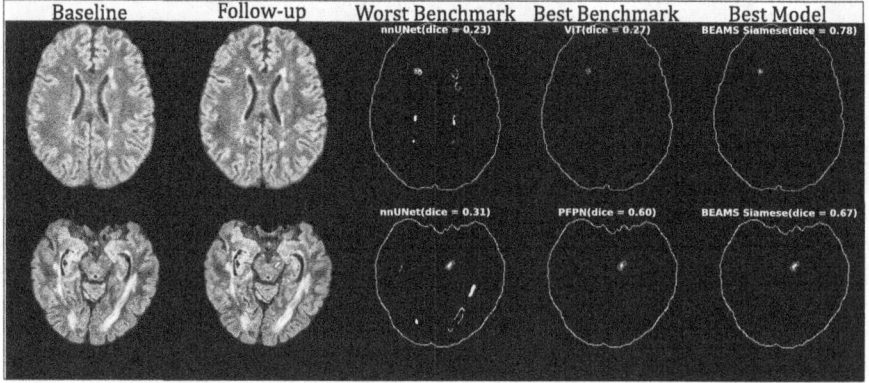

Fig. 4. Qualitative comparison of the worst performing benchmark, the best performing benchmark and the BEAMS Siamese U-Net on internal data (first row) and external data (second row). The example showcases the sensitivity of the nnUNet on structural misalignment or contrast differences between image pairs. The CD trained models focus only on new/enhancing lesions.

3.4 BEAMS-XAI

Deep Learning models are black-boxes and their decision making process is opaque to the observer. In a clinical setting it is imperative to provide the intuition behind the decisions made by the model. We make use of GradCAMs to probe the encoder network of our models to generate a visual interpretation of the attention of the network across various levels of abstraction. This also helps us to evaluate the impact of the additional boundary segmentation task on the encoder. Figure 5 shows a comparison between a Siamese U-Net and a BEAMS Siamese U-Net. We observe that the focus of the BEAMS model had refined with each layer of the encoder whereas the Siamese U-Net while able to segment the lesion, had a looser attention spread, influenced by the structure of the brain rather than the lesion itself. Figure 6 shows the comparison between PFPN and BEAMS PFPN. In this case, there is a slight error in the brain extraction causing structural misalignment between the baseline and follow-up images. The class attentions for the BEAMS PFPN show how the model focuses on the new lesion, whereas the PFPN pays more attention to the structural differences resulting in scattered attention.

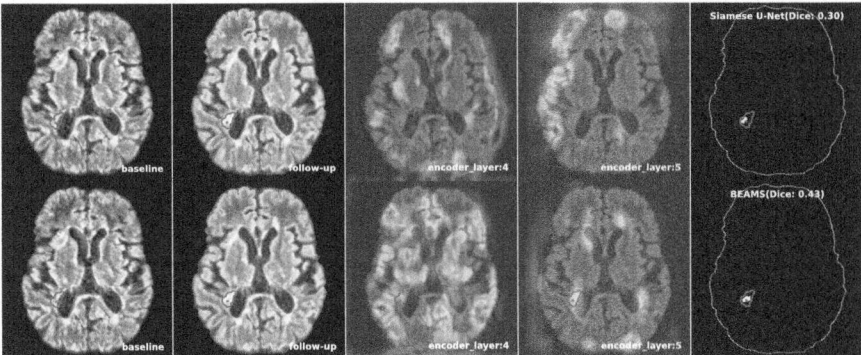

Fig. 5. Comparing Siamese U-Net(first row) and BEAMS Siamese U-Net (second row). A new lesion highlighted in red. GradCAM visualizations at final depths of the encoder illustrate attention localization on the follow-up image. The BEAMS method shows focused attention in contrast to the Siamese Network whose attention is spread around the brain structure. (Color figure online)

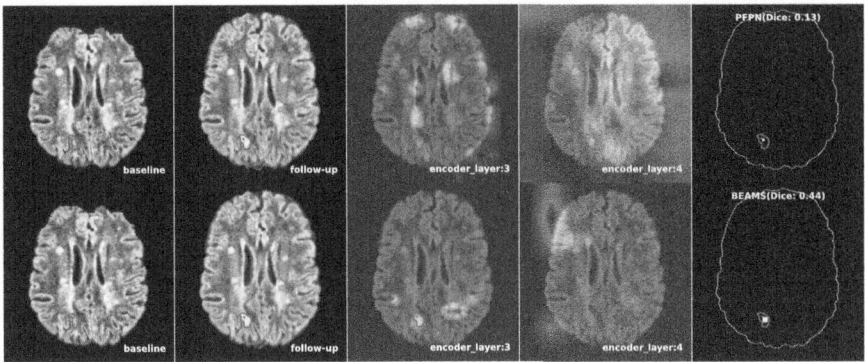

Fig. 6. Comparing PFPN(first row) and BEAMS PFPN(second row). GradCAMs show the attention of the models at penultimate and ultimate scale of the feature pyramid encoder. The BEAMS attention is concentrated and precise, whereas the PFPN attention is dispersed influenced by the structural differences between the images.

4 Conclusion

In this study, we propose a novel Boundary Enhanced Approach for MS change segmentation. This approach aids radiologists and clinicians to improve patient care by streamlining the identification of new lesions. While it is crucial to detect all lesions accurately, models identifying excessive false positives are impractical in clinical settings. Our empirically evaluated approach uses the F_β loss skewed for high precision, striking a balance between lesion identification and reducing false positives. The BEAMS model enhances traditional segmentation by incorporating a boundary segmentation task, significantly enhancing performance.

This underscores the critical importance of lesion shape and constraints in MS change segmentation. Future efforts will extend our change detection paradigm to incorporate temporal components for longitudinal tracking. This extension aims to predict MS lesion evolution, offering clinicians valuable insights into disease progression and facilitating proactive patient management.

Disclosure of Interests. This research was supported by Science Foundation Ireland (SFI) under Grant Number SFI/12/RC/2289_P2.

References

1. MSSEG-2 challenge proceedings: multiple sclerosis new lesions segmentation challenge using a data management and processing infrastructure (2021)
2. Acosta, J.N., Falcone, G.J., Rajpurkar, P.: The need for medical artificial intelligence that incorporates prior images. Radiology, 212830 (2022). https://doi.org/10.1148/radiol.212830
3. Bandara, W.G.C., Patel, V.M.: A transformer-based siamese network for change detection. arXiv (2022)
4. Basaran, B.D., Matthews, P.M., Bai, W.: New lesion segmentation for multiple sclerosis brain images with imaging and lesion-aware augmentation. Front. Neurosci. **16**, 1007453 (2022). https://doi.org/10.3389/fnins.2022.1007453
5. Canny, J.: A computational approach to edge detection. IEEE Trans. Pattern Anal. Mach. Intell. **6**, 679–698 (1986)
6. Commowick, O., et al.: Multiple sclerosis lesions segmentation from multiple experts: The MICCAI 2016 challenge dataset. Neuroimage **244**, 118589 (2021). https://doi.org/10.1016/j.neuroimage.2021.118589
7. Coronado, I., Gabr, R.E., Narayana, P.A.: Deep learning segmentation of gadolinium-enhancing lesions in multiple sclerosis. Mult. Scler. J. **27**(4), 519–527 (2020). https://doi.org/10.1177/1352458520921364
8. Daudt, R.C., Saux, B.L., Boulch, A.: Fully convolutional siamese networks for change detection. arXiv (2018)
9. Isensee, F., Jaeger, P.F., Kohl, S.A.A., Petersen, J., Maier-Hein, K.H.: nnU-Net: a self-configuring method for deep learning-based biomedical image segmentation. Nat. Methods **18**(2), 203–211 (2021). https://doi.org/10.1038/s41592-020-01008-z
10. Isensee, F., Jäger, P.F., Kohl, S.A.A., Petersen, J., Maier-Hein, K.H.: Automated design of deep learning methods for biomedical image segmentation. arXiv **18**(2), 203–211 (2019). https://doi.org/10.48550/arxiv.1904.08128
11. Jenkinson, M., Bannister, P., Brady, M., Smith, S.: Improved optimization for the robust and accurate linear registration and motion correction of brain images. Neuroimage **17**(2), 825–41 (2002). https://doi.org/10.1016/s1053-8119(02)91132-8
12. Jenkinson, M., Beckmann, C.F., Behrens, T.E., Woolrich, M.W., Smith, S.M.: FSL. NeuroImage **62**(2), 782–790 (2012). https://doi.org/10.1016/j.neuroimage.2011.09.015
13. Kamnitsas, K., et al.: Efficient multi-scale 3D CNN with fully connected CRF for accurate brain lesion segmentation. Med. Image Anal. **36**, 61–78 (2017). https://doi.org/10.1016/j.media.2016.10.004

14. Kirillov, A., Girshick, R., He, K., Dollár, P.: Panoptic Feature Pyramid Networks. arXiv (2019). https://doi.org/10.48550/arxiv.1901.02446
15. Li, M.D., et al.: Automated assessment of COVID-19 pulmonary disease severity on chest radiographs using convolutional Siamese neural networks. medRxiv p. 2020.05.20.20108159 (2020). https://doi.org/10.1101/2020.05.20.20108159
16. Li, M.D., et al.: Siamese neural networks for continuous disease severity evaluation and change detection in medical imaging. NPJ Digit. Med. **3**(1), 48 (2020). https://doi.org/10.1038/s41746-020-0255-1
17. Li, X., Morgan, P.S., Ashburner, J., Smith, J., Rorden, C.: The first step for neuroimaging data analysis: DICOM to NIfTI conversion. J. Neurosci. Methods **264**, 47–56 (2016). https://doi.org/10.1016/j.jneumeth.2016.03.001
18. Lin, T.Y., Dollar, P., Girshick, R., He, K., Hariharan, B., Belongie, S.: Feature pyramid networks for object detection. In: Proceedings of the IEEE Conference on Computer Vision and Pattern Recognition (CVPR) (2017)
19. Ma, J., et al.: Loss odyssey in medical image segmentation. Med. Image Anal. **71**, 102035 (2021). https://doi.org/10.1016/j.media.2021.102035
20. Maier-Hein, L., et al.: Metrics reloaded: recommendations for image analysis validation. arXiv **21**(2), 195–212 (2022). https://doi.org/10.48550/arxiv.2206.01653
21. McKinley, R., et al.: Simultaneous lesion and brain segmentation in multiple sclerosis using deep neural networks. Sci. Rep. **11**(1), 1087 (2021). https://doi.org/10.1038/s41598-020-79925-4
22. McNamara, C., Sugrue, G., Murray, B., MacMahon, P.: Current and emerging therapies in multiple sclerosis: implications for the radiologist, part 1-mechanisms, efficacy, and safety. Am. J. Neuroradiol. **38**(9), 1664–1671 (2017). https://doi.org/10.3174/ajnr.a5147
23. McNamara, C., Sugrue, G., Murray, B., MacMahon, P.: Current and emerging therapies in multiple sclerosis: implications for the radiologist, part 2-surveillance for treatment complications and disease progression. Am. J. Neuroradiol. **38**(9), 1672–1680 (2017). https://doi.org/10.3174/ajnr.a5148
24. Moskowitz, C.S., Welch, M.L., Jacobs, M.A., Kurland, B.F., Simpson, A.L.: Radiomic analysis: study design, statistical analysis, and other bias mitigation strategies. Radiology **304**(2), 265–273 (2022). https://doi.org/10.1148/radiol.211597
25. Pizer, S., Johnston, R., Ericksen, J., Yankaskas, B., Muller, K.: Contrast-limited adaptive histogram equalization: speed and effectiveness. In: 1990 Proceedings of the First Conference on Visualization in Biomedical Computing, pp. 337–345 (1990). https://doi.org/10.1109/vbc.1990.109340
26. Ronneberger, O., Fischer, P., Brox, T.: U-Net: convolutional networks for biomedical image segmentation. In: Navab, N., Hornegger, J., Wells, W.M., Frangi, A.F. (eds.) MICCAI 2015. LNCS, vol. 9351, pp. 234–241. Springer, Cham (2015). https://doi.org/10.1007/978-3-319-24574-4_28
27. Selvaraju, R.R., Cogswell, M., Das, A., Vedantam, R., Parikh, D., Batra, D.: Grad-CAM: visual explanations from deep networks via gradient-based localization. arXiv (2016). https://doi.org/10.48550/arxiv.1610.02391
28. Shamshad, F., et al.: Transformers in medical imaging: a survey. arXiv (2022)
29. Smith, S.M.: Fast robust automated brain extraction. Hum. Brain Mapp. **17**(3), 143–155 (2002). https://doi.org/10.1002/hbm.10062
30. Walton, C., King, R., Rechtman, L., Kaye, W., Leray, E., Marrie, R.A., Robertson, N., La Rocca, N., Uitdehaag, B., van Der Mei, I., et al.: Rising prevalence of multiple sclerosis worldwide: insights from the atlas of MS. Mult. Scler. J. **26**(14), 1816–1821 (2020)

31. Wang, H., Wang, G., Sheng, Z., Zhang, S.: Automated segmentation of skin lesion based on pyramid attention network. In: Suk, H.-I., Liu, M., Yan, P., Lian, C. (eds.) MLMI 2019. LNCS, vol. 11861, pp. 435–443. Springer, Cham (2019). https://doi.org/10.1007/978-3-030-32692-0_50
32. Wang, J., et al.: XBound-Former: toward cross-scale boundary modeling in transformers. arXiv (2022). https://doi.org/10.48550/arxiv.2206.00806
33. Wang, J., Wei, L., Wang, L., Zhou, Q., Zhu, L., Qin, J.: Boundary-aware transformers for skin lesion segmentation. arXiv (2021). https://doi.org/10.48550/arxiv.2110.03864
34. Yushkevich, P.A., et al.: User-guided 3D active contour segmentation of anatomical structures: significantly improved efficiency and reliability. Neuroimage **31**(3), 1116–1128 (2006)

A Radiological-Based Coordinate System for the Human Body: A Proof-of-Concept

Teresa M. T. Bucho[1,2], Thierry N. Boellaard[1], Mateus Taveira[3], Zuhir Bodalal[1,2], Thi D. L. Nguyen-Kim[4], Regina Beets-Tan[1,2], and Stefano Trebeschi[1,2(✉)]

[1] Department of Radiology, Netherlands Cancer Institute, Amsterdam, The Netherlands
stefano.trebeschi@maastrichtuniversity.nl
[2] GROW School for Oncology and Reproduction, Maastricht University, Maastricht, The Netherlands
[3] Department of Radiology, Memorial Sloan Kettering Cancer Center, New York, NY, USA
[4] Institute of Diagnostic and Interventional Radiology, University Hospital of Zurich, Zurich, Switzerland

Abstract. This study develops a self-supervised Siamese model to predict the relative positions of patches from thoraco-abdominal CT scans, creating an explicit 3D universal coordinate system (UCS) for the human body. The model is evaluated through experiments on body part localization, landmark detection, and longitudinal lesion tracking. Despite the moderate performance of the UCS in these experiments, this model provides a proof-of-concept system for standardized anatomical coordinates. Such a system enables robust identification and comparison of anatomical structures across different individuals and longitudinally.

Keywords: coordinate system · self-supervision · CT scans

1 Introduction

Medical images are difficult to search due to their heterogeneous nature, often requiring manual effort to identify specific anatomical features. Coordinate systems use a numbering system to uniquely identify positions in space, facilitating the tracing of objects, computation of distances, and description of changes. In human anatomy, a coordinate system would enable quick navigation during guided interventions, treatment planning, identification of organs and landmarks, tracing of their positions relative to each other and over time for patient monitoring, and simultaneously enable comparison across different subjects [6,8,9,13].

An example of a coordinate system for mapping human anatomy is the Talairach atlas [11]. It was the first widely utilized brain coordinate system in neuro-imaging, assigning unique coordinates to each location of the brain, offering a common template for registering the brains of different subjects [3]. This system was developed using specific anatomical landmarks in the postmortem brain of a single subject to define its origin and axes [1]. Later, the Montreal Neurological Institute (MNI) space was created based on the average brain of a few hundred individuals [1].

Inspired by these atlases, this study presents a proof-of-concept coordinate system for the human body. Due to its rigid structure, the brain allows for a straightforward implementation of such a system. However, the rest of the body represents a more intricate challenge due to its dynamic nature. Nonetheless, although the fixed positions of anatomical structures cannot be relied upon, unlike the consistent positioning seen in brain atlases, the natural *relative* positions of different anatomical structures with respect to each other remain consistent. Such anatomical relationships can be learned by a model and utilized to construct a Talairach-like coordinate system for the body.

Previous studies have explored self-supervised models for body part recognition in 2D based on anatomical ordering [10,12,16,17]. Zhang et al. (2017) [17] proposed a Siamese network to be trained to order 2D slices from 3D CT images. Each branch of the network processes separate axial slices, and binary classification is performed to determine their axial order. After pre-training on this task, the model was then fine-tuned in the supervised task of predicting the height of a transversal slice in a normalized body model. Yan et al. (2018) [16] also exploited the superior-inferior slice ordering in CT, improving upon Zhang et al. (2017) [17] by minimizing an order loss, enforcing spatial superior-inferior ordering and a distance loss, ensuring proportionality between slice scores and distances. Schuhegger et al. (2021) [10] built upon their work by incorporating the physical distance between slices in both the slice sampling and loss function. In the 3D context, Lei et al. 2023 [7] developed MedLAM, a self-supervised model trained to project anatomical features into a shared latent space, effectively creating an implicit unified anatomical coordinate system. Their approach involves predicting the offsets between query and reference patches of CT scans in the latent space and learning to project similar anatomical points to consistent locations in the latent space. It then refines the predicted locations by maximizing the cosine similarity between multi-scale feature vectors of the patches.

In this study, we propose a proof-of-concept self-supervised model for creating a Talairach-like whole-body coordinate system based on the relative anatomical order present in medical images. In this universal space, the positions and boundaries of any organ or landmark can be easily identified through their respective universal coordinates and mapped back to the original scan.

2 Methods

We extend previous work by predicting the relative position of two random patches - smaller crops of an axial slice - across all three imaging planes (Fig. 1). The Siamese setting first presented by Zhang et al. 2017 [17] is preserved, using a ResNet50 for the encoder. Each branch is fed with a different patch from the same CT and regresses three continuous values. These values are subtracted

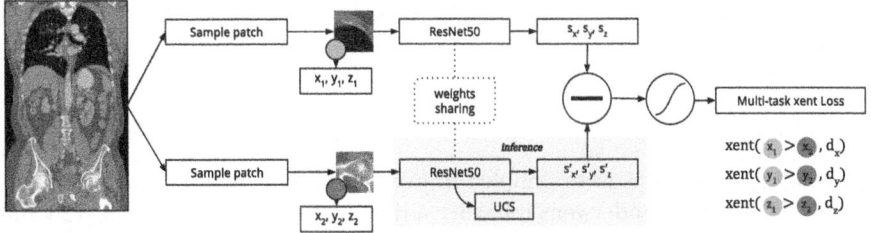

Fig. 1. Overview of our proposed model: each branch processes two patches from two different axial slices of the same scan and outputs three scores (s_i). Binary cross-entropy loss is computed for each of the sigmoid-activated score differences (d_i) compared to the true relative position of each patch.

from the ones in the counterpart branch and passed through a sigmoid function. It is followed by the classification task of predicting the relative order of the patches: class 1 indicates patch A as "above," "to the left," or "to the front" of patch B, and class 0 the opposite. In this process, each branch inherently learns the relative spatial relationships between anatomical regions within the patches, attributing three unique coordinates to each patch, based on the anatomical structures it contains.

The ground truth for this task is derived directly from the relative positions of the two patches when extracted from the same CT scan, eliminating the need for manual input. Although the model's inputs are 2D patches of axial slices, it is trained to predict the relative positions of the patches in the 3D space. After training, each identical module can output three unique anatomical scores for each voxel in a CT scan. These scores, or universal coordinates, are consistent across all CT scans, thus creating a universal coordinate system (UCS). Code is made publicly available[1].

2.1 Dataset

A total of 26,762 CT scans were collected from the publicly accessible Cancer Imaging Archive [2], selecting those with a minimum of 32 slices and a slice thickness between 0.1 and 5 mm. The CT scans in this dataset are diverse, covering various anatomical regions from the thorax to the abdomen, with differing voxel spacings [Q1=1.25mm; Q2=2.5mm; Q3=3mm] and multiple types of cancers. The CT scans from The Cancer Genome Atlas (TCGA) imaging collections were reserved as the test set (N=4,012). The remaining scans were randomly split on a patient level into training and validation sets (80% and 20%, respectively). Additionally, we collected two in-house datasets of patients undergoing therapy: 40 CT scans of 20 melanoma patients (baseline and follow-up) and 206 CT scans of 103 non-small cell lung cancer (NSCLC) patients (baseline and follow-up).

---

[1] github.com/nki-radiology/HumanCoordSystem.

In addition, we reserved 32 CT scans (32 patients) covering the thorax and abdomen from the test set.

2.2 Implementation Details

Ten random axial slices were sampled from each CT scan to construct the training set. These slices underwent intensity adjustments, clipped between -120 and +300 Hounsfield units to encompass fat to cortical bone, and normalized to a [0, 1] range. Initially, the model was trained on whole axial slices, with its weights serving as a basis for subsequent models. Data augmentation included random horizontal and vertical shifts, rotations, and zoom. The impact of slice (MxM) and patch (PxP) dimensions on model performance was assessed through experiments varying M at 256 and 512 and P at 32, 64, and 128. Training applied binary cross-entropy loss to each output, using the Adam optimizer with an initial learning rate of 10^{-4}. If the validation accuracy did not improve after ten epochs, the learning rate was reduced by 50%, with training continuing for up to 100 epochs. The model with the lowest validation loss was utilized for inference.

At inference, 1000 patches from each CT scan were randomly selected, and their corresponding universal scores were predicted. A RANSAC is then utilized to regress the universal coordinates of all voxels (positions of the axial, coronal, and sagittal slices at the patch corners). This serves two purposes: (1) eliminate outliers and (2) compute the mapping function between the scan-specific coordinates and the universal coordinates. Essentially, each voxel in a scan is mapped to its respective universal coordinate by a linear function $f : x_1 = mx_2 + b$ and inverse $f^{-1} : x_2 = (x_1 - b)m^{-1}$. We experiment with three different fittings:

1. **Linearly in one dimension**: individual mapping of the coordinates of each plane to the universal scores, followed by concatenation
2. **Linearly in three dimensions**: joint mapping of the coordinates of each plane to the universal scores
3. **Polynomial in three dimensions**: RANSAC was used to fit scan coordinates (and their second-degree polynomial combinations) to universal scores, and the inverse fitting.

2.3 Experiments

Three experiments are presented to illustrate the application and performance of the UCS.

Body Part Localization: using TotalSegmentator [14], bounding boxes were derived for the kidneys, lungs, femurs, liver, heart, aorta, spine, sacrum, and bladder in the TCGA and melanoma in-house datasets. A single scan was selected as a reference to determine the bounding box coordinates for each organ. These were then converted into UCS and used to query the remaining scans (excluding any scans from the reference patient). The 3D Intersection over Union (IoU) between the actual organ bounding boxes and those identified by

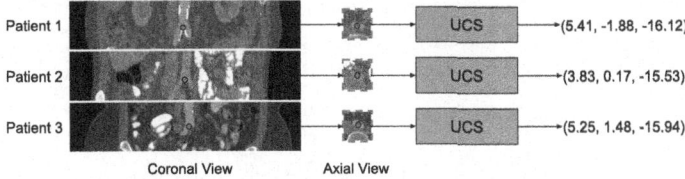

Fig. 2. The universal coordinates produced by the UCS (ResNet50) for the aorta bifurcation of three different patients

the UCS was calculated. This process was repeated with a rotating reference scan in a leave-one-reference-out manner, and the median IoUs across all scans were computed.

Landmark Detection: two experienced radiologists (T.N.B.; M.T.) manually identified and annotated 19 anatomical landmarks (Fig. 4), chosen to represent diverse regions of the thorax and abdomen, in the TCGA and melanoma in-house datasets respectively. Similar to the previous experiment, one scan was utilized as a reference. The error between the positions of the annotated landmarks and those identified by the UCS score was estimated using the Euclidean distance (in mm). This was repeated with a rotating reference scan, and the median distances across all scans were calculated.

Longitudinal Lesion Tracking: an experienced radiologist (T.K.) manually segmented lesions in the baseline and follow-up scans of the NSCLC in-house dataset. The accuracy of the UCS in tracking lesions was assessed by determining if the UCS coordinates of the lesion's center of mass remained within the same lesion's bounding box in follow-up images of the same patient [15].

3 Results

An example of the universal coordinates generated by the UCS for a specific landmark can be seen in Fig. 2: given patches from different scans containing the same anatomical region, the model will produce roughly the same universal coordinates. To better visualize and interpret the model's output, Fig. 3 shows the overlapping of the discrete values of the universal coordinates on axial slices of three different patients. The distribution of the universal coordinates for all 19 landmarks can be seen in Fig. 4, for each imaging plane. Landmarks located at opposite sides of the body will have correspondingly opposite universal coordinate values. Axial universal coordinates show less dispersion for the same landmark in different scans scans than those of the sagittal or coronal planes.

Table 1 presents the median IoU, median Euclidean distances, and median accuracy for the experiments of body part localization, landmark detection, and lesions tracking, respectively. The best performance of the UCS, across all experiments, is achieved overall when the patch size is set to 128 and the image size is 256. The performances of the two linear RANSAC fits (Linear1D and Linear3D)

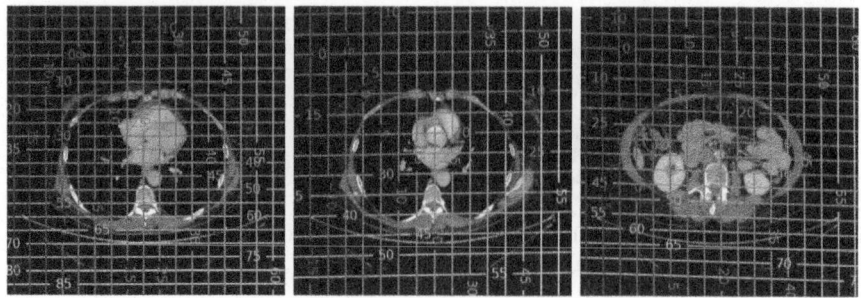

Fig. 3. Coordinate lines overlaid on CT scans for same-scoring axial slices. Discrete values were selected for a clearer visualization, although the model outputs continuous scores.

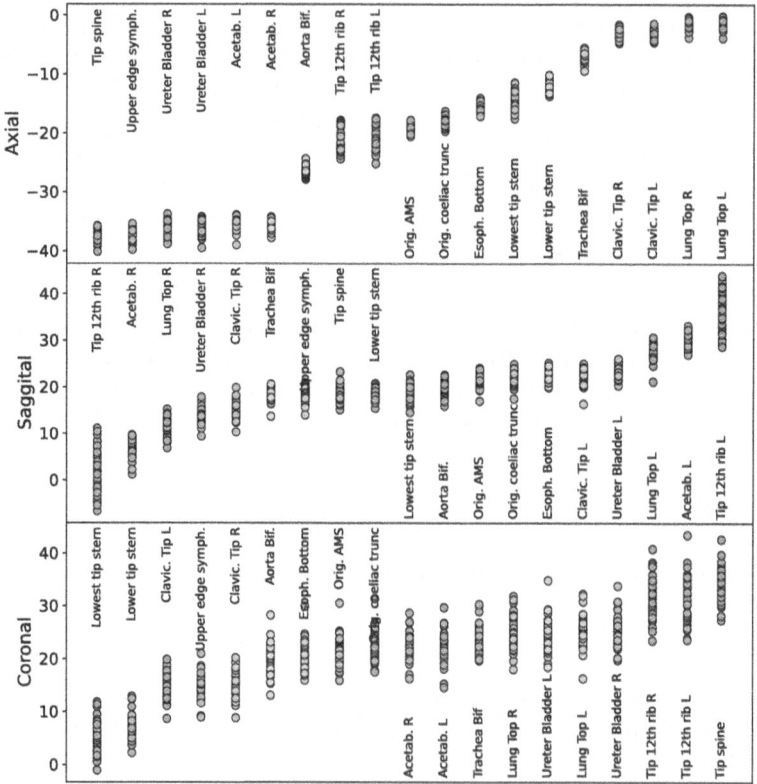

Fig. 4. Distribution of universal coordinates by landmark on the in-house melanoma cohort. L: Left; R: Right; Bif.: Bifurcation; Acetab.: Acetabulum; Clavic.: Clavicles; Symph.: Symphysis; Esoph.: Esophagus; Orig.: Origin.

are comparable, whereas the polynomial fit resulted in markedly poorer metrics. The performance for any configuration of the UCS was always poorer for the

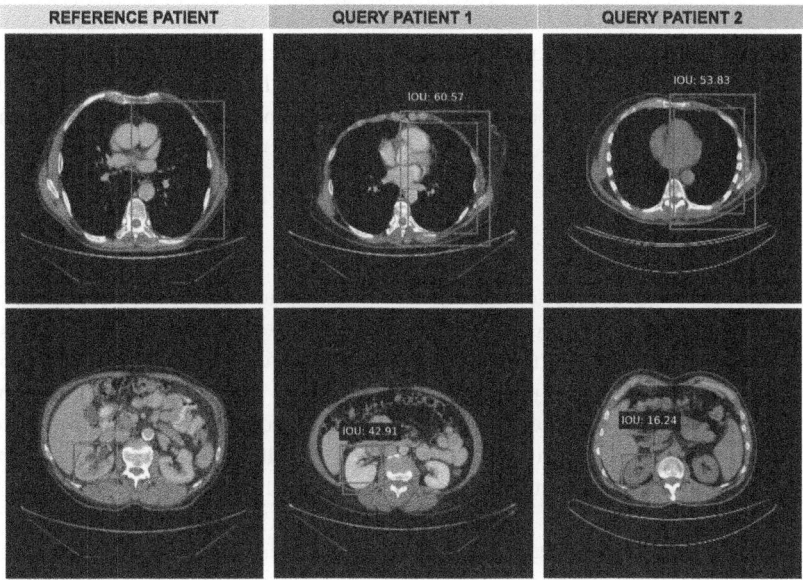

Fig. 5. Predicted (red) and ground truth (green) boundings boxes, for the right lung (top) and left kidney (bottom), and respective 3D IoU. (Color figure online)

Table 1. Results on the experiments: median 3D IoU for body part localization; median distance values in mm for landmark detection; and median accuracy for lesion tracking, for different combinations of patch and slice sizes (P-M)

Experiment		Melanoma			TCGA			NCSLC		
		64-256	128-256	128-512	64-256	128-256	128-512	64-256	128-256	128-512
IoU	Linear1D	42.1	47.9	39.6	22.1	**25.7**	10.6	-	-	-
	Linear3D	38.9	**48.0**	40.6	15.9	25.4	17.5	-	-	-
	Polynomial	16.8	26.6	24.5	9.8	10.8	9.5	-	-	-
Distance (mm)	Linear1D	48.3	27.0	47.2	59.0	**49.3**	77.1	-	-	-
	Linear3D	40.9	**25.9**	39.1	62.5	50.0	70.7	-	-	-
	Polynomial	57.6	32.8	44.4	93.2	52.7	71.4	-	-	-
Accuracy	Linear1D	-	-	-	-	-	-	24.9	22.1	14.9
	Linear3D	-	-	-	-	-	-	18.1	22.1	13.1
	Polynomial	-	-	-	-	-	-	10.5	15.2	11.2

TCGA dataset than for the in-house dataset (median z-spacing of 2 mm and 1 mm, respectively).

In Fig. 5, examples of bounding boxes predicted by UCS are compared to the ground truth. Generally, larger organ volumes result in higher IoU. For instance, across all experiments and datasets, the IoU values for the right and left lungs were in the ranges of 29.4-63.1 and 15.3-64.7, respectively, whereas the IoU for the right and left kidneys were in the ranges of 0.5-21.4 to 1.1-24.0, respectively. Similarly, accuracy is also influenced by lesion size. For lesions smaller than the 25th percentile (9 mm), accuracies ranged from 0 to 7.2%. For lesions larger than the 75th percentile (27 mm), accuracies ranged from 29.7 to 46.2%. Across all experiments and datasets, the landmark with the largest median distance between actual and predicted locations was the tip of the left 12th rib (67 mm). In comparison, the smallest was the bottom of the esophagus (28 mm).

4 Discussion

This study presents a proof-of-concept for a universal coordinate system (UCS) for the human body derived from the natural anatomical order in CT scans. Embedding this information in a neural network can translate any scan coordinate into a universal anatomical coordinate. This allows the identification of specific structures in medical images and enables comparisons across different individuals. The UCS is developed using a pair of self-supervised regression networks that inherently learn to assign a unique universal score to each voxel in a CT scan.

Previous studies utilizing self-supervised methods for body part recognition [10,16,17] have been limited to the axial plane, outputting a universal score per axial slice. In the applications we tested, our approach demonstrates limitations in performance metrics. Previous studies on landmark detection [4,15] and lesion tracking [5,15], methods have achieved accurate results. Still, these approaches do not fully leverage the concept of a universal coordinate system. To our knowledge, this is the first attempt at explicitly creating a 3D universal coordinate system for the human body. While Lei et al. (2023) [7] developed a model following a similar framework for mapping anatomical structures across different individuals to similar coordinates, their approach did not generalize the problem to an abstract representation of the human body.

Our study focuses only on the thorax and abdomen regions of patients with cancer. Future work should extend the evaluation to other anatomical regions and diseases, including healthy patients, to verify the UCS's robustness. While effective to smooth the universal scores, RANSAC may be replaced with more flexible algorithms to handle anatomical variability better. Future research should explore enforcing proportionality between slice distance and scores [10,16], as well as a continuous slice sampling strategy during training. Extending the model to actual 3D space (comparing the relative positions of cubes, not 2D patches) could further improve the UCS's accuracy and applicability. Expanding the dataset to include a more diverse population and different imaging modalities will also help validate the UCS.

In conclusion, our experiments demonstrated the UCS's potential despite its moderate performance. This proof-of-concept system sets the stage for standardized anatomical coordinates, allowing consistent and robust comparison of anatomical structures across individuals and longitudinally.

Disclosure of Interests. The authors would like to acknowledge the Research High Performance Computing facility of the NKI and the Maurits en Anna de Kock Stichting.

References

1. Chau, W., McIntosh, A.R.: The talairach coordinate of a point in the MNI space: how to interpret it. Neuroimage **25**(2), 408–416 (2005). https://doi.org/10.1016/j.neuroimage.2004.12.007, https://linkinghub.elsevier.com/retrieve/pii/S1053811904007554
2. Clark, K., et al.: The cancer imaging archive (TCIA): maintaining and operating a public information repository. J. Digit. Imaging **26**(6), 1045–1057 (2013). https://doi.org/10.1007/s10278-013-9622-7, http://link.springer.com/10.1007/s10278-013-9622-7
3. Dittrich, E., Kasprian, G., Prayer, D., Langs, G.: Atlas learning in fetal brain development. Top. Magn. Reson. Imaging **22**(3), 107–111 (2011). https://doi.org/10.1097/RMR.0b013e318267fe94, https://journals.lww.com/00002142-201105000-00004
4. Grewal, M., Deist, T.M., Wiersma, J., Bosman, P.A.N., Alderliesten, T.: An end-to-end deep learning approach for landmark detection and matching in medical images. Medical Imaging 2020: Image Processing, p. 79 (2020). https://doi.org/10.1117/12.2549302, http://arxiv.org/abs/2001.07434
5. Hering, A., et al.: Whole-body soft-tissue lesion tracking and segmentation in longitudinal CT imaging studies, p. 15
6. Hoffmann, L., Holt, M.I., Knap, M.M., Khalil, A.A., Møller, D.S.: Anatomical landmarks accurately determine interfractional lymph node shifts during radiotherapy of lung cancer patients. Radiother. Oncol. **116**(1), 64–69 (2015). https://doi.org/10.1016/j.radonc.2015.06.009
7. Lei, W., Wei, X., Zhang, X., Li, K., Zhang, S.: MedLSAM: localize and segment anything model for 3D CT images (2023). http://arxiv.org/abs/2306.14752, arXiv:2306.14752
8. Potesil, V., Kadir, T., Platsch, G., Brady, M.: Personalized graphical models for anatomical landmark localization in whole-body medical images. Int. J. Comput. Vis. **111**(1), 29–49 (2014). https://doi.org/10.1007/s11263-014-0731-7
9. Rood, J.E., et al.: Toward a common coordinate framework for the human body. Cell **179**(7), 1455–1467 (2019). https://doi.org/10.1016/j.cell.2019.11.019, https://linkinghub.elsevier.com/retrieve/pii/S0092867419312759
10. Schuhegger, S.: Body part regression for CT images. Master's thesis, Heidelberg University (2021). http://arxiv.org/abs/2110.09148
11. Talairach, J., Szikla, G.: Application of stereotactic concepts to the surgery of epilepsy. In: Advances in Stereotactic and Functional Neurosurgery 4: Proceedings of the 4 th Meeting of the European Society for Stereotactic and Functional Neurosurgery, Paris 1979, pp. 35–54. Springer (1980). https://doi.org/10.1007/978-3-7091-8592-6_5
12. Tang, Y., et al.: Body part regression with self-supervision. IEEE Trans. Med. Imaging **40**(5), 1499–1507 (2021). https://doi.org/10.1109/TMI.2021.3058281, https://ieeexplore.ieee.org/document/9350603/
13. Wang, M., Song, Z.: How does adding anatomical landmarks as fiducial points in the point-matching registration of neuronavigation influence registration accuracy? Comput. Assist. Surg. **21**(1), 39–45 (2016). https://doi.org/10.1080/24699322.2016.1180429
14. Wasserthal, J., Meyer, M., Breit, H.C., Cyriac, J., Yang, S., Segeroth, M.: TotalSegmentator: robust segmentation of 104 anatomical structures in CT images (2022). http://arxiv.org/abs/2208.05868, arXiv:2208.05868

15. Yan, K., et al.: SAM: self-supervised learning of pixel-wise anatomical embeddings in radiological images. http://arxiv.org/abs/2012.02383
16. Yan, K., Lu, L., Summers, R.M.: Unsupervised body part regression via spatially self-ordering convolutional neural networks. arXiv:1707.03891 (2018). http://arxiv.org/abs/1707.03891
17. Zhang, P., Wang, F., Zheng, Y.: Self supervised deep representation learning for fine-grained body part recognition. In: 2017 IEEE 14th International Symposium on Biomedical Imaging (ISBI 2017), pp. 578–582. IEEE (2017). https://doi.org/10.1109/ISBI.2017.7950587

MMMI-ML4MHD Workshop

Language Models Meet Anomaly Detection for Better Interpretability and Generalizability

Jun Li[1,2], Su Hwan Kim[4], Philip Müller[1], Lina Felsner[1], Daniel Rueckert[1,2,4,5], Benedikt Wiestler[1,4], Julia A. Schnabel[1,2,3,6(✉)], and Cosmin I. Bercea[1,3(✉)]

[1] Technical University of Munich, Munich, Germany
{june.li,cosmin.bercea,julia.schnabel}@tum.de
[2] Munich Center for Machine Learning, Munich, Germany
[3] Helmholtz AI and Helmholtz Munich, Munich, Germany
[4] Klinikum Rechts der Isar, Munich, Germany
[5] Imperial College London, London, UK
[6] Kings's College London, London, UK

Abstract. This research explores the integration of language models and unsupervised anomaly detection in medical imaging, addressing two key questions: *(1) Can language models enhance the interpretability of anomaly detection maps?* and *(2) Can anomaly maps improve the generalizability of language models in open-set anomaly detection tasks?* To investigate these questions, we introduce a new dataset for multi-image visual question-answering on brain magnetic resonance images encompassing multiple conditions. We propose *KQ-Former* (Knowledge Querying Transformer), which is designed to optimally align visual and textual information in limited-sample contexts. Our model achieves a 60.81% accuracy on closed questions, covering disease classification and severity across 15 different classes. For open questions, *KQ-Former* demonstrates a 70% improvement over the baseline with a BLEU-4 score of 0.41, and achieves the highest entailment ratios (up to 71.9%) and lowest contradiction ratios (down to 10.0%) among various natural language inference models. Furthermore, integrating anomaly maps results in an 18% accuracy increase in detecting open-set anomalies, thereby enhancing the language model's generalizability to previously unseen medical conditions. The code and dataset are available at: https://github.com/compai-lab/miccai-2024-junli?tab=readme-ov-file.

Keywords: Multimodal Learning · Vision-Language Models · VQA

J. A. Schnabel and C. I. Bercea—Equal contribution.

Supplementary Information The online version contains supplementary material available at https://doi.org/10.1007/978-3-031-84525-3_10.

1 Introduction

Unsupervised Anomaly Detection (UAD) plays a vital role in early disease diagnosis by identifying deviations from normal patterns. Common UAD methods in medical imaging utilize auto-encoders [7,40], generative adversarial networks [1,28], or diffusion models [3,4,37] and are typically trained on data from healthy subjects. When applied to pathological inputs, they generate counterfactual "pseudo-healthy" (PH) images that normalize anomalous features to resemble healthy tissues [6]. By comparing the pathological inputs with the generated PH images, anomaly maps can be derived, highlighting regions of interest for clinicians. However, the interpretability of UAD findings is inherently limited due to the unsupervised nature of these methods. Clinicians often lack explicit explanations of the detected anomalies, which can hinder effective decision-making.

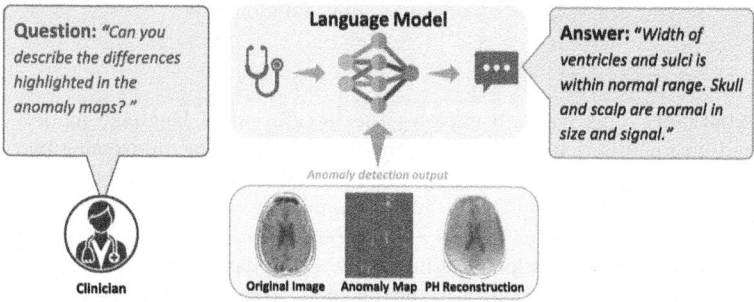

Fig. 1. Our framework is designed to process questions in conjunction with results from anomaly detection methods aiming to provide clinicians with clear, interpretable responses that render anomaly map analyses more intuitive and clinically actionable.

To provide interpretable text descriptions for clinicians, we integrate language models with UAD as shown in Fig. 1. Recent advancements in language models have achieved human-like performance in tasks such as question answering, summarizing, reasoning, and knowledge retrieval [8,25,32]. Notably, these models have demonstrated the capability to pass the United States medical licensing examination [13], showcasing their potential in the medical field [23,30,33].

However, integrating language models with UAD shifts the task from a typical single-image analysis [2,20,34] to a more complex multi-image visual question answering (VQA) challenge. While recent studies have explored generating radiology reports from frontal and lateral views of X-rays [16,31,38], the broader application of multi-image VQA remains largely unexplored. To address this gap, we propose a framework for multi-image VQA in UAD, analyzing various feature fusion strategies to effectively combine original images, anomaly maps, and PH reconstructions. Furthermore, adapting language models for multi-modal tasks introduces additional challenges due to the scarcity and high costs associated with large annotated medical datasets required for fine-tuning [17,18,24,39]. To tackle these challenges, we introduce the *KQ-Former*, a novel module designed to improve the alignment between visual and textual features, even in settings with limited data availability. In this work, we propose, to the best of our knowledge, the first multi-image question answering application for unsupervised anomaly detection (VQA-UAD). Our main contributions are as follows:

- We have developed a specialized multi-image VQA dataset for UAD, featuring brain Magnetic Resonance Imaging scans. This dataset is meticulously annotated by medical experts and covers a wide range of medical conditions.
- We introduce a model-agnostic baseline tailored for multi-image VQA-UAD, alongside a comprehensive analysis of various image fusion strategies.
- We introduce the *KQ-Former*, an innovative module designed to enhance the extraction of knowledge-related visual features, thereby improving the alignment between visual and textual information.
- Our experimental results demonstrate that language models not only render anomaly maps interpretable but can also leverage these anomaly maps to bolster the accuracy of responses in VQA. This proved particularly effective in scenarios involving previously unseen anomalies.

2 Methods

Figure 2 shows our VQA-UAD framework, which leverages multiple imaging modalities and language models to enhance diagnostic accuracy. The goal of VQA-UAD is to generate precise answers (A_i) from a set of three images-original image (I_i^o), anomaly map (I_i^a), and PH reconstruction (I_i^r)-and a question (Q_i). Section 2.1 introduces our baseline for multi-image VQA, setting the foundation for this application. Section 2.2 introduces the novel *KQ-Former*, designed to enhance both UAD and VQA through improved visual-textual alignment.

2.1 Multi-image VQA Baseline

Figure 2a provides an overview of our multi-image VQA baseline, which incorporates a visual encoder and a language decoder. Figure 2b illustrates three feature fusion methods within our module.

The visual encoder processes the image triple $\mathcal{I} = (I_i^o, I_i^a, I_i^r)$, where I_i is a tensor in $\mathbb{R}^{H \times W \times C}$ representing height, width, and channels, respectively. It transforms these images into visual embeddings $\mathcal{V} = (V_i^o, V_i^a, V_i^r)$ through the operation $\mathcal{V} = \mathcal{F}_v(\mathcal{I})$, where each V_i is an array in $\mathbb{R}^{n \times d}$, with n indicating the number of patches, and d the dimension of embeddings. Here, we implement the encoder based on two different backbones: ViT-B/16 [9] and ResNet50 [10].

The different fusion strategies are depicted in Fig. 2b. The first strategy averages the image features by computing $V_i' = \frac{1}{3} \sum_{j \in \{o,a,r\}} V_i^j$. The second strategy concatenates the visual features into $C_i = [V_i^o; V_i^a; V_i^r]$, where C_i resides in $\mathbb{R}^{3n \times d}$. Subsequently, a trainable projection model $\Phi(\cdot)$ is employed to reduce the dimension of C_i into $V_i' = \Phi(C_i)$, where $\Phi(\cdot)$ consists of a two-layer multilayer

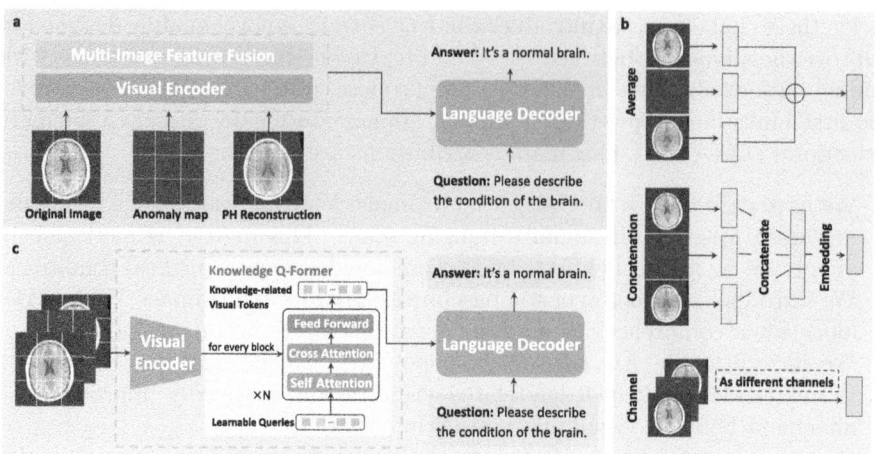

Fig. 2. An overview of our novel framework for VQA-UAD: (a) the multi-image VQA baseline; (b) multi-image feature fusion strategies; (c) the *KQ-former* module.

perception. The final fusion strategy converts each component of the image triple $\mathcal{I}$ into single-channel grayscale images. These are then concatenated channel-wise to form a combined three-channel image $\hat{I}_i = [I_i^o, I_i^a, I_i^r] \in \mathbb{R}^{H \times W \times 3}$. This transformation simplifies the multi-image VQA challenge into a single-image format, with the final integrated visual features expressed as $V_i' = \mathcal{F}_v(\hat{I}_i)$.

Language Decoder. Unlike existing methods that primarily treat VQA as a classification task [20,24], our framework approaches it as a natural language generation challenge, drawing inspiration from recent advances [16,31,38]. Our language decoder, here GPT-2 small [27], processes a question Q_i and the corresponding merged image features V_i' to generate the answer A_i, producing tokens sequentially. At each decoding step t, it calculates a probability distribution $p_\theta(A_i^t)$ over the vocabulary. Consequently, the full answer distribution for A_i with length T is defined as $p_\theta(A_i) = \prod_{t=1}^{T} p_\theta(A_i^t | Q_i, V_i', A_i^1, \ldots, A_i^{t-1})$. During training, the goal is to minimize the negative log-likelihood for N samples:

$$\mathcal{L}(\theta^*) = \arg\min_\theta \sum_{i=1}^{N} -\log p_\theta(A_i | Q_i, V_i'). \tag{1}$$

2.2 Knowledge Q-Former

We introduce the *KQ-Former* as an enhancement to our baseline multi-image VQA, specifically addressing the challenge of effectively aligning visual and textual features in contexts where datasets are typically limited. Figure 2c illustrates the design and integration of the *KQ-Former* within our VQA framework. The novel aspect of the *KQ-Former* lies in its ability to leverage knowledge embeddings that integrate pre-trained medical information, enriching its capability to understand and interpret complex medical images.

Formally, the *KQ-Former* operates by taking an input of learnable queries $L_i \in \mathbb{R}^{32 \times 768}$ and visual features V_i and processes these through a dynamic cross-attention mechanism. This interaction enables the *KQ-Former* to dynamically merge the embedded medical knowledge with the visual information, resulting in enhanced visual tokens $K_i \in \mathbb{R}^{32 \times 768}$ that carry detailed visual data alongside relevant medical insights. These tokens are then aggregated following the strategies outlined in Sect. 2.1 and fed directly into the language decoder.

Network Architecture. The architecture of the *KQ-Former* is transformer-based, inspired by the Q-Former design [17,35] but modified to consolidate image and text processing into a single transformer unit. This simplification is crucial in medical applications, where data sets are often limited to a few hundred samples. Additionally, the KQ-Former is initialized with BioBERT [14], enhancing its ability to incorporate deep medical knowledge.

3 Experiments

Dataset. We retrieved 440 T1-weighted MRI 2D mid-axial brain images from the fastMRI dataset [12], including 253 healthy and 187 unhealthy samples, featuring 13 distinct types of anomalies. For our main experiment, we focused on seven types, while the remaining six types were used to test open-set anomaly detection capabilities (refer to supplementary material for category distribution). We generated the anomaly maps and PH reconstructions using the publicly available method in [5]. Nevertheless, our framework is complementary to UAD research and can benefit from advances in this field.

We created and released VQA labels to facilitate further research. The dataset, annotated by two senior neuroradiologists with both closed and open question types as shown in Fig. 3, is organized into question-answer pairs. We divide them patient-wise into training, validation, and test sets in a 7:1:2 ratio, containing 1078, 154, and 308 samples respectively, ensuring a diverse representation of disease and question types across all sets without overlap.

Evaluation Metrics. We evaluated the performance on the closed questions using Accuracy (ACC) and F1 scores. For the open questions, we employed two types of metrics. Firstly, we used standard language evaluation metrics such as BLEU scores [26], ROUGE-L [19], and CIDEr [36] to assess the similarity between the predicted answers and the ground truths. However, since these metrics primarily measure similarity without confirming factual accuracy, we supplemented them with a second type of evaluation. We utilized four Natural Language Inference (NLI) models-BART [15], DEBERTA [11], mDeBERTa [29], and ROBERTA [21]-to determine the logical relationship between the predicted answers and the ground truths. The NLI model categorizes whether the given predicted sentence and the ground truth answer logically imply (entailment) or oppose (contradiction) each other, or are indeterminate (neutral) to each other.

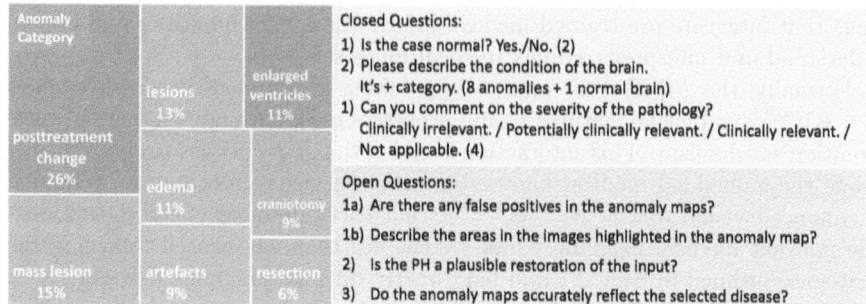

Fig. 3. Left: Distribution of anomaly categories. Right: Definitions of closed and open questions. For the closed questions, the blue text indicates the answer type, with the count of each type in parentheses. For more details, please refer to the supplementary material. Some questions are simplified here due to space constraints. (Color figure online)

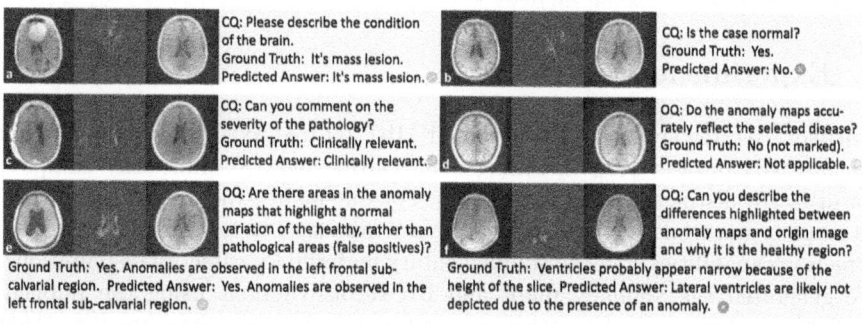

Fig. 4. Visualization examples of the *KQ-Former* module with concatenation strategy. Each example includes from left to right: the original image, anomaly map, and PH reconstruction. CQ and OQ represent closed and open questions, respectively.

Experimental Setup. Our experiments focus on two main areas. The first evaluates how well our proposed methods explain anomaly maps. The second investigates whether anomaly maps can enhance the generalizability of language models in real-world clinical scenarios, which include predominantly healthy data and some previously unseen anomalies. We trained the models on a single NVIDIA RTX A6000 for 40 epochs, using early stopping with patience of 10. We utilized the AdamW optimizer [22] with a learning rate of $1.5e^{-5}$ and a weight decay of 0.05. We used beam search with a width of 5 during the generation phase.

4 Results

4.1 Language Models Enhance the Explainability of Anomaly Maps

This section assesses the impact of language models on the explainability of anomaly maps. Figure 4 displays examples of the KQ-Former addressing radiologist queries. Instances (a, c, e) show the KQ-Former effectively describes anomaly maps. In cases (b, d, f) predictions do not fully align with expected outcomes. However, the language model still interprets these questions effectively and offers contextually relevant responses, demonstrating its capability to enhance the understanding of anomaly detection.

Table 1. Performance of the proposed Multi-Image baseline (MI) and *KQ-Former* (KQF). We experiment with different backbones: ViT and ResNet, and using different feature fusion strategies. B1 to B4 denote BLEU-1 to BLEU-4, while RL and Cr denote ROUGE-L and CIDEr. The best two performances are shown in **bold**.

	Methods	Fusion	Closed		Open					
			ACC↑	F1↑	B1↑	B2↑	B3↑	B4↑	RL↑	Cr↑
ViT	MI-baseline	average	56.76	49.30	0.49	0.38	0.32	0.27	0.62	1.94
		concat	57.43	50.14	0.45	0.35	0.29	0.24	0.61	1.79
		channel	53.38	48.33	0.44	0.34	0.28	0.24	0.58	1.77
	KQF (ours)	concat	**60.14**	**56.92**	**0.55**	**0.48**	**0.44**	**0.41**	**0.67**	**2.84**
		channel	**60.81**	**55.93**	**0.51**	**0.43**	**0.38**	**0.34**	**0.65**	**2.50**
ResNet	MI-baseline	average	36.49	38.89	0.44	0.35	0.29	0.24	0.57	1.82
		concat	40.54	**43.89**	0.35	0.26	0.21	0.18	0.56	1.48
		channel	36.49	38.89	0.38	0.29	0.24	0.20	0.54	1.69
	KQF (ours)	concat	**54.05**	**47.27**	**0.47**	**0.37**	**0.30**	**0.25**	**0.60**	**1.97**
		channel	**47.97**	41.54	**0.45**	**0.36**	**0.31**	**0.27**	**0.58**	**1.90**

Table 1 summarizes the performance metrics. Independent of the backbone architecture or fusion strategy employed, the *KQ-Former (KQF)* consistently outperforms the multi-image VQA baseline (MI) in all performance metrics. For instance, it improves accuracy by 5% for closed questions and increases the BLEU-4 score by 71% for open questions for the best variants. Among the different backbone architectures tested, the Vision Transformer (ViT) consistently outperforms the ResNet50. Specifically, switching to ViT boosts the KQ-Former's accuracy by 11.27% for closed questions and improves its BLEU-4 score by up to 26.77% for open questions. Regarding fusion strategies, the concatenation approach generally yields the highest improvements in both methods. We observe that *KQF* is more robust across different fusion strategies, likely due to its enhanced ability to utilize visual features from multiple images effectively. Additionally, the NLI model results depicted in Fig. 5 further validate the robustness of the *KQ-Former*. The model demonstrates a higher entailment ratio and a lower contradiction ratio across different configurations, indicating that its answers are not only contextually appropriate but also more aligned with the factual content of the ground truth.

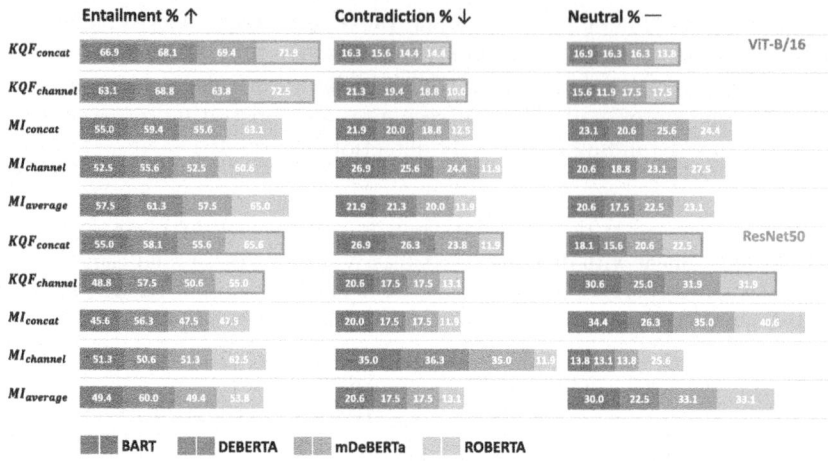

Fig. 5. Evaluation results on open questions by different NLI models show that the *KQ-Former* consistently achieves the highest entailment ratios and lower contradiction ratios compared to the baseline models across various tests.

4.2 Anomaly Maps Improve Generalizability of Language Models

In this section, we investigate how anomaly maps enhance the generalizability of language models, particularly in detecting unknown anomalies. We utilized the top-performing KQF method with a ViT backbone for this experiment. Table 2 shows that using anomaly maps with both concatenation and channel fusion strategies leads to better detection of known anomalies, with accuracy improvements of 3% and 2%, respectively. More significantly, anomaly maps greatly improve performance on previously unseen anomalies. For instance, including anomaly maps in the concatenation strategy raised overall accuracy from 69.67% to 82.35%, marking an 18% improvement in identifying open-set anomalous data.

Table 2. Performance in anomaly detection for known and unknown anomalies. The utilization of anomaly maps enhances performance in anomaly detection, particularly improving the VQA model's ability to generalize to previously unobserved pathologies.

	Method	Known		Unknown					
		Overall		Overall		Unhealthy (17%)		Healthy (83%)	
		ACC ↑	F1 ↑	ACC ↑	F1 ↑	ACC ↑	F1 ↑	ACC ↑	F1 ↑
Conc.	w/o Ano	85.29	85.29	84.13	87.50	69.67	80.00	98.70	95.00
	w Ano.	88.24	88.19	89.37	89.37	82.35▲18%	82.35▲3%	96.39	96.39
Chan.	w/o Ano	89.71	89.69	84.45	87.00	71.43	78.95	97.47	95.06
	w Ano.	91.18	91.15	85.72	88.85	72.73▲2%	82.05▲4%	98.72	95.65

These findings underscore the substantial role of anomaly maps in boosting the adaptability of language models.

5 Conclusion

In this work, we integrated language models with unsupervised anomaly detection and introduced the first multi-image Visual Question Answering benchmark for anomaly detection (VQA-UAD). We established multi-image VQA baselines and analyzed various feature fusion strategies. We then proposed the *Knowledge Querying Transformer (KQF)* module, which considerably enhanced the extraction of knowledge-related visual features when fine-tuned on a small dataset. Our findings demonstrated mutual benefits: language models provided interpretability to anomaly maps, improving clinical insights, while anomaly maps enhanced the generalizability of language models, particularly for detecting previously unseen anomalies.

Future work will explore larger language models trained on extensive medical knowledge and expand the diversity and size of our dataset. This will further enhance the generalizability and robustness of our anomaly detection framework across diverse healthcare settings. We believe our research will open new avenues for combining language models with unsupervised anomaly detection, driving innovations in this field.

Acknowledgments. C.I.B. is funded via the EVUK program (Next-generation AI for Integrated Diagnostics) of the Free State of Bavaria and partially supported by the Helmholtz Association under the joint research school Munich School for Data Science.

References

1. Akcay, S., Atapour-Abarghouei, A., Breckon, T.P.: GANomaly: semi-supervised anomaly detection via adversarial training. In: Jawahar, C.V., Li, H., Mori, G., Schindler, K. (eds.) ACCV 2018. LNCS, vol. 11363, pp. 622–637. Springer, Cham (2019). https://doi.org/10.1007/978-3-030-20893-6_39
2. Bai, L., Islam, M., Ren, H.: Cat-ViL: co-attention gated vision-language embedding for visual question localized-answering in robotic surgery. In: Medical Image Computing and Computer-Assisted Intervention, pp. 397–407. Springer (2023). https://doi.org/10.1007/978-3-031-43996-4_38
3. Behrendt, F., Bhattacharya, D., Krüger, J., Opfer, R., Schlaefer, A.: Patched diffusion models for unsupervised anomaly detection in brain MRI. In: International Conference on Medical Imaging with Deep Learning (2023)
4. Bercea, C.I., Neumayr, M., Rueckert, D., Schnabel, J.A.: Mask, stitch, and resample: enhancing robustness and generalizability in anomaly detection through automatic diffusion models. In: ICML 3rd Workshop on Interpretable Machine Learning in Healthcare (2023)
5. Bercea, C.I., Wiestler, B., Rueckert, D., Schnabel, J.A.: Generalizing unsupervised anomaly detection: towards unbiased pathology screening. In: Medical Imaging with Deep Learning (2023)

6. Bercea, C.I., Wiestler, B., Rueckert, D., Schnabel, J.A.: Reversing the abnormal: Pseudo-healthy generative networks for anomaly detection. In: International Conference on Medical Image Computing and Computer-Assisted Intervention, pp. 293–303. Springer (2023). https://doi.org/10.1007/978-3-031-43904-9_29
7. Chen, X., You, S., Tezcan, K.C., Konukoglu, E.: Unsupervised lesion detection via image restoration with a normative prior. Medical Image Analysis **64**, 101713 (2020)
8. Chowdhery, A., et al.: Palm: scaling language modeling with pathways. J. Mach. Learn. Res. **24**(240), 1–113 (2023)
9. Dosovitskiy, A., et al..: An image is worth 16×16 words: transformers for image recognition at scale. In: International Conference on Learning Representations (2021)
10. He, K., Zhang, X., Ren, S., Sun, J.: Deep residual learning for image recognition. In: Proceedings of the IEEE Conference on Computer Vision and Pattern Recognition, pp. 770–778 (2016)
11. He, P., Gao, J., Chen, W.: DeBERTav3: improving deBERTa using electra-style pre-training with gradient-disentangled embedding sharing. In: The Eleventh International Conference on Learning Representations (2022)
12. Knoll, F., et al.: fastMRI: a publicly available raw k-space and DICOM dataset of knee images for accelerated MR image reconstruction using machine learning. Radiol. Artif. Intell. **2**(1), e190007 (2020)
13. Kung, T.H., Cheatham, M., Medenilla, A., Sillos, C., De Leon, L., Elepaño, C., et al.: Performance of ChatGPT on USMLE: potential for AI-assisted medical education using large language models. PLoS Digit. Health **2**(2), e0000198 (2023)
14. Lee, J., et al.: BioBERT: a pre-trained biomedical language representation model for biomedical text mining. Bioinformatics **36**(4), 1234–1240 (2020)
15. Lewis, M., Liu, Y., Goyal, N., et al.: BART: denoising sequence-to-sequence pre-training for natural language generation, translation, and comprehension. In: Proceedings of the Association for Computational Linguistics, pp. 7871–7880 (2020)
16. Li, J., Li, S., Hu, Y., Tao, H.: A self-guided framework for radiology report generation. In: Medical Image Computing and Computer-Assisted Intervention, pp. 588–598. Springer (2022). https://doi.org/10.1007/978-3-031-16452-1_56
17. Li, J., Li, D., Xiong, C., Hoi, S.: Blip: Bootstrapping language-image pre-training for unified vision-language understanding and generation. In: International Conference on Machine Learning, pp. 12888–12900. PMLR (2022)
18. Li, P., Liu, G., He, J., Zhao, Z., Zhong, S.: Masked vision and language pre-training with unimodal and multimodal contrastive losses for medical visual question answering. In: Medical Image Computing and Computer-Assisted Intervention, pp. 374–383. Springer (2023). https://doi.org/10.1007/978-3-031-43907-0_36
19. Lin, C.Y.: Rouge: a package for automatic evaluation of summaries. In: Text Summarization Branches Out, pp. 74–81 (2004)
20. Liu, B., Zhan, L.-M., Wu, X.-M.: Contrastive pre-training and representation distillation for medical visual question answering based on radiology images. In: de Bruijne, M., et al. (eds) MICCAI 2021. LNCS, vol. 12902, pp. 210–220. Springer, Cham (2021). https://doi.org/10.1007/978-3-030-87196-3_20
21. Liu, Y., Ott, M., Goyal, N., Du, J., et al.: RoBERTa: a robustly optimized BERT pretraining approach. arXiv preprint arXiv:1907.11692 (2019)
22. Loshchilov, I., Hutter, F.: Decoupled weight decay regularization. In: International Conference on Learning Representations (2018)

23. Luo, R., Sun, L., Xia, Y., Qin, T., Zhang, S., Poon, H., Liu, T.Y.: BioGPT: generative pre-trained transformer for biomedical text generation and mining. Briefing Bioinf. **23**(6), bbac409 (2022)
24. Nguyen, B.D., Do, T.T., Nguyen, B.X., Do, T., Tjiputra, E., Tran, Q.D.: Overcoming data limitation in medical visual question answering. In: Medical Image Computing and Computer Assisted Intervention, pp. 522–530. Springer (2019). https://doi.org/10.1007/978-3-030-32251-9_57
25. OpenAI: Introducing ChatGPT (2023). https://openai.com/blog/chatgpt/. Accessed 30 Nov 2022
26. Papineni, K., Roukos, S., Ward, T., Zhu, W.J.: Bleu: a method for automatic evaluation of machine translation. In: Proceedings of the 40th Annual Meeting of the Association for Computational Linguistics, pp. 311–318 (2002)
27. Radford, A., Wu, J., Child, R., Luan, D., Amodei, D., Sutskever, I., et al.: Language models are unsupervised multitask learners. OpenAI blog **1**(8), 9 (2019)
28. Schlegl, T., Seeböck, P., Waldstein, S.M., Langs, G., Schmidt-Erfurth, U.: f-AnoGAN: fast unsupervised anomaly detection with generative adversarial networks. Med. Image Anal. **54**, 30–44 (2019)
29. Sileo, D.: TaskSource: Structured dataset preprocessing annotations for frictionless extreme multi-task learning and evaluation. arXiv preprint arXiv:2301.05948 (2023)
30. Singhal, K., et al.: Large language models encode clinical knowledge. Nature **620**(7972), 172–180 (2023)
31. Tanida, T., Müller, P., Kaissis, G., Rueckert, D.: Interactive and explainable region-guided radiology report generation. In: Proceedings of the IEEE Conference on Computer Vision and Pattern Recognition, pp. 7433–7442 (2023)
32. Touvron, H., et al.: Llama: open and efficient foundation language models. arXiv preprint arXiv:2302.13971 (2023)
33. Tu, T., et al.: Towards conversational diagnostic AI. arXiv preprint arXiv:2401.05654 (2024)
34. Van Sonsbeek, T., Derakhshani, M.M., Najdenkoska, I., Snoek, C.G., Worring, M.: Open-ended medical visual question answering through prefix tuning of language models. In: Medical Image Computing and Computer Assisted Intervention, pp. 726–736. Springer (2023). https://doi.org/10.1007/978-3-031-43904-9_70
35. Vaswani, A., et al.: Attention is all you need. In: Advances in Neural Information Processing Systems, vol. 30 (2017)
36. Vedantam, R., Lawrence Zitnick, C., Parikh, D.: Cider: Consensus-based image description evaluation. In: Proceedings of the IEEE Conference on Computer Vision and Pattern Recognition, pp. 4566–4575 (2015)
37. Wolleb, J., Bieder, F., Sandkühler, R., Cattin, P.C.: Diffusion models for medical anomaly detection. Medical Image Computing and Computer Assisted Intervention, pp. 35–45 (2022)
38. Wu, X., et al.: Deltanet: Conditional medical report generation for Covid-19 diagnosis. In: Proceedings of the 29th International Conference on Computational Linguistics, pp. 2952–2961 (2022)
39. Zhang, X., Wu, C., Zhao, Z., Lin, W.o.: PMC-VQA: visual instruction tuning for medical visual question answering. arXiv preprint arXiv:2305.10415 (2023)
40. Zimmerer, D., Isensee, F., Petersen, J., Kohl, S., Maier-Hein, K.: Unsupervised anomaly localization using variational auto-encoders. In: Medical Image Computing and Computer Assisted Intervention, pp. 289–297 (2019)

A Diffusion Model Embedded WCSAU-Net for 3D MRI Brain Tumor Segmentation

Zizhen Ji[1], Rui Chen[1], Pinyu Qiu[1], Xiaoyong Fu[1], Sheng Li[2(✉)], and Jun Tan[1,3]

[1] School of Mathematics, Sun Yat-sen University, Guangzhou, China
[2] Department of Radiology, Sun Yat-sen University Cancer Center, State Key Laboratory of Oncology in South China, Guangzhou, China
lisheng@sysucc.org.cn
[3] Guangdong Province Key Laboratory of Computational Science, Sun Yat-sen University, Guangzhou, China

Abstract. In recent years, diffusion models have achieved remarkable success in generating pixel-by-pixel semantic segmentation. In this paper, we propose a brand new end-to-end network Diff-WCSAU-Net for 3D MRI brain tumor segmentation, which integrates the Diffusion Model into WCSAU-Net to efficiently extract semantic information from the input. First, in order to extract the multi-scale features of multimodal MRI and to reduce the number of parameters of the model, a wavelet transform based on Haar wavelets is introduced in this network. Second, to incorporate conditional information into the network and to enhance the feature representation in key regions, we introduce a cross-attention mechanism in the base U-Net and the WCSAU-Net achieves feature fusion in the decoder through an improved skip connection mechanism. Finally, for the specificity of the brain tumor segmentation task, in order to instruct the model to output three different lesion regions with correct containment relationships, an asymmetric Jaccard-like coefficient as a constraint is introduced in the loss function, which improves the overall performance of the model. In comparison with the current state-of-the-art methods, our experimental results show that the proposed model can segment the multilevel anatomical structures of brain tumors with more precision, potentially facilitating the accurate diagnosis and treatment of brain tumors.

Keywords: Brain Tumor Segmentation · Jaccard Coefficient · Diffusion Model · Wavelet · Cross Self Attention

1 Introduction

1.1 Background

MRI(Magnetic Resonance Imaging), as a typical non-invasive imaging modality, has become the main and primary technical means for clinicians to diagnose and treat brain tumors due to its unique advantages such as excellent soft-tissue contrast, no radiographic damage, no bony artifacts, and the ability to perform multifaceted and multiparametric imaging [4,17]. MRI is very suitable for the examination of clinical brain lesions, and it has considerable advantages in brain tumor diagnosis [5], and has become an important component in the field of medical imaging.

Convolutional neural network-based brain tumor segmentation is a method for automatic segmentation of MRI brain images using deep learning techniques. The U-Net, proposed by Ronneberger et al. [12], has been widely adopted since its appearance. To our best knowledge, Dong et al. [3] were the first to apply the 2DU-Net network to segment brain tumor.

The Transformer architecture has gained popularity due to the ability of its global self-attention mechanism in modeling global features. TransBTS [15] uses 3D-CNN to extract local spatial features, and then applies the transformer to model global dependencies in the high-level features. UNETR [7] utilizes ViT (VisionTransformer) as an encoder to directly model the global features and output the segmentation results using a CNN-based decoder with skip connections. SwinUNETR [1] utilizes Swin-Transformer as an encoder to extract multi-scale features and uses a CNN-based decoder to generate the output. However, the ability of the above methods to extract multi-scale features is limited due to the computational complexity of the Transformer structure.

Recently, Diffusion Model has achieved significant success in various generative tasks including medical image segmentation. Med-SegDiff [18] achieved 2D medical image segmentation by denoising U-Net and inter-structure information interaction by Fourier Transform. Wolleb et al. [16] utilized the diffusion model to solve the problem of 2D medical image segmentation. However, the above methods are limited to the two-dimensional segmentation and cannot generate multi-label segmentation directly. Diff-UNet [19] utilized the diffusion model to directly solve the 3D medical image segmentation problem, and the information interaction between the networks is performed by dual U-Nets. However, the amount of parameters is too large for two 3D U-Net of equal size and its training load is very high.

1.2 Our Work

In order to solve the above problems, we propose a 3D MRI brain tumor segmentation network, Diff-WCSAU-Net, which incorporates wavelet transform and cross self attention(CSA) into Diffusion Model and U-Net. The architecture of our network is shown in Fig. 1, and details will be given in the following sections.

The primary contributions and innovations of our paper are summarized as follows:

1) Introducing Haar wavelet transform to extract the multi-scale features of MRI, to communicate the information between network structures, and to significantly reduce the number of model parameters. Wavelet Transform is a

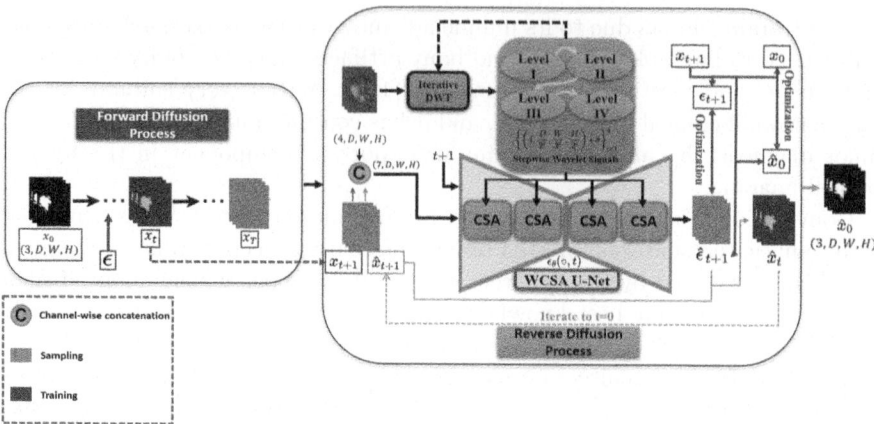

Fig. 1. Overall architecture of Diff-WCSAU-Net. In the forward diffusion process, the segmentation ground truth $x_0^{3 \times D \times W \times H}$ is transformed into x_T by adding Gaussian noise over T steps. In the reverse diffusion process, the multimodal brain tumor MRI image $I^{4 \times D \times W \times H}$ and x_{t+1} are concatenated to form $(I, x_{t+1})^{7 \times D \times W \times H}$ as the input to the WCSA U-Net. Meanwhile, 4 levels of Iterative DWT are applied to the image I, and the signals obtained at each level are fed into the WCSA U-Net.

signal processing and data analysis method that provides more detailed information in time and frequency domain and better captures the local features and time-varying nature of signals than Fourier Transform.
2) Introducing the cross-attention mechanism in U-Net, the cross-space attention between each convolutional layer of the encoder and each level of wavelet signals is computed by the self-designed CSA module, and the feature fusion of the decoder is realized by the improved skip connection mechanism in order to incorporate the conditional information into the network and to enhance the feature representation of the key regions. The core idea of cross-attention is to allow one sequence to "pay attention" to another sequence, in our case the segmentation labeling map pays attention to the image to be segmented; while spatial attention aims to enhance the feature representation of key regions, thereby increasing the importance of specific target regions while weakening irrelevant background regions.
3) A new asymmetric Jaccard-like coefficient called inclusion coefficient is designed as a constraint in the loss function to induce the model to output three different lesion regions with the correct inclusion relationship Specifically, adding this constraint for training can explicitly introduce a priori knowledge into the network and improve the overall performance of the model.

2 Preliminaries

In this section, we are going to introduce the dataset used in the paper and the loss function with "inclusion coefficient" for training.

2.1 Dataset

The BraTS dataset provides researchers with a unified and objective comparison platform for evaluating the performance of emerging brain tumor segmentation methods on multimodal MRI image data. The experimental dataset used in this paper is BraTS2020, which has 84 additional HGG cases in its training set over BraTS2017, containing a total of 294 HGG cases and 75 LGG cases.

The dataset contains four categorical labels, which, by convention, can be merged and one-hot encoded to transform the original four-categorical problem (BG, NT, ED, ET) into three binary problems (whether in WT, whether in TC, whether it is ET, and whether it is BG if none of these are true).

2.2 Inclusion Coefficient

For the specificity of the brain tumor segmentation task, inspired by Jaccard coefficients, this paper proposes a new asymmetric coefficient as a constraint, named inclusion coefficient, and introduces it into the loss function to train the model. Specifically, with the addition of this constraint, the model can be induced to output three different lesion regions (WT, TC, ET) with the correct inclusion relationship to conform to ET $\subset$ TC $\subset$ WT , and improve the overall performance of the model.

Let A, B be two different sets, then $K(A, B)$ is defined as the following expression.

$$K(A, B) = \frac{|A \cap B|}{|B|} \quad (1)$$

$$d_K(A, B) = 1 - K(A, B) \quad (2)$$

Intuitively, $K(A, B)$ describes the proportion of elements in a set B that are contained in A. Suppose $M_{\text{WT}}, M_{\text{TC}}, M_{\text{ET}}$ represent the segmentation probability mask matrices of the WT, TC, and ET regions, respectively, generated by the attention module of the model, with elements $m_{\text{WT}}, m_{\text{TC}}, m_{\text{ET}} \in [0, 1]$, and $S_{\text{WT}}, S_{\text{TC}}, S_{\text{ET}}$ represent the segmentation mask matrices of the WT, TC, and ET regions, respectively, with elements $s_{\text{WT}}, s_{\text{TC}}, s_{\text{ET}} \in \{0, 1\}$. Then, according to the inclusion relations of the three brain tumor lesion regions, for a good and correct segmentation, the following relation should hold.

$$\begin{aligned} d_K(M_{\text{WT}}, M_{\text{TC}}) &\approx 0, \ d_K(M_{\text{TC}}, M_{\text{ET}}) \approx 0 \\ d_K(S_{\text{WT}}, S_{\text{TC}}) &= d_K(S_{\text{TC}}, S_{\text{ET}}) = 0 \end{aligned} \quad (3)$$

Based on the discussion above, We consider adding d_K to the loss function during the training process. The process of continuously optimizing d_K can help the model anchor prior knowledge that is determined to be true, further increasing the model's confidence in its correctness and ultimately improving its overall performance.

Let L_t^{simple} denotes the MSE in DDPM [8], the loss function in this paper will be defined as follows.

$$L = L_t^{\text{simple}} + \frac{1}{2}\sin(\frac{e}{E}\frac{\pi}{2})(d_K(M_{\text{WT}}, M_{\text{TC}}) + d_K(M_{\text{TC}}, M_{\text{ET}})) \quad (4)$$

e, E denote the current trained and total cycles respectively, and M denotes the segmentation probability mask matrix of the corresponding region. $\sin(\frac{e}{E}\frac{\pi}{2})$ allows the weight of d_K in the loss function to gradually grow with the increase of training cycles.

3 Network Architecture

In this section, Diff-WCSAU-Net, a 3D MRI brain tumor segmentation network based on the WCSAU-Net diffusion model, will be introduced, and the key structures such as iterative wavelet transform, WCSAU-Net(Wavelet CSA U-Net), and CSA(Cross Self Attention) module will be described in detail. The overall architecture of Diff-WCSAU-Net is shown in Fig. 1.

For the iterative discrete wavelet transform(Iterative DWT) used in this paper, it is worth noting that Haar wavelet is widely used due to its simplicity, so the Iterative DWT used in this paper is based on Haar wavelet.

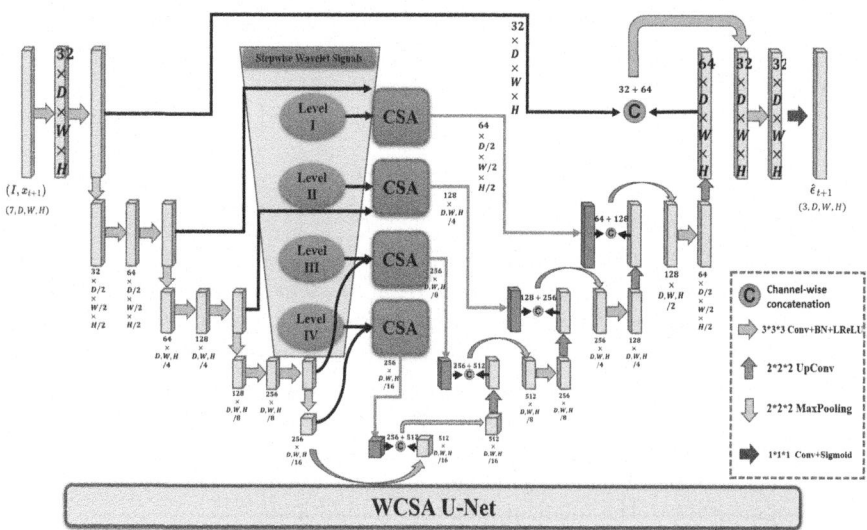

Fig. 2. Architecture of WCSA U-Net. During decoding, the decoder combines feature maps with wavelet signals from each level in the CSA module, fuses features by concatenating CSA outputs with corresponding feature maps along the channels, followed by convolution and upsampling.

WCSA U-Net is the primary structure of the network. The architecture of WCSA U-Net is shown in Fig. 2. WCSA U-Net consists of encoder, decoder and CSA module. The innovation lies in the introduction of cross-attention mechanism in U-Net. We independently designed the CSA module to calculate the cross-space attention between each convolutional layer of the encoder and each level of wavelet signals, and spliced the fusion outputs with the corresponding dimensional decoder layers to realize feature fusion of the decoder, which improves the skip connection mechanism of the traditional U-Net.

The WCSA U-Net encoder follows the traditional U-Net design, with each downsampling module containing two convolutional layers, batch normalization, an activation function layer, and a maximum pooling layer. After each downsampling, the size of the feature map is halved and the number of channels is doubled.

The decoder of WCSA U-Net is mainly responsible for performing up-sampling operations, and each up-sampling module contains two convolutional layers, batch normalization, an activation function layer and an inverse convolutional layer. After each upsampling, the size of the feature map is doubled and the number of channels is halved. Finally, the feature map is mapped to the predicted step $t+1$ noise $\hat{\epsilon}_{t+1}$ through a $1 \times 1 \times 1$ convolutional and Sigmoid layer. It is worth noting that, unlike the conventional U-Net, instead of performing feature fusion directly through skip connections when performing up-sampling, the decoder is first fed into the CSA module along with all levels of the wavelet signals and then the output of the corresponding CSA module and the corresponding encoder section are spliced through channels to realize feature fusion.

Furthermore, in practice, in order to let the network know the time step corresponding to the noise ϵ_t, a time-dependent U-Net (Time-Conditional U-Net) [2] is used in the model. It encodes the time t into the network by incorporating a TE (Time Embedding) similar to PE (Position Embedding) [14] (see Fig. 3), thus making it possible to train only one U-Net that is shared for all times. The embedding takes the following form:

$$TE_{(t,2i)} = \sin\left(\tfrac{t}{10000^{2i/c}}\right), \quad TE_{(t,2i+1)} = \cos\left(\tfrac{t}{10000^{2i/c}}\right) eALT \quad (5)$$

where t denotes the time step, i denotes the position of the ith channel and c is the number of channels.

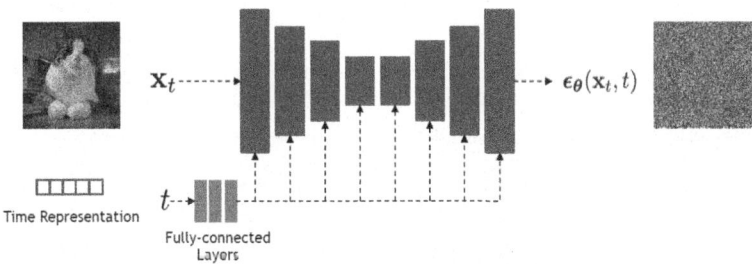

Fig. 3. The mechanism of Time Embedding in the reverse diffusion process of our method, where x_t denotes the image with time step t and $\epsilon_\theta(x_t, t)$ represents the predicted noise in this image.

Finally, the architecture of CSA Module is shown in Fig. 4 below.

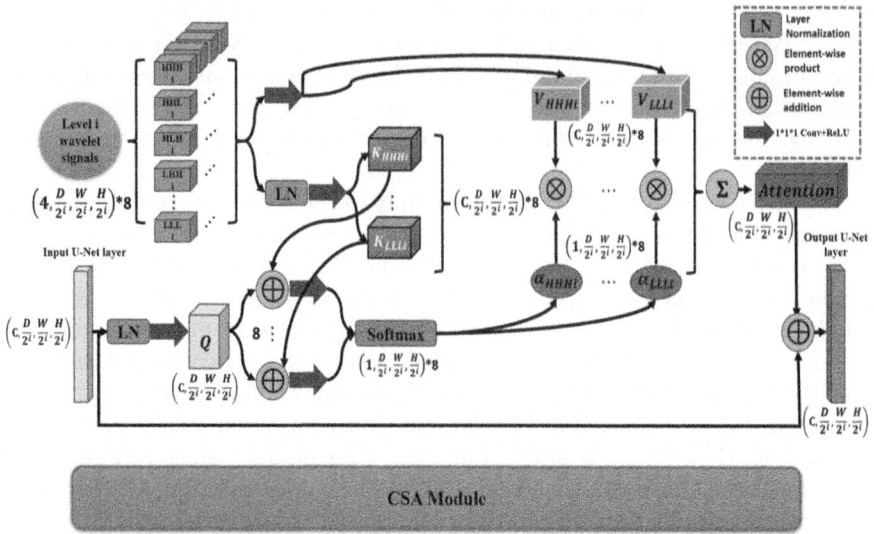

Fig. 4. Architecture of CSA Module. In the computation involving Q and the layer-normalized and then convolved wavelet signals K, Q is element-wise added to 8 different Ks, while in the computation of the convolved wavelet signals V and the attention weights α, the 8 weights are element-wise multiplied with their corresponding V, followed by summation to obtain the fused attention.

4 Experiments and Results

In this section, brain tumor segmentation experiments will be performed on BraTS2020 based on the methods introduced in Sect. 3, visualizations will be presented, metrics will be displayed and compared with other SOTA methods, and finally ablation experiments will be performed and results will be presented.

4.1 Experimental Settings

The network is built by PyTorch and MONAI and runs on 2 x NVIDIA GeForce RTX 3080 Ti GPUs.

In this paper, the hyperparameter $\bar{\alpha}_t$ [10] is defined as follows:

$$\bar{\alpha}_t = \frac{f(t)}{f(0)}, \quad f(t) = \cos\left(\frac{t/T + s}{1 + s} \cdot \frac{\pi}{2}\right)^2 \qquad (6)$$

The AdamW optimizer is used in the training phase. The epoch is 300 and the batch size is 8. The warmup period is set to 1/10 of the total number of epochs, and the learning rate is updated using the cosine annealing schedule. The number of forward diffusion steps $T = 1000$. In the sampling phase, this paper uses DDIM [13] skip-step accelerated sampling for inference sampling, the sampling step is set to 10.

4.2 Evaluation Metrics

In this paper, DSC and HD95 (Hausdorff Distance 95%) are mainly used as metrics to evaluate the segmentation results.

DSC (Dice Similarity Cofficient) is used to measure the similarity of two sets, the value range is [0,1]. The larger DSC is, the more similar the two sets are. Hausdorff distance is a measure that describes the degree of similarity between two sets of points, the larger the Hausdorff distance is, the lower the segmentation accuracy is. In particular, their specific expressions are as follows.

$$DSC(A,B) = \frac{2|A \cap B|}{|A|+|B|} \quad (7)$$

$$h(A,B) = \max\left(\max_{a \in A}\min_{b \in B} d(a,b), \{\max_{b \in B}\min_{a \in A} d(a,b)\}_{0.95}\right) \quad (8)$$

$$h_{0.95}(A,B) = \max\left(\{\min_{b \in B} d(a,b)\}_{0.95}, \{\min_{a \in A} d(a,b)\}_{0.95}\right) \quad (9)$$

where A and B denote two different sets of points.

4.3 Results

Figure 5 demonstrates several brain tumor segmentation results obtained by applying the method proposed, and it can be seen that the segmentation given with the baseline truth value is basically consistent with the good results. Where Axial denotes the transverse plane, Coronal denotes the coronal plane, Sagittal

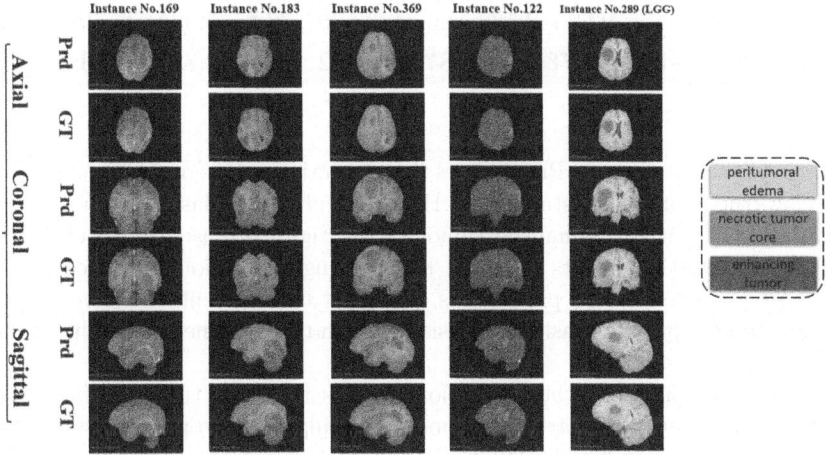

Fig. 5. Brain tumor segmentation results (axial, coronal, sagittal views). "Prd" indicates predicted segmentation and "GT" represents ground truth. Yellow: peritumoral edema; Green: necrotic tumor core; Red: enhancing tumor. All cases are HGG except No. 289. (Color figure online)

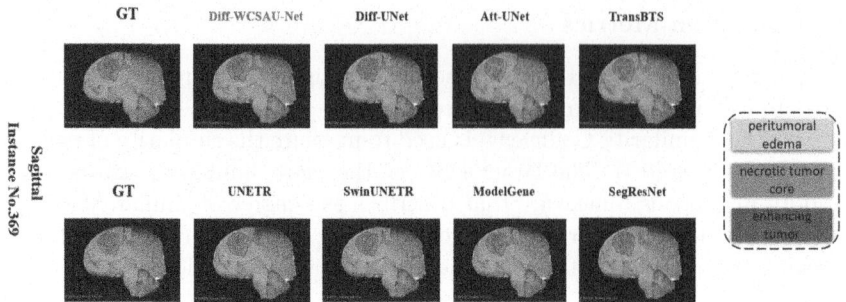

Fig. 6. Comparison of brain tumor segmentation results for instance No. 369 from the sagittal view. "GT" represents ground truth labels. Yellow: peritumoral edema; Green: necrotic tumor core; Red: enhancing tumor. (Color figure online)

Table 1. Quantitative comparison of our model (Diff-WCSAU-Net) with reference methods

Method	WT		TC		ET		Average	
	Dice↑	HD95↓	Dice↑	HD95↓	Dice↑	HD95↓	Dice↑	HD95↓
SwinUNETR [6]	91.68	2.856	82.60	4.314	74.85	4.503	83.04	3.891
UNETR [7]	90.15	4.305	81.26	5.740	73.23	4.643	81.55	4.896
TransBTS [15]	91.06	3.360	83.60	2.986	74.03	**3.403**	82.90	3.249
SegResNet [9]	91.54	3.2275	83.61	3.769	73.04	3.486	82.73	3.494
Attention-UNet [11]	84.49	15.174	78.17	16.380	71.62	9.095	78.09	13.549
ModelsGenesis [20]	91.98	2.799	84.31	**2.836**	73.84	4.333	83.38	**3.096**
Diff-UNet [19]	92.23	2.588	86.94	3.596	76.87	3.984	85.35	3.389
Diff-WCSAU-Net	**92.78**	**2.513**	**87.85**	3.232	**78.41**	3.724	**86.34**	3.156

denotes the sagittal plane, Prd denotes the prediction result, and GT denotes the baseline true value. All instances are HGG except for the last column (No.289) which is LGG without enhanced tumor (ET). Figure 6 illustrates several brain tumor segmentation results obtained by applying the various methods including those proposed in this paper. It is clear that the segmentation given by the methods in this paper is basically consistent with the baseline truth value, which gives the best results.

Table 1 demonstrates the evaluation metrics for brain tumor segmentation obtained by applying the various methods including those proposed in this paper. It can be seen that under the DICE metric, the method of this paper maintains the best performance on all regions segmentation. Under the HD95 metric, the segmentation given by this paper's method is optimal on the WT region. The effect of segmentation on TC region ranks the second. For ET region, the segmentation effect ranks the third, and the average of the three region segmentation effect metrics ranks the second among all the methods.

4.4 Ablation Study

Table 2. Ablation study of different conditioning mechanisms of Diff-WCSAU-Net

Module	WT	TC	ET	Average
w/o DWT&CSA	90.27	85.61	75.43	83.77
w/o d_K	92.25	87.01	77.24	85.50
Diff-WCSAU-Net	**92.78**	**87.85**	**78.14**	**86.34**

Table 2 demonstrates the metrics of the ablation experiments. "w/o" denotes no module followed by and "w/o DWT&CSA" denotes the removal of the wavelet transform and CSA modules and the training of the denoising network using only the base U-Net as a diffusion model, and "w/o d_K" denotes no introduction of d_K, the result of training with the loss function in DDPM [8] instead of Eq. 4. It can be seen that the introduction of each module and the improved design all contribute to the performance improvement of the model, proving its effectiveness. Figure 7 demonstrates the effect of adding d_K or not on the segmentation results during training. It can be seen that adding d_K to train the model helps the model to output segmentation results with correct inclusion relationships.

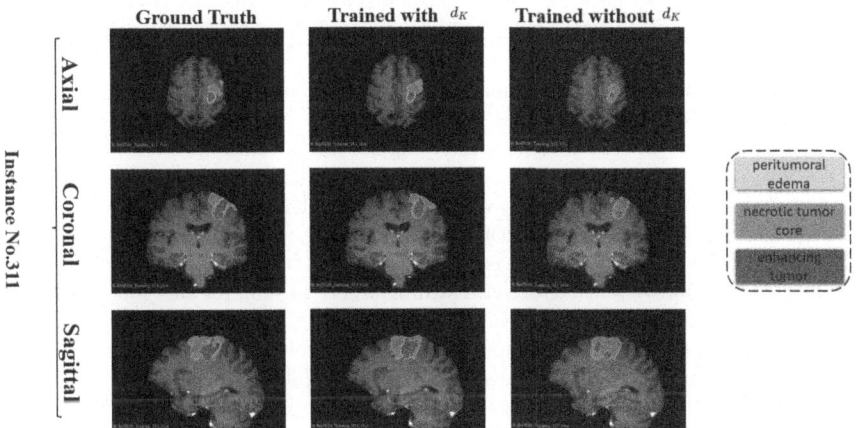

Fig. 7. Comparison of segmentation results with and without the inclusion of d_K during training

5 Conclusion

In this paper, we innovatively propose a 3D MRI brain tumor segmentation method Diff-WCSAU-Net based on diffusion model and deep learning models such as U-Net. Experimental results on BraTS2020 show that Diff-WCSAU-Net outperforms the existing methods. The ablation experiments demonstrate the effectiveness of the proposed modules and the improved design. In conclusion, the work in this paper demonstrates the effectiveness of the diffusion model in the task of MRI brain tumor segmentation, and the proposed method has the potential to facilitate more accurate diagnosis.

References

1. Cao, H., et al.: SWIN-Unet: Unet-like pure transformer for medical image segmentation. In: European Conference on Computer Vision, pp. 205–218. Springer (2022). https://doi.org/10.1007/978-3-031-25066-8_9
2. Dhariwal, P., Nichol, A.: Diffusion models beat GANs on image synthesis (2021)
3. Dong, H., Yang, G., Liu, F., Mo, Y., Guo, Y.: Automatic brain tumor detection and segmentation using U-Net based fully convolutional networks. In: Valdés Hernández, M., González-Castro, V. (eds.) MIUA 2017. CCIS, vol. 723, pp. 506–517. Springer, Cham (2017). https://doi.org/10.1007/978-3-319-60964-5_44
4. Ge, T., MU, N., Li, L.: A brain tumor segmentation method based on softmax regression and graph cut. Acta Electonica Sin. **45**(3), 644 (2017)
5. Gordillo, N., Montseny, E., Sobrevilla, P.: State of the art survey on MRI brain tumor segmentation. Magn. Reson. Imaging **31**(8), 1426–1438 (2013)
6. Hatamizadeh, A., Nath, V., Tang, Y., Yang, D., Roth, H.R., Xu, D.: Swin UNETR: Swin transformers for semantic segmentation of brain tumors in mri images. In: International MICCAI Brainlesion Workshop, pp. 272–284. Springer (2022). https://doi.org/10.1007/978-3-031-08999-2_22
7. Hatamizadeh, A., et al.: UNETR: transformers for 3D medical image segmentation. In: Proceedings of the IEEE/CVF Winter Conference on Applications of Computer Vision. pp. 574–584 (2022)
8. Ho, J., Jain, A., Abbeel, P.: Denoising diffusion probabilistic models. Adv. Neural. Inf. Process. Syst. **33**, 6840–6851 (2020)
9. Myronenko, A.: 3D MRI brain tumor segmentation using autoencoder regularization. In: Crimi, A., Bakas, S., Kuijf, H., Keyvan, F., Reyes, M., van Walsum, T. (eds.) BrainLes 2018. LNCS, vol. 11384, pp. 311–320. Springer, Cham (2019). https://doi.org/10.1007/978-3-030-11726-9_28
10. Nichol, A., Dhariwal, P.: Improved denoising diffusion probabilistic models (2021)
11. Oktay, O., et al.: Attention U-Net: learning where to look for the pancreas. arXiv preprint arXiv:1804.03999 (2018)
12. Ronneberger, O., Fischer, P., Brox, T.: U-Net: convolutional networks for biomedical image segmentation. In: Navab, N., Hornegger, J., Wells, W.M., Frangi, A.F. (eds.) MICCAI 2015. LNCS, vol. 9351, pp. 234–241. Springer, Cham (2015). https://doi.org/10.1007/978-3-319-24574-4_28
13. Song, J., Meng, C., Ermon, S.: Denoising diffusion implicit models. arXiv preprint arXiv:2010.02502 (2020)
14. Vaswani, A., et al.: Attention is all you need. In: Advances in Neural Information Processing Systems, vol. 30 (2017)

15. Wang, W., Chen, C., Ding, M., Yu, H., Zha, S., Li, J.: TransBTS: multimodal brain tumor segmentation using transformer. In: de Bruijne, M., et al. (eds.) MICCAI 2021. LNCS, vol. 12901, pp. 109–119. Springer, Cham (2021). https://doi.org/10.1007/978-3-030-87193-2_11
16. Wolleb, J., Sandkühler, R., Bieder, F., Valmaggia, P., Cattin, P.C.: Diffusion models for implicit image segmentation ensembles. In: International Conference on Medical Imaging with Deep Learning, pp. 1336–1348. PMLR (2022)
17. Wong, K.P.: Medical image segmentation: methods and applications in functional imaging. In: Handbook of Biomedical Image Analysis: Volume II: Segmentation Models Part B, pp. 111–182. Springer (2005). https://doi.org/10.1007/0-306-48606-7_3
18. Wu, J., et al.: MedSegDiff: medical image segmentation with diffusion probabilistic model. In: Medical Imaging with Deep Learning, pp. 1623–1639. PMLR (2024)
19. Xing, Z., Wan, L., Fu, H., Yang, G., Zhu, L.: Diff-UNet: a diffusion embedded network for volumetric segmentation. arXiv preprint arXiv:2303.10326 (2023)
20. Zhou, Z., Sodha, V., Pang, J., Gotway, M.B., Liang, J.: Models genesis. Med. Image Anal. **67**, 101840 (2021)

Predicting Human Brain States with Transformer

Yifei Sun[1,2(✉)], Mariano Cabezas[2,3,4], Jiah Lee[1], Chenyu Wang[2,3,5], Wei Zhang[6], Fernando Calamante[1,2,7], and Jinglei Lv[1,2]

[1] School of Biomedical Engineering, University of Sydney, Sydney, NSW 2008, Australia
{yifei.sun,jinglei.lv}@sydney.edu.au
[2] Brain and Mind Center, University of Sydney, Sydney, NSW 2050, Australia
[3] Central Clinical School, University of Sydney, Sydney, NSW 2050, Australia
[4] Macquarie University Hearing, Macquarie University, Sydney, NSW 2109, Australia
[5] Sydney Neuroimaging Analysis Centre, University of Sydney, Sydney, NSW 2050, Australia
[6] School of Computer and Cyber Sciences, Augusta University, Augusta, GA 30901, USA
[7] Sydney Imaging, University of Sydney, Sydney, NSW 2006, Australia

Abstract. The human brain is a complex and highly dynamic system, and our current knowledge of its functional mechanism is still very limited. Fortunately, with functional magnetic resonance imaging (fMRI), we can observe blood oxygen level-dependent (BOLD) changes, reflecting neural activity, to infer brain states and dynamics. In this paper, we ask the question of whether the brain states represented by the regional brain fMRI can be predicted. Due to the success of self-attention and the transformer architecture in sequential auto-regression problems (e.g., language modelling or music generation), we explore the possibility of the use of transformers to predict human brain resting states based on the large-scale high-quality fMRI data from the human connectome project (HCP). Current results have shown that our model can accurately predict the brain states up to 5.04 s with the previous 21.6 s. Furthermore, even though the prediction error accumulates for the prediction of a longer time period, the generated fMRI brain states reflect the architecture of functional connectome. These promising initial results demonstrate the possibility of developing generative models for fMRI data using self-attention that learns the functional organization of the human brain. Our code is available at: https://github.com/syf0122/brain_state_pred.

Keywords: fMRI · brain states · transformer · prediction

1 Introduction

The human brain is an intricate dynamic system with tens of billions of neurons and trillions of synaptic connections [1]. Understanding the dynamic mechanisms of the human brain [2] is always a top priority of neuroscience, as it is essential for uncovering the origins of cognition, emotion, language and other higher-level human intelligence [3]. Additionally, this understanding is crucial for deciphering the mechanisms behind brain disorders such as Alzheimer's Disease [4, 5] and Schizophrenia [6, 7]. Moreover, as brain-computer interfaces (BCI) and brain-inspired artificial intelligence become the current technology trend, learning the mechanisms for brain dynamics [8, 9] becomes an essential step to mimicking them.

Functional magnetic resonance imaging (fMRI) is a widely used non-invasive and in-vivo technique to observe whole brain dynamics spatially at the meso-scale and temporally at the second scale [10]. Despite significant progression in mapping the brain's functional organization [11] (e.g., the intrinsic networks were reconstructed with resting-state fMRI [12]), understanding its functional connectivity (FC) has become an important biomarker for healthy brains and mental health research [4, 6]. While recent deep learning approaches to model the hierarchical organization of brain function have become critical achievements in the field [13, 14], the question of how brain activity emerges even when we are not performing a specific task (i.e., resting state) still remains unanswered [15]. Moreover, whether specific future sequential brain states from a resting state acquisition can be predicted still remains unknown. Addressing this technology and knowledge gap could potentially reduce the fMRI scan time for patients with difficulties or disabilities. If the brain states can be predicted, the pain and harm from certain fatal brain disorders, such as epilepsy, can also be avoided or at least reduced [16, 17]. Furthermore, the ability to predict brain states paves the way for BCI technologies, potentially enabling more intuitive and effective communication. This capability could transform not only medical therapeutics but also how to interact with technology, making artificial intelligence systems more adaptive to our cognitive and emotional states.

Since the introduction of multi-headed self-attention blocks by Vaswani et al. [18] in 2017, transformer architectures have become ubiquitous in deep learning for multiple tasks focusing on sequences [19, 20] and images [21, 22]. A recent success story is Chat-GPT [23], which exemplifies the power of transformers in processing sequential information in natural language that learns patterns from a knowledge pool and gives answers within the context of a continuous conversation. Given their ability to find long-distance relationships between data tokens (in our case, brain states) grounded in correlations and with links to graph theory, we believe that self-attention-based architectures have the ability to learn patterns from sequential brain activity and predict the upcoming brain states. More recently, Peter et al. [24] and Malkiel et al. [25] demonstrated the potential of the transformer framework in analyzing fMRI data for age prediction, gender classification, and disease classification. Furthermore, a brain language model (BrainLM) [26] was proposed as a foundation model for brain dynamic activities, especially focusing on the fMRI data. The BrainLM is pre-trained for masked prediction and then fine-tuned for future brain state prediction, outperforming other state-of-the-art architectures. This further shows the use of self-attention-based frameworks is promising in brain state prediction. However, the BrainLM needs the use of a large dataset for pretraining and the brain states prediction requires a relatively long time series (180 time points). If we can train a model to predict future brain states depending on a shorter input time series, we can largely shorten the scanning time.

In this paper, we frame the brain state prediction problem as an auto-regression task where given a sequence, we predict the next temporal element. Specifically, we propose a novel method based on the time series transformer [27] architecture to predict future brain states comprising 379 grey matter regions of a whole brain given a sequence of previous time points as observed in an fMRI acquisition. We train our model on high-quality data from the Human Connectome Project (HCP) and present a set of promising results on brain state prediction. Briefly, the model can accurately predict the immediate brain state, predict the brain states of 5.04 s with low error, and predict brain states of over 10 min agreeing with the average human functional connectome.

2 Method

2.1 Data and Preprocessing

In this study, the resting-state fMRI (rs-fMRI) data from the HCP young adults dataset [28] were used. We employed the 3 T fMRI data of 1003 healthy young adults, excluding 110 subjects with missing or incomplete rs-fMRI scans. For each subject, four rs-fMRI scans, with 1200 time points each in the CIFTI [29] format that stores surface-based gray matter data, were utilized. The HCP rs-fMRI data has an isotropic spatial resolution of 2 mm and a temporal resolution of 0.72 s.

Aside from the minimal preprocessing already provided with the HCP dataset [29], we carried out several additional preprocessing steps to further clean the data and prepare the data for training and testing the transformer. First, we spatially smoothed the fMRI data using a Gaussian filter with the full width at the half maximum (FWHM) set to 6mm in the CIFTI format, in order to reduce noise and improve signal-to-noise ratio [30]. Then, a bandpass filter was employed to filter out some uninterested noises while retaining the temporal signal within the 0.01 to 0.1 Hz range [31]. In order to bring all the samples onto a common scale, we applied the z-score transformation on time series to get zero temporal mean and unit standard deviation. Finally, the mean fMRI time series were calculated for 379 brain regions, including 360 cortical regions and 19 subcortical regions, using the multi-modal parcellation (MMP) atlas [32]. Therefore, we use a vector with the signal intensity of 379 regions at each time point to represent a brain state.

2.2 Transformer Model

The human brain is a dynamic system, where its current state is related to the previous ones. In this paper, we explore the possibility of predicting a single brain state given a sequence of previous brain states. To model these predictions, we re-designed an existing time series transformer developed for influenza forecasting [18, 19, 27]. Our model comprises a combination of transformer encoders and decoders, with the whole architecture illustrated in Fig. 1.

The transformer takes as input time series data represented by a sequence of tokens with a given window size. As self-attention treats token relationships as a graph (ignoring token order), positional encoding with the sine and cosine functions is used to add relative temporal information [18, 27]. The encoder of the network contains four encoding layers with self-attention and feed-forward. These layers contain eight attention heads. Ultimately, this encoding stack generates the encoder output.

The last time point of the encoder input combined with the encoder output serves as the input of the decoder, which is defined as a stack of four decoding layers, which are also comprised of self-attention (with eight attention heads) and feed-forward layers. Finally, a fully connected layer maps the output from the decoder layers stack to the target output shape. Our model, unlike the time series transformer for influenza prevalence cases [27] that predicts a series of future time points and employs look-ahead masking to ensure that the predictions are based on past data [18], focuses on predicting a single future time point $(i + 1)$ using the immediate previous time point (i) and the encoder output. Therefore, we have omitted the use of look-ahead masking, simplifying the prediction process.

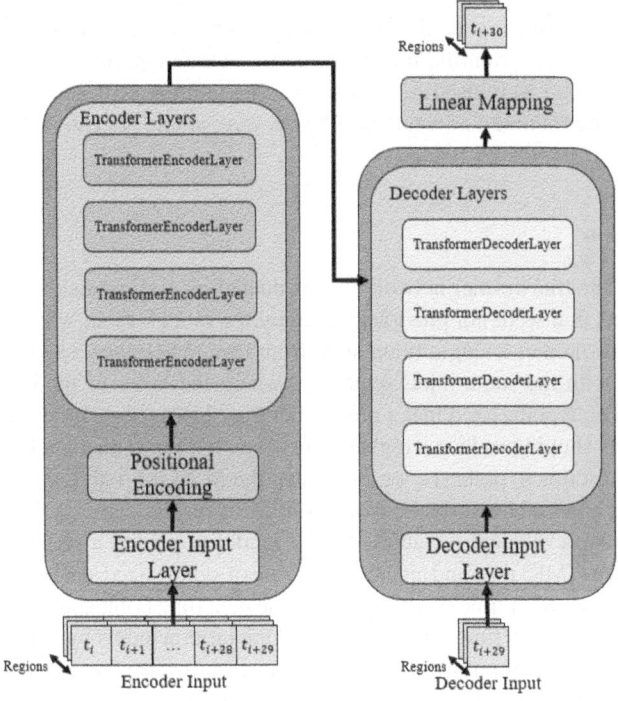

Fig. 1. Scheme of the transformer architecture for predicting brain states. The encoder takes an input of 30 $(t_i - t_{i+29})$ time points of 379 regions, the decoder takes the last input time point (t_{i+29}), and the encoder output to predict the next time point (t_{i+30}) of 379 regions.

2.3 Training

As we framed the brain state prediction problem as an autoregression task, we used the mean squared error (MSE) as the loss function and the Adam optimizer [33] with an initial learning rate of 10^{-4} to train our model.

We first conducted a primary test with different window sizes, i.e. the number of input timepoints, (5, 10, 15, 20, 30, 40, and 50) and the number of epochs per run (20, 25, 30, and 50) with forty subjects' data. All transformers started their prediction on the 51st time point to ensure a fair comparison. We allowed the overlap between input time series, so there are 1150 training samples for each rs-fMRI session data. During training, samples were randomly chosen from all training data across all subjects and all sessions, with a batch size of 512 to speed up the training. The model performance was then evaluated and compared using ten independent subjects not previously seen.

After the preliminary test, the best model was determined to be the one with a window size of 30, and after 20 epochs the model converged with the data of forty subjects. Thus, the window size was set to 30 for training the model with a much larger dataset. Additionally, ten-fold cross-validation was employed for model training and validation. In each fold, among the 1003 subjects, 90% of subjects (roughly 901 or 902 subjects) were used to train the model, while the remaining 10% of subjects (around 102 or 101 subjects) were used for validation. The number of training epochs was set to 10 because the training and validation losses were stable after the 6 epochs without overfitting.

2.4 Evaluation

After training the transformer network, we evaluated its performance with the rs-fMRI data of subjects that were not previously seen by the model. First, we tested the ability of the model to predict a single brain state from true fMRI data. Then, we performed a similar test with the same input sequences where the order of the brain states was randomized. We hypothesized that a model that truly learns sequential information and brain dynamics should produce a higher error when fed the same data in a randomized sequence. To test this hypothesis, we calculated the MSE for both tests for comparison and conducted a paired t-test on the two sets of MSE results.

After that, we evaluated the ability of our model to predict a series of brain states using limited true fMRI data and an increasing rate of synthesized states. Specifically, we used the thirty true fMRI time points to predict the next time point and then concatenated this prediction to the true time series and shifted the input window by one step to include the new predicted time point in an iterative manner until a sequence of the same length of time series as the true data (1200 time points) was synthesized. This resulted in the prediction of a synthetic time series of 1150 time points. MSE was calculated between the predicted time series and the true fMRI data together with Spearman's correlation between each predicted and true brain state to test for monotonic correlations.

Finally, the FC matrices for both true and predicted fMRI time series were calculated using Pearson's correlation between regional time series. Only the predicted portion of the brain states (1150 time points) was used for the FC analysis to avoid leakage from the true signal. To measure the similarity between the predicted FC matrices and the group average FC matrix based on the true fMRI data, we first calculated the mean absolute difference between the predicted FC matrix of each individual and the group average FC matrix calculated with true data. Spatial correlations between the predicted and true FC matrices were also calculated using the flattened upper triangle of FC matrices.

3 Results and Discussion

3.1 Model Selection

To select the proper window size and the number of training epochs, we evaluated the error of the trained models in predicting single brain states at one time point and the whole time series prediction using a subset of the dataset as a preliminary experiment.

As shown in Fig. 2a, when the model was trained for twenty epochs, it predicted single brain states with the least MSE, and using window sizes of fifteen and thirty showed a lower MSE. By looking at the MSE of the whole time series of generated brain states (Fig. 2b), models with window sizes of twenty and thirty showed the best performance. Thus, for the rest of the experiments, we used the model trained with a window size of thirty, but the number of epochs was set based on the observation of the actual training and validation losses of the model on the entire dataset because there are more training samples.

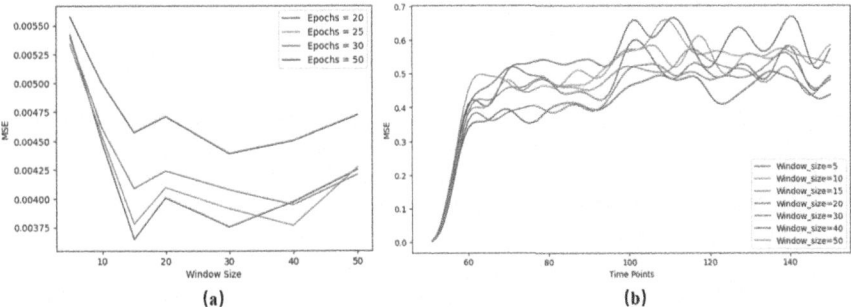

Fig. 2. Performance of the model using different window sizes. (a) The MSE of the models trained with different numbers of epochs and window sizes when predicting a single time point using true fMRI data. (b) The MSE of the models trained with 20 epochs and different window sizes when predicting long time series using the previous predicted time points (predicted brain states are used for future prediction).

3.2 Single Next Time Point Prediction

When we evaluated the model on the true fMRI data for single next time point predictions, the average MSE for all time points was 0.0013. However, when we shuffled the time points in the input time sequence, the MSE increased to 0.97 (more than 700 times higher, p-value $< 10^{-10}$). These results provide strong evidence that the transformer model effectively learned and leveraged the temporal dependencies present in the fMRI time series. The substantial increase in error upon shuffling indicates that the brain state prediction accuracy is indeed driven by its ability to understand the sequential nature of the data, which is crucial for accurately modelling brain activity patterns over time. Thus, this shows the transformer's potential for applications in studying the functional dynamics of the human brain.

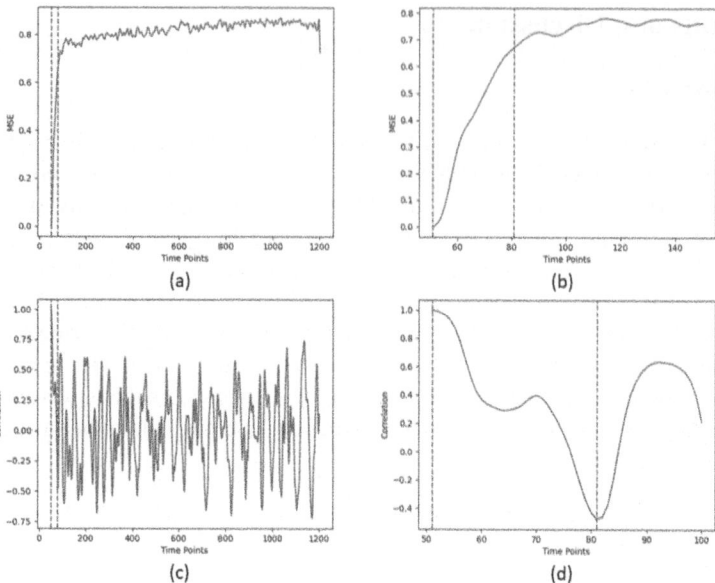

Fig. 3. Time series prediction MSE and correlation between the predicted and true brain states. The red dashed line specifies the first prediction starting point, which is the MSE of the 51st time points. The green dash line shows the point where the time points after it (on the right-hand side) are predicted purely depending on previously predicted data. Time points between two dashed lines are predicted partially based on real data. (a) The MSE of all predicted time points averaged across all test subjects. (b) The zoomed-in version of (a), showing the MSE of the first 100 predicted time points averaged across all test subjects. (c) The correlation coefficients of all 1150 predicted brain states averaged across all test subjects. (d) The zoomed-in version of (c), showing the correlation coefficients of the first 50 predicted brain states averaged across all test subjects. The red and green dash lines possess correspondence across the 4 sub-figures. (Color figure online)

3.3 Time Series Prediction

As shown in Fig. 3b, the prediction MSE rises after predicting several sequential time points (after ~20 timepoints). We hypothesized that this is caused by cascading errors that accumulate as we sequentially predict brain states with more synthetic states as input. The accumulation of prediction errors can be understood similar as a Markov chain [34], where each state is predicted based on previous states. As more previously predicted states are incorporated into subsequent predictions, the accumulated errors from prior steps propagate through the chain, leading to an increased overall prediction error. Figure 3a shows that after the input to the transformer comprises only predicted data, the error slightly increases and starts to fluctuate. More importantly, the first seven predicted time points (within the time of 5.04 s) have relatively low MSE (<0.15) and the MSE for the first 20 time points is roughly 0.26. After that, the MSE increases to around the level of 0.80. The similar phenomenon is observed in BrainLM [26], where the prediction MSE rises gradually after the prediction of the first 20 time points. In comparison, their 20-time-point MSE is 0.568, larger than ours. Overall, our results of the time series prediction show that future brain states of around 5.04 s can be accurately predicted using a short fMRI sequence of only 21.6 s.

We also calculated Spearman's correlation between the predicted brain states and the true fMRI data for all predictions. According to Fig. 3c and 3d, the first five time points have high correlation coefficients > 0.85 (especially the first time point with a correlation of 0.997 with the true data). After that, even though the correlation drops quickly and starts to fluctuate, it is evident that our method can accurately predict at least seven consecutive brain states (5.04 s) based on 30 fMRI time points (21.6 s).

3.4 Functional Connectivity

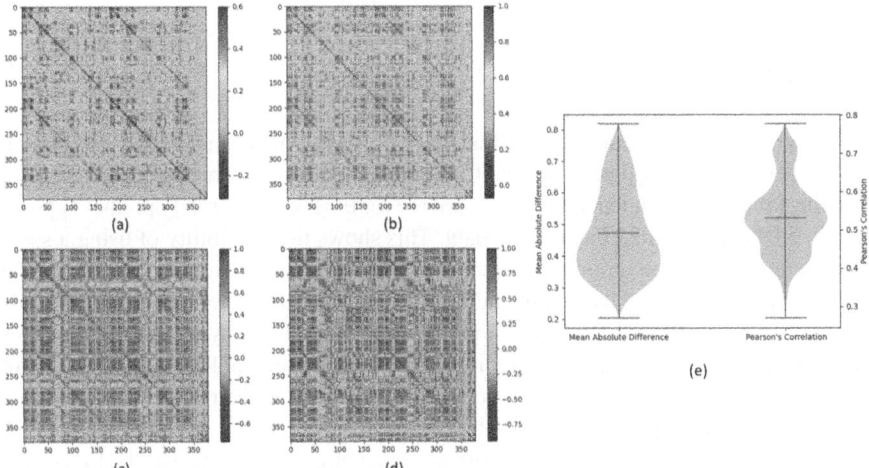

Fig. 4. FC matrices, mean absolute difference, and Pearson's correlation. (a) The group average FC calculated based on the true fMRI (b) The group average FC calculated based on predicted fMRI. (c) The FC calculated based on the predicted fMRI for one session of a subject. (d) The FC calculated based on the predicted fMRI for one session of another subject (e) Distribution of the mean absolute differences and Pearson's correlation coefficients between predicted and true group average FC. The mean absolute difference is shown on the left, and Pearson's correlation is shown on the right. The three horizontal lines specify the minimum, maximum, and mean of the mean absolute difference and Pearson's correlation, respectively.

FC matrices were calculated for both the true and predicted data. Figure 4a and 4b show the group average FC matrices calculated from the HCP rs-fMRI data and the predicted time series for the same set of subjects. Although they have a different range, true and predicted FC show similar global patterns. Figure 4c and 4d are the predicted FC of two individuals, that show similarity with the group average in Fig. 4b, but clear individual variability.

The distribution of the mean absolute differences and spatial correlation between the predicted and true group average FC matrix is shown in Fig. 4e. From the figure plot, it is obvious that most of the predicted FC matrices have relatively low mean absolute differences and relatively strong correlations, with MSE from 0.35 to 0.45 and correlation from 0.50 to 0.60, respectively.

The relatively low mean absolute differences and relatively strong correlations confirm that the transformer model was able to capture the group-level functional organization. By predicting the group average connectivity patterns, this transformer captures the collective patterns shared by individuals in the HCP dataset, which can be beneficial for understanding the underlying principles of healthy brain function at the group level. In clinical cohorts, getting the group average FC allows the identification of common patterns that may serve as biomarkers of certain neurological conditions, aiding the development of diagnostic tools or treatment strategies.

4 Conclusion

In this work, we presented a novel method that employs a transformer network to predict brain states using fMRI data. The results demonstrated that our method could actually learn the temporal dependencies of brain states over time and accurately predict approximately 5.04s based on 21.6s of fMRI data. This shows the possibility of using a short fMRI segment for future brain state prediction. Furthermore, the model could learn the functional organization of the healthy human brain. In the future, we aim to improve this transformer architecture to generate more accurate predictions by mitigating the error accumulation issue. The improved prediction would be beneficial for studying the brain functions of vulnerable individuals who are not able to have their fMRI scanned for a long period. We also plan to develop the personalized model by using transfer learning. The explainability of our method will also be explored to understand the functional principles of the human brain.

Acknowledgements. J. Lv is supported by Brain and Mind Centre Research Development Grant, USYD-Fudan Brain and Intelligence Science Alliance Flagship Research Program, Moyira Elizabeth Vine Fund for Research into Schizophrenia Program and ARC Discovery Project (DP240102161).

References

1. Herculano-Houzel, S.: The human brain in numbers: a linearly scaled-up primate brain. Front. Hum. Neurosci. 31 (2009)
2. Shine, J.M., et al.: The dynamics of functional brain networks: integrated network states during cognitive task performance. Neuron **92**(2), 544–554 (2016)
3. Barch, D.M., et al.: Function in the human connectome: task-fMRI and individual differences in behavior. Neuroimage **80**, 169–189 (2013)
4. Dennis, E.L., Thompson, P.M.: Functional brain connectivity using fMRI in aging and Alzheimer's disease. Neuropsychol. Rev. **24**, 49–62 (2014)

5. Lupton, M.K., et al.: A prospective cohort study of prodromal Alzheimer's disease: prospective imaging study of ageing: genes, brain and behaviour (PISA). NeuroImage Clin. **29**, 102527 (2021)
6. Yu, Q., et al.: Assessing dynamic brain graphs of time-varying connectivity in fMRI data: application to healthy controls and patients with schizophrenia. Neuroimage **107**, 345–355 (2015)
7. Rashid, B., et al.: Classification of schizophrenia and bipolar patients using static and dynamic resting-state fMRI brain connectivity. Neuroimage **134**, 645–657 (2016)
8. Hou, Y., et al.: GCNs-net: a graph convolutional neural network approach for decoding time-resolved EEG motor imagery signals. IEEE Trans. Neural Netw. Learn. Syst. (2022)
9. Hou, Y., et al.: Deep feature mining via the attention-based bidirectional long short term memory graph convolutional neural network for human motor imagery recognition. Front. Bioeng. Biotechnol. **9**, 706229 (2022)
10. Deng, F., et al.: FMRI signal analysis using empirical mean curve decomposition. IEEE Trans. Biomed. Eng. **60**(1), 42–54 (2012)
11. Lv, J., et al.: Holistic atlases of functional networks and interactions reveal reciprocal organizational architecture of cortical function. IEEE Trans. Biomed. Eng. **62**(4), 1120–1131 (2014)
12. Lv, J., et al.: Sparse representation of whole-brain fMRI signals for identification of functional networks. Med. Image Anal. **20**(1), 112–134 (2015)
13. Huang, H., et al.: Latent source mining in FMRI data via deep neural network. In: 2016 IEEE 13th International Symposium on Biomedical Imaging (ISBI). IEEE (2016)
14. Dong, Q., et al.: Modeling hierarchical brain networks via volumetric sparse deep belief network. IEEE Trans. Biomed. Eng. **67**(6), 1739–1748 (2019)
15. Zhang, S., et al.: An explainable deep learning framework for characterizing and interpreting human brain states. Med. Image Anal. **83**, 102665 (2023)
16. Waites, A.B., et al.: Functional connectivity networks are disrupted in left temporal lobe epilepsy. Ann. Neurol. Off. J. Am. Neurol. Assoc. Child Neurol. Soc. **59**(2), 335–343 (2006)
17. Bubic, A., Von Cramon, D.Y., Schubotz, R.I.: Prediction, cognition and the brain. Front. Hum. Neurosci. 25 (2010)
18. Vaswani, A., et al.: Attention is all you need. In: Advances in Neural Information Processing Systems, vol. 30 (2017)
19. Huang, C.-Z.A., et al.: Music transformer. arXiv preprint arXiv:1809.04281 (2018)
20. Stiennon, N., et al.: Learning to summarize with human feedback. Adv. Neural. Inf. Process. Syst. **33**, 3008–3021 (2020)
21. Liu, Z., et al.: Swin transformer: hierarchical vision transformer using shifted windows. In: Proceedings of the IEEE/CVF International Conference on Computer Vision (2021)
22. Dosovitskiy, A., et al.: An image is worth 16x16 words: transformers for image recognition at scale. arXiv preprint arXiv:2010.11929 (2020)
23. OpenAI, GPT-4 Technical Report. arXiv, abs/2303.08774 (2023)
24. Kim, P., et al.: SwiFT: Swin 4D fMRI transformer. In: Advances in Neural Information Processing Systems, vol. 36 (2024)
25. Malkiel, I., et al.: Self-supervised transformers for fMRI representation. In: International Conference on Medical Imaging with Deep Learning. PMLR (2022)
26. Ortega Caro, J., et al.: BrainLM: A foundation model for brain activity recordings. bioRxiv (2023), p. 2023.09.12.557460
27. Wu, N., et al.: Deep transformer models for time series forecasting: the influenza prevalence case. arXiv preprint arXiv:2001.08317 (2020)
28. Van Essen, D.C., et al.: The WU-Minn human connectome project: an overview. Neuroimage **80**, 62–79 (2013)

29. Glasser, M.F., et al.: The minimal preprocessing pipelines for the Human Connectome Project. Neuroimage **80**, 105–124 (2013)
30. Molloy, E.K., Meyerand, M.E., Birn, R.M.: The influence of spatial resolution and smoothing on the detectability of resting-state and task fMRI. Neuroimage **86**, 221–230 (2014)
31. Lin, P., et al.: Dynamic default mode network across different brain states. Sci. Rep. **7**(1), 46088 (2017)
32. Glasser, M.F., et al.: A multi-modal parcellation of human cerebral cortex. Nature **536**(7615), 171–178 (2016)
33. Kingma, D.P., Ba, J.: Adam: a method for stochastic optimization. arXiv preprint arXiv:1412.6980 (2014)
34. Agbinya, J.I.: Markov chain and its applications. In: Applied Data Analytics-Principles and Applications, pp. 1–15. River Publishers (2022)

Cross-Modality Image Quality Prediction for Time-Resolved CT from Breathing Signals

Annette Schwarz[1,2](✉), Jannis Dickmann[2], Christian Hofmann[2], Juliane Szkitsak[3,4], Christoph Bert[3,4], Andreas Maier[1], and Tomás Arias-Vergara[1]

[1] Pattern Recognition Lab, Friedrich-Alexander-Universität Erlangen-Nürnberg, Erlangen, Germany
Annette.Schwarz@fau.de
[2] Siemens Healthineers AG, Forchheim, Germany
[3] Department of Radiation Oncology, Universitätsklinikum Erlangen, Friedrich-Alexander-Universität Erlangen-Nürnberg, Erlangen, Germany
[4] Comprehensive Cancer Center Erlangen-EMN (CCC ER-EMN), Erlangen, Germany

Abstract. Four-dimensional computed tomography (4DCT) is a time-resolved, multi-modal imaging method that captures respiratory signals synchronised with the CT scan in order to track the movement of the lung. It is routinely used in radiation therapy treatment planning for lung or liver cancer patients. However, image artifacts during 4DCT scans caused by irregular patient breathing negatively impact treatment outcomes. This work proposes a method to automatically detect patients at high risk for severe image artifacts even before the scan is conducted based on an pre-scan analysis of their breathing. This can help to take proactive measures to improve image quality, such as changing the scan mode or providing in-depth patient coaching. A deep neural network is trained to predict the image quality score of 28 lung CT phantom scans, each rated by ten clinical experts. Different pretrained networks are investigated for feature generation and combined with two linear output heads to predict the average expert image quality score of unseen scans. We were able to predict the quality of a 4DCT with a mean absolute error of 8% using only the one-dimensional breathing signal as input. This accuracy is comparable to the rating consistency of our clinical experts, which were rating the images directly.

Keywords: Computed tomography · Breathing signals · Time series · Radiation therapy · Multi-modal · 4DCT

1 Introduction

Lung cancer is the most common cause of cancer death with 1.8 million deaths worldwide in 2020 [15]. After it is identified, treatment options include surgery, radiation therapy, targeted therapy, and chemotherapy [8]. One challenge for radiation therapy planning is that the lungs as well as the surrounding anatomy are constantly in motion as a person breathes, which means that tumors within the lungs can also move significantly during breathing. This makes it harder to target the radiation treatment on the tumor and spare healthy tissue, which is necessary to avoid acute and late side effects and reduce the likelihood of secondary cancer later on. One of the most common imaging modalities in this field is time-resolved, four-dimensional computed tomography (4DCT). It has emerged as an essential tool for accurate radiation therapy treatment planning and delivery on motion affected organs like heart, lung and liver. This allows for delineation of the tumor's spatial extent and location throughout the breathing cycle [7]. It was shown, that this allows for more effective targeting of the tumour while sparing healthy tissue, improving treatment outcomes and quality of life for patients by reducing radiation dose to healthy tissue [3]. This is particularly crucial for lung tumors due to their proximity to vital structures like the heart.

A 4DCT scan captures images of the patient's anatomy over multiple phases (i.e. at multiple time points) of the breathing cycle. To achieve this synchronous, multi-modal image and sensor acquisition is required. During image acquisition the patient's respiratory motion is tracked, which generally results in a one-dimensional time series of the breathing amplitude. After scanning, the signal is then used to identify a sequence of intermediate motion states, for each of which a corresponding 3D CT volume is reconstructed. In this way, we obtain a time-resolved sequence of 3D volumes that are used to monitor the tumor's movement and delineate the tumor volume.

One challenge of this method specifically in lung and liver imaging are the large variations between multiple instances of the breathing motion even in the same patient. The motion of the heart follows a stable pattern with only gradual changes regarding motion frequency and motion amplitude. Breathing is a much more volatile motion affecting much larger organs which leads to challenges for time-resolved imaging. Since most 4DCT approaches can't scan the entire lung during the duration of a patient's breathing cycle, a volume needs to be assembled from data of multiple breathing cycles. Hence, irregular breathing can strongly influence the image quality at intersections of data stacks, which adds uncertainty to treatment planning [17,21]. The occurrence of 4DCT artifacts has even been shown to correlate with local metastasis control, which is an important measure of treatment success in cancer patients [13]. Multiple techniques were introduced to avoid these so-called stair-step or stacking artifacts, some trying to restrict image acquisition to regular breathing cycles during the image acquisition [6,18], others trying to counter them through specific strategies, so-called binning methods, for identifying the breathing states [11,17].

In contrast to the previously presented methods, the approach proposed in this paper steps in before any radiation is emitted, giving the medical personnel the chance to prevent unusable or bad images and possibly avoid unnecessary repeat scans. The idea is to analyze the breathing signal of the patient before the scan is started. If breathing patterns are detected that hold a high risk for image artifacts, appropriate countermeasures can be taken in the form of patient breathing coaching or selection of a different scan mode [2,4].

Li et al. tried to solve the same problem using discrete Fourier transforms to measure the periodicity of the signals and estimate image quality [9]. A correlation was found between the sum of the largest five Fourier coefficients and their image quality metric. We could not reproduce the correlation for the artifacts in our data. It might be because CT scanner technology evolved in the nine years since the publishing of this paper: our data was acquired on a 64-slice scanner while their data stems from a 8-slice scanner, which means that in their data there are more chances for stacking artifacts. When collecting our data, other methods of artefact avoidance, such as i4DCT [18], were also used. This probably causes the relationship between breath signal and image artefacts to be quite different in the new data and explains the missing correlation.

We propose a method to predict the occurrence of 4DCT image artifacts based on a patient's breathing. This can be used to avoid artifacts and help improve the treatment of lung cancer. The main contributions can be summarised as follows:

- A deep learning approach to predict patients at risk of image artifacts during 4DCT using breathing signals.
- Using 3D spectrograms and pretrained image networks to extract dynamic breathing information.
- Exploring the interplay of 3D spectrograms and different network architectures.
- Building a pipeline capable of predicting image quality for two distinct reconstruction methods with different artifact probabilities based on only 30 s of breathing signal.
- A system capable of achieving a rating performance comparable to the clinical experts.

2 Methods

2.1 Data

Our dataset contains 56 4DCT volumes with image quality blindly assessed by five medical physicists and five physicians for a previous study [19]. These 4D volumes were generated by reconstructing 28 4DCT scans with two different binning methods routinely used in clinical practice (amplitude based binning and phase based binning) [16]. The radiation therapy experts had an inter observer agreement of Fleiss' Kappa of 0.33, which is considered fair. Our goal in this study is to automatically predict the average rating of those ten clinical experts only using the corresponding breathing signal. All scans were acquired on a SOMATOM go.Open Pro scanner (Siemens Healthineers, Forchheim, Germany) using the motion tracking system RGSC (Varian Medical Systems, Palo Alto,

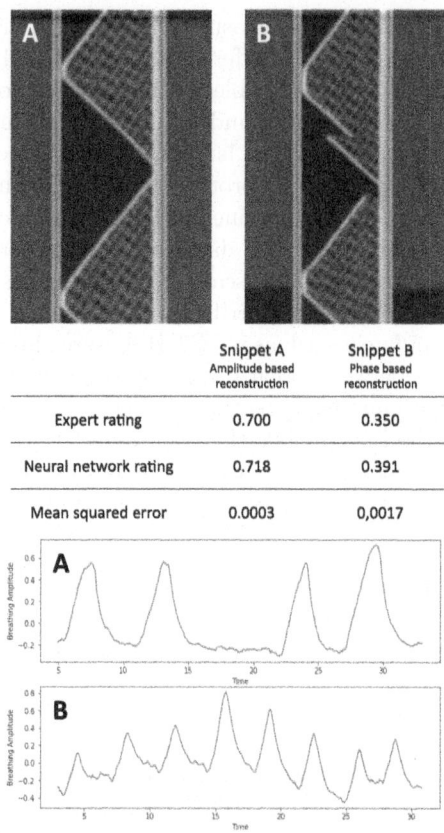

Fig. 1. Two examples of 4DCT scans with the 3D-printed phantom and two different breathing signals. Example A has almost no artifacts with a high image quality rating of 0.7. The breathing curve shown in the lower part is relatively regular. Example B has a low rating of 0.35 and the example slice shows a strong irregularity. The corresponding breathing signal shows more variation, especially regarding amplitude.

CA, USA) to acquire breathing signals. In the phantom dataset, 28 challenging patient breathing patterns were investigated for their influence on the resulting image quality while using a 4DCT approach called i4DCT [19]. This method analyses the breathing during the scan so that scans are only started in regular inhale breathing phases and, once started, continue until sufficient data are acquired, which prevents artifacts. The used phantom inlay has an internal 3D-printed triangular structure that makes it easy to identify 4DCT artifacts. Different strengths of image artifacts and the corresponding image quality rating can be seen in Fig. 1. Data are available for two commonly used binning techniques, amplitude-based and phase-based binning, depending on whether time points were selected based on the breathing amplitude or the time between two peaks, which also affects artifact magnitude. The breathing patterns used

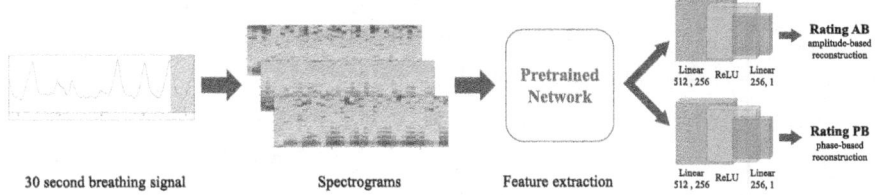

Fig. 2. Framework Flowchart

were selected from real patient breathing curves acquired during 4DCT image acquisition to represent different types of irregularity like variations in amplitude or frequency, baseline drift, and breathing pauses. Figure 1 shows examples of breathing patterns.

2.2 Preprocessing

Labeling data, especially with multiple raters, is very time-consuming. Expanding our data through public sources was also not possible due to the lack of sufficient open source datasets showing a correlation between breathing patterns and 4DCT image quality. To make better use of the available data, we augmented the data by selecting four 30-second segments from the breathing curve. The segments were chosen so that they always ended with a respiratory cycle during which scans were acquired. The idea is for the algorithm to learn the position of the important respiratory cycle and gives it some context through the previous respiratory signal.

2.3 Baseline Method

Feature Extraction: Multiple descriptors can be used to extract the most relevant information from the breathing signals. In this work, we used a feature generator called *tsfresh*, proposed by [1] to compute more than 700 features such as absolute energy, auto-correlation, Fourier coefficients, linear trend, and others.

Regression Analysis: The features computed from the breathing signals were used as input to train three classical regression models: Ridge, Random Forest, and a Support Vector Regressor (SVR). A grid search was conducted to determine the best parameters for ridge regression (with $2^{-5} \leq \alpha \leq 2^5$), Random Forest Regression (with $N : \{25, \ldots, 200\}$ trees and $D : \{5, \ldots, 50\}$ depths), and SVR (with $2^{-5} \leq \epsilon, C \leq 2^5$). The scikit-learn implementation of these models was used [12].

2.4 Proposed Approach

The proposed framework for image quality prediction (see Fig. 2) consists of spectrogram generation, a feature extraction module and a multitask regression

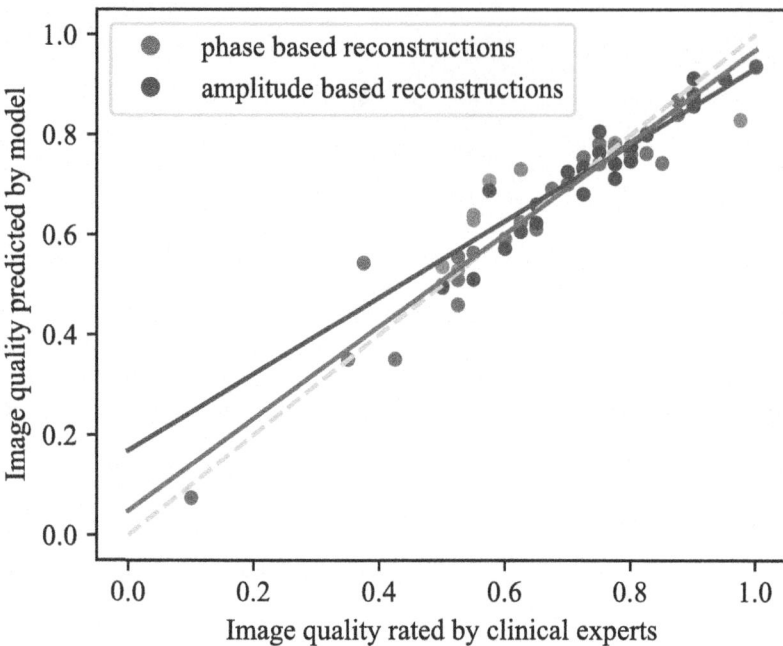

Fig. 3. All predictions were made using one *Resnet18* model that performed best regarding mean absolute error on our test set. Darker dots are from the training set and lighter dots are from the test set.

network. Initially, 30 s long segments of the breathing curve are selected. These segments are then transformed into spectrograms, which represent the frequency content of a signal over time. Next, this time-frequency representation is processed for feature generation. To generate these features two networks typically used for image recognition are explored *Resnet-18* [5] and *VGG* [14]. As the networks expects three channels of input data, we used 3D spectrograms formed with the power, real, and imaginary parts of the short-time Fourier transform and compared them with spectrograms only containing power on all three channels. The networks were selected to investigate different deep learning architectures, but also to explore the performance of 3D spectrograms in these different settings. Both architectures were already shown to perform well with spectrograms containing only the power of signals in other use cases outside of respiratory motion tracking [10, 20].

The features generated by the second to last layer of the network are subsequently fed into a multitask regression network. The regression network consists of two regression output heads, each comprising two linear layers connected by rectifier linear units (ReLUs). Two heads are needed since each CT scan was reconstructed twice using different binning methods resulting in two different image quality ratings per breathing curve: one head was tasked with learning to rate the phase-based reconstruction, the other head the amplitude-based reconstruction. Five-fold cross-validation and early stopping were performed to prevent overfitting. The best performing parametrization for learning rate η, the number of epochs N and batch size B were determined through grid search.

2.5 Performance Metrics

We measured the performance of the baseline and proposed methods using error and correlation metrics. In particular, we computed the Mean Squared Error (MSE), Mean Absolute Error (MAE), Spearman's (ρ) and Pearson's (r) correlation coefficients.

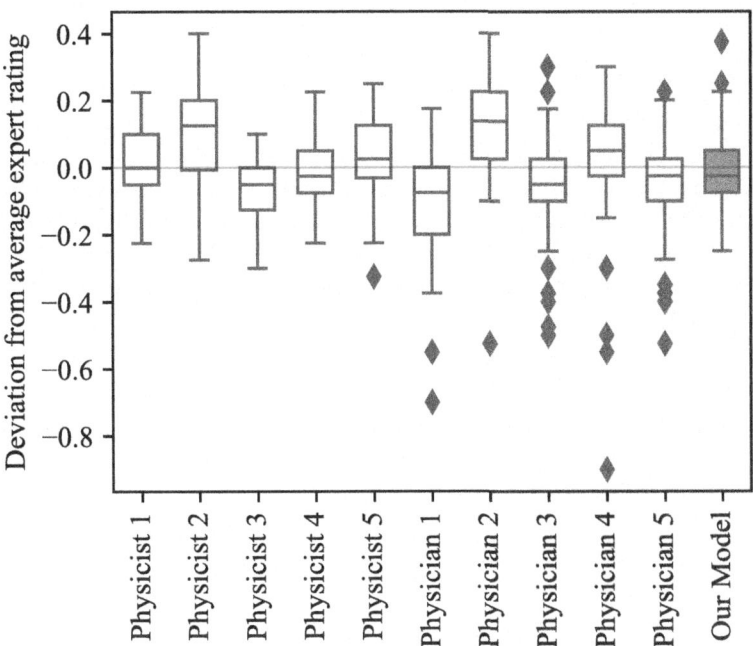

Fig. 4. Deviation from the average expert rating for each clinical expert and our approach using *Resnet18* and 3D spectrograms (blue). (Color figure online)

3 Experiments and Results

We used 28 breathing signals for training and testing the image quality prediction models. The baseline and proposed methods were trained using 24 breathing signals and the remaining four were used for test. The parameters of the models were optimized during training with an internal five-fold cross-validation. The results were reported in Table 1. Regarding the baseline methods, i.e., *tfresh* and classical machine learning algorithms, the best performance was obtained with the Random Forest Regressor (MAE:0.1404; ρ:0.667); however, the lowest error (and highest correlation) was achieved with our proposed 3D spectrogram approach and a *Resnet18* feature extractor (MAE: 0.0839; ρ: 0.895). These results are not surprising, considering our method has a special focus on capturing the dynamic information of the signals without using handcrafted features, which are limited to covering specific characteristics. In our case, such information is embedded in spectrograms, thus providing information about how the energy, distributed in the frequency domain, changes over time.

To further illustrate the results, the model with the best MAE and Spearman's correlation (*Resnet18* with 3D spectrogram) is evaluated as an exemplary case in the following Figures. The parametrization was optimized through grid search ($\eta = 0.0001$, $N = 50$, $B = 8$). Figure 3 shows that our approach correlates well with the ground truth average ratings assigned by the medical experts. The error analysis shows that our model can predict the ratings from the amplitude-based reconstruction with MAE = 0.1052. For the phase-based reconstruction, we obtained a lower error MAE = 0.0626. Figure 4 shows the target and predicted rating distributions. Some raters exhibit a considerable deviation from the average expert rating, which is supported by a 'fair' interobserver agreement of Fleiss' Kappa at 0.33. Our model, shown in blue, has a similar deviation and spread from the average rating as most experts. Statistical analysis (t-test) showed no significant difference from the four raters (p-values = $\{0.671, 0.400, 0.689, 0.320\}$), who are deviating least from the average ratings.

Table 1. Regression results for prediction of the 4DCT scan image quality. **MSE:** Mean Squared Error. **MAE:** Mean Absolute Error. ρ: Spearman's correlation coefficient. r: Pearson's correlation coefficient.

Regression Model	MSE	MAE	ρ	r
Ridge	0.0251	0.1511	0.471	0.467
Random Forest	0.0279	0.1404	0.667	0.628
RBF-SVR	0.0241	0.1444	0.459	0.665
VGG (only Power)	0.0128	0.1105	0.513	0.516
VGG (3D)	0.0121	0.0861	0.823	0.728
Resnet (only Power)	**0.0103**	0.0980	0.834	0.608
Resnet (3D)	0.0108	**0.0839**	**0.895**	**0.773**

4 Discussion

The approximation of the image quality from breathing signals provides valuable information. On the one hand, it can be used for targeted countermeasures for patients where bad image quality is expected before the scan is even started.

On the other hand, it can be used to rapidly estimate image quality after the scan is taken. Using out-of-the-box machine learning techniques we were able to achieve a mean absolute error regarding the average expert rating of 14.0%. By turning the breathing signals into 3D spectrograms and using a Resnet18 image classification network as a feature generator we were able to improve the performance to a MAE of 8.4%. Across the investigated network architectures, the switch from 1D to 3D spectrograms did improve the mean absolute error and the spearman's as well as the pearson's correlation coefficient. In future work, we will consider that even strong irregularities may not cause image artifacts if they correlate to scan regions with little motion like the shoulders. Training on the phantom scan data is important for accurate risk assessment, since artifacts that might be caused by the breathing pattern are almost certainly present and quantifiable in the phantom scans, which is not true for patient scans. The step that must now be taken in cooperation with medical experts on radiation therapy is to find thresholds for those risks that make sense in a clinical environment and evaluate them on patient data. This is why our experiments were formulated as a regression task instead of classification, since these thresholds should be set after evaluating and improving our model with more data. Also, the preferred threshold settings might vary between clinics and clinical indications.

5 Conclusion

Image artifacts caused by irregular breathing considerably impact 4DCT scans for lung cancer radiation therapy. The approach presented in this paper can successfully predict image quality based on corresponding breathing patterns. With this knowledge, countermeasures can be initiated. Additional work with more data is needed to translate this into clinical practice.

References

1. Time series feature extraction on basis of scalable hypothesis tests (tsfresh - a python package). Neurocomputing **307**, 72–77 (2018). https://doi.org/10.1016/j.neucom.2018.03.067. https://www.sciencedirect.com/science/article/pii/S0925231218304843
2. Aznar, M.C., Persson, G.F., Kofoed, I.M., Nygaard, D.E., Korreman, S.S.: Irregular breathing during 4DCT scanning of lung cancer patients: is the midventilation approach robust? Physica Med. **30**(1), 69–75 (2014)
3. Bai, T., et al.: How does four-dimensional computed tomography spare normal tissues in non-small cell lung cancer radiotherapy by defining internal target volume? Thoracic Cancer **5**(6), 537–542 (2014)
4. Goossens, S., Senny, F., Lee, J.A., Janssens, G., Geets, X.: Assessment of tumor motion reproducibility with audio-visual coaching through successive 4D CT sessions. J. Appl. Clin. Med. Phys. **15**(1), 47–56 (2014)
5. He, K., Zhang, X., Ren, S., Sun, J.: Deep residual learning for image recognition. CoRR abs/1512.03385 (2015). http://arxiv.org/abs/1512.03385

6. Keall, P.J., Vedam, S., George, R., Williamson, J.: Respiratory regularity gated 4D CT acquisition: concepts and proof of principle. Australas. Phys. Eng. Sci. Med. **30**, 211–220 (2007)
7. Korreman, S., Persson, G., Nygaard, D., Brink, C., Juhler-Nøttrup, T.: Respiration-correlated image guidance is the most important radiotherapy motion management strategy for most lung cancer patients. Int. J. Radiat. Oncol. Biol. Phys. **83**(4), 1338–1343 (2012)
8. Lemjabbar-Alaoui, H., Hassan, O.U., Yang, Y.W., Buchanan, P.: Lung cancer: biology and treatment options. Biochimica et Biophysica Acta (BBA)-Reviews on Cancer **1856**(2), 189–210 (2015)
9. Li, G., et al.: Rapid estimation of 4DCT motion-artifact severity based on 1D breathing-surrogate periodicity. Med. Phys. **41**(11), 111717 (2014)
10. Neili, Z., Sundaraj, K.: A comparative study of the spectrogram, scalogram, mel-spectrogram and gammatonegram time-frequency representations for the classification of lung sounds using the ICBHI database based on CNNs. Biomedical Engineering/Biomedizinische Technik **67**(5), 367–390 (2022)
11. Olsen, J.R., et al.: Effect of novel amplitude/phase binning algorithm on commercial four-dimensional computed tomography quality. Int. J. Radiat. Oncol. Biol. Phys. **70**(1), 243–252 (2008)
12. Pedregosa, F., et al.: Scikit-learn: machine learning in python. J. Mach. Learn. Res. **12**, 2825–2830 (2011)
13. Sentker, T., et al.: 4D CT image artifacts affect local control in SBRT of lung and liver metastases. Radiother. Oncol. **148**, 229–234 (2020)
14. Simonyan, K., Zisserman, A.: Very deep convolutional networks for large-scale image recognition. arXiv preprint arXiv:1409.1556 (2014)
15. Sung, H., et al.: Global cancer statistics 2020: globocan estimates of incidence and mortality worldwide for 36 cancers in 185 countries. CA Cancer J. Clin. **71**(3), 209–249 (2021)
16. Werner, R., Hofmann, C., Gauer, T.: Optimized projection binning for improved helical amplitude-and phase-based 4DCT reconstruction in the presence of breathing irregularity. In: Medical Imaging 2016: Physics of Medical Imaging, vol. 9783, pp. 271–276. SPIE (2016)
17. Werner, R., Hofmann, C., Mücke, E., Gauer, T.: Reduction of breathing irregularity-related motion artifacts in low-pitch spiral 4D CT by optimized projection binning. Radiat. Oncol. **12**, 1–8 (2017)
18. Werner, R., Sentker, T., Madesta, F., Gauer, T., Hofmann, C.: Intelligent 4D CT sequence scanning (I4DCT): concept and performance evaluation. Med. Phys. **46**(8), 3462–3474 (2019)
19. Werner, R., et al.: Comparison of intelligent 4D CT sequence scanning and conventional spiral 4D CT: a first comprehensive phantom study. Phys. Med. Biol. **66**(1), 015004 (2021)
20. Wyse, L.: Audio spectrogram representations for processing with convolutional neural networks. arXiv preprint arXiv:1706.09559 (2017)
21. Yamamoto, T., Langner, U., Loo Jr, B.W., Shen, J., Keall, P.J.: Retrospective analysis of artifacts in four-dimensional CT images of 50 abdominal and thoracic radiotherapy patients. Int. J. Radiat. Oncol. Biol. Phys. **72**(4), 1250–1258 (2008)

RATNUS: Rapid, Automatic Thalamic Nuclei Segmentation Using Multimodal MRI Inputs

Anqi Feng[1,2], Zhangxing Bian[1], Blake E. Dewey[3], Alexa Gail Colinco[4], Jiachen Zhuo[4], and Jerry L. Prince[1(✉)]

[1] Department of Electrical and Computer Engineering, Johns Hopkins University, Baltimore, MD 21218, USA
prince@jhu.edu
[2] Laboratory of Behavioral Neuroscience, National Institute on Aging, National Institutes of Health, Baltimore, MD 21224, USA
[3] Department of Neurology, Johns Hopkins School of Medicine, Baltimore, MD 21287, USA
[4] Department of Diagnostic Radiology and Nuclear Medicine, University of Maryland School of Medicine, Baltimore, MD 21218, USA

Abstract. Accurate segmentation of thalamic nuclei is important for better understanding brain function and improving disease treatment. Traditional segmentation methods often rely on a single T1-weighted image, which has limited contrast in the thalamus. In this work, we introduce RATNUS, which uses synthetic T1-weighted images with many inversion times along with diffusion-derived features to enhance the visibility of nuclei within the thalamus. Using these features, a convolutional neural network is used to segment 13 thalamic nuclei. For comparison with other methods, we introduce a unified nuclei labeling scheme. Our results demonstrate an 87.19% average true positive rate (TPR) against manual labeling. In comparison, FreeSurfer and THOMAS achieve TPRs of 64.25% and 57.64%, respectively, demonstrating the superiority of RATNUS in thalamic nuclei segmentation. The source code and pretrained models are available at: https://github.com/ANQIFENG/RATNUS.

1 Introduction

The thalamus is a vital brain structure located between the cortex and brain stem, composed of multiple functional clusters called nuclei [7,19,28]. These nuclei have significant relevance to diseases such as Parkinson's diseases, Alzheimer's disease, multiple sclerosis, and frontotemporal dementia [4,5,9,14], making their segmentation crucial for targeted research and the development of therapies. Despite this, many studies typically segment the thalamus as one entity in part because the exclusive use of standard T1-weighted and T2-weighted images lack the contrast necessary to distinguish the small nuclei within the thalamus [3,10,29,31].

Existing methods that provide segmentations of certain thalamic nuclei include FreeSurfer [11] and THOMAS [22]. FreeSurfer uses a Bayesian segmentation approach with a probabilistic atlas of the human thalamus as prior knowledge; however, its use of only the Magnetization Prepared Rapid Gradient Echo (MPRAGE) sequence [16] limits the contrast between nuclei. THOMAS uses multi-atlas segmentation and label fusion techniques on high-contrast, white-matter-nulled MPRAGE scans, also known as Fast Gray Matter Acquisition T1 Inversion Recovery (FGATIR) [23], collected at 7T to segment 12 thalamic nuclei. While it achieves good results on 7T images, its effectiveness on 3T scans has not been quantitatively validated. None of these methods use multiple T1-weighted images with different inversion times (multi-TI), which provide higher thalamus contrast not achievable by MPRAGE or FGATIR alone.

Diffusion Magnetic resonance imaging (MRI) [2,20,21,25,26,30,32,33] has been used for thalamic nuclei segmentation. One approach [21] develops a hierarchical random forest framework to parcellate the thalamus into 6 nuclei, utilizing inputs such as fractional anisotropy (FA), the Knutsson 5D vector and edge map, and connectivity with cortical regions. However, its manual labeling was based on FA and Knutsson edge maps, which does not align perfectly with labels derived from T1-weighted images. Two approaches [25,26] extend the previous FreeSurfer method by incorporating the FA and principal eigenvector with MPRAGE images. The first approach [26] uses Bayesian segmentation but lacks a model for partial volume effects, leading to poor performance at resolutions worse than 1mm. The second approach [25], based on a convolutional neural network (CNN), has not been quantitatively compared with ground truth for its segmentation of 23 histological labels. When evaluating its performance on a 10-label grouping, Dice scores were below 0.6, indicating limitations in their segmentation accuracy.

In this paper, we present a new approach to thalamic nuclei segmentation, named RATNUS. Its innovation lies in the integration of multi-TI images and features derived from diffusion images, providing enhanced contrast for accurate thalamic nuclei segmentation. Our contributions are threefold: (1) We present a method to correctly synthesize multi-TI images from MPRAGE and FGATIR images. (2) We develop a CNN-based network to identify 13 distinct thalamic nuclei, trained using novel manual delineations. (3) We establish a protocol for unifying different labeling schemes across methods to facilitate comparison. RATNUS achieves superior performance compared to benchmark methods, demonstrating its outstanding capability in the segmentation of thalamic nuclei.

2 Methods

2.1 Data and Manual Labels

Our dataset is derived from a study on mild traumatic brain injury (MTBI), which was approved by the University of Maryland's ethics review board. The datasest contains 24 subjects, including 14 healthy controls and 10 people with MTBI. Each participant underwent MRI, including MPRAGE, FGATIR, and diffusion sequences. The MPRAGE and FGATIR images were acquired using the same sequence protocol: an isotropic resolution of 1 mm, repetition time (TR): 4000 ms, echo time (TE): 3.37 ms, and inversion time (TI): MPRAGE 1400 ms and FGATIR 400 ms. Diffusion images were acquired with an isotropic resolution of 2 mm, with 136 directions, at b-values of 0, 1000, and 2500, using an anterior-posterior (AP) phase-encoding direction with additional posterior-anterior (PA) b0 images for distortion correction. All data were collected using a 3T Siemens Prisma scanner.

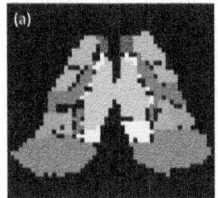

Grouping	Manual Label Color Map				
Anterior Nuclear Group	AN			LD	
Medial Nuclear Group	MD		CM		CL
Lateral Nuclear Group	VA	VPL	VPM	VLP	VLA
Posterior Nuclear Group	PuA		PuI		LP

Fig. 1. (a) Our manual labels of thalamic nuclei are sparse. (b) Color-coded labeling scheme for thalamic nuclei according to the Morel atlas.

Manual thalamic nuclei delineation was guided by the Morel Atlas [15]. Referencing both the T_1 map and multi-TI images, labels were assigned only to those voxels for which the rater had high confidence of correct label assignment. This led to sparse labels, ensuring high confidence in the labeled voxels but leaving many voxels unlabeled, particularly in boundaries between nuclei, as illustrated in Fig. 1(a). Our study focuses on 13 nuclei (and nuclear groups): Anterior Nucleus (AN), Central Lateral (CL), Center Median (CM), Lateral Dorsal (LD), Lateral Posterior (LP), Mediodorsal (MD), Anterior Pulvinar (PuA), Inferior Pulvinar (PuI), Ventral Anterior (VA), Ventral Lateral Anterior (VLA), Ventral Lateral Posterior (VLP), Ventral Posterior Lateral (VPL), and Ventral Posterior Medial (VPM). The labeling scheme of these thalamic nuclei with color coding is shown in Fig. 1(b).

2.2 Data Processing Pipeline

We developed a pipeline to synthesize multi-TI images. We also generated comprehensive features from the diffusion images. These processed images and features greatly enhance the visibility of details within the thalamus and are concatenated together to form the input to the models.

Structural MRI Processing. Our processing of MPRAGE and FGATIR images begins with a coarse-to-fine registration, using ANTS [1] for rigid registration specific to each subject. Initially, MPRAGE images are registered to the MNI space. This is followed by the registration of FGATIR images to their corresponding MPRAGE images, transforming both images to the same atlas space.

Following registration, the MPRAGE and FGATIR images go through two processing steps: N4 Bias Field Correction [27] and White Matter Mean Normalization [18]. To accurately derive proton density (PD) and T_1 maps from the MPRAGE and FGATIR images, as described below, it is important to process these images together, as separate adjustments in brightness or contrast will introduce errors in computation of the PD and T_1 maps [24]. Consequently, we use a harmonic bias field computed as the geometric mean of the two N4 bias fields, found separately from the MPRAGE and FGATIR images, for uniform intensity normalization. We also create a white matter mask from the MPRAGE image using Fuzzy C-means clustering [18] and then adjust the two images with the same scaling factor, determined by the average white matter intensity within the MPRAGE image.

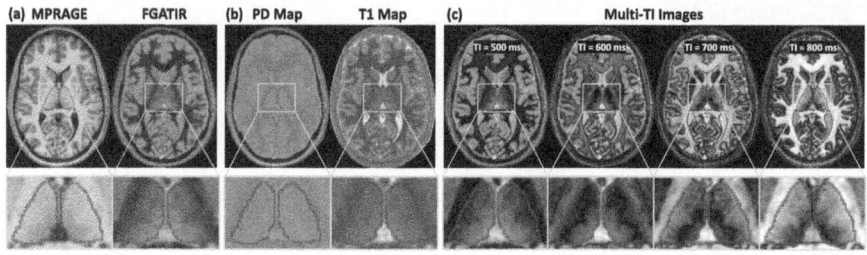

Fig. 2. Different T1-weighted images. (a) MPRAGE and FGATIR images after registration, N4 bias field correction and white matter mean normalization. (b) PD and T_1 maps derived from MPRAGE and FGATIR images. (c) Example multi-TI images at TIs: 500 ms, 600 ms, 700 ms, and 800 ms. Thalamus regions are highlighted with yellow boxes and delineated with red contours. (Color figure online)

For a given voxel within a T1-weighted image, the signal intensity can be expressed as

$$I^{(i)} = \text{PD}^{(i)}[1 - 2e^{(-\text{TI}/T_1^{(i)})} + e^{(-\text{TR}/T_1^{(i)})}], \tag{1}$$

where $I^{(i)}$ denotes the image intensity for the i-th voxel, $\text{PD}^{(i)}$ the proton density map value for the i-th voxel, $T_1^{(i)}$ the T_1 map value for the i-th voxel, TI the inversion time, and TR the repetition time. As the MPRAGE and FGATIR images were acquired in identical fashion except for their different TIs, we are able to write two distinct equations based on Eq. 1 for each image and then solve for the PD and T_1 maps using nonlinear least squares. We then proceed to synthesize a series of multi-TI images by keeping PD and T_1 values constant and systematically varying the TI value. Specifically, we varied TI from 400 to 1400 ms in increments of 20 ms, resulting in a set of 51 images, revealing contrast between different nuclei in different images. Figure 2 shows examples of MPRAGE and FGATIR images after processing, corresponding PD and T_1 maps, and some computed multi-TI images.

Diffusion MRI Processing. We processed our diffusion MRI data using the Tortoise software [17], starting with the DIFFPREP module for denoising, motion, and distortion corrections, followed by DR-BUDDI module for EPI distortion correction leveraging opposite phase encoding directions. These two steps also registered the diffusion data to their corresponding T2-weighted images in MNI space. We then used the DIFFCALC module to perform tensor fitting and calculate key metrics, including axial diffusivity (AD), fractional anisotropy (FA), radial diffusivity (RD), Trace, Eigenvalues, and Eigenvectors, along with the three Westin measures (WS, WP, WL). Following this, we applied the Knutsson mapping to convert the principal eigenvector into a 5-dimensional (5D) vector [12,21]. Moreover, we generated an edge map based on these orientations, serving as a visual representation of the changes in direction of the principal eigenvectors. Using the Knutsson 5D vector and the Knutsson edge map helps to better define the boundaries and reveal more subtle details within the thalamus, surpassing the conventional eigenvector depictions.

2.3 Thalamic Nuclei Segmentation

Our work focuses on segmenting 13 distinct nuclei (and nuclear groups) within the thalamus. We implemented a two-step approach, with two networks each built upon a 5-level 3D U-Net [6]. The first network identifies the region of interest (ROI) and the second delineates the ROI into 13 nuclei classes, as illustrated in Fig. 3. For both models, the input consists of a 68-channel image per subject, derived from the processing pipeline described in Sect. 2.2, as shown in Fig. 3(a). Volumes are center-cropped to $96 \times 96 \times 96$ voxels (specified in MNI coordinates), which always includes the entire thalamus.

The first model, the ROI model, generates foreground masks that identify the areas of interest for the thalamic nuclei we aim to segment. Before training, we convert the nuclei labels into a binary format to create a binary ground truth. Given our sparse manual labels, we used the paint tool in the 3D Slicer Segmentation Editor to fill the holes within the binary ground truth without altering its overall external shape, as depicted in Fig. 3(b). The second model, the Nuclei model, segments the entire data into 13 classes, with each voxel being classified into one of the thalamic nuclei. The last step is to multiply the foreground mask from the ROI model with the nuclei mask from the Nuclei model to generate the 13 thalamic nuclei predictions.

Loss. We trained the ROI model using Dice Loss [13]. When training the Nuclei model, we aim to minimize the Dice Loss for the 13 nuclei classes. However, given the sparse ground truth, where the rater only labeled voxels with high confidence, leaving many voxels in the thalamus unlabeled, we applied a masking technique during the Dice Loss calculation. Specifically, we multiplied both the numerator and denominator of the Dice Loss by a ground truth mask (where labeled voxels are 1 and unlabeled voxels are 0) to ensure that only labeled voxels contributed to the loss calculation, thereby excluding the influence of unlabeled voxels. This naturally leads to the maximization of the true positive rate. The loss function for the Nuclei model is then formed as:

$$\mathcal{L}_{\text{Nuclei}} = 1 - \frac{1}{13} \sum_{c=1}^{13} \frac{\sum_i T_{c,i} P_{c,i} + \varepsilon}{\sum_i T_{c,i} + \varepsilon},\tag{2}$$

where $T_{c,i}$ denotes the true label for class c at voxel i, $P_{c,i}$ is the predicted probability for class c at voxel i, and ε is a smoothing factor set to 1e-6.

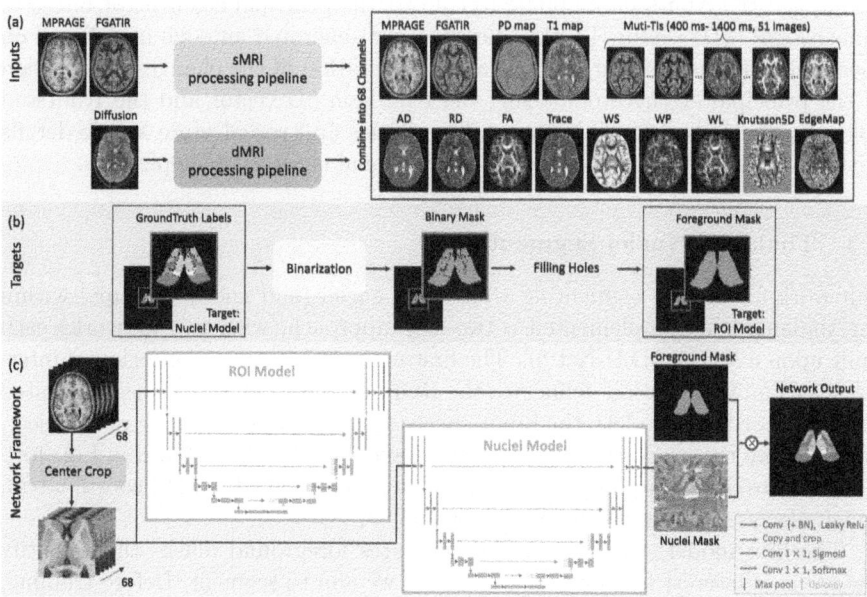

Fig. 3. Overview of the thalamic nuclei segmentation framework. (a) The processing for the structural (sMRI) and diffusion MRI (dMRI), leading to a combined 68-channel network input. (b) The generation of the foreground mask (ground truth of the ROI model) using the thalamic nuclei labels (ground truth of the Nuclei model). (c) The network framework, consists of the ROI model and the Nuclei model, both built upon a 5-level 3D U-Net. The final segmentation is produced by multiplying the foreground mask from the ROI model with the nuclei mask from the Nuclei model.

Implementation Details. We performed an 8-fold cross-validation on 24 subjects with a training, validation, testing split ratio of 19:2:3, ensuring that all subjects were included in the testing process once. Both models are 3D U-Nets with 5 levels, trained using the Adam optimizer with a weight decay of 1e-4, and an initial learning rates of 1e-3, reduced by 20% if the validation loss does not improve over 5 epochs. We employed Leaky ReLU activation and Batch Normalization across all convolutional blocks. The random seed was set to 1234. The

ROI model was trained using a sigmoid activation in the final layer, with a batch size of 4 and stopped training if the validation loss does not decrease within 10 epochs. The Nuclei model was trained using a softmax activation in the final layer, with a batch size of 1, and the same stopping criterion as the ROI model.

2.4 Labeling Schemes Unifying Protocol

We compared RATNUS to FreeSurfer [11] and THOMAS [22], two popular approaches for thalamic nuclei segmentation. Since each method uses a unique set of rules for labeling thalamic nuclei, we used the Morel atlas [15] as a structural guide to propose a unified labeling scheme for comparison. After reviewing

Grouping	RATNUS	THOMAS	Freesurfer
Anterior	AN	AV	AV
	LD		LD
Medial		MD	MDl
	MD		MDm
			CL
	CL		CeM
			pc
Midline	CM	CM	CM
Ventral Anterior	VA	VA	VA
			VAmc
Ventral Posterior	VPL	VPL	VPL
	VPM		VM
Ventral Lateral	VLp	VLp	VLp
	VLa	VLa	VLa
Posterior	PuA		PuA
			PuI
	PuI	PuI	PuL
			PuM
	LP		LP
MTT		MTT	None
Hb		Hb	
LGN		LGN	LGN
MGN	None	MGN	MGN
Pf			Pf
Lsg		None	Lsg
MV			MV

Fig. 4. An exhaustive mapping of thalamic nuclei classes between RATNUS, and those defined by THOMAS and FreeSurfer. The first column lists the major categories derived from our grouping strategy, each of which corresponds to the merging of several nuclei in the second, third and, forth column. All major categories and individual instances are assigned a unique color for clear differentiation. Abbreviations for THOMAS and FreeSurfer nuclei are carefully extracted from [22] and [11].

correspondences between the schemes, we formed the following seven main categories: Anterior group, Medial group, Midline group, Ventral Anterior group, Ventral Posterior group, Ventral Lateral group, and Posterior group. Nuclei that do not have a corresponding match—e.g., the MTT is labeled in the THOMAS atlas but is not represented in either our atlas or the FreeSurfer atlas, and the Lsg is labeled in FreeSurfer but is missing from ours and the THOMAS atlas— were marked as distinct classifications. The grouping and color-coding scheme is shown in Fig. 4.

3 Experiments and Results

In this section, we evaluate the performance of the RATNUS model. We first compare RATNUS' segmentation results with ground truth labels to measure accuracy. Then, we benchmark RATNUS against FreeSurfer [11] and THOMAS [22] to highlight its advantages. As our ground truth labels are sparse, where the rater only labeled voxels with high confidence, leaving many voxels in the thalamus unlabeled, using Dice Score as the evaluation metric could be inappropriate, since it may count predictions as incorrect if they match the nuclei class but lack corresponding ground truth labels. Therefore, we adopt the TPR as the evaluation metric for the following experiments. Additionally, as mentioned in the implementation details, we performed an 8-fold cross-validation on 24 subjects. This ensures that each subject is included in the testing process once, and the results presented below are the average and standard deviation calculated across all 24 subjects.

3.1 Comparison Against Ground Truth

We evaluated the RATNUS's segmentation results by comparing them with ground truth labels using TPR. The quantitative results, summarized in Table 1, illustrates RATNUS's consistently high TPR across all thalamic nuclei. Figure 5, provides a visual comparison, showing close alignments between our model's predictions and the ground truth, demonstrating RATNUS's capability in accurate thalamic nuclei segmentation.

Table 1. TPRs for 13 thalamic nuclei, shown in percentages. "Average" indicates the volume-weighted mean across all nuclei.

AN	CM	LD	LP	MD	PuA	PuI	VA	VLa	VLp	VPL	VPM	CL	Average
86.32	80.65	80.75	85.30	91.08	61.91	94.36	91.79	79.43	88.10	83.16	75.60	68.43	87.19
±	±	±	±	±	±	±	±	±	±	±	±	±	±
1.58	5.10	4.06	3.53	1.31	7.82	0.92	2.21	4.77	1.93	3.64	7.98	2.53	1.47

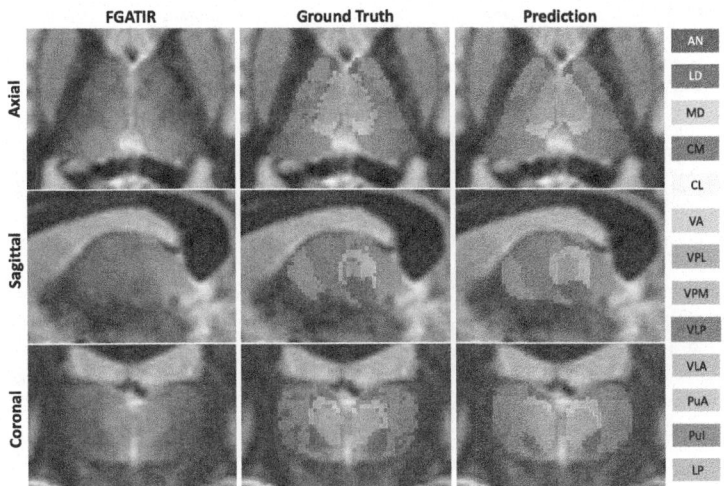

Fig. 5. Comparisons between model's predictions and ground truth labels. From left to right, each column shows the FGATIR scans, the ground truth, and our model predictions. The provided color codes is consistent with Fig. 1.

3.2 Comparisons Against FreeSurfer and THOMAS Segmentation

We compared our model's predictions with those of FreeSurfer and THOMAS after unifying them to a common ground using the protocol described in Sect. 2.4. The quantitative comparison focuses only on seven main groups and excludes unique labels and background. Figure 6 shows that RATNUS consistently achieves higher TPR in all major thalamic groups, with an average TPR of 75.80%, greatly surpassing THOMAS at 57.64% and FreeSurfer at 64.25%. Qualitatively, as shown in Fig. 7, RATNUS's predictions are more contiguous with fewer misclassified voxels and better adherence to the boundary of the thalamus, whereas FreeSurfer appears to over-segment (highlighted by the yellow

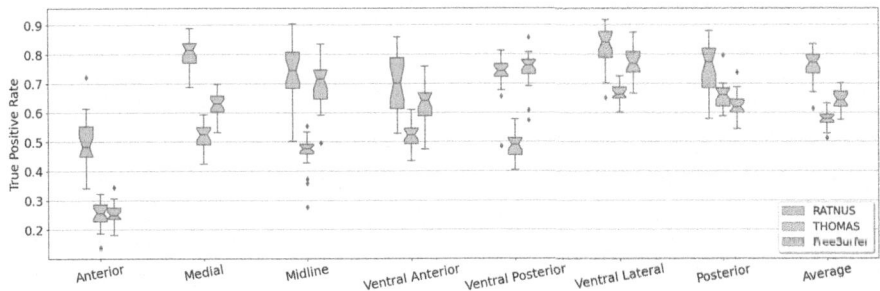

Fig. 6. Boxplot showing RATNUS's TPR compared with FreeSurfer and THOMAS. The horizontal axis lists major thalamic groups from Anterior to Posterior, with "Average" showing the volume-weighted mean of all the groups.

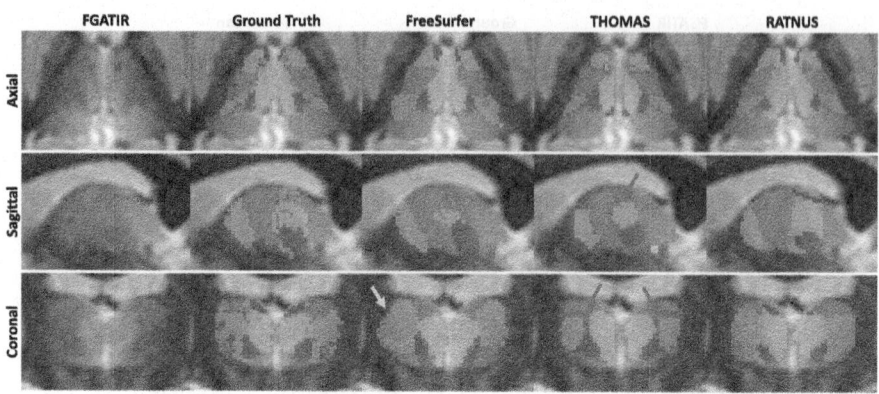

Fig. 7. Comparative visualization of our model predictions against FreeSurfer and THOMAS across seven major thalamic regions. Unique instances, such as MGN, are also included. Color codes for each thalamic group are provided in Fig. 4. (Color figure online)

arrow), and THOMAS tends to under-segment (highlighted by the red arrows) the thalamus.

4 Conclusions and Discussions

We propose RATNUS, a method that segments 13 thalamic nuclei within a CNN framework using the combination of multi-TI images and diffusion-derived features, which provide enhanced contrast within the thalamus. It achieves superior performance over FreeSurfer and THOMAS, demonstrating RATNUS's potential for precise thalamic nuclei segmentation.

Our method has some limitations. First, the approach benefits greatly from multimodal data, particularly multi-TI images, which provide detailed information about thalamic nuclei. These multi-TI images require both MPRAGE and FGATIR sequences to generate. If either MPRAGE or FGATIR is unavailable, the multi-TI images cannot be produced, and the method cannot utilize the valuable information they provide. Second, we compared our method to FreeSurfer and THOMAS, both of which use different labeling schemes. To ensure fairness, we proposed a unifying protocol based on the Morel atlas to standardize these schemes. However, since our model was trained using our specific labels and tested on the same distribution, it is more likely to perform better than THOMAS and FreeSurfer, introducing some bias despite our unifying efforts. Third, delineating thalamic nuclei is difficult and costly due to their small size and low contrast. As a result, in this work, we only trained and tested models using 24 pairs of data and thalamic nuclei labels. Although this is comparable to the 28 delineations used to develop THOMAS, it is still somewhat limited for training deep learning models, potentially restricting model's generalization ability and robustness.

To address these limitations, our future work will focus on several key areas. First, in order to eliminate the dependence on FGATIR, we plan to develop a network to synthesize multi-TI images from alternative multi-contrast imaging data, similar to [8]. Second, we plan to perform out-of-distribution tests to evaluate the generalization capabilities of FreeSurfer, THOMAS, and RATNUS. Third, we plan to implement semi-supervised training techniques to leverage a larger amount of data which does not have ground truth labels.

Acknowledgments. This work was supported in part by the Intramural Research Program of the National Institutes of Health (NIH), National Institute on Aging. It is also supported in part by the NIH through the National Institute of Neurological Disorders and Stroke grant R01-NS105503 (PIs: Zhuo & Prince).

References

1. Avants, B.B., Tustison, N., Song, G.: Advanced normalization tools (ANTS). Insight J. **2**(365), 1–35 (2009)
2. Battistella, G., et al.: Robust thalamic nuclei segmentation method based on local diffusion magnetic resonance properties. Brain Struct. Funct. **222**, 2203–2216 (2017)
3. Billot, B., et al.: SynthSeg: segmentation of brain MRI scans of any contrast and resolution without retraining. Med. Image Anal. **86**, 102789 (2023)
4. Bocchetta, M., et al.: Thalamic nuclei in frontotemporal dementia: mediodorsal nucleus involvement is universal but pulvinar atrophy is unique to C9ORF72. Hum. Brain Mapp. **41**(4), 1006–1016 (2020)
5. Braak, H., Braak, E.: Alzheimer's disease affects limbic nuclei of the thalamus. Acta Neuropathol. **81**(3), 261–268 (1991)
6. Çiçek, Ö., et al.: 3D U-Net: learning dense volumetric segmentation from sparse annotation. In: Medical Image Computing and Computer-Assisted Intervention–MICCAI 2016: 19th International Conference, Athens, Greece, 17–21 October 2016, Proceedings, Part II 19, pp. 424–432. Springer (2016)
7. Fama, R., Sullivan, E.V.: Thalamic structures and associated cognitive functions: relations with age and aging. Neurosci. Biobehav. Rev. **54**, 29–37 (2015)
8. Hays, S.P., et al.: Revisiting registration-based image synthesis: a focus on unsupervised MR image synthesis. In: Proceedings of SPIE Medical Imaging (SPIE-MI 2024), San Diego, CA, 18–22 February 2024, vol. 12926, pp. 257–265 (2024)
9. Henderson, J., Carpenter, K., Cartwright, H., Halliday, G.: Loss of thalamic intralaminar nuclei in progressive supranuclear palsy and Parkinson's disease: clinical and therapeutic implications. Brain **123**(7), 1410–1421 (2000)
10. Huo, Y., et al.: 3D whole brain segmentation using spatially localized atlas network tiles. Neuroimage **194**, 105–119 (2019)
11. Iglesias, J.E., et al.: A probabilistic atlas of the human thalamic nuclei combining ex vivo MRI and histology. Neuroimage **183**, 314–326 (2018)
12. Knutsson, H.: Producing a continuous and distance preserving 5-D vector representation of 3-D orientation. In: IEEE Computer Society Workshop on Computer Architecture for Pattern Analysis and Image Database Management, pp. 175–182 (1985)

13. Milletari, F., Navab, N., Ahmadi, S.A.: V-Net: fully convolutional neural networks for volumetric medical image segmentation. In: 2016 Fourth International Conference on 3D Vision (3DV), pp. 565–571. IEEE (2016)
14. Minagar, A., et al.: The thalamus and multiple sclerosis: modern views on pathologic, imaging, and clinical aspects. Neurology **80**(2), 210–219 (2013)
15. Morel, A.: Stereotactic atlas of the human thalamus and basal ganglia. CRC Press (2007)
16. Mugler, J.P., III., Brookeman, J.R.: Three-dimensional magnetization-prepared rapid gradient-echo imaging (3D MPRAGE). Magn. Reson. Med. **15**(1), 152–157 (1990)
17. Pierpaoli, C., et al.: TORTOISE: an integrated software package for processing of diffusion MRI data. In: ISMRM 18th Annual Meeting, vol. 1597. Stockholm (2010)
18. Reinhold, J.C., et al.: Evaluating the impact of intensity normalization on MR image synthesis. In: Medical Imaging 2019: Image Processing, vol. 10949, pp. 890–898. SPIE (2019)
19. Sherman, S.M., Guillery, R.W.: Exploring the thalamus. Elsevier (2001)
20. Stough, J.V., et al.: Thalamic parcellation from multi-modal data using random forest learning. In: 10th International Symposium on Biomedical Imaging (ISBI 2013), pp. 852–855 (2013)
21. Stough, J.V., et al.: Automatic method for thalamus parcellation using multi-modal feature classification. In: Medical Image Computing and Computer-Assisted Intervention–MICCAI 2014, vol. 8675, pp. 169–176. Springer (2014)
22. Su, J.H., et al.: Thalamus optimized multi atlas segmentation (THOMAS): fast, fully automated segmentation of thalamic nuclei from structural MRI. Neuroimage **194**, 272–282 (2019)
23. Sudhyadhom, A., et al.: A high re solution and high contrast MRI for differentiation of subcortical structures for DBS targeting: the fast gray matter acquisition T1 inversion recovery (FGATIR). Neuroimage **47**, T44–T52 (2009)
24. Tohidi, P., et al.: Joint synthesis of WMn MPRAGE and parameter maps using deep learning and an imaging equation. In: Medical Imaging 2023: Image Processing, vol. 12464, pp. 558–564. SPIE (2023)
25. Tregidgo, H.F., Soskic, S., Olchanyi, M.D., et al.: Domain-agnostic segmentation of thalamic nuclei from joint structural and diffusion MRI. arXiv preprint arXiv:2305.03413 (2023)
26. Tregidgo, H.F., et al.: Accurate Bayesian segmentation of thalamic nuclei using diffusion MRI and an improved histological atlas. Neuroimage **274**, 120129 (2023)
27. Tustison, N.J., et al.: N4ITK: improved N3 bias correction. IEEE Trans. Med. Imaging **29**(6), 1310–1320 (2010)
28. Van Der Werf, Y.D., et al.: Contributions of thalamic nuclei to declarative memory functioning. Cortex **39**(4–5), 1047–1062 (2003)
29. Wachinger, C., Reuter, M., Klein, T.: DeepNAT: deep convolutional neural network for segmenting neuroanatomy. Neuroimage **170**, 434–445 (2018)
30. Wiegell, M.R., Tuch, D.S., Larsson, H.B., Wedeen, V.J.: Automatic segmentation of thalamic nuclei from diffusion tensor magnetic resonance imaging. Neuroimage **19**(2), 391–401 (2003)
31. Woolrich, M.W., et al.: Temporal autocorrelation in univariate linear modeling of FMRI data. Neuroimage **14**(6), 1370–1386 (2001)

32. Yan, C., et al.: Segmenting thalamic nuclei from manifold projections of multi-contrast MRI. In: Proceedings of SPIE Medical Imaging (SPIE-MI 2023), San Diego, CA, 19–23 February 2023, vol. 12464, pp. 727–734 (2023)
33. Ziyan, U., Tuch, D., Westin, C.F.: Segmentation of thalamic nuclei from DTI using spectral clustering. In: Medical Image Computing and Computer-Assisted Intervention–MICCAI 2006: 9th International Conference, Copenhagen, Denmark, 1–6 October 2006. Proceedings, Part II 9, pp. 807–814. Springer (2006)

HyperMM: Robust Multimodal Learning with Varying-Sized Inputs

Hava Chaptoukaev[1]([✉]), Vincenzo Marcianó[1,2], Francesco Galati[1], and Maria A. Zuluaga[1]

[1] Data Science Department, EURECOM, Biot, France
{chaptouk,marciano,galati,zuluaga}@eurecom.fr
[2] School of Biomedical Engineering and Imaging Sciences, Kings College London, London, UK

Abstract. Combining multiple modalities carrying complementary information through multimodal learning (MML) has shown considerable benefits for diagnosing multiple pathologies. However, the robustness of multimodal models to missing modalities is often overlooked. Most works assume modality completeness in the input data, while in clinical practice, it is common to have incomplete modalities. Existing solutions that address this issue rely on modality imputation strategies before using supervised learning models. These strategies, however, are complex, computationally costly and can strongly impact subsequent prediction models. Hence, they should be used with parsimony in sensitive applications such as healthcare. We propose HyperMM, an end-to-end framework designed for learning with varying-sized inputs. Specifically, we focus on the task of supervised MML with missing imaging modalities without using imputation before training. We introduce a novel strategy for training a *universal* feature extractor using a conditional hypernetwork, and propose a permutation-invariant neural network that can handle inputs of varying dimensions to process the extracted features, in a two-phase *task-agnostic* framework. We experimentally demonstrate the advantages of our method in two tasks: Alzheimer's disease detection and breast cancer classification. We demonstrate that our strategy is robust to high rates of missing data and that its flexibility allows it to handle varying-sized datasets beyond the scenario of missing modalities. We make all our code and experiments available at github.com/robustml-eurecom/hyperMM.

Keywords: Multimodal learning · Missing modalities · Multi-resolution data

1 Introduction

Multimodal imaging techniques are widely used both in clinical practice and medical research. Simultaneous acquisition and analysis of multiple imaging modalities, such as Emission Tomography (PET), Computed Tomography (CT), or Magnetic Resonance Imaging (MRI), has shown to be beneficial in the diagnosis of Alzheimer's disease [24], or detection of cancers [25], among others. Accordingly, deep learning methods designed to learn from multimodal medical images [4,16], and more generally multimodal medical data [22], have seen rapid growth. This development has been favored by the emergence of multimodal learning (MML), a field of machine learning combining modalities from various sources that depict a single subject from multiple views, thus providing both shared and complementary information. MML has shown considerable advantages in multiple domains [1,29]. However, most current models [6,26,28,31,35] assume completeness of the training and testing data, which is rare for real-world datasets. In particular, in routine clinical practice obtaining several modalities for the same subject is not a standard. Incomplete datasets can occur for multitudes of reasons including databases fusion, unavailability of acquisition material, or simply patient refusal to partake in specific examinations. As a result, having varying numbers of modalities per patient is common, which results in multimodal datasets where one or more modalities can be missing. This makes MML challenging as it prevents the straightforward use of the existing methods. Moreso, multimodal models trained on complete datasets become unusable (without complex additional processing steps) if modalities are missing at testing time, which severely restricts their usage to complete samples only. Therefore, the robustness of multimodal models to missing modalities is of paramount importance for the use of MML in real-life applications.

1.1 Related Work

MML aims to build models that process and combine information from multiple sources [1], i.e. multiple modalities. The most prominent way to combine multi-source information resides in fusion methods that can be classified in three categories: early fusion, mid-level fusion, and decision-level fusion of modalities [29]. In practice, summation and averaging are common and straightforward techniques used for fusion. However, when modalities are missing, these operations are impossible for early and mid-level fusion in classical multimodal architectures. They are usually not designed to handle varying-sized inputs and fail to account for missing data.

A vast majority of existing solutions to missing modalities in supervised learning consists of first training a generative model on a complete dataset, and using it to impute missing modalities before learning a discriminative model for prediction [2,10,21,32]. This approach has considerable limitations in practice. First, an unreasonable number of samples may be needed for training a good missing-modality imputation model. For instance, generative adversarial networks (GANs) [8,34], often used for image generation and imputation, can typically require up to 10^6 samples for efficient training [9]. This considerably limits their uses in medical applications where data is often scarce. Second, the complexity of the prediction model strongly depends on the choice of the imputation model. The imputer and predictor networks need to be adapted to each other [11,13], which can be difficult to ensure in practice. Some studies [23,27] address this limitation by focusing on jointly learning the modality imputation and prediction tasks, but these models rely on complex and computationally costly training strategies. Lastly, poorly imputed data can compromise the interpretability of subsequent predictors [18], which is a crucial aspect to consider in sensitive applications, such as healthcare, where it can lead to incorrect conclusions about the impact of a feature on the outcome.

Some recent works have proposed handling missing data without using imputation [3,17,33]. Instead of directly imputing the missing modalities, they replace them with *dummy* inputs, such as a constant or generated data (e.g., zeros or Gaussian noise), and then learn to ignore these during training. In contrast, we propose to learn with varying-sized inputs to avoid model degradation caused by poor imputations or the presence of *dummy* data.

1.2 Contributions

In this work, we address the limitations of existing methods by proposing an end-to-end *imputation-free* strategy for multimodal supervised learning with missing imaging modalities. Building on conditional hypernetworks [5], we formulate a novel strategy for training a *universal* modality-agnostic feature extractor using a large pre-trained network. We then reformulate the problem of predicting multimodal observations with missing modalities as one of predicting *sets* of observations of varying size, thus relaxing the requirement of fixed-dimensional data inputs of most machine learning models. We implement this approach through a permutation-invariant neural network [30], allowing the mid-level fusion of varying-sized multimodal inputs, hence eliminating the need to impute [2,21,32] or mask missing modalities using dummy data [3,17,33] as done in previous works. By combining these elements into a two-step training framework, we formulate HyperMM, a novel *task* and *model agnostic* strategy for MML from incomplete datasets, without the use of imputation or dummy data in the training process. To the best of our knowledge, our work is the first proposing such an approach for multimodal learning with missing modalities.

2 Methodology

2.1 Overview of the Method

We consider a dataset $\mathcal{D}$ of $n \in \mathbb{N}$ independent input and output pairs such that $\mathcal{D} := \{(X_1, Y_2), \ldots, (X_n, Y_n)\}$, and for which the goal is to predict Y given X. Each $X := \{x_1, \ldots, x_d\}$ corresponds to a d-modal observation, where each x_i represents one of the available modalities. Let us now introduce the indicator vector $v \in \{0,1\}^d$ to denote the positions of missing modalities in X, such that $v_i = 1$ if x_i is missing, and 0 otherwise. The observed data of X can be expressed as $X_{obs} = (1-v) \odot X + v \odot \mathbf{na}$, where $\odot$ is the term-by-term product. In this setting, the learning goal becomes the prediction of Y given X_{obs}.

We intend on learning without the use of any form of imputation of missing modalities, and therefore, with entries of different dimensions. However, standard

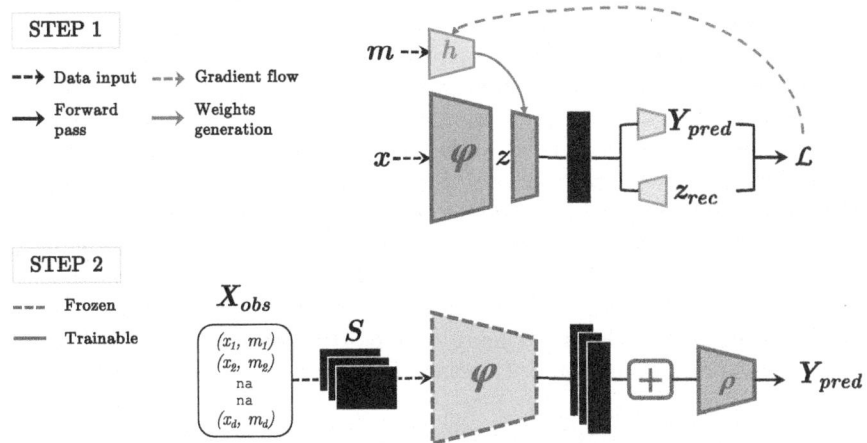

Fig. 1. Overview of our HyperMM framework. A network φ is trained to extract features from any modality in $\mathcal{D}$ by jointly optimizing feature reconstruction and unimodal prediction (step 1). The learned φ is frozen, and used to process multimodal inputs, the latent features are then aggregated and processed through a network ρ for prediction (step 2).

machine learning models, including MML models, are built to handle data inputs of a fixed size. In contrast, we aim to learn a sum-decomposable function f of the form $f = \rho(\sum \varphi(x_i))$, operating on *sets* and thus relaxing the requirement of fixed-dimensional data. We propose a two-step framework that we call HyperMM to implement our method. Figure 1 presents an overview of our strategy. In a first step, we learn a neural network φ that can extract features from any modality present in $\mathcal{D}$. Then in a second step, we freeze the learned φ, use it to encode each element of X_{obs}, and feed the combination of the encoded inputs to a classifier ρ through a permutation-invariant architecture.

2.2 Universal Feature Extractor

A single network φ that can encode all observed modalities in $\mathcal{D}$ is a requirement for learning a set function as described in Sect. 2.1. We propose to achieve this by first learning such a universal feature extractor φ using a conditional hypernetwork [5]. In this first step, we train a network on all available images x in the dataset, without any modality pairing. As illustrated in Fig. 1, we introduce an *auxiliary* network h that takes as input m, the modality identifier corresponding to the image x, and generates conditional weights for the last layer of the encoder φ. By doing so, the last feature extraction step is different for each modality but still performed by the same network. Specifically, modality-specific layers are generated through a common hypernetwork, which facilitates information sharing across modality-specific layers.

In practice, our universal feature extractor φ can be implemented using transfer learning and networks pre-trained on natural images such as VGGs [19]. First, we use the pre-trained encoding layers of a VGG to extract features from our dataset. Then, we adapt the obtained general features into medical ones by training an additional layer on top of the VGG extractor, that is conditioned using the auxiliary network h. By stacking these elements together, we obtain our universal feature extractor φ that is adapted to the modalities of our dataset.

To ensure that the features learned by φ are relevant, the network is trained to both predict y from the single modality images, and reconstruct z, the features outputed by the second-to-last layer of φ. This is achieved by optimising a loss function of the form $\mathcal{L} = \mathcal{L}_{MSE} + \mathcal{L}_{CE}$, where $\mathcal{L}_{MSE}$ denotes the mean squared error between z and z_{rec}, and $\mathcal{L}_{CE}$ the cross-entropy loss between y and y_{pred}. This optimisation loss has been chosen by cross-validation, as it yielded better performances than optimising on the classification or reconstruction only.

2.3 Permutation Invariant Architecture

Once we have learned φ, we freeze it, and use it to implement a permutation invariant network for supervised MML with missing modalities. To do so, we define S, the set representation of the $q = |S|$ observed elements of X_{obs}, such that $S := \{s_1, \ldots, s_q\}$, with $q \leq d$. Each element s_j is represented as a tuple (x_i, m_i) consisting of an observed modality x_i, and the corresponding modality identifier m_i. This reformulation allows observations of varying dimensions. Thereby, it does not require nor expects all observations to have the same number of elements and it fully allows observations with missing modalities. A d-modal observation X_{obs} containing **na** values can simply be expressed as a set S of size $q \leq d$ where the **na** values are not represented anymore.

Using this definition, we leverage on the findings of [30], who proposed a learning framework that considers permutation invariant functions operating over sets. We reformulate our learning goal as one of learning a set function f of the form

$$f(X_{obs}) = \rho\left(\sum_{s_k \in S} \varphi(s_k)\right), \qquad (1)$$

where the function $\varphi : \mathbb{R} \times \{r \times r\}^d \to \mathbb{R}^{d_l}$ corresponds the encoder obtained from the pre-training phase, the function $\rho : \mathbb{R}^{d_l} \to \mathbb{R}$ is implemented as neural network, r is the size of each image and $d_l \in \mathbb{N}^+$ is the dimensionality of the latent space of φ.

As illustrated in Fig. 1, a given observation X_{obs} with missing modalities is encoded as a set S. Each element $s_k \in S$ is then transformed into a representation $\varphi(s_k) := \varphi(x_i|m_i)$ through the frozen network φ conditioned by the modality identifier m. The representations $\varphi(s_k)$ are aggregated using a permutation invariant operation such as the sum, the mean or the maximum. The aggregation is processed through the network ρ, which allows to predict the target Y corresponding to the input X_{obs}. The proposed architecture interprets each observation S of a dataset as a set of unordered modalities, where all information available in X_{obs} is conserved and no new information, such as imputed images, is added. By transforming individual elements s_k of S at a time and then aggregating the transformations, our network encodes sets of arbitrary sizes into a fixed representation $\sum \varphi(s_k)$. This aspect is particularly relevant and further justifies handling our dataset with missing modalities as unordered sets.

Our permutation invariant model is learned by optimising the loss function

$$\mathcal{L}(\theta) := \mathbb{E}_{(S,Y) \in \mathcal{D}} \left[\ell \left(Y, \rho_\theta \left(\sum_{s_k \in S} \varphi(s_k) \right) \right) \right], \tag{2}$$

where ρ is parametrised by θ, and ℓ is the cross-entropy loss. As φ is optimised in the pre-training step, its weights are not updated in this step.

3 Experiments

3.1 Alzheimer's Disease Detection

In a first application, we illustrate the performances of HyperMM and its robustness to missing modalities on the task of binary classification of Alzheimer's disease (AD) using multimodal images from the ADNI dataset [15]. We select a subset of 300 patients for which both T1-weighted MRIs and FDG-PET images are available, resulting in 165 cognitively normal (CN) and 135 AD observations. Before learning, all the samples are skull stripped using HD-BET [7], resampled through bicubic interpolation to set an uniform voxel size, standardised, and normalised using min-max scaling.

Baselines. We first evaluate the advantages of our strategy for MML with complete data. We compare the performances of HyperMM against: **Uni-CNN**, an unimodal CNN as implemented by [12]; **Multi-CNN**, a multimodal CNN as proposed by [26]; and **Multi-VAE**, a multimodal VAE [28] that we adapt for classification. Then, we compare our method against state-of-the-art techniques for MML with missing modalities in two scenarios: complete MRIs +50% of PETs available for training and testing, and complete PETs +50% of MRIs available. Specifically we compare to: **pix2pix**, a strategy where an image-to-image translation model [8] is trained on the subset of the training data containing only modality-complete samples, is then used to impute the missing modality of the incomplete data, and once imputed the data is classified using a Multi-CNN; and **cycleGAN**, the same strategy, only using a cycleGAN [34] for imputation.

Implementation Details. We randomly split the data into train, validation and test sets with a 6:1:3 ratio on the patient-level, and repeat all experiments 3 times. For simplicity and fairness, we use the same feature extraction strategy (Fig. 2) in all baselines, following [12]. Specifically, 3D MRI and PET images are processed as batches of 2D slices that are each fed to a pre-trained frozen VGG11 [19] feature extractor. We feed all 2D slices of a 3D volume to the VGG, and apply a 1D max pooling on the slice dimension to the resulting feature blocks to obtain a single block per 3D image. The resulting block is passed through a 1×1 convolution layer after the pre-trained VGG encoder, allowing us to adapt the pre-trained features into AD-specific ones. This corresponds to the training

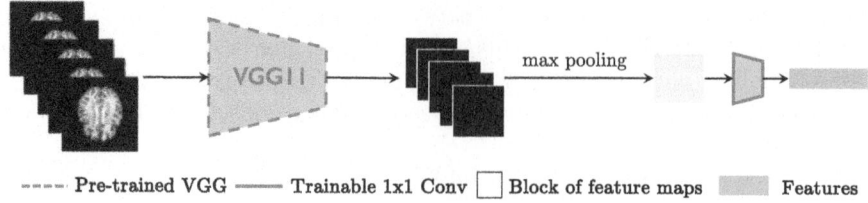

Fig. 2. Feature extraction strategy used in the ADNI baselines (see [12]). All 2D slices of one 3D volume are fed to a VGG11. A 1D max pooling on the slice dimension is applied to the resulting feature blocks to obtain a single block per 3D image. The latter is passed through a 1×1 convolution layer to obtain AD-specific features that can then be fed to a classifier.

Table 1. Performances (mean ± std) on the ADNI dataset. **Bold** means best.

	Acc. (↑)	AUC (↑)	F1 (↑)	Prec. (↑)	Rec. (↑)	Time (↓)
Complete unimodal						
Uni-CNN PET	0.61 ± .05	0.58 ± .05	0.58 ± .06	0.65 ± .06	0.31 ± .05	< 20 min
Uni-CNN MRI	0.71 ± .02	0.69 ± .02	0.58 ± .02	**0.85 ± .03**	0.43 ± .05	< 20 min
Complete multimodal						
Multi-VAE classifier	0.66 ± .03	0.65 ± .03	0.54 ± .04	0.74 ± .04	0.41 ± .03	< 30 min
Multi-CNN	0.70 ± .02	0.70 ± .01	0.67 ± .01	0.67 ± .02	0.68 ± .02	< 30 min
HyperMM w/o 2-steps (ours)	0.62 ± .03	0.61 ± .02	0.53 ± .02	0.61 ± .03	0.46 ± .03	< 20 min
HyperMM w/ 2-steps (ours)	**0.74 ± .02**	**0.73 ± .02**	**0.70 ± .01**	0.70 ± .02	**0.70 ± .02**	< 1 h
100% MRI + 50% PET						
pix2pix	0.65 ± .02	0.64 ± .02	**0.62 ± .02**	**0.62 ± .03**	**0.61 ± .02**	> 14+1 h
cycleGAN	0.62 ± .09	0.60 ± .07	0.57 ± .07	0.61 ± .08	0.54 ± .08	> 30+1 h
HyperMM (ours)	**0.67 ± .02**	**0.66 ± .02**	0.61 ± .03	0.61 ± .03	0.61 ± .03	< 1 h
100% PET + 50% MRI						
pix2pix	0.62 ± .04	0.62 ± .03	0.53 ± .03	0.61 ± .05	0.48 ± .05	> 14+1 h
cycleGAN	0.62 ± .09	0.59 ± .1	0.47 ± .07	0.60 ± .07	0.39 ± .07	> 30+1 h
HyperMM (ours)	**0.64 ± .02**	**0.63 ± .02**	**0.61 ± .02**	**0.61 ± .03**	**0.61 ± .03**	< 1 h

of the φ network in the step 1 of our framework, where we simply make the last 1×1 convolution layer conditional. In step 2, the ρ network is implemented by 3 linears layers separated by ReLU activations. All models are implemented with PyTorch, and trained on an Nvidia TITAN Xp GPU for a maximum of 100 epochs using an early stopping strategy, where training stops after 10 iterations without a decrease in the validation loss. We use a batch size of 1 and an Adam optimiser with an initial learning rate of 1e−4.

Results. Performances of all models are reported in Table 1. Several observations can be drawn from these results. First, MML shows considerable improvements over unimodal baselines. In particular, HyperMM achieves the best performances for binary classification of AD using complete multimodal data and considerably improves the F1-score, recall metric, and precision/recall balance.

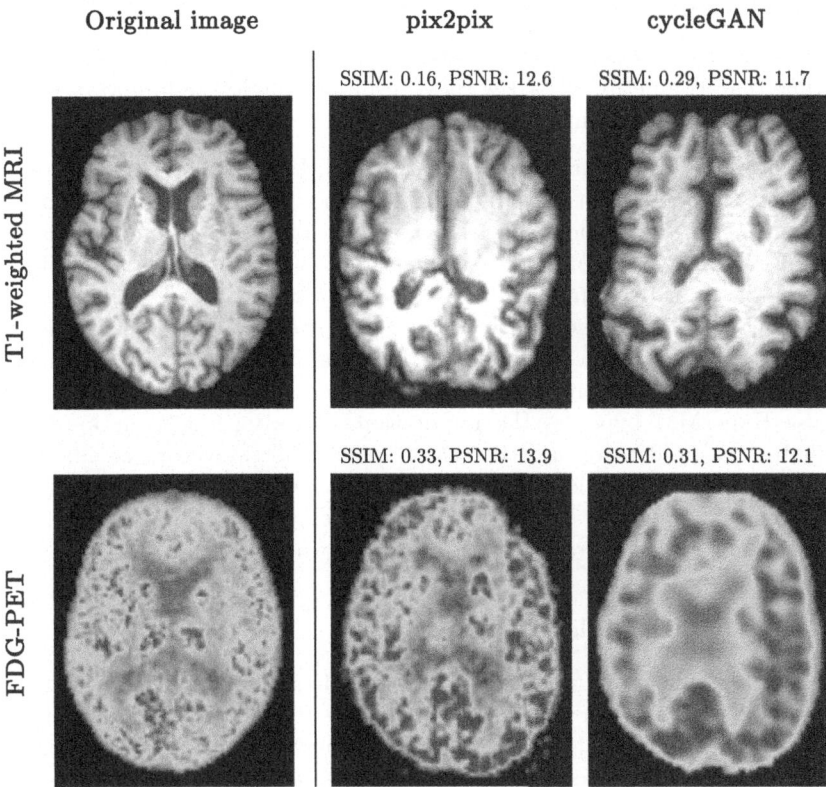

Fig. 3. Examples of real and imputed slices of MRI and PET images for one patient. While the PET reconstructions (bottom right) translated from the corresponding MRI (top left) are reasonably similar to the original PET image (bottom left), the MRI reconstructions (top right) translated from the low-resolution PET (bottom left) are much less consistent with reality (top left).

Second, MML with missing modalities still achieves better results than unimodal models. Notably, HyperMM trained on MRIs available even for only 50% of the patients performs better than an unimodal model trained on PETs only. Inversely, having access to PETs for 50% of the patients improves the F1-score and recall of learning from MRIs only. Third, HyperMM outperforms state-of-the-art strategies on MML with missing modalities. While GAN-based strategies can handle missing PETs in the input data, they are considerably less efficient in terms of precision/recall balance when the missing modality is MRI. In this scenario, the missing high-resolution MRIs need to be translated from the available low-resolution PETs before learning. This limitation is further illustrated in Fig. 3. While PET imputation yields realistic images, the imputed MRIs are of poor quality: they suffer from important structural deformations and a great loss of information (as highlighted by the SSIM and PSNR scores between the imputations and the original images). In contrast, as HyperMM does not rely on any imputation, it performs well in both scenarios, and trains in significantly less time than competitors. Lastly, these results highlight the importance of the pre-training and conditioning step of the HyperMM framework.

Discussion. The results illustrate how HyperMM tackles the main limitations of existing methods. First, as our model does not require training an imputation model prior to prediction, it does not call for the large amounts of data typically required for training GANs efficiently. The results observed in Table 1 highlight the poor performances of cycleGAN for translating PETs into MRIs, which could be due to insufficient training data. Second, our model is agnostic to the missing modality, whereas the prediction and imputation quality in other approaches strongly depends on it, as highlighted by our experiments. Indeed, because HyperMM bypasses the imputation step altogether, our approaches eliminates the need to ensure that the imputer and predictor are adapted to each other. This, in turn, leads to drastically reduced computing time and learning complexity. Lastly, as our method does not employ any imputed or dummy data, it avoids model degradation caused by poor imputations or noisy data.

3.2 Breast Cancer Classification

In a second application, we demonstrate the flexibility of HyperMM and its benefits for learning with varying-sized datasets, beyond the scenario of missing modalities. We investigate the usage of HyperMM for the slightly different task of analysing multi-resolution histopathological images. Because potential tumors are typically acquired at multiple magnification levels, the numbers of samples per patients in histopathology datasets are often highly varying. We perform binary classification of breast cancer using histopathological images from the BreaKHis dataset [20]. BreaKHis contains multiple images per sample (i.e. patient) of benign or malignant tumors observed through different microscopic magnifications: 40×, 110×, 200×, and 400×. We select a balanced subset of the data composed of samples of 24 benign and 29 malignant tumors, resulting in 5,575 images in total. We use the images as they are for learning, and do not perform any pre-processing or data augmentation.

In clinical practice, pathologists combine the complimentary information present in images captured under different magnifications in order to make a patient-level decision. Nonetheless, most current learning approaches consist of magnification-specific models, due to the difficulty of processing images of different natures with a single model. Moreover, because the number of available images can vary a lot from one patient to another, traditional algorithms cannot be applied at the patient-level. Existing methods rather predict from individual images, and later combine the predictions in order to form a global decision. Instead, we propose to tackle this problem using HyperMM, conditioning the universal feature extractor on the different magnification levels. We classify tumors at patient-level by combining all available images during training directly.

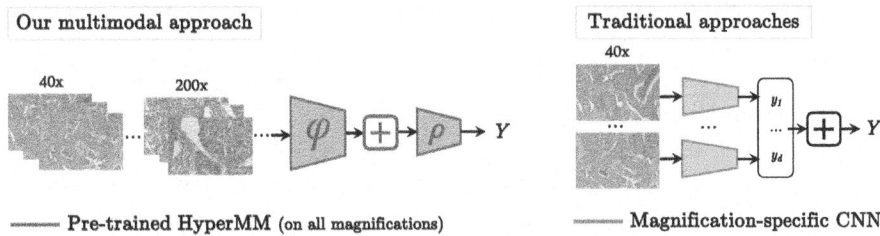

Fig. 4. Comparison of decision strategies for patient-level tumor classification. Our method (left) enables the combination of a subject's available images during training, regardless of the magnification level to obtain a patient-level decision. In opposition, traditional approaches (right) make prediction on the image-level, and combine the final predictions to obtain a patient-level decision.

Baselines. We evaluate the benefits of HyperMM for learning from histopathology data, and compare its performances with: **CNN**, where a magnification-specific CNN is trained to classify tumor types from individual images, and patient-level prediction is obtained by averaging the classification scores of individual images [20]; and **Incremental-CNN**, in which a magnification-agnostic CNN is trained by incrementally updating its weights on successive batches of $40\times, 100\times, 200\times$ then $400\times$ magnifications, as proposed in [14]. The patient-level decision is obtained similarly to the previous baseline. The differences between our approach and traditional ones are further illustrated in Fig. 4.

Implementation Details. We randomly split the data into train and test sets with a 8:2 ratio at the patient-level, and repeated all experiments 5 times. We use a pre-trained VGG11 [19] feature extractor for all baselines, and adapted the features to our application by adding a 1×1 convolution block on top of the frozen VGG encoder. All models are trained for a maximum of 50 epochs using an early stopping strategy such that training stops after 10 iterations without a decrease in the validation loss. We train the model with an Adam optimiser with an initial learning rate of 1e−4. We use a batch size of 16 for image-level baselines (i.e. CNN and Incremental-CNN) and 1 for HyperMM.

Results. All performances averaged over 5 repetitions are reported in Table 2. They underline the clear benefits of HyperMM for cancer classification from histopathological images. In particular, our method outperforms magnification-specific models, and is closely followed by Incremental-CNN, which highlights the benefits of combining the information carried by different magnifications. Moreover, while Incremental-CNN maximises the recall score of the task, HyperMM maximises precision, and overall improves upon Incremental-CNN. This shows that learning to predict an early latent combination of features (i.e. combining multiple images of a same patient during model training directly) yields better performances than combining predictions made on individual images.

Discussion. While the analysis of multi-resolution images is not a multimodal application by definition, our method is designed to enable mid-level fusion of

Table 2. Performances (mean ± std) on the BreaKHis dataset. **Bold** means best.

	Acc. (↑)	AUC (↑)	F1 (↑)	Prec. (↑)	Rec. (↑)
Magnification-specific					
CNN 40×	0.83 ± 0.07	0.81 ± 0.07	0.83 ± 0.06	0.85 ± 0.08	0.83 ± 0.08
CNN 100×	0.85 ± 0.08	0.85 ± 0.08	0.87 ± 0.06	0.85 ± 0.07	0.90 ± 0.07
CNN 200×	0.84 ± 0.07	0.84 ± 0.09	0.84 ± 0.05	0.80 ± 0.11	0.90 ± 0.09
CNN 400×	0.83 ± 0.09	0.83 ± 0.09	0.85 ± 0.10	0.88 ± 0.11	0.83 ± 0.15
Magnification-agnostic					
Incremental-CNN	0.89 ± 0.11	0.88 ± 0.12	0.90 ± 0.10	0.88 ± 0.12	**0.93 ± 0.09**
HyperMM (ours)	**0.92 ± 0.06**	**0.91 ± 0.07**	**0.90 ± 0.08**	**0.94 ± 0.09**	0.88 ± 0.10

latent features of varying-sized inputs, and is therefore adapted for this use case. Because of the varying number of images per patient in histopathology datasets, traditional approaches are not equiped to combine multiple resolutions directly during training to make patient-level decisions, and instead rely on the late fusion of image-level decisions. In contrast, HyperMM offers this possibility. It opens a new and different way to classify cancer patients. Moreso, our experiments suggest that mid-level fusion even considerably improves the performances of existing late fusion models.

4 Conclusion

We have demonstrated the advantages of HyperMM for robust MML with missing modalities: our method eliminates the need to use complex and computationally costly imputation strategies, thus significantly decreasing model training time; and unlike competitors, its performances are not dependant on which modality is missing in the data. In particular, unlike imputation-based methods, our approach is end-to-end: HyperMM eliminates the time-consuming steps of manually imputing the missing modalities using a previously trained imputation model, before finally training a prediction model. On the contrary, our two-step model is trained without interruption or human intervention. Moreover, by only utilising the observed images of the incomplete dataset, HyperMM avoids prediction bias caused by poor imputation or the presence or generated dummy data. In addition, we have shown that the flexibility of HyperMM alleviates the constraints usually met in applications with varying-sized datasets and opens up a whole new range of possible learning strategies. Our framework is *task-agnostic*, and can be easily used beyond the two applications we have presented. For instance, it could be extended to multivariate time series analysis, where incomplete data is common (e.g. damaged channels in EEG recordings). Moreover, while we used pre-trained feature extractors in all our experiments for simplicity, HyperMM is *model-agnostic* and adaptable to any neural network-based feature extractor or predictor.

Acknowledgments. This work has been supported by the French government, through the 3IA Côte d'Azur Investments in the Future project managed by the National Research Agency (ANR) (ANR-19- P3IA-0002) and by TRAIN (ANR-22-FAI1-0003-02).

References

1. Baltrušaitis, T., Ahuja, C., Morency, L.-P.: Multimodal machine learning: a survey and taxonomy. IEEE Trans. Pattern Anal. Mach. Intell. **41**(2), 423–443 (2018)
2. Cai, L., Wang, Z., Gao, H., Shen, D., Ji, S.: Deep adversarial learning for multimodality missing data completion. In: Proceedings of the 24th ACM SIGKDD International Conference on Knowledge Discovery & Data Mining, pp. 1158–1166 (2018)
3. Chen, B., Oliva, J., Niethammer, M.: A unified model for longitudinal multi-modal multi-view prediction with missingness. arXiv preprint arXiv:2403.12211 (2024)
4. Fu, X., Bi, L., Kumar, A., Fulham, M., Kim, J.: Multimodal spatial attention module for targeting multimodal PET-CT lung tumor segmentation. IEEE J. Biomed. Health Inform. **25**(9), 3507–3516 (2021)
5. Ha, D., Dai, A.M., Le, Q.V.: Hypernetworks. CoRR (2016)
6. Huang, Y., Xu, J., Zhou, Y., Tong, T., Zhuang, X., Alzheimer's Disease Neuroimaging Initiative (ADNI). Diagnosis of Alzheimer's disease via multi-modality 3D convolutional neural network. Front. Neurosci. **13**, 509 (2019)
7. Isensee, F., et al.: Automated brain extraction of multisequence MRI using artificial neural networks. Hum. Brain Mapp. **40**(17), 4952–4964 (2019)
8. Isola, P., Zhu, J.Y., Zhou, T., Efros, A.A.: Image-to-image translation with conditional adversarial networks. In: Proceedings of the IEEE Conference on Computer Vision and Pattern Recognition, pp. 1125–1134 (2017)
9. Karras, T., Aittala, M., Hellsten, J., Laine, S., Lehtinen, J., Aila, T.: Training generative adversarial networks with limited data. Adv. Neural. Inf. Process. Syst. **33**, 12104–12114 (2020)
10. Kim, J.-C., Chung, K.: Multi-modal stacked denoising autoencoder for handling missing data in healthcare big data. IEEE Access **8**, 104933–104943 (2020)
11. Le Morvan, M., Josse, J., Scornet, E., Varoquaux, G.: What's a good imputation to predict with missing values? Adv. Neural. Inf. Process. Syst. **34**, 11530–11540 (2021)
12. Liang, G., et al.: Alzheimer's disease classification using 2D convolutional neural networks. In: 43rd Annual International Conference of the IEEE Engineering in Medicine & Biology Society (EMBC), pp. 3008–3012 (2021)
13. Lu, Z.: A theory of multimodal learning. In: Advances in Neural Information Processing Systems, vol. 36 (2024)
14. Mayouf, M.S., Dupin de Saint-Cyr, F.: Curriculum incremental deep learning on breakhis dataset. In: Proceedings of the 2022 8th International Conference on Computer Technology Applications, pp. 35–41 (2022)
15. Mueller, S.G., et al.: Ways toward an early diagnosis in Alzheimer's disease: the Alzheimer's disease neuroimaging initiative (ADNI). Alzheimer's Dementia **1**(1), 55–66 (2005)
16. Odusami, M., Maskeliūnas, R., Damaševičius, R., Misra, S.: Machine learning with multimodal neuroimaging data to classify stages of Alzheimer's disease: a systematic review and meta-analysis. Cogn. Neurodyn. 1–20 (2023)

17. Parthasarathy, S., Sundaram, S.: Training strategies to handle missing modalities for audio-visual expression recognition. In: Companion Publication of the 2020 International Conference on Multimodal Interaction, pp. 400–404 (2020)
18. Shadbahr, T., et al.: The impact of imputation quality on machine learning classifiers for datasets with missing values. Commun. Med. **3**(1), 139 (2023)
19. Simonyan, K., Zisserman, A.: Very deep convolutional networks for large-scale image recognition. arXiv preprint arXiv:1409.1556 (2014)
20. Spanhol, F.A., Oliveira, L.S., Petitjean, C., Heutte, L.: A dataset for breast cancer histopathological image classification. IEEE Trans. Biomed. Eng. **63**(7), 1455–1462 (2015)
21. Sun, W., Ma, F., Li, Y., Huang, S.L., Ni, S., Zhang, L.: Semi-supervised multimodal image translation for missing modality imputation. In: ICASSP 2021-2021 IEEE International Conference on Acoustics, Speech and Signal Processing (ICASSP), pp. 4320–4324 (2021)
22. Sun, Z., et al.: A scoping review on multimodal deep learning in biomedical images and texts. J. Biomed. Inform. 104482 (2023)
23. Suo, Q., Zhong, W., Ma, F., Yuan, Y., Gao, J., Zhang, A.: Metric learning on healthcare data with incomplete modalities. In: IJCAI, vol. 3534, p. 3540 (2019)
24. Teipel, S., et al.: Multimodal imaging in Alzheimer's disease: validity and usefulness for early detection. Lancet Neurol. **14**(10), 1037–1053 (2015)
25. Tempany, C.M., et al.: Multimodal imaging for improved diagnosis and treatment of cancers. Cancer **121**(6), 817–827 (2015)
26. Venugopalan, J., Tong, L., Hassanzadeh, H.R., Wang, M.D.: Multimodal deep learning models for early detection of Alzheimer's disease stage. Sci. Rep. **11**(1), 3254 (2021)
27. Wang, H., Chen, Y., Ma, C., Avery, J., Hull, L., Carneiro, G.: Multi-modal learning with missing modality via shared-specific feature modelling. In: Proceedings of the IEEE/CVF Conference on Computer Vision and Pattern Recognition, pp. 15878–15887 (2023)
28. Wu, M., Goodman, N.: Multimodal generative models for scalable weakly-supervised learning. In: Advances in Neural Information Processing Systems, vol. 31 (2018)
29. Xu, P., Zhu, X., Clifton, D.A.: Multimodal learning with transformers: a survey. IEEE Trans. Pattern Anal. Mach. Intell. **45**(10), 12113–12132 (2023)
30. Zaheer, M., Kottur, S., Ravanbakhsh, S., Poczos, B., Salakhutdinov, R.R., Smola, A.J.: Deep sets. In: Advances in Neural Information Processing Systems, vol. 30 (2017)
31. Zhang, T., Shi, M.: Multi-modal neuroimaging feature fusion for diagnosis of Alzheimer's disease. J. Neurosci. Methods **341**, 108795 (2020)
32. Zhang, Y., Peng, C., Wang, Q., Song, D., Li, K., Zhou, S.K.: Unified multi-modal image synthesis for missing modality imputation. arXiv preprint arXiv:2304.05340 (2023)
33. Zhou, Q., Zou, H., Jiang, H., Wang, Y.: Incomplete multimodal learning for visual acuity prediction after cataract surgery using masked self-attention. In: International Conference on Medical Image Computing and Computer-Assisted Intervention, pp. 735–744. Springer, Cham (2023)

34. Zhu, J.-Y., Park, T., Isola, P., Efros, A.A.: Unpaired image-to-image translation using cycle-consistent adversarial networks. In: Proceedings of the IEEE International Conference on Computer Vision, pp. 2223–2232 (2017)
35. Zuo, Q., Lei, B., Shen, Y., Liu, Y., Feng, Z., Wang, S.: Multimodal representations learning and adversarial hypergraph fusion for early Alzheimer's disease prediction. In: Ma, H., et al. (eds.) PRCV 2021. LNCS, vol. 13021, pp. 479–490. Springer, Cham (2021). https://doi.org/10.1007/978-3-030-88010-1_40

HEMIT: H&E to Multiplex-Immunohistochemistry Image Translation with Dual-Branch Pix2pix Generator

Chang Bian[1(✉)], Beth Phillips[2], Tim Cootes[1], and Martin Fergie[1]

[1] Division of Informatics, Imaging and Data Sciences, School of Health Sciences, University of Manchester, Manchester, UK
chang.bian@postgrad.manchester.ac.uk
[2] Division of Cancer Sciences, University of Manchester, Manchester, UK

Abstract. Computational analysis of multiplexed immunofluorescence histology data is emerging as an important method for understanding the tumour micro-environment in cancer. This work presents HEMIT, a dataset designed for translating Hematoxylin and Eosin (H&E) sections to multiplex-immunohistochemistry (mIHC) images, simultaneously featuring DAPI, CD3, and panCK markers. Distinctively, HEMIT's mIHC images are multi-component and cellular-level aligned with H&E, enriching supervised stain translation tasks. To our knowledge, HEMIT is the first publicly available cellular-level aligned dataset that enables H&E to multi-target mIHC image translation. This dataset provides the computer vision community with a valuable resource to develop novel computational methods which have the potential to gain new insights from H&E slide archives.

We also propose a new dual-branch generator architecture combining residual Convolutional Neural Networks (CNNs) and Swin Transformers, with a feature map fusion module to integrate information from both branches. This architecture achieves superior translation outcomes compared to other popular algorithms. Evaluations on the HEMIT dataset show it outperforms pix2pixHD, pix2pix, U-Net, and ResNet, with the highest scores in Structural Similarity Index Measure (SSIM), Pearson correlation (R), and Peak Signal-to-Noise Ratio (PSNR). Additionally, we discuss the limitations of commonly used metrics in certain stain translation scenarios and provide recommendations for future use. Additionally, we also designed a downstream analysis to further validate the quality and utility of the generated mIHC images from a clinical-focused perspective. These results set a new benchmark in the field of stain translation tasks.

The proposed dataset can be accessed at: https://github.com/BianChang/HEMIT-DATASET.

Supplementary Information The online version contains supplementary material available at https://doi.org/10.1007/978-3-031-84525-3_16.

Keywords: HEMIT dataset · Hematoxylin and Eosin (H&E) · Multiplex-immunohistochemistry (mIHC) · stain translation · Swin Transformers · Downstream analysis

1 Introduction

Multiplex immunohistochemistry/immunofluorescence (mIHC/IF) technologies have revolutionized the study of the tumor microenvironment (TME), providing critical insights for cancer research and immunotherapy [1,3,28,29,31]. These technologies enable the detection of multiple markers in a single tissue slice, revealing intricate spatial interactions. However, the complexity and cost of mIHC limits its accessibility [27]. Deep learning offers a promising solution to these challenges, with recent advancements in stain translation and virtual staining allowing for better exploitation of existing H&E slides [4,5,7,9,12,23,24,32].

Capitalizing on the ease and cost-efficiency of producing H&E images, this paper aims to develop an image-to-image translation method that can convert H&E images into their corresponding mIHC counterparts.

Image-to-image translation algorithms are well-established across a range of image analysis domains. Specifically, pix2pix [11] employs a conditional generative adversarial network (cGAN) approach for paired images, adeptly generating high-fidelity translations. Building upon this, pix2pixHD [30] has demonstrated significant outcomes with high-resolution paired images. Notably, a recent study [16] introduced a multi-scale loss term, improving the translation performance for HER2 images. Furthermore, other methods [13,15,21] have been designed specifically for image-to-image translation tasks, underscoring the breadth and depth of research in this domain.

High-quality datasets are essential for effective supervised image translation, yet the realm of pathological image translation lacks comprehensive resources. The BCI dataset [16] is proposed for H&E to HER2 IHC image translation. However, it is limited in use as staining is performed on consecutive tissue sections so there is no cell-to-cell mapping across stains. Further, it is limited to one target stain (HER2) unlike mIHC where multiple stains can be predicted simultaneously. In response, we present HEMIT: A dataset for H&E to mIHC Translation. This is the first publicly-available cellular-level aligned dataset for stain translation. Concurrently, we propose a specialized method tailored for this task which we compare to various state-of-the-art image translation algorithms. This work makes the following contributions:

1. Introduction of HEMIT: a paired dataset for H&E to mIHC image translation. To the best of our knowledge, HEMIT is the first publicly available cellular-level aligned dataset that enables H&E to multi-target mIHC image translation.
2. Development of a SwinTransformer-CNN-based dual-branch pix2pix strategy to convert H&E images into mIHC versions. Our methodology assimilates both global information and spatial details, culminating in superior outcomes, setting benchmark results for the proposed dataset.

3. A thorough empirical evaluation was conducted on the newly introduced HEMIT dataset, setting a benchmark for future investigations within the research community. We also discussed on the limitations of commonly used metrics in certain scenarios of stain translation. This discussion provides insights into the appropriateness and applicability of these metrics for different use cases.
4. Further downstream analysis from clinical focused perspective, employing QuPath [2], substantiated the quality and utility of the images produced. This establishes a solid foundation for subsequent studies and applications, encouraging a deeper exploration into the dataset's potential.

2 HEMIT Dataset

We present HEMIT: A cellular-level aligned dataset for H&E to mIHC Image Translation. A schematic of our dataset's construction pipeline is provided in Fig. 1a. The proposed dataset can be accessed at: https://github.com/BianChang/HEMIT-DATASET.

2.1 Data Collection

HEMIT's raw data is sourced from ImmunoAIzer [6] which we have adapted to make it suitable for the computer vision community. Notably, HEMIT distinguishes itself from other datasets: the H&E and mIHC slide pairs are derived from the identical tissue section, not consecutive slides. Consecutive slides often suffer from misalignment and variations in tissue morphology due to differences in the depths at which sectioning happens. This may affect the network's ability to learn accurate feature mappings between H&E and mIHC stains. This misalignment leads to errors in translating the stains, which can degrade the model's performance and reliability in medical imaging applications. Examples of this misalignment are shown in Fig. 2(b) using examples of existing datasets that rely on consecutive sections [14,16]. The tissue of HEMIT was first stained with mIHC protocols and then bleached before the H&E staining. This feature leads to higher fidelity and alignment between the matched image pairs and better translation outcomes [8]. Example images demonstrating accurate pixel-level alignment of the HEMIT dataset and given in Fig. 2(a).

In the mIHC images, three pivotal cell type identification markers are incorporated: DAPI to signify cell nuclei, pan-cytokeratin (panCK) to highlight tumor regions, and CD3 to pinpoint T cells-all of which are integral to TME analysis. These specific markers serve as the foundation for our H&E to mIHC stain translation benchmark. We have collated a selection of publicly available datasets that leverage H&E images for predicting IHC expressions. A comparative overview of their characteristics is presented in Table 1.

Table 1. Summary of publicly available datasets

Datasets	Staining Types	Sectioning Approach	IHC/mIHC Markers	Ground Truths
HEMIT	H&E & mIHC	same slide	DAPI, CD3, panCK	cellular level
BCI [16]	H&E & IHC	consecutive slides	HER2	structural level
HEROHE [10]	H&E	H&E only	Clinical HER2 status	slide level
MIST [14]	H&E & IHC	consecutive slides	HER2, Ki67, PR, ER	structural level

2.2 Data Preprocessing

Despite both H&E and mIHC staining being performed on the same tissue slide, the re-staining and scanning processes mean that the captured images do not align perfectly. We employ a 2-step registration process to ensure cellular-wise alignment of the image pairs which is crucial for optimal training performance. All registration steps are conducted under 40 times magnification. Implementation details of the registration process are given in the supplementary material.

Upon concluding the registration, a margin of 50 pixels from each edge is trimmed to account for rotational transformations, following methods established in previous work [24]. Subsequently, the block pairs are cropped into 1024 × 1024 patches, maintaining a 50% overlap. Color normalization [20] is then applied to all H&E patches to mitigate stain variations. Visualizations of the final registered image pairs are shown in Fig. 2a. This process resulted in 5292 matched image patch pairs. This processed data is distributed into three partitions: *training*, *validation*, and *testing*. The division yields 3717 patches designated for training, 630 for validation, and 945 for the testing phase. Importantly, to prevent data leakage of our evaluation, patches across these subsets are derived from unique patient samples, precluding potential data overlap.

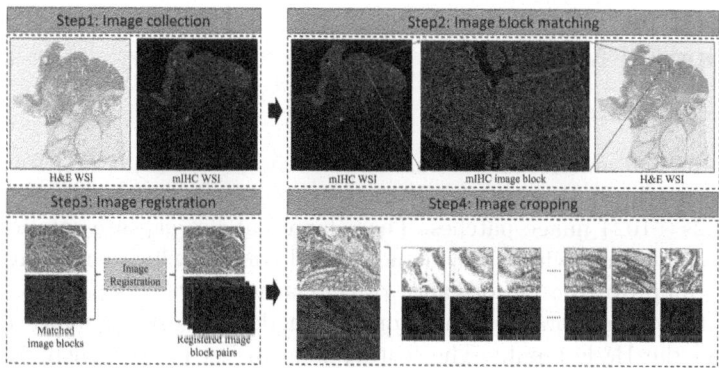

Fig. 1. Overview of dataset processing pipeline of the HEMIT dataset.

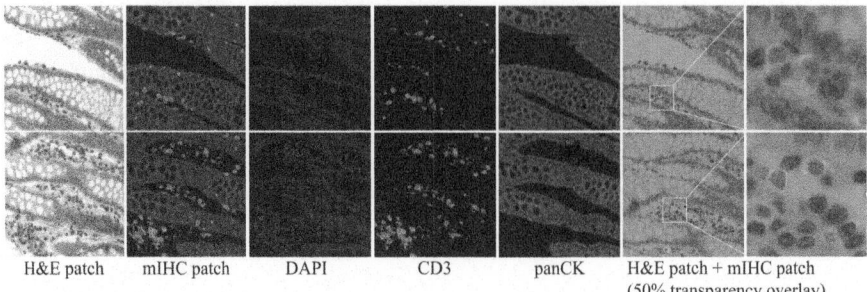

H&E patch mIHC patch DAPI CD3 panCK H&E patch + mIHC patch
(50% transparency overlay)

(a) Visualization of registered HEMIT image pairs and their constituent channels.

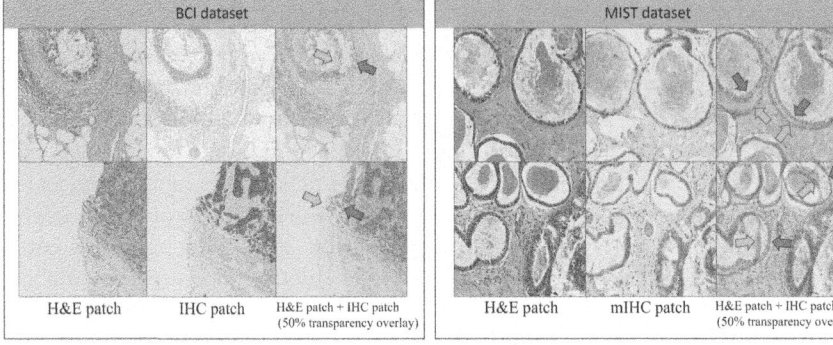

BCI dataset — H&E patch, IHC patch, H&E patch + IHC patch (50% transparency overlay)
MIST dataset — H&E patch, mIHC patch, H&E patch + IHC patch (50% transparency overlay)

(b) Visualization of misaligned image pairs from consecutive sectioning datasets.

Fig. 2. Alignment comparison of HEMIT and other datasets: (a) Visualization of registered image pairs of HEMIT dataset. (b) Visualization of the misaligned image pairs in BCI dataset [16] and MIST [14] dataset which used consecutive sectioning. Yellow arrows point to the edges of tissues in HER2 IHC images, and blue arrows point to the edges of tissues in H&E images to enhance visualization of the misalignment. (Color figure online)

3 Proposed Method

3.1 Architecture

Our dual-branch architecture is based on the original pix2pix [11] framework, designed with the motivation to fully leverage the detailed information contained within 1024×1024 image patches. These large patches capture comprehensive tissue compartments which provide additional context which has been demonstrated to improve the performance of cellular-level prediction tasks [26]. By incorporating a dual-branch generator, our model can extract multi-scale features from the H&E inputs. The feature map fusion module then adaptively integrates the information from the 2 branches to boost translation performance. The overall framework is shown in Fig. 3.

We developed a dual-branch generator architecture. The main branch with residual blocks of the generator is to extract spatial nuances from the input H&E

images, and an auxiliary branch powered by Swin Transformer block [18] is incorporated to integrate information across multiple scales. The features extracted by each stage of the Swin Transformer branch are fused with the feature maps of the CNN branch by the Feature Map Fusion (FMF) module. This architecture caters to the multi-scale nature of pathological images. This design captures information from the structure of individual cells to the interaction of cell clusters, vital for interpreting complex tissue environments.

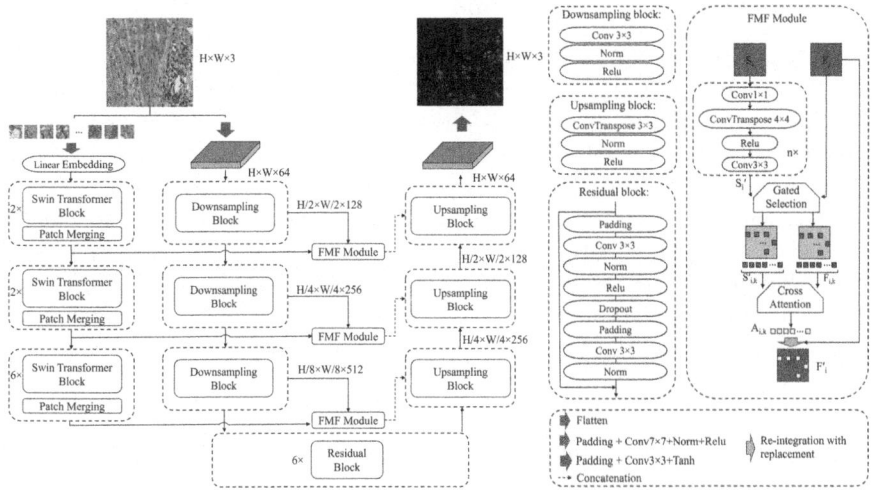

Fig. 3. Overall structure of the proposed generator.

3.2 Swin Transformer-Based Auxiliary Branch

The auxiliary branch, operating in parallel with the main branch, leverages Swin Transformer modules [18] to adeptly capture multi-scale features. Notably, the Swin Transformer introduces both Window-based Multi-head Self Attention (W-MSA) and Shifted Window-based MSA (SW-MSA). Prior to each MSA module and MLP, a Layer Normalization (LN) is applied. $\hat{s}_l$ and s_l denote the outputs of W-MSA and MLP respectively, at the lth layer. These are computed as:

$$\hat{s}_l = \text{W-MSA}(\text{LN}(s_{l-1})) + s_{l-1}; s_l = \text{MLP}(\text{LN}(\hat{s}_l)) + \hat{s}_l, \\ \hat{s}_{l+1} = \text{SW-MSA}(\text{LN}(\hat{s}_l)) + s_l; s_{l+1} = \text{MLP}(\text{LN}(\hat{s}_{l+1})) + \hat{s}_{l+1} \quad (1)$$

The Swin Transformer module is particularly suitable for H&E images due to its ability to effectively handle different scales of information inherent in these images. H&E images contain various levels of information, such as cell shape, cell cluster organization, tissue compartments, and cell-stroma interactions, each requiring different levels of resolution for accurate interpretation. The window-based approach of the Swin Transformer allows it to focus on local features within a window, while the shifted window mechanism enables the capture of global context by aggregating information across different windows. This multi-scale feature extraction is crucial for capturing the complex and hierarchical nature of tissue structures in H&E images, ultimately improving the model's ability to distinguish subtle histological details and interactions.

3.3 Feature Map Fusion Module

The FMF module integrates features from the two branches by utilizing Gated Cross Attention, which emphasizes spatially significant regions. For the ith stage, the Swin Transformer output, S_i, is aligned with the CNN feature map, F_i, in both dimensions and resolution to form S'_i. To identify the most informative regions within F_i, a gating layer is introduced. This gating layer, which can be trained during the training phase, processes F_i through convolution and sigmoid activation to produce a gating map G_i. The gating map G_i highlights areas of importance within F_i, enabling the model to focus on spatially significant regions while also managing the computational burden by selectively processing only the most relevant parts of the input.

$$G_i = \sigma(\text{Conv}(F_i)) \qquad (2)$$

The top k pixels in G_i with the highest values represent the most informative regions. Subsets $F_{i,k}$ and $S'_{i,k}$ are extracted from F_i and S'_i correspondingly for cross attention operation in Eq. 3. Focusing on these k points allows the cross-attention to exchange information primarily in regions crucial for the model's performance, thereby improving efficiency. The choice of k is based on empirical analysis, details in the supplementary materials. The cross attention function is given by:

$$A_{i,k} = \text{Attention}(F_{i,k}, S'_{i,k}, S'_{i,k}), \qquad (3)$$

where:

- $F_{i,k}$ serves as the query, representing the top k elements from the CNN feature maps.
- $S'_{i,k}$ serves as the key and value, derived from the corresponding elements in the Swin Transformer output.

After the cross-attention operation, the resulting attention matrix $A_{i,k}$ is re-integrated into the original F_i, replacing original values correspondingly. This re-integration process integrates the spatial context learned from the auxiliary Swin Transformer branch into the primary CNN feature maps, enriching F_i with complementary tissue spatial information and enhancing the overall feature representation.

3.4 Loss Functions

The adversarial loss is adopted from the pix2pix framework:

$$\mathcal{L}_{cGAN}(G, D) = \mathbb{E}_{x,y}[\log D(x, y)] + \mathbb{E}_{x,z}[\log(1 - D(x, G(x, z)))]. \tag{4}$$

The terms x, y, and z denote the input H&E image, the ground truth mIHC image, and random noise, respectively. Additionally, the L1 loss from pix2pix is employed to preserve structural consistency:

$$\mathcal{L}_1 = \mathbb{E}_{x,y,z}[\|y - G(x, z)\|_1]. \tag{5}$$

Thus, our overarching objective function becomes:

$$G^* = \arg \min_G \max_D \mathcal{L}_{cGAN}(G, D) + \lambda \mathcal{L}_1(G), \tag{6}$$

where λ balances the contributions of the adversarial loss and the L_1 loss.

4 Experiments

We used the Adam optimizer over 100 epochs, with an initial learning rate of 0.00003 for 50 epochs, and then linearly decayed to zero over the remaining epochs, on an NVIDIA Tesla V100 16GB GPU.

4.1 Benchmark Results

Following established benchmarks in image-to-image translation [7,9,16,17], we adopt the Structural Similarity Index Measure (SSIM), Pearson correlation score (R), and Peak Signal to Noise Ratio (PSNR) as evaluation metrics to gauge the quality of the synthesized images.

SSIM assesses the perceived quality by comparing luminance, contrast, and structural information, capturing structural content and visual quality. Pearson correlation score (R) measures the linear correlation between the synthesized and reference images, indicating overall consistency in pixel intensity distribution. PSNR quantifies the ratio between the maximum possible signal power and the power of corrupting noise, reflecting the accuracy and precision of image synthesis. Employing these three metrics provides a comprehensive evaluation, capturing different aspects of image quality for robust performance analysis.

Our method demonstrated superior performance on the HEMIT dataset, achieving the highest scores in SSIM (0.875), Pearson correlation (0.746), and PSNR (29.886), as shown in Table 2. This indicates its effectiveness in image translation quality compared to other models. Visualization examples are shown in Fig. 4. The images generated by our methods demonstrate good overall alignment with the ground truth and consistency in marker expression. This indicates that our dual-branch architecture effectively handles stain translation by maintaining structural integrity and marker accuracy across the translated images.

Table 2. Comparison of evaluation metrics across different methods.

Methods	SSIM				R				PSNR (dB)			
	DAPI	CD3	panCK	Average	DAPI	CD3	panCK	Average	DAPI	CD3	panCK	Average
U-Net	0.791	**0.907**	0.901	0.866	0.659	0.005	0.949	0.538	27.929	24.733	33.773	28.695
ResNet	0.790	**0.907**	0.898	0.865	0.677	0.005	0.949	0.544	27.531	24.733	33.212	28.268
pix2pix_UNet	0.775	0.879	0.903	0.852	0.652	0.455	0.943	0.683	27.691	25.659	34.306	29.219
pix2pix_ResNet	0.723	0.906	**0.914**	0.848	0.668	0.553	0.946	0.723	27.152	26.225	34.359	29.189
pix2pixHD	0.786	0.900	0.888	0.858	**0.721**	0.530	0.943	0.731	28.156	26.281	34.033	29.471
ours	**0.815**	0.898	0.913	**0.875**	0.716	**0.571**	**0.951**	**0.746**	**28.610**	**26.349**	**34.875**	**29.886**

While SSIM is commonly used in previous works regarding stain translation tasks [14,16], it has limitations when used alone. SSIM may offer misleading results, especially in cases where marker expression is highly imbalanced. For instance, as shown in Fig. 4, the UNet and ResNet models completely ignore the CD3 marker in their predictions, focusing only on the dominant markers (DAPI and PanCK). Despite this, these models achieve the highest SSIM scores. This indicates that SSIM alone is insufficient for evaluating the quality of stain translation tasks and highlights the importance of using multiple metrics to obtain a more accurate and reliable assessment.

While U-Net and ResNet scored well in SSIM and PSNR, they fell short in Pearson correlation due to insufficient emphasis on less dominant markers, such as CD3. This highlights the importance of Pearson correlation for evaluating multi-stain translations and demonstrates that GAN-based frameworks significantly improve the realism of image translations, particularly for low-expression markers.

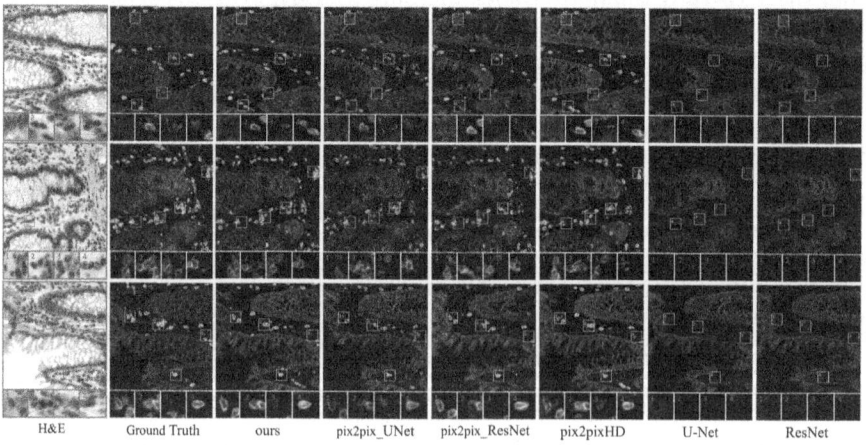

Fig. 4. Visualization of different methods on HEMIT dataset. DAPI is shown in blue, panCK in red, and CD3 in green. Below each patch, four zoomed-in regions are displayed to provide a more detailed view. (Color figure online)

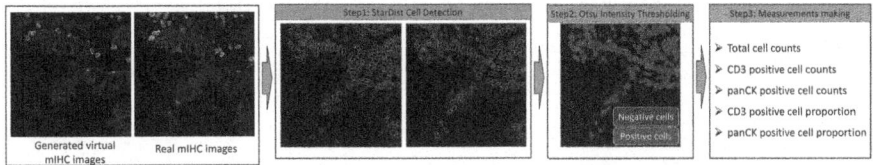

Fig. 5. Downstream analysis pipeline: Real and generated virtual mIHC images are analyzed using the Qupath StarDist model for cell detection. Following cell detection, the Otsu thresholding method is applied to identify positive cell groups. Finally, measurements are taken for evaluation purposes.

4.2 Downstream Analysis

To further evaluate the performance of the HEMIT model's generated mIHC images and to give an indication for it's potential utility in clinical studies, we compared the cell overall counts obtained between the generated and real images using an mIHC image analysis pipeline. Both real and generated images were analyses using the QuPath application [2,19] along with the nuclear segmentation system Stardist [25] to identify individual cell nuclei. For each cell, the mean stain expression was extracted for each marker and Otsu segmentation [22] was applied to identify marker positivity enabling a comparison of the positive cell proportions between real and generated images. A schematic of the downstream analysis pipeline is shown in Fig. 5.

We calculated the mean absolute error ratios of positive cell proportions for all methods. The mean absolute error ratios are shown in Fig. 6A. Our method shows considerable improvement over the existing state-of-the-art methods, especially on the challenging CD3 marker. Further comparative results of our method are shown in Fig. 6B-D. Figure 6C and Fig. 6D showcase the close correspondence between real and generated images, evidenced by the tight distribution around the identity line in scatter plots and marginal deviations in Bland-Altman plots. The mean absolute error ratio is calculated using the formula:

$$\text{Mean Absolute Error Ratio} = \frac{1}{n}\sum_{i=1}^{n}\left|\frac{p_i^{\text{real}} - p_i^{\text{generated}}}{p_i^{\text{real}}}\right| \tag{7}$$

where p_i^{real} and $p_i^{\text{generated}}$ represent the positive cell proportions of the real and generated images for the i-th sample, respectively, and n is the total number of test samples.

5 Conclusion

In this study, we introduced HEMIT, a pioneering dataset tailored for pathology image translation tasks. HEMIT is specifically designed to bridge the gap between H&E stained sections and their mIHC counterparts, showcasing multiple markers including DAPI, CD3, and panCK. Notably, the mIHC images in

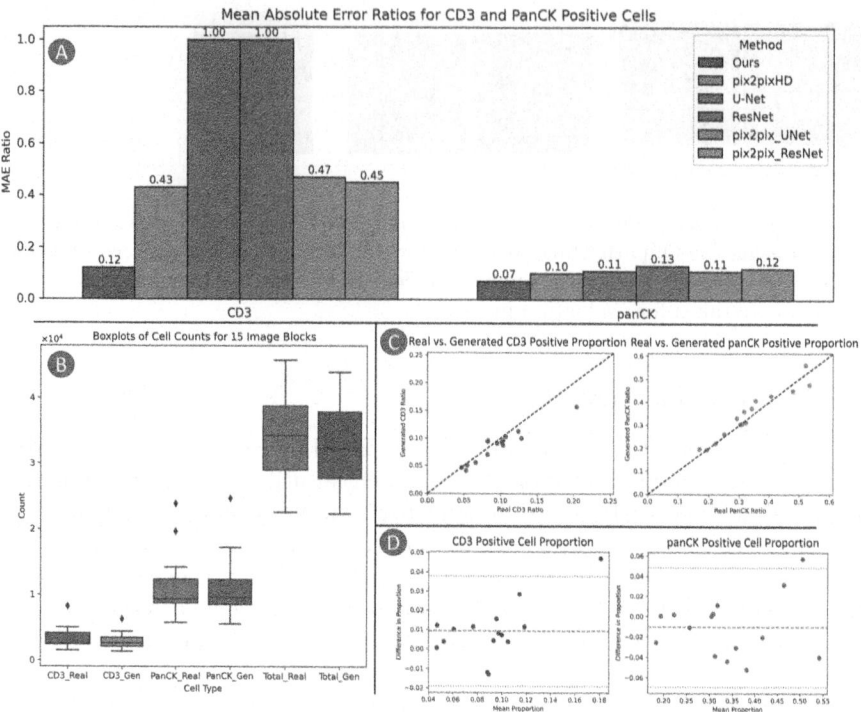

Fig. 6. Downstream Analysis Results: (A) Comparative MAE Ratios for CD3 and PanCK; (B) shows boxplots of cell counts for CD3, panCK, and total of the generated images of our method and real images; (C) and (D) provide scatter plots and Bland-Altman plots for CD3 and panCK positive cell proportions of the generated images of our method and the real images.

our dataset are multi-component, providing a cellular-level registration with the associated H&E images. This unique alignment presents an invaluable opportunity for supervised stain translation research.

Complementing our dataset contribution, we proposed a dual-branch generator architecture optimized for pathology image analysis. Through extensive experimentation, we contrasted our approach with several SOTA algorithms. The empirical outcomes with downstream analysis underscore the efficacy of our method, establishing a new benchmark for the H&E to mIHC translation domain. We hypothesise that the significant performance improvement is due to the spatial context provided by the Swin Transformer where the tissue compartment can inform the cell protein expression. This is in line with other work [26] which has demonstrated that tissue context can inform cell classification leading to improved accuracy. In addition, we also discussed the limitation of the commonly used metrics in certain scenarios, and provided a comprehensive evaluation scheme which could offer guidance for future research.

Moreover, in addition to the metrics commonly used in the computer vision field, we proposed a downstream analysis pipeline from a clinically-focused perspective. The downstream analysis demonstrated that while traditional metrics showed marginal improvements, significant enhancements were observed at the cellular level. This downstream pipeline not only proved the efficacy of our proposed method but also provided a supplementary evaluation approach for stain translation tasks.

This work provides an opportunity for further exploration in the use of predicting biomarkers from H&E pathology images to accelerate research in biomarker prediction.

References

1. An, Y., et al.: A fast and automated FMT/XCT reconstruction strategy based on standardized imaging space. IEEE Trans. Med. Imaging **41**(3), 657–666 (2021)
2. Bankhead, P., et al.: Qupath: open source software for digital pathology image analysis. Sci. Rep. **7**(1), 1–7 (2017)
3. Bian, C., et al.: Integrating spatial and morphological characteristics into melanoma prognosis: a computational approach. Cancers **16**(11), 2026 (2024)
4. Bian, C., Cootes, T., Fergie, M.: A transformer-based computational approach for h and e to multiplexed immunohistochemistry stain translation. In: Medical Imaging 2023: Digital and Computational Pathology, vol. 12471, pp. 42–52. SPIE (2023)
5. Bian, C., Wang, Y., An, Y., Wang, H., Du, Y., Tian, J.: A computational prediction method based on modified u-net for cell distribution in tumor microenvironment. In: Medical Imaging 2021: Digital Pathology, vol. 11603, pp. 64–69. SPIE (2021)
6. Bian, C., et al.: Immunoaizer: a deep learning-based computational framework to characterize cell distribution and gene mutation in tumor microenvironment. Cancers **13**(7), 1659 (2021)
7. Burlingame, E.A., Margolin, A.A., Gray, J.W., Chang, Y.H.: Shift: speedy histopathological-to-immunofluorescent translation of whole slide images using conditional generative adversarial networks. In: Medical Imaging 2018: Digital Pathology, vol. 10581, p. 1058105. International Society for Optics and Photonics (2018)
8. Burlingame, E.A., et al.: Shift: speedy histological-to-immunofluorescent translation of a tumor signature enabled by deep learning. Sci. Rep. **10**(1), 17507 (2020)
9. Christiansen, E.M., et al.: In silico labeling: predicting fluorescent labels in unlabeled images. Cell **173**(3), 792–803 (2018)
10. Conde-Sousa, E., et al.: Herohe challenge: predicting her2 status in breast cancer from hematoxylin-eosin whole-slide imaging. J. Imaging **8**(8), 213 (2022)
11. Isola, P., Zhu, J.Y., Zhou, T., Efros, A.A.: Image-to-image translation with conditional adversarial networks. In: Proceedings of the IEEE Conference on Computer Vision and Pattern Recognition, pp. 1125–1134 (2017)
12. Jen, K.Y., et al.: In silico multi-compartment detection based on multiplex immunohistochemical staining in renal pathology. In: Medical Imaging 2021: Digital Pathology, vol. 11603, pp. 294–301. SPIE (2021)

13. Kong, L., Lian, C., Huang, D., Hu, Y., Zhou, Q., et al.: Breaking the dilemma of medical image-to-image translation. Adv. Neural. Inf. Process. Syst. **34**, 1964–1978 (2021)
14. Li, F., Hu, Z., Chen, W., Kak, A.: Adaptive supervised patchnce loss for learning H&E-to-IHC stain translation with inconsistent groundtruth image pairs. In: International Conference on Medical Image Computing and Computer-Assisted Intervention, pp. 632–641. Springer (2023)
15. Liu, M.Y., Breuel, T., Kautz, J.: Unsupervised image-to-image translation networks. In: Advances in Neural Information Processing Systems, vol. 30 (2017)
16. Liu, S., Zhu, C., Xu, F., Jia, X., Shi, Z., Jin, M.: BCI: breast cancer immunohistochemical image generation through pyramid pix2pix. In: Proceedings of the IEEE/CVF Conference on Computer Vision and Pattern Recognition, pp. 1815–1824 (2022)
17. Liu, Y., Yuan, H., Wang, Z., Ji, S.: Global pixel transformers for virtual staining of microscopy images. IEEE Trans. Med. Imaging **39**(6), 2256–2266 (2020)
18. Liu, Z., et al.: Swin transformer: hierarchical vision transformer using shifted windows. In: Proceedings of the IEEE/CVF International Conference on Computer Vision, pp. 10012–10022 (2021)
19. Loughrey, M.B., et al.: Validation of the systematic scoring of immunohistochemically stained tumour tissue microarrays using qupath digital image analysis. Histopathology **73**(2), 327–338 (2018)
20. Macenko, M., et al.: A method for normalizing histology slides for quantitative analysis. In: 2009 IEEE International Symposium on Biomedical Imaging: from Nano to Macro, pp. 1107–1110. IEEE (2009)
21. Menze, B.H., et al.: The multimodal brain tumor image segmentation benchmark (brats). IEEE Trans. Med. Imaging **34**(10), 1993–2024 (2014)
22. Ostu, N.: A threshold selection method from gray-level histograms. IEEE Trans. SMC **9**, 62 (1979)
23. Peng, Z., Bian, C., Du, Y., Tian, J.: A deep learning-based computational prediction model for characterizing cellular biomarker distribution in tumor microenvironment. In: Medical Imaging 2022: Digital and Computational Pathology, vol. 12039, pp. 326–331. SPIE (2022)
24. Rivenson, Y., et al.: Virtual histological staining of unlabelled tissue-autofluorescence images via deep learning. Nat. Biomed. Eng. **3**(6), 466–477 (2019)
25. Schmidt, U., Weigert, M., Broaddus, C., Myers, G.: Cell detection with star-convex polygons. In: Medical Image Computing and Computer Assisted Intervention–MICCAI 2018: 21st International Conference, Granada, Spain, 16–20 September 2018, Proceedings, Part II 11, pp. 265–273. Springer (2018)
26. Shephard, A.J., et al.: Simultaneous nuclear instance and layer segmentation in oral epithelial dysplasia. In: Proceedings of the IEEE/CVF International Conference on Computer Vision, pp. 552–561 (2021)
27. Stack, E.C., Wang, C., Roman, K.A., Hoyt, C.C.: Multiplexed immunohistochemistry, imaging, and quantitation: a review, with an assessment of tyramide signal amplification, multispectral imaging and multiplex analysis. Methods **70**(1), 46–58 (2014)
28. Tan, W.C.C., et al.: Overview of multiplex immunohistochemistry/immunofluorescence techniques in the era of cancer immunotherapy. Cancer Commun. **40**(4), 135–153 (2020)
29. Wang, H., Bian, C., Kong, L., An, Y., Du, Y., Tian, J.: A novel adaptive parameter search elastic net method for fluorescent molecular tomography. IEEE Trans. Med. Imaging **40**(5), 1484–1498 (2021)

30. Wang, T.C., Liu, M.Y., Zhu, J.Y., Tao, A., Kautz, J., Catanzaro, B.: High-resolution image synthesis and semantic manipulation with conditional GANs. In: Proceedings of the IEEE Conference on Computer Vision and Pattern Recognition, pp. 8798–8807 (2018)
31. Wang, Y., et al.: Graph convolution based residual connected network for morphological reconstruction in fluorescence molecular tomography. In: Medical Imaging 2022: Biomedical Applications in Molecular, Structural, and Functional Imaging, vol. 12036, pp. 527–533. SPIE (2022)
32. Weinstein, J.N., et al.: The cancer genome atlas pan-cancer analysis project. Nat. Genet. **45**(10), 1113–1120 (2013)

Physics-Informed Latent Diffusion for Multimodal Brain MRI Synthesis

Sven Lüpke[1], Yousef Yeganeh[1,2(✉)], Ehsan Adeli[3], Nassir Navab[1,2], and Azade Farshad[1,2]

[1] Technical University of Munich, Munich, Germany
y.yeganeh@tum.de
[2] Munich Center for Machine Learning, Munich, Germany
[3] Stanford University, Stanford, USA

Abstract. Recent advances in generative models for medical imaging have shown promise in representing multiple modalities. However, the variability in modality availability across datasets limits the general applicability of the synthetic data they produce. To address this, we present a novel physics-informed generative model capable of synthesizing a variable number of brain MRI modalities, including those not present in the original dataset. Our approach utilizes latent diffusion models and a two-step generative process: first, unobserved physical tissue property maps are synthesized using a latent diffusion model, and then these maps are combined with a physical signal model to generate the final MRI scan. Our experiments demonstrate the efficacy of this approach in generating unseen MR contrasts and preserving physical plausibility. Furthermore, we validate the distributions of generated tissue properties by comparing them to those measured in real brain tissue.

Keywords: Medical Image Synthesis · Brain MRI Generation · Physics-Informed · Multimodal · Denoising Diffusion

1 Introduction

Synthetic data generation has emerged as a critical research area in the medical domain, where real data samples are often scarce due to limited availability, strict privacy regulations, or ethical considerations. State-of-the-art (SOTA) generative models for medical images increasingly employ denoising diffusion models [11,18,22], which generate images by iteratively denoising Gaussian noise. Due to the high computational demands of these models, the latent diffusion model (LDM) [20] performs denoising in a lower dimensional latent space by first encoding images with a variational autoencoder (VAE). The increasing integration of multimodal data [9] necessitates the creation of multimodal synthetic datasets.

S. Lüpke and Y. Yeganeh—Equal contribution.

© The Author(s), under exclusive license to Springer Nature Switzerland AG 2025
A. Schroder et al. (Eds.): MICCAI 2024 Workshops, LNCS 15401, pp. 198–207, 2025.
https://doi.org/10.1007/978-3-031-84525-3_17

Recent multimodal generative models in the medical imaging domain are limited to the fixed set of modalities used to train these models [17,25]. However, the availability of modalities varies drastically across different datasets in the medical domain, limiting the general applicability of the data synthesized by these models.

Multimodal variational autoencoders [23] can process a varying number of modalities by aggregating unimodal inference distributions of the individual modalities into a joint multimodal distribution. Shi et al. [21] propose to model the inference distribution as a mixture of experts, creating shared and private sub-spaces in the joint distribution. Alternatively, the joint multimodal distribution can be modeled by a product of unimodal experts [10]. Joshi et al. [14] generalized the product of experts for multimodal inference in the presence of noise by adaptively weighting each modality.

Physics-informed methods [19] combine neural networks with physical equations, ensuring their predictions respect the given physical laws. In contrast to purely data-driven solutions, they offer improved extrapolation capabilities [4]. Trask et al. [24] integrate a product-of-experts into a physics-informed framework for disentangling multimodal data in the latent space using a Gaussian mixture prior over the latent variables.

In this paper, we propose a novel physics-informed diffusion-based generative model for multimodal brain MR scans. Inspired by quantitative MRI techniques [12,13], we utilize the acquisition parameters [6] in combination with a physical signal model [2] and a latent diffusion model to synthesize images in a two-step process: (1) The generation of modality shared physical tissue property maps, namely the proton density, the longitudinal relaxation time, and the transverse relaxation time, (2) The application of a physical signal model with a desired set of scanner acquisition parameters to the tissue property maps to obtain the final MRI scan.

We showcase the versatility of our approach by generating MRI contrasts not present in the training data. This is achieved by combining generated tissue property maps with acquisition parameters unseen during training, effectively expanding the variety of images while preserving physical plausibility. Additionally, we compare the distributions of generated tissue properties against those measured in real brain tissue, highlighting the potential for future research on a unified generative model for multimodal medical images.

2 Method

2.1 MRI Signal Model

The signal intensity in an MRI scan is mainly influenced by two factors: the scanner configuration and the tissue properties. Given the tissue properties, an MRI simulator can generate a variety of MR contrasts based on the chosen MR sequence and the acquisition parameters. However, due to the high computational cost of a full MRI simulation, the relationship between tissue properties, which are given by the proton density (PD), the longitudinal relaxation time

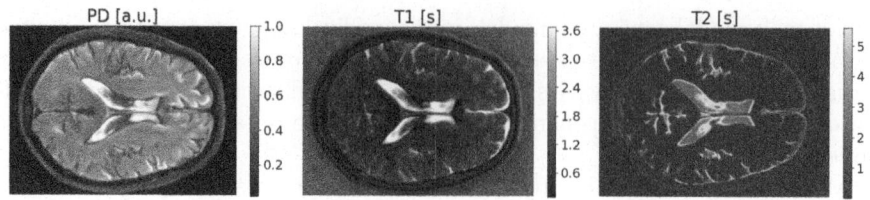

Fig. 1. Unobserved tissue property maps generated by our model.

(T1) and the transverse relaxation time (T2), and the signal intensity is instead modeled by a set of signal equations. These equations only depend on a subset of all possible acquisition parameters, namely the echo time (TE), the repetition time (TR), and the inversion time (TI). For T1-weighted MPRAGE [5], T2-weighted spin-echo (SE) [8] and FLAIR [8] sequences, the equations modeling the signal intensity s at a spatial location x are given by:

$$s_{MPRAGE}(x) = G \cdot PD(x)\left(1 - \frac{2e^{\frac{-TI}{T1(x)}}}{1 + e^{\frac{-TR}{T1(x)}}}\right)$$

$$s_{SE}(x) = G \cdot PD(x)\left(1 - e^{\frac{-TR}{T1(x)}}\right)e^{\frac{-TE}{T2(x)}} \quad (1)$$

$$s_{FLAIR}(x) = G \cdot PD(x)\left(1 - 2e^{\frac{-TI}{T1(x)}} + e^{\frac{-TR}{T1(x)}}\right)e^{\frac{-TE}{T2(x)}}$$

The tissue properties T1, T2, and PD depend on the location x, whereas G is a global parameter that models the scanner gain. Our model ignores the scanner gain and assumes $G = 1$. Since the signal depends linearly on PD and G, any scanner-specific signal scaling is absorbed into the proton density map.

2.2 Multimodal Physics-Informed Variational Autoencoder

To efficiently perform denoising diffusion to generate tissue property maps containing PD, T1, and T2, we design a multimodal physics-informed variational autoencoder that downsamples N multimodal MRI scans by a factor of 8 into a shared lower dimensional latent representation.

We use a single shared convolutional encoder to encode the input modalities independently into unimodal latent distributions $q_\phi(z|x_i)$. The encoder is conditioned on the acquisition parameters corresponding to each input image using adaptive group normalization [7] in the residual blocks:

$$AdaGN(h, s, b) = s \cdot GroupNorm(h) + b \quad (2)$$

where h is the hidden feature and $(s, b) \in \mathbb{R}^{2 \times N} = MLP(TE, TR, TI)$ is the output of a multilayer perceptron given the acquisition parameters.

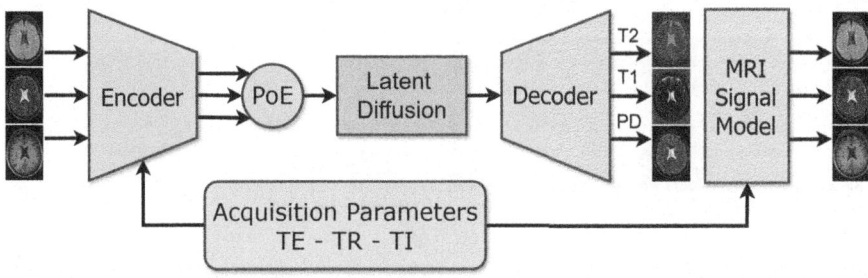

Fig. 2. Overview of our physics-informed generative model. We combine an MRI signal model with a product-of-experts (PoE) multimodal variational autoencoder and a latent diffusion model.

To combine the unimodal latent distributions $q_\phi(z|x_i)$ into a shared multimodal distribution $q(z|X)$, we use a product-of-experts:

$$q(z|X) \propto \prod_{i=1}^{N} q_\phi(z|x_i) \qquad (3)$$

The unimodal distributions $q_\phi(z|x_i)$ are assumed to be Gaussian, with their mean μ_i and standard deviation σ_i being predicted by the encoder. Thus, the product of the unimodal distributions is also a Gaussian and is given by (Fig. 2):

$$q(z|X) = \mathcal{N}(\mu, \sigma^2) \qquad (4)$$

$$\sigma^{-2} = \sum_{i=1}^{N} \sigma_i^{-2}, \qquad \mu = \sigma^2 \sum_{i=1}^{N} \frac{\mu_i}{\sigma_i^2} \qquad (5)$$

We decode the shared latent representation using a convolutional network into tissue property maps by passing its output through the exponential function, ensuring that the property values are greater than zero, and transforming the resulting values by the signal model (Eq. 1) to reconstruct the input. Following previous work [18,20], we combine an L2 reconstruction loss with a perceptual loss, a patch-wise adversarial loss, and a KL-regularization loss on the latent distribution.

Because the tissue property values that reconstruct the input are not unique, we employ a prior over T1 and T2. More specifically, we employ a light L2-regularization on the output values o_{T1} and o_{T2} of the decoder and apply a constant bias before passing them through the exponential function:

$$T1 = exp(o_{T1} + b_{T1}) \qquad (6)$$
$$T2 = exp(o_{T2} + b_{T2}) \qquad (7)$$

We set $s_{T1} = ln(1)$ and $s_{T2} = ln(0.1)$ based on the median of the property value distribution measured in real brain tissue [1], corresponding to a log-normal prior with a median of 1 on T1 and a median of 0.1 on T2.

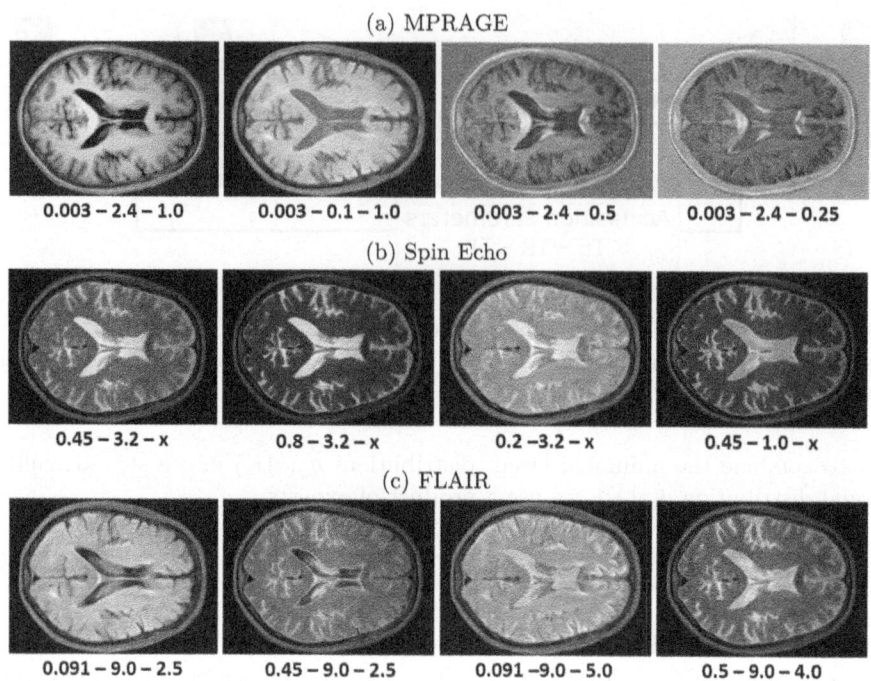

Fig. 3. Images of a single brain, represented by the tissue property maps in Fig. 1 generated with different signal models and varying acquisition parameters TE-TR-TI. Spin-Echo sequences do not use inversion recovery. The leftmost images use parameters commonly found in the OASIS-3 dataset, whereas the other images use parameter combinations not present in the training data.

2.3 Latent Diffusion Model

To generate new tissue properties maps, we train a latent diffusion model [20] on the joint multimodal representation we obtain through Eq. 3. Given a sample $z \sim q(z|X)$, the objective function is:

$$L_{LDM} = \mathbb{E}_{z, \epsilon \sim \mathcal{N}(0,1), t}\left[||\epsilon - \epsilon_\theta(z_t, t)||_2^2\right] \quad (8)$$

where ϵ_θ is a UNet that predicts the noise added at each timestep t.

3 Experiments and Results

Dataset and Preprocessing. Our experiments used T1-weighted MPRAGE, T2-weighted spin-echo, and FLAIR scans from the OASIS-3 dataset [15]. The MRI volumes were co-registered to a common MNI space using UniRes [3] and cropped to a resolution of $160 \times 224 \times 160$. Due to memory limitations, we did not use the entire brain volumes but only the 2D axial slices, each having a

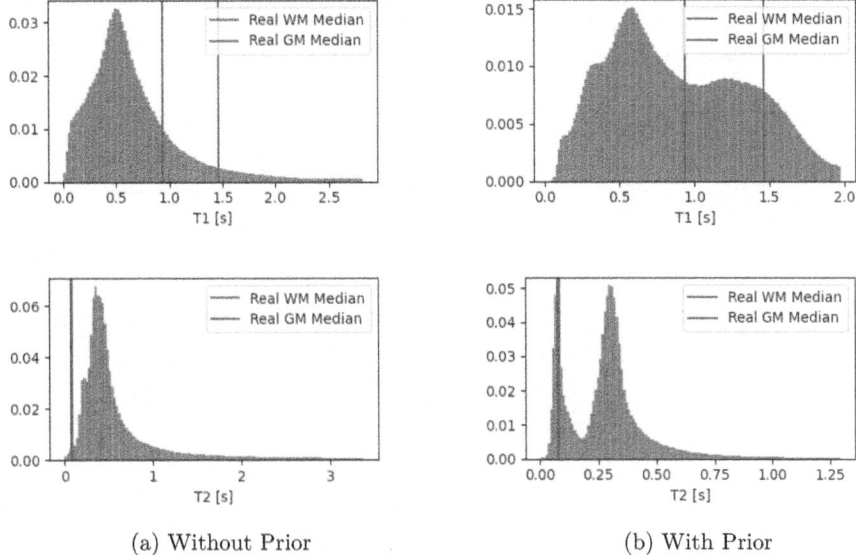

(a) Without Prior (b) With Prior

Fig. 4. Distribution of T1 and T2 values in the generated images compared to the median T1 and T2 of white matter (WM) and grey matter (GM) in real brains reported by [1]. For visualization purposes, we clipped the distributions of the generated properties to the 95th percentile. The results show that the introduction of the prior leads to the generation of more realistic property distributions.

resolution of 224 × 160. At the input of the VAE, we scaled the image value to the range $[-1, 1]$, only considering the 99.5^{th} percentile of the pixel intensities due to the long upside tails in the signal intensity distribution of MR images. As targets for reconstruction during the VAE training, we used unscaled images because our signal model is designed to predict the raw signal intensity produced by the scanner.

Training Details. For training the networks, we mainly adopt the hyperparameters used by Pinaya et al. [18] and train all networks with the Adam optimizer. We trained the VAE for 50 epochs using a batch size of 4, where the encoder and decoder used a learning rate of $5e-5$ and the discriminator used a learning rate of $1e-4$. The latent diffusion UNet was trained with a learning rate of $2.5e-5$ for 100 epochs using a batch size of 16. All models were trained on a Nvidia Titan Xp GPU with 12 GB of VRAM.

3.1 Results

Synthesis of Unseen Modalities. A key advantage of our physics-informed generative model over previous methods is the ability to synthesize modalities not present in the training data. Figure 3 shows how changes in the acquisition

Table 1. Quantitative results of our ablation study, showing the reconstruction performance of our physics-informed VAE model. The best metrics are marked **bold**, and the second best is underlined.

G Regression	Modality Dropout	T1 & T2 Prior	AdaGN	MSE ↓	MAE ↓	MS-SSIM ↑	PSNR ↑
✓	✓	✓	✓	1542	25.35	0.9577	30.89
	✓	✓	✓	1268	22.94	0.9603	31.67
✓		✓	✓	1367	24.11	0.9609	31.39
		✓	✓	**996**	**20.25**	**0.9632**	**32.70**
✓	✓		✓	1592	25.67	0.9565	30.75
	✓		✓	1365	23.63	0.9528	31.38
✓			✓	1401	24.12	0.9607	31.30
			✓	1084	20.76	0.9617	32.40
✓	✓	✓		1531	25.42	0.9554	30.91
	✓	✓		1179	21.67	0.9596	32.00
✓		✓		1436	24.64	0.9565	31.18
		✓		1083	20.85	0.9613	32.35
✓	✓			1635	25.94	0.9527	30.63
	✓			1391	23.58	0.9578	31.37
✓				1537	25.16	0.9579	30.90
				1388	23.65	0.9577	30.89

parameters affect the generated images using different signal models given a single tissue property map generated by our model. Although we can generate various novel MR contrasts, some acquisition parameter combinations can still lead to unrealistic images with bright backgrounds.

Analysis of the Tissue Property Distribution. To ensure that our model can extrapolate to unseen modalities, it is crucial that the tissue property maps contain physically plausible values. In Fig. 4, we compare the distribution of T1 and T2 values generated by our model to the average T1 and T2 values of white matter and grey matter in actual brain tissue. The results highlight the importance of the prior on the predicted T1 and T2 values, as it guides the model towards generating tissue properties that are, on average, more realistic. However, it is essential to note that the generated distribution includes tissue types beyond white matter and grey matter, such as cerebrospinal fluid and bones.

Reconstruction Performance. We evaluated the impact of the encoder conditioning via adaptive group normalization and the prior on T1 and T2 on the reconstruction performance of our VAE model measured by the mean squared error (MSE), the mean absolute error (MAE), the multi-scale structural similarity index (MS-SSIM), and the peak signal-to-noise ratio (PSNR). The results

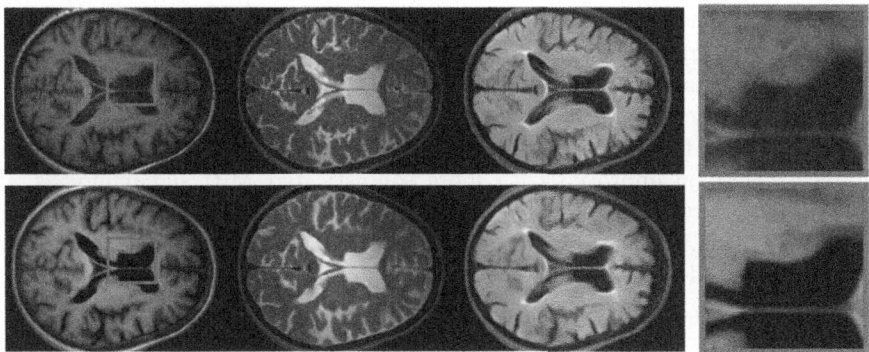

Fig. 5. Images from the data set (top) and their physics-informed VAE reconstructions (bottom), showing the absence of scanner noise in the images generated by our model.

in Table 1 show that encoder conditioning improves the model's performance in the majority, whereas the prior improves its performance in all cases.

We also experimented with modality dropout, a method commonly employed by multimodal models [2,25], which randomly removes modalities from the input to encourage the encoder to extract information from all modalities. However, this did not provide any benefits, which can likely be attributed to our use of the product-of-experts for multimodal fusion. Additionally, we attempted to regress the scanner gain G using a convolutional neural network, which has not benefited our model's performance either.

3.2 Limitations

The employed signal model only considers a perfect MR scanner that does not add any noise to images. Thus, the MRI scans generated by our model do not contain any noise either Fig. 5. While this might be desirable for some applications, noise is required to create realistic MRI scans. One solution could be to model the residual noise separately using another diffusion model conditioned on the noise-free MRI scan [16]. Additionally, the accuracy of the tissue property maps is limited by the number of available MR contrasts per scanning session. This issue could be addressed by introducing location-dependent priors based on the expected tissue type, such as white matter, grey matter, and cerebrospinal fluid. A more robust evaluation of the generated tissue properties would furthermore require access to real tissue property maps, which advanced quantitative MRI techniques can obtain [13].

4 Conclusion

We have presented a physics-informed approach to the generative modeling of MRI scans. By combining physical MR signal models with a variational autoencoder and a latent diffusion model, we separated the generative process into two steps: the generation of unobserved physical tissue properties and a scanner model that transforms the tissue properties to signal intensities in the final MRI scans. Our results show that our model can generate MRI modalities beyond those seen by the model during training. However, the precise evaluation of the intermediate tissue property maps remains challenging. In the future, our approach could be improved with more sophisticated MRI signal models. It could theoretically be extended to develop physics-informed generative models for other medical imaging modalities beyond MRI, such as computed tomography or ultrasound scans.

References

1. Bojorquez, J.Z., Bricq, S., Acquitter, C., Brunotte, F., Walker, P.M., Lalande, A.: What are normal relaxation times of tissues at 3 T? Magn. Reson. Imaging **35**, 69–80 (2017)
2. Borges, P., Fernandez, V., Tudosiu, P.D., Nachev, P., Ourselin, S., Cardoso, M.J.: Unsupervised heteromodal physics-informed representation of MRI data: tackling data harmonisation, imputation and domain shift. In: International Workshop on Simulation and Synthesis in Medical Imaging, pp. 53–63. Springer, Cham (2023)
3. Brudfors, M., Balbastre, Y., Nachev, P., Ashburner, J.: A tool for super-resolving multimodal clinical MRI. arXiv preprint arXiv:1909.01140 (2019)
4. David Davini, Bhargav Samineni, Benjamin Thomas, Amelia Huong Tran, Cherlin Zhu, Kyung Ha, Ganesh Dasika, and Laurent White. Using physics-informed regularization to improve extrapolation capabilities of neural networks. In *Fourth Workshop on Machine Learning and the Physical Sciences (NeurIPS 2021)*, 2021
5. Deichmann, R., Good, C.D., Josephs, O., Ashburner, J., Turner, R.: Optimization of 3-D MP-rage sequences for structural brain imaging. Neuroimage **12**(1), 112–127 (2000)
6. Denck, J., Guehring, J., Maier, A., Rothgang, E.: MR-contrast-aware image-to-image translations with generative adversarial networks. Int. J. Comput. Assist. Radiol. Surg. **16**, 2069–2078 (2021)
7. Dhariwal, P., Nichol, A.: Diffusion models beat GANs on image synthesis. Adv. Neural. Inf. Process. Syst. **34**, 8780–8794 (2021)
8. Hashemi, R.H., Bradley, W.G., Lisanti, C.J.: MRI: the basics: The Basics. Lippincott Williams & Wilkins (2012)
9. Hatamizadeh, A., Nath, V., Tang, Y., Yang, D., Roth, H.R., Xu, D.: Swin unetr: swin transformers for semantic segmentation of brain tumors in MRI images. In: International MICCAI Brainlesion Workshop, pp. 272–284. Springer, Cham (2021)
10. Hinton, G.E.: Training products of experts by minimizing contrastive divergence. Neural Comput. **14**(8), 1771–1800 (2002)
11. Ho, J., Jain, A., Abbeel, P.: Denoising diffusion probabilistic models. Adv. Neural. Inf. Process. Syst. **33**, 6840–6851 (2020)
12. Jacobs, L., Mandija, S., Liu, H., van den Berg, C.A., Sbrizzi, A., Maspero, M.: Generalizable synthetic MRI with physics-informed convolutional networks. arXiv preprint arXiv:2305.12570 (2023)
13. Jara, H., et al.: Primary multiparametric quantitative brain MRI: state-of-the-art relaxometric and proton density mapping techniques. Radiology **305**(1), 5–18 (2022)

14. Joshi, A., Gupta, N., Shah, J., Bhattarai, B., Modi, A., Stoyanov, D.: Generalized product-of-experts for learning multimodal representations in noisy environments. In: Proceedings of the 2022 International Conference on Multimodal Interaction, pp. 83–93 (2022)
15. LaMontagne, P.J., et al.: Oasis-3: longitudinal neuroimaging, clinical, and cognitive dataset for normal aging and Alzheimer disease. MedRxiv (2019)
16. Mardani, M., et al.: Residual diffusion modeling for KM-scale atmospheric downscaling (2024)
17. Na, Y., Kim, K., Ye, S.-J., Kim, H., Lee, J.: Generation of multi-modal brain tumor MRIs with disentangled latent diffusion model. In: Medical Imaging with Deep Learning, short paper track (2023)
18. Pinaya, W.H.L., et al.: Brain imaging generation with latent diffusion models. In: MICCAI Workshop on Deep Generative Models, pp. 117–126. Springer, Cham (2022)
19. Raissi, M., Perdikaris, P., Karniadakis, G.E.: Physics-informed neural networks: a deep learning framework for solving forward and inverse problems involving nonlinear partial differential equations. J. Comput. Phys. **378**, 686–707 (2019)
20. Rombach, R., Blattmann, A., Lorenz, D., Esser, P., Ommer, B.: High-resolution image synthesis with latent diffusion models. In: Proceedings of the IEEE/CVF Conference on Computer Vision and Pattern Recognition, pp. 10684–10695 (2022)
21. Shi, Y., Paige, B., Torr, P., et al.: Variational mixture-of-experts autoencoders for multi-modal deep generative models. In: Advances in Neural Information Processing Systems, vol. 32 (2019)
22. Sohl-Dickstein, J., Weiss, E., Maheswaranathan, N., Ganguli, S.: Deep unsupervised learning using nonequilibrium thermodynamics. In: International Conference on Machine Learning, pp. 2256–2265. PMLR (2015)
23. Suzuki, M., Matsuo, Y.: A survey of multimodal deep generative models. Adv. Robot. **36**(5–6), 261–278 (2022)
24. Trask, N., Martinez, C., Lee, K., Boyce, B.: Unsupervised physics-informed disentanglement of multimodal data for high-throughput scientific discovery. arXiv preprint arXiv:2202.03242 (2022)
25. Zhou, T., Canu, S., Vera, P., Ruan, S.: Feature-enhanced generation and multimodality fusion based deep neural network for brain tumor segmentation with missing mr modalities. Neurocomputing **466**, 102–112 (2021)

ML-CDS Workshop

MedPromptX: Grounded Multimodal Prompting for Chest X-Ray Diagnosis

Mai A. Shaaban[1,2]( ), Adnan Khan[3], and Mohammad Yaqub[1]

[1] Mohamed Bin Zayed University of Artificial Intelligence, Abu Dhabi, UAE
mai.kassem@mbzuai.ac.ae
[2] Department of Mathematics and Computer Science, Faculty of Science, Alexandria University, Alexandria, EG, Egypt
[3] School of Computer Science, Carleton University, Ottawa, CA, Canada

Abstract. Chest X-ray images are commonly used for predicting acute and chronic cardiopulmonary conditions, but efforts to integrate them with structured clinical data face challenges due to incomplete electronic health records (EHR). This paper introduces MedPromptX, the first clinical decision support system that integrates multimodal large language models (MLLMs), few-shot prompting (FP) and visual grounding (VG) to combine imagery with EHR data for chest X-ray diagnosis. A pre-trained MLLM is utilized to complement the missing EHR information, providing a comprehensive understanding of patients' medical history. Additionally, FP reduces the necessity for extensive training of MLLMs while effectively tackling the issue of hallucination. Nevertheless, the process of determining the optimal number of few-shot examples and selecting high-quality candidates can be burdensome, yet it profoundly influences model performance. Hence, we propose a new technique that dynamically refines few-shot data for real-time adjustment to new patient scenarios. Moreover, VG narrows the search area in X-ray images, thereby enhancing the identification of abnormalities. We also release MedPromptX-VQA, a new in-context visual question answering dataset encompassing interleaved images and EHR data derived from MIMIC-IV and MIMIC-CXR-JPG databases. Results demonstrate the SOTA performance of MedPromptX, achieving an 11% improvement in F1-score compared to the baselines. Code and data are publicly available on https://github.com/BioMedIA-MBZUAI/MedPromptX.

Keywords: Medical Diagnosis · Multimodal Large Language Models · Few-shot Learning · Visual Grounding · Visual Question Answering

1 Introduction

Emerging machine learning and deep learning advancements are assisting radiologists in detecting chest X-ray abnormalities, streamlining diagnostic processes [9,16]. While traditional diagnosis based solely on imaging data can be effective, incorporating patients' clinical history can significantly improve diagnostic outcomes, underscoring the importance of multimodal approaches [21]. The integration of electronic health records (EHR) has been challenged by its inherent incompleteness [18]. For instance, the missing values of normal ranges for laboratory tests can complicate the interpretation of medical datasets like MIMIC-IV [8]. Hence, processing textual descriptions of static EHR events can help complement the missing information by leveraging the capabilities of large language models pre-trained on large-scale medical data. We provide a subset from the MIMIC-IV dataset in Table 1 that exemplifies undefined upper and lower thresholds for some lab tests. To this end, large language models (LLMs), as in [27], have shown promise in clinical prediction by fine-tuning with prompts leveraging structured EHR data. While multimodal LLMs like BiomedGPT [25] represent a major advancement in biomedical AI by handling various tasks across modalities and surpassing SOTA results, there is limited research on exploring the capabilities of LLMs with structured EHR data, particularly lab test results. Additionally, multimodal techniques, specifically visual grounding techniques, as explored in [6], further exemplify progress in automating associations between image features and descriptive reports in CT imaging. Despite these advancements, there remains a gap in the integration of multimodal data for enhancing diagnostic accuracy in chest X-ray analysis [11].

Table 1. Example of incomplete information about lab test results in electronic health records.

Value	Unit	Label	Low	High
479	mL	Tidal Volume (observed)	299	750
9	L/min	Minute Volume	-	12
39.9	L/min	Flow Rate (L/min)	-	-
24	cmH2O	Plateau Pressure	-	31

Training LLMs or even fine-tuning can be computationally expensive [26]. Therefore, a crucial breakthrough lies in few-shot prompting [4], which enables rapid adaptation to new diagnostic tasks with minimal labelled data and without parameter updates. This empowers medical professionals to efficiently use accurate diagnostic solutions tailored to specific patient cases [15]. In addition, few-shot prompting addresses the challenge of hallucination in LLMs, guiding the output and ensuring the reliability of diagnostic results [23]. Nevertheless, the quality and the quantity of the few-shot data play a pivotal role in influencing performance [1, 22].

To this end, we introduce **MedPromptX** and a new multimodal in-context learning dataset. To the best of our knowledge, MedPromptX is the first model to integrate multimodal LLMs, few-shot prompting, and visual grounding for chest X-ray diagnosis. MedPromptX addresses the challenge of incomplete EHR by complementing missing information through a pre-trained multimodal LLM and focusing on relevant image regions through visual grounding. Additionally,

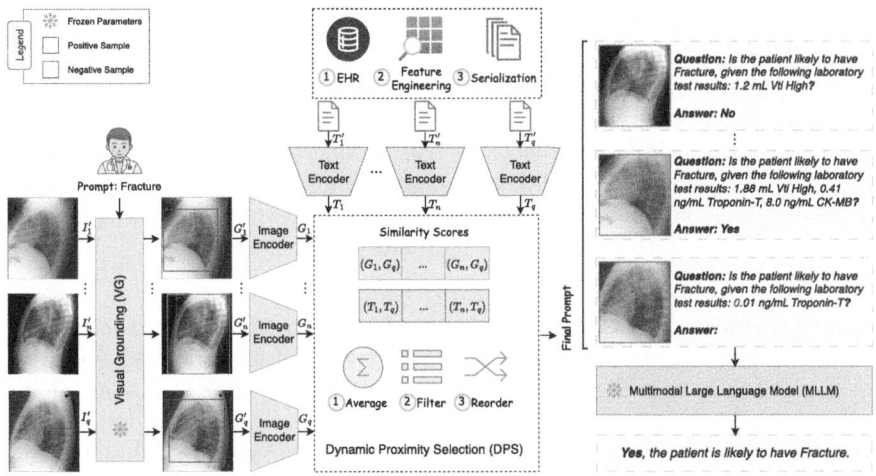

Fig. 1. MedPromptX: each input sample consists of an image I' and corresponding text T' containing tabular features. (1) The VG model takes I' and generates a grounded image G' by prompting the desired output. (2) The grounded image embeddings G and text embeddings T of the candidates are processed by the DPS technique to calculate their relevancy scores to a query sample q. (3) MLLM ingests a few-shot prompt and predicts whether a patient is likely to have a targeted disease.

we propose a dynamic proximity selection (DPS) technique that refines few-shot data in real-time. DPS involves analyzing a few examples of positively and negatively diagnosed patients. This technique allows the model to capture the nuanced relationships between patient history and patient outcomes, enhancing diagnostic accuracy while reducing the dependency on extensive labelled datasets, positioning our framework as a significant advancement in the field. Our main contributions are as follows:

- Introducing **MedPromptX**, a novel diagnostic model for chest X-ray images that harnesses multimodal LLMs (MLLMs), few-shot prompting (FP) and visual grounding (VG), enabling more accurate prediction of abnormalities.
- Mitigating the incompleteness in EHR data by transforming inputs into a textual form, adopting pre-trained MLLMs.
- Extracting the logical patterns discerned from the few-shot data efficiently by implementing DPS, allowing for the capture of the underlying semantics.
- Constructing MedPromptX-VQA, a new in-context learning dataset tailored for VQA with interleaved chest X-ray images and structured medical data.

2 Methodology

2.1 McdPromptX for Diagnosis

The workflow of MedPromptX in Fig. 1 can be conceptualized as a four-phase process. Let $\mathcal{C} = \{(I'_1, T'_1), \ldots, (I'_n, T'_n)\}$ denotes a set of n candidates and

$q = (I'_q, T'_q)$ denotes the query sample. I' is a chest X-ray image and T' is the corresponding text containing EHR data. First, the visual grounding (VG) module crops irrelevant parts in each sample and generates grounded image G' by prompting the class. Then, frozen image and text encoders generate image G and text T embeddings, respectively. Next, the dynamic proximity selection (DPS) module refines the candidates, resulting in $\mathcal{E}$, where $\mathcal{E} \subseteq \mathcal{C}$. Finally, the multimodal large language model (MLLM) ingests the final prompt containing a reordered subset $\mathcal{E}$ to predict the abnormality in query patient q.

Visual Grounding (VG). Conventional object detection methods often confront limitations regarding their capacity to recognize predefined classes of objects [10,12]. Integrating new classes into these models necessitates an exhaustive process of data collection, annotation and model retraining. We use Grounding DINO (GDINO) [12] (the VG component in Fig. 1) to address this challenge by detecting arbitrary objects in real-time delineated through human language inputs, a concept commonly referred to as zero-shot detection.

GDINO uses DINO [24], a SOTA transformer-based object detection algorithm, with GLIP [10] pre-training that focuses on grounding textual descriptions to visual elements in a given image. GDINO is a two-stream framework where multi-scale image and text features are extracted separately using backbone architectures such as Swin Transformer [13] and BERT [5], respectively. These features are then transformed into a unified representation space through multiple layers of feature enhancers, incorporating deformable self-attention for image features and regular self-attention for text features.

To detect visual evidence (i.e., grounded image) denoted as G', a clinician passes a textual input e of a pathological condition (e.g., *Pneumonia*) along with an X-ray image I' to the VG model. The model assigns scores to particular regions based on their prominence in the image $VG(I', e) = \{p(G'_1), \ldots, p(G'_k)\}$, where k is the total number of detected regions and p is the score. We then consider G' with the highest score for the subsequent phases of our model. This approach narrows the search area in an X-ray image.

Dynamic Proximity Selection (DPS). The performance of FP is highly sensitive to the design of the prompt. This includes the choice of examples, their order, and how well they align with the desired task. Misleading, ambiguous, or poorly chosen examples can lead to suboptimal or entirely incorrect outputs [1, 22]. The DPS method leverages a distance function d, such as cosine similarity to order candidate instances $\mathcal{C} = \{(G'_1, T'_1), \ldots, (G'_n, T'_n)\}$, based on their proximity to a query instance q. Applying a similarity threshold dynamically filters out noisy candidates, enhancing the robustness and adaptability of the FP technique. Thus, the number of n candidate samples can be reduced $(n-1, n-2, \ldots, 1)$. Mathematically, the approach can be represented as:

$$\text{DPS}(\mathcal{C}, q) = \left\{ \frac{d(G_c, G_q) + d(T_c, T_q)}{2} \geq th \right\}_{c \in \mathcal{C}} \quad (1)$$

The result is a refined subset $\mathcal{E}$ where each candidate has a similarity score greater than or equal to a threshold th. In this method, an instance $c \in \mathcal{C}$ can be decomposed into either grounded image embeddings G_c or text embeddings T_c containing laboratory test results of a patient. After computing the similarity scores for text and images separately, the final score is obtained by averaging the scores from both modalities. Motivated by [1,22], DPS positions the most closely related candidate directly before the query instance rather than allocating it at a greater distance. This order enhances the precision of the FP process.

Multimodal LLM (MLLM). Incorporating descriptive information about clinical events can provide valuable context for understanding the reasoning behind model predictions, unlike classical machine learning algorithms, which treat input as numerical attributes without considering the semantic meaning. There are limited examples of open-source models that can ingest FP with interleaved modalities. One notable model is Med-Flamingo [15], which has undergone pre-training on a vast array of medical data. Therefore, Med-Flamingo, which is based on Flamingo [1], serves as the MLLM component in Fig. 1. The Flamingo [1] framework can process inputs consisting of both textual and visual content and produce coherent textual output. Flamingo adopts a strategy of freezing the language model and vision encoder weights and establishing connections through learnable architectures. The key component is the perceiver resampler module, introduced in Flamingo to convert spatiotemporal features from the vision encoder into a fixed-size set of visual tokens, facilitating their integration into the language model's processing pipeline. Additionally, cross-attention layers are inserted between pre-trained language model layers, enabling the model to incorporate visual cues for tasks such as next-token prediction. The pivotal aspect of Flamingo is that it predicts the likelihood of text sequences y when conditioned on accompanying images x as follows:

$$p(y|x) = \prod_{\ell=1}^{L} p(y_\ell | y_{<\ell}, x_{\leq \ell}). \qquad (2)$$

The notation y_ℓ represents the ℓ-th token in the sequence of L language tokens constituting our input text, while $y_{<\ell}$ denotes all preceding language tokens, and $x_{\leq \ell}$ symbolizes the corresponding sequence of images.

2.2 MedPromptX-VQA Dataset

Our methodology involves constructing the MedPromptX-VQA dataset derived from a unified multimodal dataset, denoted as HAIM-MIMIC-MM [19]. HAIM-MIMIC-MM is a fusion of information sourced from MIMIC-IV [8] and MIMIC-CXR-JPG [7] databases, meticulously curated to focus solely on patients with at least one chest X-ray procedure. This dataset encapsulates records from 7,279 hospitalization stays involving 6,485 distinct patients, thereby establishing a multimodal link encompassing tabular, textual and visual representations of patient health data.

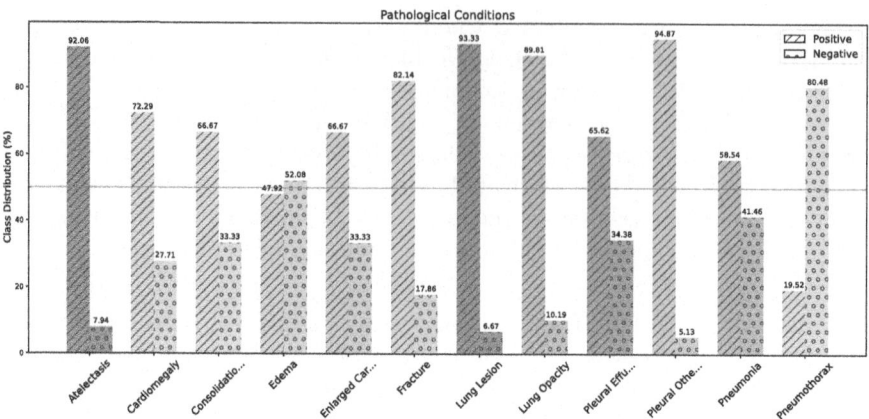

Fig. 2. The "Positive" and "Negative" representations for 12 pathological conditions.

In MedPromptX-VQA, patients are labelled with 12 pathological conditions: *Atelectasis, Cardiomegaly, Consolidation, Edema, Enlarged Cardiomediastinum, Fracture, Lung Lesion, Lung Opacity, Pleural Effusion, Pleural Other, Pneumonia and Pneumothorax*. To alleviate the challenges of limited context length and hallucination in LLMs [23], we transformed these labels into a binary single-label classification framework to ensure that the input fits the context length and to acquire a controlled output, rather than acquiring an open set of possible diagnoses. For each label, if a patient exhibits the condition, the corresponding label is assigned the value 1; otherwise, it is given the value 0. For this study, we specifically selected patients diagnosed with the aforementioned conditions, resulting in 968 records split into 501 positive and 467 negative samples. Figure 2 shows the representations of the labels in the final dataset.

The creation of MedPromptX-VQA involves three steps: (1) extraction of laboratory test results from the *chartevents* table within the MIMIC-IV dataset [8], resulting in 357 features in total, (2) feature engineering, which includes identification of the most strongly correlated features in relation to the label using Pearson method, and (3) transformation of clinical charts into textual representations using comma-separated values (i.e., serialization). Finally, the dataset is structured to support the in-context learning task, where each record has interleaved images and texts, encompassing both positive and negative samples of patients. The motivation for feature selection is to maintain input consistency between the few-shot data and the query sample. This means that the features present in the query sample should already be represented by the candidates while also adhering to the context length. Hence, we set a maximum of 10 features per label. The selected features are presented in Table 6 in *Appendix*.

3 Experimental Setup

We employed a randomized order strategy for the input sequences across several SOTA models, namely Med-Flamingo [15], OpenFlamingo [2], BioMedLM [3] and Clinical-T5-Large [14]. Moreover, the number of few-shot samples remained consistent at 6 across all the models and they were chosen randomly. For MedPromptX, the number of few-shot candidates is dynamically reduced by the DPS technique, resulting in a unique configuration for each query instance. The exclusion criteria for a candidate involve eliminating instances where the cosine similarity falls below a certain threshold, set at 70%. Furthermore, all experiments were conducted using NVIDIA A100-SXM GPU equipped with 40GB of dedicated memory. For MedPromptX, the frozen language encoder employed is LLaMA-7B [20], while the frozen visual encoder is CLIP ViT-L-14 [17]. Table 5 in *Appendix* shows detailed descriptions of the used models.

The prompt design for each model differs based on its capability. Accordingly, Med-Flamingo and OpenFlamingo ingest interleaved images and texts, excluding EHR data, whereas BioMedLM and Clinical-T5 use text, including EHR data. MedPromptX stands out as the sole model that processes interleaved grounded or original images and EHR text prompts. Below are examples for each type:

- Image, Text: "< *image*> *Question:* Is the patient likely to have Cardiomegaly?"
- EHR Text: "*Question:* Is the patient likely to have Cardiomegaly, given the following laboratory test results: 0.52 sec QTc?"
- Image, EHR Text: "< *image*> *Question:* Is the patient likely to have Cardiomegaly, given the following laboratory test results: 0.52 sec QTc?"

4 Results and Discussion

The results in Table 2 emphasize the complex nature of medical diagnosis, wherein multiple data modalities can provide complementary information leading to better model performance. The combination of imaging data with clinical text via MedPromptX seems significant in providing the model with a richer context, leading to more informed predictions. However, initial attempts yielded lower results, emphasizing the challenges in effectively integrating diverse data sources. With the implementation of DPS and VG, subsequent improvements were observed, suggesting that these strategies are crucial in overcoming the obstacles encountered when processing complex prompts. Although some clinical features may not significantly impact the final decision, refining the prompt using DPS could limit the ambiguity. However, it is also recommended to explore strategies such as causal inference in the future.

DPS enhances the model's ability to learn from limited data by reducing the number of ambiguous examples to 4 on average, contributing to better understanding. On the other hand, a random configuration of FP may introduce unintended biases or result in irrelevant guidance for the model. Moreover, the activation of VG empowers the model to restrict the search area within an image

Table 2. Performance of MedPromptX against SOTA baselines. Without DPS, candidate prompts in the 6-shot setting are randomly ordered. In contrast, with DPS, the ordering is determined by cosine similarity scores between the embeddings of each candidate and the test prompt, potentially reducing the number of candidates per record given a threshold. When VG is activated, the model processes images with contextual grounding. Conversely, when VG is deactivated, the model ingests original images.

Model	DPS Setting	VG Setting	Precision	Recall	F1-score	Accuracy
BioMedLM			0.665	0.210	0.484	0.536
Clinical-T5-Large	✗	N/A	0.707	0.371	0.576	0.595
Med-Flamingo			0.545	0.220	0.461	0.501
OpenFlamingo	✗	✗	0.523	0.291	0.476	0.496
MedPromptX (ours)	✗	✗	0.520	0.381	0.493	0.498
	✗	✓	0.511	0.379	0.486	0.491
	✓	✗	0.708	0.581	0.658	0.659
	✓	✓	**0.773**	0.565	**0.686**	**0.689**

by generating output embeddings that encode semantic information instead of dealing with raw pixel data.

The performance gap observed when using VG solely may be attributed to training the VG model on general domain data rather than on chest X-ray images, particularly in handling the complexity inherent in cases where abnormalities are present in small regions. Providing additional context could bridge the gap, which was achieved by refining EHR data with DPS alongside VG.

4.1 Ablations

Table 3. Comparing model performance using different number of instances for DPS initialization. The threshold is set at 0.7, and VG is enabled.

Prompt Setting	Precision	Recall	F1-score	Accuracy
4-shot	0.640	0.565	0.609	0.609
6-shot	0.773	0.565	0.686	0.689
8-shot	**0.789**	0.556	0.689	0.693
10-shot	0.732	0.541	0.690	0.705
12-shot	0.735	**0.654**	**0.733**	**0.740**

Initializing DPS with an increased number of shots provides the model with a broader range of context and examples to learn from, enabling it to generalize more effectively, as shown in Table 3. However, the 6-shot setting strikes a balance between performance and ensuring the inclusion of all classes. In contrast, using

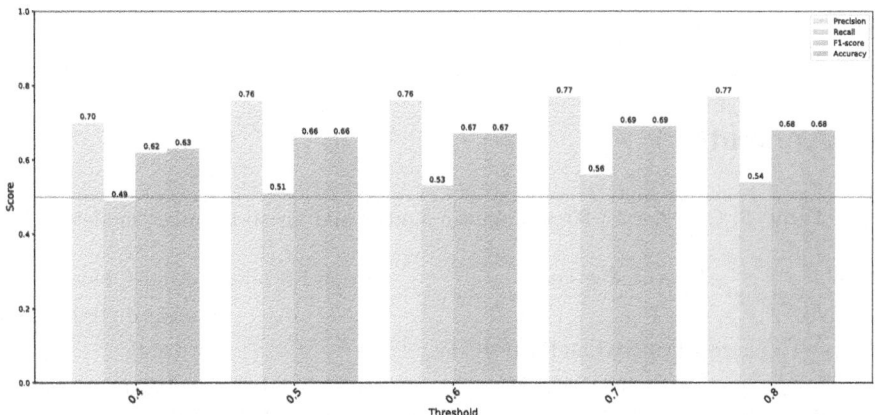

Fig. 3. Comparison of MedPromptX under different DPS thresholds while the VG module is enabled.

Table 4. Comparison of employing DPS with averaged similarity scores from two modalities versus employing similarity scores based on a single modality.

DPS Modality	Precision	Recall	F1-score	Accuracy
Text	0.558	0.391	0.518	0.525
Image	0.748	0.463	0.632	0.642
Multimodal	**0.773**	**0.565**	**0.686**	**0.689**

a higher number of examples would necessitate dropping classes with insufficient positive or negative examples. Moreover, zero-shot assessment was unattainable due to the hallucination of the models, giving entirely incorrect output for some patient cases. This underscores the necessity for employing FP.

Adjusting the threshold for DPS can significantly affect performance; an extremely high threshold restricts the model from including meaningful examples, while an extremely low threshold retains nearly the same examples as in Fig. 3. Moreover, the utilization of multimodal similarity, as shown in Table 4, enhances the instance selection process by capturing a more comprehensive representation of the data compared to single-modality approaches.

5 Conclusion

This paper introduced MedPromptX, a novel prompting strategy that integrates clinical history with imaging data to support decision-making by clinicians for more accurate chest X-ray diagnosis. MedPromptX demonstrated an approach to address the challenges associated with medical data incompleteness, adaptability to new patient cases with limited labelled data and abnormality detection in X-ray images. Nevertheless, further improvements could be obtained by using fine-tuned backbones, which is beyond the scope of this study. Future work can include the accessibility of diverse and well-annotated datasets. Additionally, rigorous clinical trials and real-world deployment are necessary to validate the framework's real-world effectiveness and clinical utility.

A Appendix

Table 5. Overview of large language models and visual-language models.

Model	Pre-training Data	Visual Encoder	Language Model	Size
BioMedLM	The Pile		Standard GPT-2	2.7B
Clinical-T5-Large	MIMIC-III and MIMIC-IV	N/A	T5-Large	0.8B
Med-Flamingo	MTB and PMC-OA	CLIP ViT-L-14	LLaMA-7B	8.3B
OpenFlamingo	LAION-2B and Multimodal C4	CLIP ViT-L-14	MPT-1B	3.0B

Table 6. Summary of the top correlated features that contribute to each label's prediction, providing a clear understanding of the significant variables.

Label	No. Features	Top Features
Atelectasis	10	CO (Arterial), HDL, Cholesterol, ELWI (PiCCO), T Low (APRV), GEDI (PiCCO), LDL measured, T High (APRV), LDL calculated, Serum Osmolality
Cardiomegaly	10	BiPap bpm (S/T -Back up), LDL measured, ELWI (PiCCO), D-Dimer, Impaired Skin Length #5, Impaired Skin Width #5, Uric Acid, GEDI (PiCCO), QTc, Cholesterol
Consolidation	9	Manual Blood Pressure Diastolic Right, Manual Blood Pressure Systolic Right, ELWI (PiCCO), GEDI (PiCCO), CFI (PiCCO), Manual Blood Pressure Diastolic Left, Negative Insp. Force, Cholesterol, PCA basal rate (mL/hour)
Edema	10	SV (Arterial), CO (Arterial), ELWI (PiCCO), CFI (PiCCO), GEDI (PiCCO), Bladder Scan Estimate, SVV (Arterial), Gentamicin (Random), LDL measured, BiPap bpm (S/T -Back up)
Enlarged Cardiomediastinum	5	ELWI (PiCCO), GEDI (PiCCO), SVV (Arterial), D-Dimer, RCexp (Measured Time Constant)
Fracture	10	Absolute Count - Monos, CK-MB, Absolute Count - Neuts, Troponin-T, CO2 production, Differential-Bands, Vti High, Absolute Count - Lymphs, Chloride (whole blood), Total Bilirubin
Lung Lesion	10	Temporary Ventricular Sens Setting mV, Temporary Venticular Sens Threshold mV, PCV Level, Absolute Count - Neuts, GI #1 Tube Mark (CM), Temporary Pacemaker Rate, Glucose (whole blood), Ionized Calcium, Total Bilirubin, Absolute Count - Eos

continued

Table 6. continued

Label	No. Features	Top Features
Lung Opacity	6	Cardiac Output (thermodilution), Bladder Scan Estimate, Ammonia, Serum Osmolality, PBP (Prefilter) Replacement Rate, Current Goal
Pleural Effusion	10	SV (Arterial), CO (Arterial), ELWI (PiCCO), Permanent Pacemaker Rate, GEDI (PiCCO), Gentamicin (Random), SVV (Arterial), Arctic Sun/Alsius Temp #2 C, Feeding Weight, Arctic Sun/Alsius Temp #1 C
Pleural Other	10	PCV Level, Impaired Skin Length #2, Temporary Ventricular Sens Setting mV, Temporary Ventricular Stim Threshold mA, Temperature Celsius, Temporary Ventricular Sens Threshold mV, Troponin-T, Total Bilirubin, Mixed Venous O2% Sat, PeCO2
Pneumonia	9	ELWI (PiCCO), Recruitment Duration, T Low (APRV), CO (PiCCO), HDL, Cholesterol, SV (Arterial), Impaired Skin Width #5, LDL measured
Pneumothorax	10	HDL, Impaired Skin Width #3, Cardiac Output (thermodilution), Temporary Ventricular Stim Threshold mA, TCO2 (calc) Venous, Total Bilirubin, Tidal Volume (set), Venous CO2 Pressure, Differential-Monos, Absolute Count - Eos

References

1. Alayrac, J.B., Donahue, J., Luc, P., et al.: Flamingo: a visual language model for few-shot learning. In: Advances in Neural Information Processing Systems, vol. 35 (2022). https://arxiv.org/abs/2204.14198v2
2. Awadalla, A., Gao, I., Gardner, J., et al.: OpenFlamingo: an open-source framework for training large autoregressive vision-language models. arXiv preprint arXiv:2308.01390 (2023)
3. Bolton, E., Hall, D., Yasunaga, M., et al.: Stanford CRFM: Biomedlm (2022). https://crfm.stanford.edu/2022/12/15/biomedlm.html
4. Brown, T.B., Mann, B., Ryder, N., et al.: Language models are few-shot learners. In: Advances in Neural Information Processing Systems, vol. 2020-Decem (2020). https://arxiv.org/abs/2005.14165v4
5. Devlin, J., Chang, M.W., Lee, K., et al.: BERT: pre-training of deep bidirectional transformers for language understanding. arXiv preprint arXiv:1810.04805 (2018)
6. Ichinose, A., Hatsutani, T., Nakamura, K., et al.: Visual grounding of whole radiology reports for 3D CT images, p. 611–621. Springer Nature Switzerland (2023). https://doi.org/10.1007/978-3-031-43904-9_59
7. Johnson, A.E.W., Pollard, T.J., Greenbaum, N.R., et al.: MIMIC-CXR-JPG, a large publicly available database of labeled chest radiographs (2019). https://arxiv.org/abs/1901.07042v5

8. Johnson, A.E., Bulgarelli, L., Shen, L., et al.: MIMIC-IV, a freely accessible electronic health record dataset. Sci. Data **10**(1), 1–9 (2023). https://doi.org/10.1038/s41597-022-01899-x
9. van Leeuwen, K.G., de Rooij, M., Schalekamp, S., van Ginneken, B., Rutten, M.J.C.M.: How does artificial intelligence in radiology improve efficiency and health outcomes? Pediatr. Radiol., 1–7 (2021). https://doi.org/10.1007/s00247-021-05114-8
10. Li, L.H., Zhang, P., Zhang, H., et al.: Grounded language-image pre-training. In: Proceedings of the IEEE/CVF Conference on Computer Vision and Pattern Recognition, pp. 10965–10975 (2022)
11. Li, Y., Liu, Y., Wang, Z., et al.: A comprehensive study of GPT-4V's multimodal capabilities in medical imaging. medRxiv, pp. 2023–11 (2023)
12. Liu, S., Zeng, Z., Ren, T., et al.: Grounding DINO: marrying DINO with grounded pre-training for open-set object detection. arXiv preprint arXiv:2303.05499 (2023)
13. Liu, Z., Lin, Y., Cao, Y., et al.: Swin transformer: hierarchical vision transformer using shifted windows. In: Proceedings of the IEEE/CVF International Conference on Computer Vision, pp. 10012–10022 (2021)
14. Lu, Q., Dou, D., Nguyen, T.H.: ClinicalT5: a generative language model for clinical text. findings of the association for computational linguistics: EMNLP 2022, pp. 5436–5443 (2022). https://doi.org/10.18653/V1/2022.FINDINGS-EMNLP.398
15. Moor, M., Huang, Q., Wu, S., et al.: Med-Flamingo: a multimodal medical few-shot learner (2023). https://arxiv.org/abs/2307.15189v1
16. Najjar, R.: Redefining radiology: a review of artificial intelligence integration in medical imaging. Diagnostics **13**(17), 2760 (2023)
17. Radford, A., Kim, J.W., Hallacy, C., et al.: Learning transferable visual models from natural language supervision. In: International Conference on Machine Learning, pp. 8748–8763. PMLR (2021)
18. Shah, S.M., Khan, R.A.: Secondary use of electronic health record: opportunities and challenges. IEEE Access **8**, 136947–136965 (2020)
19. Soenksen, L.R., Ma, Y., Zeng, C., et al.: Integrated multimodal artificial intelligence framework for healthcare applications. NPJ Digit. Med. **5**(1), 1–10 (2022). https://doi.org/10.1038/s41746-022-00689-4
20. Touvron, H., Lavril, T., Izacard, G., et al.: Llama: open and efficient foundation language models. arXiv preprint arXiv:2302.13971 (2023)
21. Tu, T., Azizi, S., Driess, D., et al.: Towards generalist biomedical AI (2023). https://arxiv.org/abs/2307.14334v1
22. Yang, Z., Gan, Z., Wang, J., et al.: An empirical study of GPT-3 for few-shot knowledge-based VQA
23. Yin, S., Fu, C., Zhao, S., et al.: Woodpecker: hallucination correction for multimodal large language models (2023). https://doi.org/10.48550/ARXIV.2310.16045
24. Zhang, H., Li, F., Liu, S., et al.: Dino: DETR with improved denoising anchor boxes for end-to-end object detection. arXiv preprint arXiv:2203.03605 (2022)
25. Zhang, K., Yu, J., Adhikarla, E., et al.: BiomedGPT: a unified and generalist biomedical generative pre-trained transformer for vision, language, and multimodal tasks (2024)
26. Zhou, H., Liu, F., Gu, B., et al.: A survey of large language models in medicine: principles, applications, and challenges (2023). https://arxiv.org/abs/2311.05112v2
27. Zhu, Y., et al.: Prompting large language models for zero-shot clinical prediction with structured longitudinal electronic health record data. arXiv preprint arXiv:2402.01713 (2024)

Predicting Stroke Through Retinal Graphs and Multimodal Self-supervised Learning

Yuqing Huang[1], Bastian Wittmann[3], Olga Demler[1,4], Bjoern Menze[3], and Neda Davoudi[1,2,3](✉)

[1] Department of Computer Science, ETH Zürich, Zürich, Switzerland
[2] ETH AI Center, ETH Zürich, Zürich, Switzerland
neda.davoudi@ai.ethz.ch
[3] Department of Quantitative Biomedicine, University of Zurich, Zürich, Switzerland
[4] Harvard Medical School, Boston, MA, USA

Abstract. Early identification of stroke is crucial for intervention, requiring reliable models. We proposed an efficient retinal image representation together with clinical information to capture a comprehensive overview of cardiovascular health, leveraging large multimodal datasets for new medical insights. Our approach is one of the first contrastive frameworks that integrates graph and tabular data, using vessel graphs derived from retinal images for efficient representation. This method, combined with multimodal contrastive learning, significantly enhances stroke prediction accuracy by integrating data from multiple sources and using contrastive learning for transfer learning. The self-supervised learning techniques employed allow the model to learn effectively from unlabeled data, reducing the dependency on large annotated datasets. Our framework showed an AUROC improvement of 3.78% from supervised to self-supervised approaches. Additionally, the graph-level representation approach achieved superior performance to image encoders while significantly reducing pre-training and fine-tuning runtimes. These findings indicate that retinal images are a cost-effective method for improving cardiovascular disease predictions and pave the way for future research into retinal and cerebral vessel connections and the use of graph-based retinal vessel representations.

Keywords: Multimodal Learning · Self-supervised Learning · Graph

1 Introduction

Cardiovascular diseases (CVDs) are the leading cause of death worldwide [16], which makes proactive monitoring of risk factors a critical task in medical research. One of the major subclasses of CVDs is stroke, a medical condition in which poor blood flow to the brain causes cell death and makes the brain stop functioning properly. Deep learning (DL) contributes to stroke treatment by detecting infarcts or hemorrhages, segmenting images, identifying large vessel occlusions, early detection, and providing prognostic insights [26,29].

Recent studies suggest that retinal microvascular changes reflect cerebral small vessel disease (CSVD) [11] and cardiovascular disease (CVD) [20,27]. The RETFound model was developed to generalize disease detection from retinal images [32]. Retinal microvascular biomarkers may indicate systemic cardiovascular diseases like hypertension, atherosclerosis, and heart failure [12]. Retinal vessel thickness is linked to intracranial hypertension [13], while retinal vessel geometry is associated with MRI markers and CVD phenotypes in elderly participants [2]. Recent works focus on early diagnosis and risk management of CVD using retinal images with DL algorithms [23].

To leverage the huge amount of unannotated data and assess the risk of CVDs more efficiently, we propose a contrastive learning framework on fundus photographs (FPs) and clinical information in tabular format. Our framework is developed upon a general contrastive learning model using tabular and imaging data [9]. In addition, we provide three different modules to extract embeddings from fundus photographs. The first module, based on ResNet [10], takes the raw fundus photographs as input. The second module transforms retinal images into probabilistic vessel masks, which are then processed by a ResNet model. Finally, the third module constructs a vessel graph representation from the fundus photograph and uses Graph Neural Networks (GNNs) to learn the feature embedding. This is the first time, to the best of our knowledge, that retinal images are represented as vessel graphs and further utilized in a contrastive learning framework. We show the effectiveness of the contrastive pre-training by comparing it against other baseline approaches for stroke prediction. Our code is publicly available at https://github.com/yuqinghuang01/MMCL-Tabular-Fundus.

1.1 Multimodal Learning

Integrating patient data from diverse sources in real-time facilitates more effective prevention and treatment strategies. Previous work showed that the fused clinical and imaging models outperformed models that included only one modality [17]. DL models, leveraging extensive data, are recognized as valuable tools for enhanced diagnosis and multimodal prognostication, particularly in the rapidly advancing field of stroke imaging [4]. Current models are limited by being trained on a single modality and not translating between different modalities. To fully capture the complexity of human biology, it's necessary to go beyond traditional expert-curated features and include other important data types that doctors also rely on [8]. ML models can leverage the complementary information present in different modalities to develop a joint characterization of physiological states and further enhance their effectiveness. Lee et al. developed an AI model to identify CVD using multimodal data, including clinical risk factors and fundus photographs via supervised learning [14].

1.2 Self-supervised Learning

Recent models excel in biomedical tasks, but overfitting risks persist due to limited annotated medical datasets for supervised learning. Results of generative models such as Autoencoders (AEs) [1] on multimodal clinical measurements show that they perform well on aligning the embeddings from diverse modalities and constructing a holistic representation for characterizing physiological states [22]. AEs are employed to learn cross-modal representations from large multimodal datasets. The UK Biobank [25] serves as an excellent resource for learning clinically relevant representations. Hager et al. attempted to combine images and tabular data for pre-training of representation by optimizing a CLIP loss and predicting myocardial infarction (MI) [9]. Diaz et al. estimated risks of future events of MI using diagnostic features from retinal images that may be undiscovered by human experts [5]. The study estimates cardiac indices, such as left ventricular mass (LVM) and left ventricular end-diastolic volume (LVEDV), and predicts future MI events with multi-channel variational autoencoder. The learned latent space is used to train the ResNet model with cardiac MRI reconstructed from the retinal images plus the demographic data to estimate LVM and LVEDV. Finally, they predict the MI risk using logistic regression.

1.3 Graph Representation of Vessels

Graphs efficiently represent vessel structures, enabling GNNs to model their topological and geometric properties for accurate segmentation. Unlike Convolutional Neural Networks (CNNs), which work on a regular image grid, GNNs excel in capturing complex vascular connectivity globally. Shin et al. proposed Vessel Graph Network (VGN) that combines a GNN into a comprehensive CNN architecture for vessel segmentation [24]. They showed that VGN performs better at segmenting thinner vessels and suppressing false positives by considering the graphical vessel structure. Mishra et al. exploited graph convolutional networks (GCN) such that the model can benefit from vessel topological features for retinal artery/vein classification [19]. Recent research converted vessels into graph representations to efficiently enhance the accuracy and connectivity of vessel segmentation [15,31]. Drees et al. provide an open-source tool for scalable, robust graph and feature extraction from vessel segmentations [7]. The method generates node features including position and degree as well as edge features such as length, curveness, and volume. This tool, among others [3], is a versatile solution for generating graph-level representations for segmented vasculatures.

2 Contrastive Learning Frameworks

Our proposed framework (Fig. 1) is based on the backbone of multimodal contrastive learning [9] where the data sample pair $x = (x_i, x_t)$ consists of imaging data x_i and tabular data x_t. The encoder module for imaging data is denoted as f_i and that for tabular data as f_t. In the following subsections, we discuss three

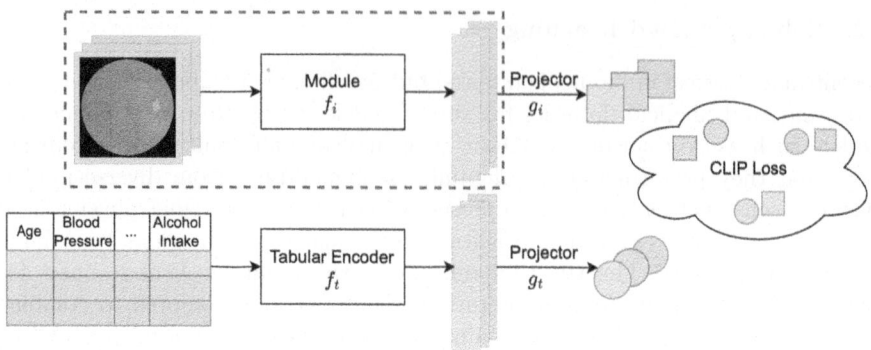

Fig. 1. The overall contrastive learning framework with fundus photographs and tabular data. The Module in the dotted box will be further specified in the subsections depending on the strategy used.

encoder modules proposed for the imaging modality. The modules are introduced in the order of increasing preprocessing steps to condense the information in fundus photographs. The projectors for imaging and tabular data are g_i and g_t, respectively. The projected embeddings for the two data modalities are

$$x'_i = g_i(f_i(x_i)) \quad \text{and} \quad x'_t = g_t(f_t(x_t))$$

As x'_i and x'_t are projections in the same latent space, a CLIP loss [21] is employed to pull projections from the same sample closer and push away projections from different samples. Considering a batch $\mathcal{B}$ of data pairs, the total loss is therefore a weighted sum of imaging modality loss $\ell_{i,t}$ and tabular modality loss $\ell_{t,i}$. Note that $\ell_{t,i}$ is defined symmetrically to $\ell_{i,t}$, and τ, λ are both hyperparameters.

$$\mathcal{L} = \lambda \ell_{i,t} + (1-\lambda)\ell_{t,i} \tag{1}$$

$$\ell_{i,t} = -\sum_{x \in \mathcal{B}} \log \frac{\exp\left(\cos\left(x'_i, x'_t\right)/\tau\right)}{\sum_{y \in \mathcal{B}\setminus\{x\}} \exp\left(\cos\left(x'_i, y'_t\right)/\tau\right)} \tag{2}$$

2.1 Raw Fundus Photographs

Firstly, we use ResNet50 [10] as the imaging encoder. As illustrated in Fig. 2, the encoder directly takes raw fundus images and generates embeddings of fixed size. We name this contrastive learning method Multimodal-CL-raw.

2.2 Retinal Vessel Probability Mask

We propose a two-step processing module (Fig. 3). The first part consists of generating vessel probability masks from raw retinal images using the Automorph pipeline [33]. The second part is a ResNet-based encoder producing embedding vectors. This contrastive learning method is referred to as Multimodal-CL-prob.

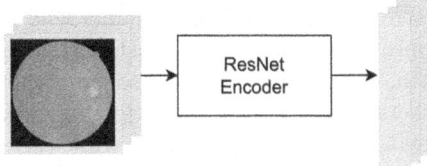

Fig. 2. Module that directly learns from raw fundus images.

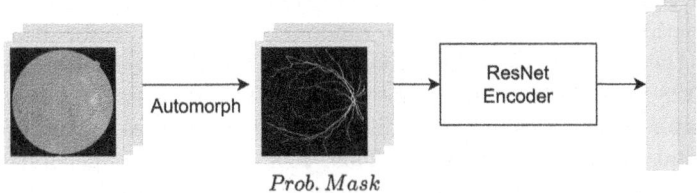

Fig. 3. Module that extracts probabilistic masks from fundus images.

2.3 Retinal Vessel Graph

As illustrated in Fig. 4, the third module exploits graph-level representation for retinal vessels. Pre-processing steps generate binary vessel segmentations using Automorph [33] and extract vessel graphs and features using Voreen tools [18]. Finally, the graphs are processed by a graph encoder consisting of graph attention layers [28] and a global pooling layer to produce the feature embedding. We name this contrastive learning method Multimodal-CL-graph.

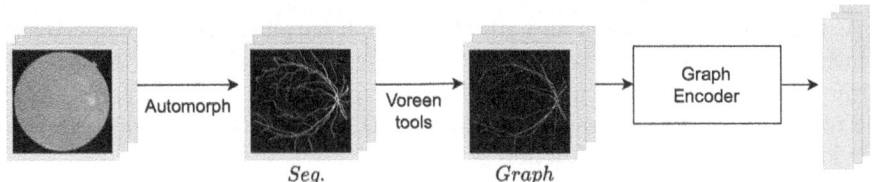

Fig. 4. Module that turns fundus images into vessel segmentations and further into graph representations. A graph encoder is used for feature extraction from graphs.

3 Experiments and Results

3.1 Dataset

Our analyses were performed on UK Biobank, which is a prospective cohort study of over 500,000 individuals' data from across the United Kingdom [25]. This massive database includes patients' information as well as fundus images. To demonstrate the effectiveness of the contrastive pre-training, our goal was to predict future risk of stroke. Therefore, participants who have stroke diagnosed after data collection were labeled as positive instances in the dataset.

For the tabular data, 49 features are selected from the following categories: demographics, biomarkers, comorbidities, lifestyles, and medications. The binary and categorical data fields were one-hot encoded, while the continuous data fields were normalized to a mean value of 0 and standard deviation of 1. Missing values in the tabular data were imputed using an iterative imputer. For the imaging data, the raw fundus photographs were cropped at the center to remove the unnecessary background and min-max normalized to the range between 0 and 1. Transformations such as random flip, random rotation, and color jittering were applied to the images in the contrastive training. Finally, the images were resized to 128 × 128 using bicubic interpolation. No data augmentations were applied for the graph modality as we would like to preserve the vessel structures.

The total size of the dataset is 82569. 20% was used for generating a test set, while the rest are further split with an 80-20 ratio into a training set and a validation set. After enriching our embedding with multimodal contrastive learning, we fine-tune the encoders in a supervised fashion by training on a balanced dataset comprises all patients with diagnosed disease and randomly chosen individuals from the healthy cohort.

3.2 Experimental Setup

The imaging encoder is based on ResNet50 [10], while the tabular encoder, tabular projector, and imaging projector are multilayer perceptions (MLPs) with one hidden layer. The tabular encoder is an MLP with a hidden layer of size 1024 and an output layer of size 1024. In the method Multimodal-CL-graph, the graph encoder consists of three graph attentional layers, using both node and edge features from the vessel graphs. The three layers were defined to have 4, 4, and 2 attention heads and 10, 50, and 256 output channels, respectively. Hence, the graph encoder generates embeddings of dimension 512. Adam optimizer was used with a batch size of 64 in all experiments. We report area under the receiver operating characteristic curve (AUROC) on the test set, as used in previous works on CVD prediction [5,9,14,22].

For downstream task, the three contrastive learning methods used both tabular features and images as inputs. Our goal was to investigate whether contrastive pre-training on all available data pairs could be beneficial for stroke prediction. To evaluate the performance of our methods Multimodal-CL-raw, Multimodal-CL-prob, and Multimodal-CL-graph, we compared them against three fully supervised baselines on stroke prediction. We also tested the XGBoost on tabular data, which gives much lower AUROC comparing to neural networks (NNs). Therefore, we focused on NN-based methods in the experiments for consistency. For these supervised methods, we used the same 80-20 train-test split ratio. Furthermore, the train and validation sets are balanced so that the supervised baselines are in fair comparison with the self-supervised methods.

Tabular-NN. We defined a neural network (NN) with one hidden layer of size 256 and an output of size 2. The model was developed using tabular data only.

Imaging-NN. Imaging-NN is composed of an encoder network and a classifier. For the encoder network, we used the architecture and pre-trained weights taken from a foundation model, RETFound [32]. The RETFound model is a masked autoencoder trained on millions of color fundus photographs. Specifically, the encoder uses a Vision Transformer (ViT) [6] with 24 Transformer blocks and creates an embedding vector of size 1024. The classifier takes 1024-dimension inputs, features a width-512 hidden layer, and outputs a prediction of size 2. The weights of the pre-trained RETFound encoder were frozen throughout the training and testing phases.

Multimodal-NN. Multimodal-NN takes both the tabular and imaging modality. For the tabular data, the model learns feature embeddings of size 256 using an MLP. Embeddings for the imaging modality were learned the same way as in Imaging-NN method, using the pre-trained RETFound encoder. In addition, we projected the size-1024 imaging embedding vectors to dimension 256 and concatenated them with the tabular embeddings to make the final prediction using a fully connected layer.

3.3 Stroke Prediction

Table 1 shows the evaluation metrics reported on the test set. The results of Tabular-NN, Imaging-NN, and Multimodal-NN indicate that tabular data plays an important role in stroke prediction. Compared to using tabular modality only, concatenating the learned features from tabular and imaging modality in a fully supervised setting seemed not sufficient for improving the AUROC. With contrastive pre-training, our proposed approaches outperformed all supervised baselines, with Multimodal-CL-graph achieving the best AUROC 71.92%. Multimodal-CL-prob also demonstrated better performance than Multimodal-CL-raw on the test set.

Furthermore, we showed a visualization (Fig. 5) of the receiver operating characteristic (ROC) curves of three methods: Imaging-NN, Multimodal-NN, and Multimodal-CL-graph. Out of the two fully supervised methods, multimodal training with tabular and imaging data outperformed unimodal training with imaging data, which shows that fundus images are best used as an additional modality rather than the only data modality for prediction. Compared to the multimodal supervised baseline, making use of unlabelled paired data in self-supervised pre-training gives further improvement in predicting future risk of stroke.

Table 1. A summary table of evaluation metrics for different configurations of supervised and self-supervised methods. Our methods are highlighted in gray.

Method	AUROC(%)
Tabular-NN	70.02
Imaging-NN	62.46
Multimodal-NN	69.30
Multimodal-CL-raw	71.54
Multimodal-CL-prob	71.73
Multimodal-CL-graph	**71.92**

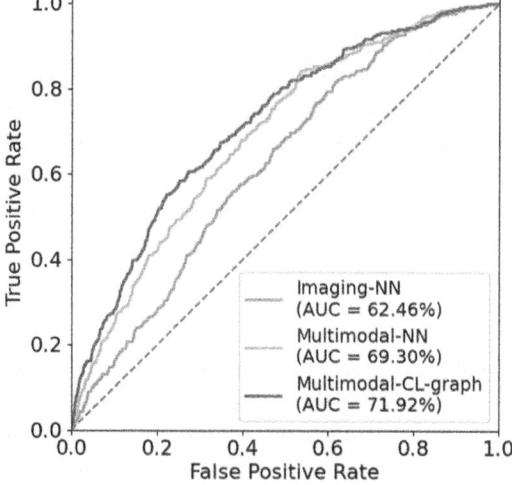

Fig. 5. Comparison of test-time ROC curves for Imaging-NN, Multimodal-NN, and Multimodal-CL-graph methods.

3.4 Efficiency Comparison

In Table 2, we compare the sizes of the networks and the runtimes per epoch when using image encoder versus when using graph encoder in the contrastive learning framework. Vessel graphs with node and edge features are compact representations of the vessel structure in retinal images. The number of trainable parameters in the contrastive pre-training with graph encoder is 3.4 M, which is about 12% of those needed for contrastive pre-training with image encoder. In terms of training time, pre-training takes about 840 s per epoch with ResNet50 encoder and about 90 s per epoch with graph attention network (GAT) encoder. Similarly, during fine-tuning, Multimodal-CL-graph requires significantly fewer trainable parameters and thus less training time per epoch compared to Multimodal-CL-image or Multimodal-CL-prob while outperforming the test-time AUROCs of the latter two.

Table 2. Comparison of computational efficiency for image and graph encoders by trainable parameters and runtime per epoch during pre-training and fine-tuning.

	Pre-training		Fine-tuning	
	Parameters	Per epoch	Parameters	Per epoch
Multimodal-CL-raw/ Multimodal-CL-prob	28.2 M	840 s	24.8 M	13 s
Multimodal-CL-graph	3.4 M	90 s	1.5 M	2 s

4 Discussion and Conclusion

In this work, we presented self-supervised methods leveraging retinal images and medical information in tabular format to improve stroke prediction. Moreover, we proposed the first contrastive framework that combines graph and tabular data. In particular, vessel graphs were extracted from retinal images for a more efficient representation and were paired with tabular features in multimodal contrastive learning. The contrastive pre-training step allowed us to use all available paired tabular-fundus data, even in the absence of labels, by jointly learning a latent space. We improved the AUROC from supervised to self-supervised methods by 3.78%. In addition, compared to the methods using image encoders, the method using graph-level representations achieves superior performance while being more efficient with regard to number of parameters and around ten times faster in terms of pre-training and fine-tuning runtimes.

Here are a few directions for improving the study. First, our experiments focus on the downstream task of stroke prediction. Future work can also examine the effectiveness on other cardiovascular diseases as downstream classification tasks such as myocardial infraction prediction. Second, for the fine-tuning datasets, we randomly sampled the healthy people with the same number of people having stroke. Further ablation studies can be conducted to investigate how the ratio between the positive and negative cases in the fine-tuning set would affect the performance of downstream tasks. Third, the graph encoder used in our experiments consists of graph attention layers and a global pooling layer to extract the final embedding vector. Future studies can explore the use of other graph encoder architectures and test their effectiveness. For example, Ying et al. [30] proposed a differentiable graph pooling module that generates hierarchical representations of graphs. This method offers an alternative solution to global pooling and can be adapted to aggregate features in vessel graphs in a hierarchical manner.

In conclusion, we proposed novel approachs to integrate the fundus photographs in a contrastive learning framework. Our findings suggest that retinal images could be a cost-effective modality for improving stroke predictions. We believe these results are clinically meaningful and would motivate future research exploring the relation between retinal and cerebral vessels as well as using graphs as a compact representation of retinal vessels.

Acknowledgments. This research used UK Biobank under application number 81959. We thank Prof. Samia Mora from Harvard Medical School for her invaluable medical insight and guidance. This project was supported by the grant #2023-N-306 of the 1st Joint Call of the Swiss Data Science Center (SDSC) and the Strategic Focus Area "Personalized Health and Related Technologies (PHRT)" of the ETH Domain (Swiss Federal Institutes of Technology). N.D. is partially supported by the ETH AI Center postdoctoral fellowship. B.M., B.W., and N.D. acknowledge support of the Helmut-Horten-Foundation.

Disclosure of Interests. The authors have no competing interests to declare that are relevant to the content of this article.

References

1. Alain, G., Bengio, Y.: What regularized auto-encoders learn from the data-generating distribution. J. Mach. Learn. Res. **15**(1), 3563–3593 (2014)
2. Arnould, L., Soumare, A., Delcourt, C., Helmer, C., Creuzot-Garcher, C., Debette, S.: The retinal vascular network with Singapore I vessel assessment (siva) software and brain magnetic resonance imaging markers of cerebral small vessel disease in the elderly: the montrachet study. Invest. Ophthalmol. Vis. Sci. **64**(8), 4668–4668 (2023)
3. Bumgarner, J.R., Nelson, R.J.: Open-source analysis and visualization of segmented vasculature datasets with vesselvio. Cell Rep. Methods **2**(4), 100189 (2022). https://doi.org/10.1016/j.crmeth.2022.100189, https://www.sciencedirect.com/science/article/pii/S2667237522000443
4. Cui, L., et al.: Deep learning in ischemic stroke imaging analysis: a comprehensive review. BioMed Res. Int. **2022**, 2456550 (2022)
5. Diaz-Pinto, A., et al.: Predicting myocardial infarction through retinal scans and minimal personal information. Nat. Mach. Intell. **4**(1), 55–61 (2022)
6. Dosovitskiy, A., et al.: An image is worth 16×16 words: transformers for image recognition at scale. In: International Conference on Learning Representations (2021). https://openreview.net/forum?id=YicbFdNTTy
7. Drees, D., Scherzinger, A., Hägerling, R., Kiefer, F., Jiang, X.: Scalable robust graph and feature extraction for arbitrary vessel networks in large volumetric datasets. BMC Bioinf. **22**(1), 1–28 (2021)
8. Gong, W., Bai, S., Zheng, Y.Q., Smith, S.M., Beckmann, C.F.: Supervised phenotype discovery from multimodal brain imaging. IEEE Trans. Med. Imaging **42**(3), 834–849 (2022)
9. Hager, P., Menten, M.J., Rueckert, D.: Best of both worlds: multimodal contrastive learning with tabular and imaging data. In: Proceedings of the IEEE/CVF Conference on Computer Vision and Pattern Recognition, pp. 23924–23935 (2023)
10. He, K., Zhang, X., Ren, S., Sun, J.: Deep residual learning for image recognition. In: 2016 IEEE Conference on Computer Vision and Pattern Recognition (CVPR), pp. 770–778 (2015). https://api.semanticscholar.org/CorpusID:206594692
11. Ji, C., et al.: Predicting cerebral small vessel disease through retinal scans and demographic data with bayesian feature selection. In: Medical Imaging 2024: Computer-Aided Diagnosis, vol. 12927, pp. 830–837. SPIE (2024)

12. Kellner, R.L., et al.: The eye as the window to the heart: optical coherence tomography angiography biomarkers as indicators of cardiovascular disease. J. Clin. Med. **13**(3), 829 (2024)
13. Kwapong, W.R., et al.: Retinal microvascular and structural changes in intracranial hypertension patients correlate with intracranial pressure. CNS Neurosci. Ther. **29**(12), 4093–4101 (2023)
14. Lee, Y.C., et al.: Multimodal deep learning of fundus abnormalities and traditional risk factors for cardiovascular risk prediction. NPJ Digit. Med. **6**(1), 14 (2023)
15. Li, R., et al.: 3D graph-connectivity constrained network for hepatic vessel segmentation. IEEE J. Biomed. Health Inform. **26**(3), 1251–1262 (2022). https://doi.org/10.1109/JBHI.2021.3118104
16. Lindstrom, M., et al.: Global burden of cardiovascular diseases and risks collaboration, 1990–2021. J. Am. Coll. Cardiol. **80**(25), 2372–2425 (2022)
17. Liu, Y., et al.: Functional outcome prediction in acute ischemic stroke using a fused imaging and clinical deep learning model. Stroke **54**(9), 2316–2327 (2023)
18. Meyer-Spradow, J., Ropinski, T., Mensmann, J., Hinrichs, K.: Voreen: a rapid-prototyping environment for ray-casting-based volume visualizations. IEEE Comput. Graphics Appl. **29**(6), 6–13 (2009). https://doi.org/10.1109/MCG.2009.130
19. Mishra, S., Wang, Y.X., Wei, C., Chen, D., Hu, X.: VTG-Net: a CNN based vessel topology graph network for retinal artery/vein classification. Front. Med. **8**, 750396 (2021). https://doi.org/10.3389/fmed.2021.750396
20. Poplin, R., et al.: Prediction of cardiovascular risk factors from retinal fundus photographs via deep learning. Nat. Biomed. Eng. **2**(3), 158–164 (2018)
21. Radford, A., et al.: Learning transferable visual models from natural language supervision. In: Meila, M., Zhang, T. (eds.) Proceedings of the 38th International Conference on Machine Learning. Proceedings of Machine Learning Research, vol. 139, pp. 8748–8763. PMLR (18–24 Jul 2021) (2021). https://proceedings.mlr.press/v139/radford21a.html
22. Radhakrishnan, A., et al.: Cross-modal autoencoder framework learns holistic representations of cardiovascular state. Nat. Commun. **14**(1), 2436 (2023)
23. Sheela, A.J., Krishnamurthy, M.: Revolutionizing cardiovascular risk prediction: a novel image-based approach using fundus analysis and deep learning. Biomed. Signal Process. Control **90**, 105781 (2024)
24. Shin, S.Y., Lee, S., Yun, I.D., Lee, K.M.: Deep vessel segmentation by learning graphical connectivity. Med. Image Anal. **58**, 101556 (2019). https://doi.org/10.1016/j.media.2019.101556, https://www.sciencedirect.com/science/article/pii/S1361841519300982
25. Sudlow, C., et al.: UK biobank: an open access resource for identifying the causes of a wide range of complex diseases of middle and old age. PLoS Med. **12**(3), e1001779 (2015)
26. Tan, K., Marvell, Y.A., Gunawan, A.A.S.: Early ischemic stroke detection using deep learning: a systematic literature review. In: 2023 International Seminar on Application for Technology of Information and Communication (iSemantic), pp. 7–11. IEEE (2023)
27. Tseng, R.M.W.W., et al.: Validation of a deep-learning-based retinal biomarker (RETI-CVD) in the prediction of cardiovascular disease: data from uk biobank. BMC Med. **21**(1), 28 (2023)
28. Veličković, P., Cucurull, G., Casanova, A., Romero, A., Liò, P., Bengio, Y.: Graph attention networks. In: International Conference on Learning Representations (2018). https://openreview.net/forum?id=rJXMpikCZ

29. Wardlaw, J.M., Mair, G., Von Kummer, R., Williams, M.C., Li, W., Storkey, A.J., Trucco, E., Liebeskind, D.S., Farrall, A., Bath, P.M., et al.: Accuracy of automated computer-aided diagnosis for stroke imaging: a critical evaluation of current evidence. Stroke **53**(7), 2393–2403 (2022)
30. Ying, Z., You, J., Morris, C., Ren, X., Hamilton, W., Leskovec, J.: Hierarchical graph representation learning with differentiable pooling. In: Bengio, S., Wallach, H., Larochelle, H., Grauman, K., Cesa-Bianchi, N., Garnett, R. (eds.) Advances in Neural Information Processing Systems, vol. 31. Curran Associates, Inc. (2018), https://proceedings.neurips.cc/paper_files/paper/2018/file/e77dbaf6759253c7c6d0efc5690369c7-Paper.pdf
31. Yu, H., Zhao, J., Zhang, L.: Vessel segmentation via link prediction of graph neural networks. In: Li, X., Lv, J., Huo, Y., Dong, B., Leahy, R.M., Li, Q. (eds.) Multiscale Multimodal Medical Imaging, pp. 34–43. Springer Nature Switzerland, Cham (2022). https://doi.org/10.1007/978-3-031-18814-5_4
32. Zhou, Y., et al.: A foundation model for generalizable disease detection from retinal images. Nature **622**(7981), 156–163 (2023)
33. Zhou, Y., et al.: AutoMorph: automated retinal vascular morphology quantification via a deep learning pipeline. Transl. Vis. Sci. Technol. **11**(7), 12–12 (2022)

Multimodality for Diagnosis of Asian Choroidal Vasculopathy: Results from a Novel Dataset and Deep-Learning Experiments

Daehyun Cho[1], Young Ho Kim[2], Somin Ahn[3], Jaeryung Oh[2], and Christian Wallraven[1,4(✉)]

[1] Department of Artificial Intelligence, Korea University, Seoul, Korea
wallraven@korea.ac.kr
[2] Department of Ophthalmology, Korea University College of Medicine, Seoul, Korea
[3] Department of Ophthalmology, Dongguk University Ilsan Hospital, Goyang, South Korea
[4] Department of Artificial Intelligence and Department of Brain and Cognitive Engineering, Korea University, Seoul, Korea

Abstract. Deep learning algorithms show tremendous potential for clinical decision-making - for example, in providing automated diagnoses of imaging data. However, typical clinical datasets often are limited in size, modalities, and contain heterogeneous, incomplete data, which presents challenges for deep learning frameworks that necessitate larger, uniform datasets, complicating their deployment especially with new types of disease models. In this work, we present a case study for deep learning in such a challenging setting in the context of diagnosing Asian choroidal Vasculopathy (ACV), which is a retinopathy profile currently under discussion in ophthalmology to be differentiated from age-related macular degeneration (AMD). We first introduce a novel, human-annotated multimodal dataset for ACV versus AMD diagnosis incorporating four different imaging modalities. We next explore the usefulness of "foundation models" for this data, compared to traditional dataset-specific training. Most importantly, we investigate which of the four modalities is most discriminative and whether bi-modal classification is able to enhance performance across multiple fusion approaches. We also discuss first results of salient features using explainability techniques.

Keywords: Deep Learning · Multimodal Imaging · Retinopathy

1 Introduction

As the complexity of diseases demands more sophisticated detection methods, multimodal imaging has become an indispensable tool. This is especially true in ophthalmology, where integration of diagnostic tools such as optical coherence tomography (OCT), fundus photography, and fluorescein angiography can provide a more holistic view of affected tissues, facilitating accurate diagnosis [5].

One of the focal points of our research is the diagnosis of a relatively new concept termed "Asian choroidal vasculopathy" (ACV), which is a pathology that is proposed to be distinct from Age-related macular degeneration (AMD), one of the most common retinal diseases world-wide. Variations in AMD presentations, such as the higher prevalence of distinct soft drusen in Asian populations compared to the predominance of indistinct or reticular drusen in non-Asians, necessitate population-specific screening and treatment protocols [14]. Additionally, the presence of pachydrusen linked to pachychoroid diseases in Asians underscores the need for tailored diagnostic criteria, influencing disease progression and treatment response [17]. Age-related macular degeneration (AMD) and Asian choroidal vasculopathy (ACV) require distinct approaches for effective diagnosis and management, and critically need to make use of multimodal imaging [16,19–21] to provide a comprehensive view of the retina and choroid. This diagnosis strategy should help practitioners to distinguish AMD and ACV, which may appear similar in one single imaging modality but show differentiated characteristics across multiple modalities. Recognizing these differences is essential for tailoring treatment to the specific condition and demographic, leading to better patient outcomes.

However, the application of deep learning in this context is constrained by the availability of appropriate datasets. Most publicly available datasets cater to high-prevalence conditions, even fewer are available that include multiple modalities. Importantly as well, multimodal datasets rarely include multiple modalities from *the same patient*, leading to increased cross-domain variability, which hampers generalization for deep learning algorithms. Further research on the ACV pathology is in need of such a homogeneous, multimodal dataset, including three or more types of imaging modalities. Recognizing this gap, our team has been working on creating a new dataset specifically geared towards enabling (automated) diagnosis of ACV, incorporating recordings from patients across multiple modalities, and contrasting it against AMD. This dataset allows for a detailed analysis of the nuanced differences and similarities between these conditions in diverse populations, facilitating the development of more effective, evidence-based diagnostic criteria and treatments. Through this dataset, our research aims to refine the classification systems for AMD and ACV, ensuring they are sensitive to the variations presented by these distinct pathology profiles.

Our contributions are as follows: First, we present an initial snapshot of a new, larger-scale dataset containing four different modalities, specifically designed to address the complexities of ACV, including its subtle distinctions from AMD. Second, we provide a deep learning analysis of how well "foundation" models would fare on this dataset, compared to the more traditional approach of fine-tuning standard image classification models on the data. Third, we present results that test which of the four modalities fares best in terms of diagnosing AMD versus ACV (versus normal). Fourth, we test the degree to which bimodal models are able to improve performance over unimodal models and analyze differences in performance pattern. Overall, our research aims not only to enhance our understanding of ACV for clinical decision-making, but also hopes to inspire further studies into multimodal medical imaging.

2 Related Works

Multimodal Data in Neural Networks. The integration of multimodal data has become pivotal for enhancing model robustness and accuracy across a spectrum of applications: for instance, Baltrušaitis et al. [1] show that multimodal networks leverage diverse data types - such as text, images, and audio - by capturing a richer array of features and reducing the impact of noisy or incomplete data in any single mode. When developing models for multimodal classification, different approaches for fusing information across modalities become important (see [15], for a review), including from pixel-level fusions to decision-level fusion. To avoid variability across modalities, the ideal case especially for multimodal datasets would be to have every modality available from every source (i.e., patient). However, especially in clinical settings, this is rarely the case, which has led to approaches trying to deal with missing modalities, such as SMIL [24], or ShaSpec [29]. However, these methods also have limitations when applied to datasets with incomplete data: SMIL assumes that one modality is complete (present for all patients), whereas ShaSpec requires complete data in the training phase in order to deal with missing ones in the inference phase.

Deep Learning for Retinopathy. Early works of deep learning in retinopathy primarily addressed specific tasks without incorporating multimodality (e.g. [6,18]. Multimodal imaging has been used, for example, to better understand and diagnose disease progression of AMD, as detailed anatomical features are better elucidated [7]. Consequently, deep learning models that employ multimodal imaging, such as those combining fundus photography (FP) and OCT, have demonstrated superior diagnostic accuracy in classifying AMD [11]. Similarly, the work in [30], showed that combining FP and OCT scans significantly improved the accuracy of distinguishing AMD from normal eyes and drusen. Thakoor [28] extended this approach by using OCT, OCTA, HD 5-line B-scan cubes and 2D B-Scan modality in detecting late-stage AMD, achieving higher performance in the combined case. Importantly, however, these studies relied on fully homogenized datasets with complete data across all modalities, which is unrealistic in typical clinical settings where data is more heterogeneous.

Foundation Models in Retinal Imaging Analysis. One recent solution to limited sample sizes has been to employ "foundation models" [2] - models that are trained on large datasets and then fine-tuned to downstream tasks. In the context of retinal imaging, we highlight two such recent models: RETFound [32] is a transformer-based model, pre-trained using a masked autoencoder [8] approach. Its release contains one model trained on 904,170 fundus photography

(FP) images, and another model trained on 736,442 Optical Coherence Tomography (OCT) scans. Given that restoration-based self-supervised learning can capture domain-specific characteristics, this model may hold potential also in our case, given that we use similar modalities. The second model, FLAIR [27], is a convolutional-based foundational model, enriched with co-trained expert textual knowledge. Its vision encoder leverages a Resnet [9] architecture that has been pre-trained in a CLIP [25] style, focusing on contrastive learning between image-text pairs. This integration of expert knowledge is intended to enhance model robustness and interpretability in clinical applications.

3 Methods

3.1 Dataset

The dataset we are collecting in our team is aimed at distinguishing ACV from AMD pathologies and at present contains a total of 3,811 recordings from 570 patients[1]. To better discriminate between AMD and ACV, the dataset includes the following modalities: Fundus Photography (FP), Fundus Autofluorescence (FAF), Optical Coherence Tomography (OCT), Optical Coherence Tomography Angiography (OCTA), Fluorescein Angiography (FA) and Indocyanine Green Angiography (ICGA). Since the recording protocol of FA and ICGA results in varying-length video streams and data was not available yet for the majority of cases, at present we exclude these two modalities.

The dataset comprises images from both eyes, and for some patients, identical images are captured at different times. Each visit was labeled by experts as one of 3 classes - Normal, Age-related Macular Degeneration (AMD) and Asian Choroidal Vasculopathy (ACV). For details of each modality, refer to Table 1 (left); Table 1 (right) shows the age and gender distribution of the dataset.

Table 1. Left: Dataset demographics. #N = number of scans per visit. Right: Age distribution across genders.

Modality	HC	AMD	ACV	#N
FP	88	956	315	1
FAF	25	370	143	1
OCT	76	616	224	10
OCTA	91	653	254	4

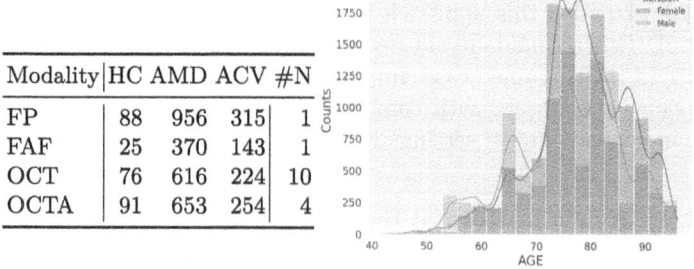

[1] We note that due to Institutional Review Board (IRB) restrictions, public access to this dataset cannot be granted at present. For access to the dataset, the corresponding author should be contacted.

To conduct evaluations, we first created a stratified, 10% hold-out test set. The remaining data was again split into a 90/10 train/validation dataset. Given the presence of patients with multiple clinical visits and the similarity between the left and right retinal images, all splits were managed so as to prevent accidental leakage.

3.2 Models

We first tested two foundation models derived from large-scale fundus photography databases - RETfound and FLAIR models. To benchmark foundation models, we employed two standard convolutional models, a Resnet50d and a Resnet101d [10] model, as well as two ConvNext [23] models, all pre-trained on the ImageNet-1k dataset. We use these pre-trained models, as it is well-documented that pre-training on non-medical domain images can enhance the classification of medical images [13]. For parameter specifications, see Table 2.

3.3 Modality Fusion

Since methods such as SMIL [24] or ShaSpec [29] are not applicable on our heterogeneous dataset, we employed three different strategies for modality fusion, following [15]. The first approach involved concatenating all images along the channel dimension, allowing models to perform channel-wise embedding of different modalities, substituting missing modalities with a null image. The second strategy involved embedding each modality into separate branches, which were then concatenated to generate the final predictions. In case of missing modalities, predictions were made using only the available modalities, bypassing the absent ones. The third strategy mirrored the second in terms of initial modality-specific embeddings. However, for any missing modality, we introduced a trainable representation-vector specific to each modality. This representation-vector was concatenated in place of the missing modality's contribution, allowing the model to maintain structural integrity. The three methods will be referred to as channel concatenation, branching, and adaptive vector fusion, respectively.

3.4 Training Configuration

When training the foundation models, we used a learning rate of $1e^{-5}$ to avoid forgetting of its encoded domain knowledge. All other (ImageNet pre-trained) models were trained with $1e^{-4}$. All experiments used the Adam optimizer with standard settings and did not freeze layers to enable information to backpropagate to the feature level. For the multimodal fusion experiments, we used the Resnet50d as our backbone, as the Convnext model - especially in its standard version - did not converge on extended data. In order to avoid overfitting on the (relatively) small dataset, we applied augmentation via the standard FundusAug method used in [3]. To deal with imbalanced classes, we applied label smoothing (weight of 0.05) and weighted cross entropy. We used batch sizes of

64/32 and gradient accumulations of 8/16 in unimodal and multimodal training, respectively. The validation set was used for all models to implement an early stopping criterion via monitoring the F1-score (see below). For detailed training recipes, refer to our training codebase: github link[2].

3.5 Evaluation

Due to the significant label imbalance, we focus on the weighted-F1 score as our main performance metric. For evaluating the effectiveness of unimodal versus multimodal approaches, we compared performance of individual modalities as well as their combined impact across all possible bimodal combinations. For instance, the results of multimodal training combining Fundus Photography (FP) and Fundus Autofluorescence (FAF) were compared in terms of the overall Weighted-F1 score, and the individual scores for FP and FAF, respectively.

Table 2. Model specification and weighted F1 score of unimodality tertiary classification. $\#P$ refers to trainable parameters of a model.

Dataset	Model	#P	FP	FAF	OCT	OCTA	Avg.
Medical	RETFound: FP	303 M	46.7	62.4	53.2	54.5	54.1
	RETFound: OCT	303 M	56.6	56.7	61.8	52.4	56.9
	FLAIR	25 M	69.9	54.5	*73.9*	58.7	64.3
ImageNet	Resnet-50d	25 M	65.4	78.3	**73.9**	52.7	67.6
	Resnet-101d	43 M	65.0	67.7	73.1	53.6	64.8
	Convnext-small	50 M	67.2	78.7	71.5	**62.3**	69.9
	Convnext-base	88 M	**71.3**	**84.2**	72.7	52.0	**70.0**

While performance metrics, such as F1 are important, we also wanted to characterize the degree to which the different models agree in their predictions, i.e., would a multimodally-trained model result in different prediction patterns compared to a unimodally-trained one? For this, we compared prediction patterns using Cohen's Kappa, that measures agreements of two "raters" (models).

4 Results

We first focus on unimodal training results, contrasting performance of the foundation models with the "standard" pre-trained convolutional models. Next, we trained on multi-modal inputs and compared performance changes to unimodal training results, investigating the interactions between modalities. Lastly, we focus on binary classification, contrasting AMD versus ACV, to better understand model performance and to analyze explainability results crucial for clinical decision-masking.

---

[2] https://github.com/1pha/retinopathy.

4.1 Unimodal Training

As Table 2 shows, none of the two RETFound models yielded high performance, potentially due to the propensity of transformers to overfit specific domain data and limited data points [22]. Interestingly, in our training setup, the OCT-trained model performed better also on FP data, compared to the fundus-trained model. In contrast, FLAIR significantly outperformed RETFound across all modalities except for FAF. Although FLAIR was anticipated to excel due to its training on fundus photography, the ImageNet-pretrained ConvNeXt model surpassed FLAIR's performance on FP, perhaps due to the difference in model capacities (24.6M for FLAIR versus 98.3M for ConvNeXt). Importantly, however, across all modalities, we found the best performances either for the dataset-specific-trained Resnet or the Convnext models. In addition, we observe that overall the best-performing modality for unimodal prediction was FAF, followed by OCT, for which all convolutional models showed high performance - a potential indicator also for the clinical importance of these two modalities in diagnosing ACV.

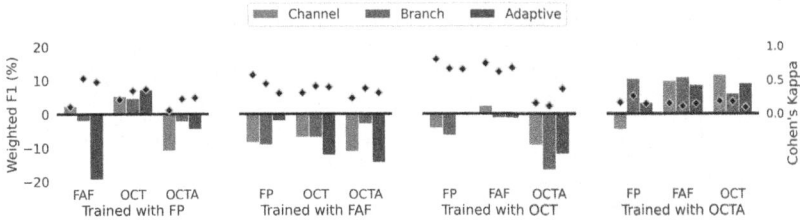

Fig. 1. Modality interaction via modality fusion. The bargraph depicts weighted F1 of modality in x-axis. Diamond markers illustrates Cohen's Kappa value.

4.2 Multimodal Fusion

Performance of the Resnet50d models trained with different fusion strategies for all six different bimodal combinations is summarized in Table 3. The baseline performance is taken from unimodal training. To illustrate the effects of bimodal training, we further plot the difference to unimodal performance in Fig. 1.

We observe first that overall, performance of FAF and OCT are somewhat *degraded* when combined with other modalities. In contrast, FP gained improvements when co-trained with OCT across all different fusion types, but not from other modalities. Likewise, OCTA - the overall worst-performing modality in unimodal training - showed improvements across almost all cases. Overall, these results show that it is possible to find a bimodal combination that outperforms the unimodal results for three out of four modalities. We further find no clear advantage across the three different fusion methods - showing that further, larger-scale experiments are needed to evaluate their (potential) effectiveness.

Table 3. Multimodality Weighted F1 Score and Cohen's Kappa. The F1 score represents overall performance and the influence of individual modalities on paired modalities. Cohen's kappa measures agreement between predictions from unimodal and multimodal test sets for each modality.

	Fusion	Weighted-F1					Cohen's Kappa			
		Total	FP	FAF	OCT	OCTA	FP	FAF	OCT	OCTA
Baseline		-	65.3	**78.2**	73.8	52.6				
FP & FAF	Cha	68.7	67.6	69.7	-	-	0.47	0.31	-	-
	Bran.	64.0	63.3	69.1	-	-	0.53	0.45	-	-
	Ada.	49.1	45.9	76.2	-	-	0.11	0.58	-	-
	Avg.	60.6	58.9	71.7	-	-	0.37	0.45	-	-
FP & OCT	Cha	71.0	70.6	-	69.6	-	0.37	-	0.66	-
	Bran.	69.3	70.0	-	67.5	-	0.34	-	0.67	-
	Ada.	72.9	**72.5**	-	73.5	-	0.21	-	0.81	-
	Avg.	71.1	71.0	-	70.2	-	0.31	-	0.71	-
FP & OCTA	Cha	54.7	54.4	-	-	48.0	0.24	-	-	0.15
	Bran.	64.0	63.1	-	-	63.0	0.22	-	-	0.26
	Ada.	61.2	60.8	-	-	55.8	0.06	-	-	0.17
	Avg.	60.0	59.4	-	-	55.6	0.17	-	-	0.19
FAF & OCT	Cha	72.4	-	71.3	72.6	-	-	0.40	0.68	-
	Bran.	71.4	-	71.3	72.6	-	-	0.41	0.62	-
	Ada.	67.9	-	66.0	**76.2**	-	-	0.31	0.75	-
	Avg.	70.6	-	69.5	73.8	-	-	0.37	0.68	-
FAF & OCTA	Cha	62.4	-	67.1	-	62.4	-	0.31	-	0.15
	Bran.	63.4	-	75.3	-	**63.4**	-	0.38	-	0.11
	Ada.	61.2	-	63.8	-	61.2	-	0.23	-	0.16
	Avg.	62.3	-	68.7	-	62.3	-	0.31	-	0.14
OCT & OCTA	Cha	63.7	-	-	64.5	64.2	-	-	0.37	0.10
	Bran.	59.0	-	-	57.2	58.6	-	-	0.11	0.18
	Ada.	62.0	-	-	61.9	61.6	-	-	0.16	0.19
	Avg	61.6	-	-	61.2	61.5	-	-	0.21	0.16

We also list the Cohen's Kappa assessing the alignment of predictions of unimodal versus multimodal trained outputs in Table 3 - a kappa value of 0 would indicate chance-level alignment, whereas larger values indicate increasing levels of similarity. In conjunction with the F1-score, for example, an increased F1 and lower kappa value would suggest that the prediction was significantly affected by the added modality, at the same time moving closer to the ground truth. Based on the unimodal classification results, one might as well anticipate that modalities with superior performance (FAF, OCTA) would enhance their counterparts (FP, OCT), which we partially observe for FP, for example. Conversely, interactions of other modalities (FAF, OCT) appear antagonistic. OCTA again benefited positively from other modalities in multimodal training in this interpretation as well. FAF, in contrast, seemed not to get enhanced, indicating a high susceptibility to influence from other modalities. We also observed a certain asymmetry: whereas OCT results do not differ much from the addition of FAF, the opposite setting significantly affects performance.

4.3 Binary Classification: AMD vs. ACV

In order to dive deeper into classification of the pathology of Asian choroidal Vasculopathy, we next re-trained classifiers to do a direct two-class comparison, discriminating AMD and ACV, for the four unimodal models. The confusion matrices shown in Fig. 2 together with the weighted F1-scores indicate that all models are above chance. However, importantly, we clearly see that FAF and OCT are more discriminative overall for the ACV case, enabling better separation of the two classes.

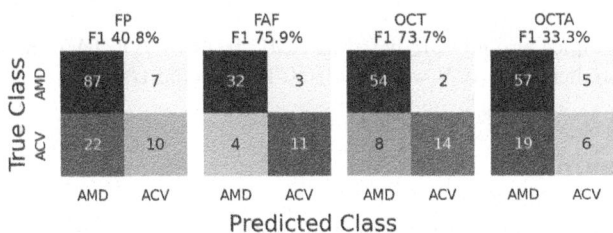

Fig. 2. Binary classification performance with Resnet50d. Task performed discriminating AMD vs. ACV

For practical aid in clinical decision-making, models need to offer explainability. To illustrate the learned features that helped the model to discriminate the two classes of AMD versus ACV, Fig. 3 shows Grad-CAM [26] reconstructions of four ACV samples contrasting a FP-trained model versus a FAF-trained model and an OCTA model versus an OCT model. In all cases, the samples were incorrectly predicted as AMD by the FP/OCTA-trained model while correctly recognized as ACV by the FAF/OCT-trained model. All samples were diagnosed as ACV as they are part of the pachychoroid spectrum (one symptom telling it apart from classical AMD [21]), which goes along with increased subfoveal choroidal thickness [4]. Accordingly, the Grad-CAM results of the FAF model show highlights around the foveal area, whereas the FP model focuses on arterial structures. Likewise, the OCT-samples show the presence of pachydrusen (again one of the symptoms accompanying ACV [31]) located between two membranes, which is picked up by the Grad-CAM saliency maps. Conversely, although such pachydrusen may appear in OCTA as small, hyperreflective dots [12], the OCTA-trained model fails to detect the relevant structures. Overall, these results highlight the superiority of FAF and OCT for diagnosis.

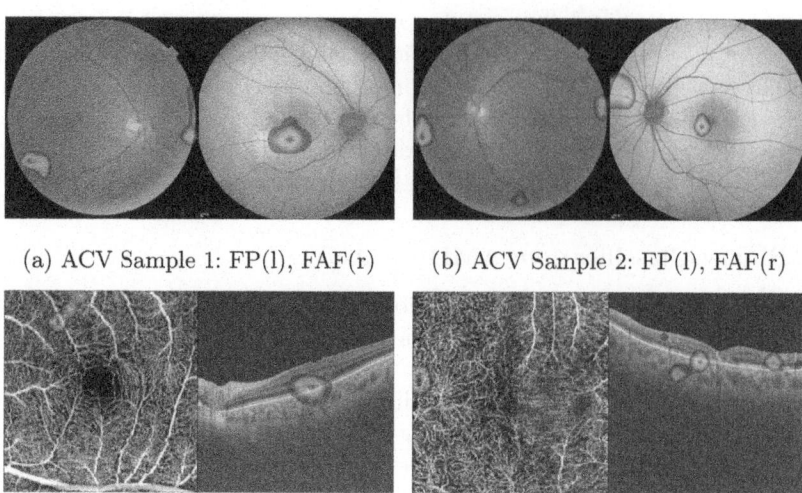

(a) ACV Sample 1: FP(l), FAF(r) (b) ACV Sample 2: FP(l), FAF(r)

(c) ACV Sample 3: OCTA(l), OCT(r) (d) ACV Sample 4: OCTA(l), OCT(r)

Fig. 3. ACV samples wrongly predicted as AMD from FP/OCTA unimodal training, but correctly predicted as ACV with FAF/OCT unimodal training.

5 Discussion

In this work, we introduced a novel, multimodal dataset aimed at the diagnosis of ACV (versus AMD). Using this resource, we showed that Fundus Autofluorescence (FAF) and Optical Coherence Tomography (OCT) yield superior performance in binary and tertiary classifications compared to Fundus Photography (FP) and OCT Angiography (OCTA). Interestingly, performance was *not improved* by fine-tuning two foundation models on our dataset, which indicates further need for research on optimizing such models for downstream tasks - one potential reason may be that our images are still too much out-of-distribution compared to the source training images.

We also showed that - except for the best-performing FAF modality - bimodal training is beneficial in terms of performance. The fact that none of the bimodal models were able to outperform the unimodal FAF model will need to be explored in future work with a larger dataset. Although our in-house collection constitutes a comparatively large dataset compared to other publicly available resources - and is the only dataset so far explicitly labeling ACV - a larger corpus of data is needed for further research, an effort that is currently underway.

Across all our experiments, we observed several instances in which predicted labels (no matter the modality or fusion method) did not match the human annotations. Given that ACV is a novel pathology, this may suggest issues with the labeling, warranting further research into the annotations. This (automated) method may be used together with the saliency maps (e.g. Fig. 3) to determine whether they are mislabeled or whether these images exhibit additional symptoms that complicate differentiation between AMD and ACV, hence informing clinical practice.

Overall, with our work we have broken new ground for a deeper exploration into ACV as a new pathology to be distinguished from AMD. Our deep learning experiments have yielded first new insights into the modalities that may be important for diagnosis, and have set stage for future inquiries that may lead to significant advancements in both diagnostic and therapeutic strategies for decision-making in retinal diseases.

Acknowledgments. This study was supported by the National Research Foundation (NRF) of Korea under project BK21 FOUR (Fostering Outstanding Universities for Research) and 2022R1A2C2092118, as well as by Institute of Information & Communications Technology Planning & Evaluation (IITP) grants funded by the Korea government (MSIT) (RS-2019-II190079, Department of Artificial Intelligence, Korea University; RS-2021-II212068, Artificial Intelligence Innovation Hub).

Disclosure of Interests. The authors have no competing interests to declare that are relevant to the content of this article.

References

1. Baltrušaitis, T., Ahuja, C., Morency, L.P.: Multimodal machine learning: a survey and taxonomy. IEEE Trans. Pattern Anal. Mach. Intell. **41**(2), 423–443 (2018)
2. Bommasani, R., et al.: On the opportunities and risks of foundation models. arXiv preprint arXiv:2108.07258 (2021)
3. Che, H., Cheng, Y., Jin, H., Chen, H.: Towards generalizable diabetic retinopathy grading in unseen domains. In: International Conference on Medical Image Computing and Computer-Assisted Intervention, pp. 430–440. Springer (2023). https://doi.org/10.1007/978-3-031-43904-9_42
4. Cheung, C.M.G., Lee, W.K., Koizumi, H., Dansingani, K., Lai, T.Y., Freund, K.B.: Pachychoroid disease. Eye **33**(1), 14–33 (2019)
5. Garrity, S.T., Sarraf, D., Freund, K.B., Sadda, S.R.: Multimodal imaging of non-neovascular age-related macular degeneration. Invest. Ophthalmol. Vis. Sci. **59**(4), AMD48–AMD64 (2018)
6. Gulshan, V., et al.: Development and validation of a deep learning algorithm for detection of diabetic retinopathy in retinal fundus photographs. JAMA **316**(22), 2402–2410 (2016)
7. Guymer, R., Wu, Z.: Age-related macular degeneration (AMD): more than meets the eye. the role of multimodal imaging in today's management of AMD-a review. Clin. Exp. Ophthalmol. **48**(7), 983–995 (2020)
8. He, K., Chen, X., Xie, S., Li, Y., Dollár, P., Girshick, R.: Masked autoencoders are scalable vision learners. In: Proceedings of the IEEE/CVF Conference on Computer Vision and Pattern Recognition, pp. 16000–16009 (2022)
9. He, K., Zhang, X., Ren, S., Sun, J.: Deep residual learning for image recognition. In: Proceedings of the IEEE Conference on Computer Vision and Pattern Recognition, pp. 770–778 (2016)

10. He, T., Zhang, Z., Zhang, H., Zhang, Z., Xie, J., Li, M.: Bag of tricks for image classification with convolutional neural networks. In: Proceedings of the IEEE/CVF Conference on Computer Vision and Pattern Recognition, pp. 558–567 (2019)
11. He, X., Deng, Y., Fang, L., Peng, Q.: Multi-modal retinal image classification with modality-specific attention network. IEEE Trans. Med. Imaging **40**(6), 1591–1602 (2021)
12. Hua, R., Zhang, M.: Imaging characteristics of neovascular and atrophic pachychoroidal spectrum diseases. Front. Med. **9**, 891397 (2022)
13. Islam, N.U., Zhou, Z., Gehlot, S., Gotway, M.B., Liang, J.: Seeking an optimal approach for computer-aided diagnosis of pulmonary embolism. Med. Image Anal. **91**, 102988 (2024)
14. Joachim, N., et al.: Ethnic variation in early age-related macular degeneration lesions between white Australians and Singaporean Asians. Invest. Ophthalmol. Vis. Sci. **55**(7), 4421–4429 (2014)
15. Kalamkar, S., et al.: Multimodal image fusion: a systematic review. Decis. Anal. J. **9**, 100327 (2023)
16. Kang, S.W., et al.: Investigation of precursor lesions of polypoidal choroidal vasculopathy using contralateral eye findings. Graefe's Arch. Clin. Exp. Ophthalmol. **255**, 281–291 (2017)
17. Kawasaki, R., et al.: The prevalence of age-related macular degeneration in Asians: a systematic review and meta-analysis. Ophthalmology **117**(5), 921–927 (2010)
18. Kermany, D.S., et al.: Identifying medical diagnoses and treatable diseases by image-based deep learning. cell **172**(5), 1122–1131 (2018)
19. Kim, Y.H., et al.: Optical coherence tomographic features of macular telangiectasia type 2: Korean macular telangiectasia type 2 study-report no. 1. Sci. Rep. **10**(1), 16594 (2020)
20. Kim, Y.H., Lee, B., Kang, E., Oh, J.: Clustering of eyes with age-related macular degeneration or pachychoroid spectrum diseases based on choroidal thickness profile. Sci. Rep. **11**(1), 4999 (2021)
21. Kim, Y.H., Lee, B., Kang, E., Oh, J.: Comparison of regional differences in the choroidal thickness between patients with pachychoroid neovasculopathy and classic exudative age-related macular degeneration. Curr. Eye Res. **46**(9), 1398–1405 (2021)
22. Lee, S.H., Lee, S., Song, B.C.: Vision transformer for small-size datasets. arXiv preprint arXiv:2112.13492 (2021)
23. Liu, Z., Mao, H., Wu, C.Y., Feichtenhofer, C., Darrell, T., Xie, S.: A convnet for the 2020s. In: Proceedings of the IEEE/CVF Conference on Computer Vision and Pattern Recognition, pp. 11976–11986 (2022)
24. Ma, M., Ren, J., Zhao, L., Tulyakov, S., Wu, C., Peng, X.: SMIL: multimodal learning with severely missing modality. In: Proceedings of the AAAI Conference on Artificial Intelligence, vol. 35, pp. 2302–2310 (2021)
25. Radford, A., et al.: Learning transferable visual models from natural language supervision. In: International Conference on Machine Learning, pp. 8748–8763. PMLR (2021)
26. Selvaraju, R.R., Cogswell, M., Das, A., Vedantam, R., Parikh, D., Batra, D.: Gradcam: Visual explanations from deep networks via gradient-based localization. In: Proceedings of the IEEE International Conference on Computer Vision, pp. 618–626 (2017)
27. Silva-Rodriguez, J., Chakor, H., Kobbi, R., Dolz, J., Ayed, I.B.: A foundation language-image model of the retina (flair): encoding expert knowledge in text supervision. arXiv preprint arXiv:2308.07898 (2023)

28. Thakoor, K.A., et al.: a multimodal deep learning system to distinguish late stages of AMD and to compare expert vs. AI ocular biomarkers. Sci. Rep. **12**(1), 2585 (2022)
29. Wang, H., Chen, Y., Ma, C., Avery, J., Hull, L., Carneiro, G.: Multi-modal learning with missing modality via shared-specific feature modelling. In: Proceedings of the IEEE/CVF Conference on Computer Vision and Pattern Recognition, pp. 15878–15887 (2023)
30. Yoo, T.K., Choi, J.Y., Seo, J.G., Ramasubramanian, B., Selvaperumal, S., Kim, D.W.: The possibility of the combination of oct and fundus images for improving the diagnostic accuracy of deep learning for age-related macular degeneration: a preliminary experiment. Med. Biol. Eng. Comput. **57**, 677–687 (2019)
31. Zhang, X., Sivaprasad, S.: Drusen and pachydrusen: the definition, pathogenesis, and clinical significance. Eye **35**(1), 121–133 (2021)
32. Zhou, Y., et al.: A foundation model for generalizable disease detection from retinal images. Nature **622**(7981), 156–163 (2023)

Multimodality Frequency Feature Customized Learning for Pediatric Ventricular Septal Defects Identification

Feifei Jin[1], Cheng Zhao[1], Peng Yang[1], Zhuo Xiang[1], Xunyi Chen[2], Yu Zhang[2], Shumin Fan[2], Luyao Zhou[2], Weiling Chen[2(✉)], Tianfu Wang[1(✉)], and Baiying Lei[1(✉)]

[1] School of Biomedical Engineering, Guangdong Key Laboratory for Biomedical Measurements and Ultrasound Imaging, Shenzhen University, National-Regional Key Technology Engineering Laboratory for Medical Ultrasound, Shenzhen, China
{tfwang,leiby}@szu.edu.cn
[2] Ultrasound Department, Shenzhen Children Hospital, Shenzhen, China
chenwl2007@qq.com

Abstract. Ventricular septal defects (VSD) can be more effectively identified by combining anatomical structural features from 2D grayscale images and blood flow information from Doppler images. Most current algorithms only perform the same operation on features and do not take into account that different frequency features focus on the expression of different information. Starting from the perspective of frequency and multi-modality, this paper designs a method called multimodality frequency feature customized learning (MFCL) for the identification of VSD. Specifically, this paper first constructs a frequency decomposition module (FD) based on the Fourier transform to extract high-frequency and low-frequency features corresponding to different modes. Secondly, this paper designs a cross-pooling fusion Transformer (CPFT) module tailored for multi-modality low-frequency features, which can achieve the fusion of multi-modality global information while reducing computational costs. This paper designs a cross-convolution fusion (CCF) module tailored for multi-modality high-frequency features to achieve the fusion of anatomical structure detail features of 2D grayscale images and blood flow information of color Doppler images. Experimental results show that the proposed algorithm is superior to the comparison methods for VSD identification.

Keywords: VSD Identification · Frequency Decomposition · Cross-pooling Fusion Transformer Module · Cross-convolution Fusion Module

1 Introduction

Ventricular septal defect (VSD) is a birth defect of the heart in which there is a hole in the wall (septum) that separates the two lower chambers of the heart. It is the most common type, accounting for about 50% of all congenital heart diseases [1, 2]. Echocardiography is the preferred diagnostic method for clinical screening of VSD [3]. In clinical practice, doctors usually need to use 2D grayscale images (Gray images), color Doppler images (Doppler images) and other methods to identify VSD. Doctors who identify VSD by only a single modality may make a diagnostic error (Fig. 1). Moreover, the medical level of different hospitals varies greatly, and the differences in professional knowledge and clinical experience of different doctors often lead to misjudgments. Therefore, there is an urgent need to develop an automatic VSD identification solution to improve clinician's screening efficiency.

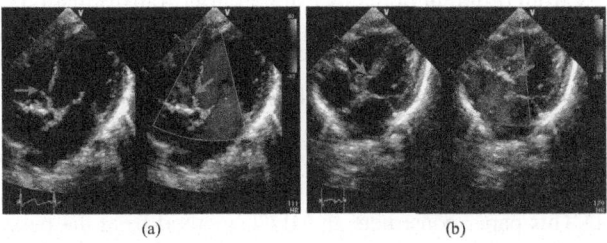

Fig. 1. Examples where VSD cannot be identified with a single modality. (a) Doppler image fails to detect VSD. (b) Gray image fails to detect VSD. Each image pair consists of a Gray image on the left and a Doppler image on the right. Green arrows indicate normal and red arrows indicate VSD.

Convolutional Neural Networks (CNNs) have demonstrated significant capability in various disease identification tasks due to their effectiveness in extracting local detailed features. For example, Liu et al. [4] realized the automatic monitoring of thyroid nodules using a region-based multi-scale detection network; Chen et al. [5] achieved the segmentation of breast lesions by introducing a hybrid adaptive attention module to replace the traditional convolution operation. However, the above methods typically analyze single-modality data and lack effective analysis of multi-modality data. In addition, CNN-based methods often focus on the expression of local features and fail to consider global features. In the task of VSD identification, capturing global information about cardiac structure is crucial. Transformers [6] excel in extracting global features through mechanisms like self-attention and multi-layer perceptron, facilitating effective modeling of large-scale dependencies. However, the computational demands of the multi-head self-attention computing module increase training and inference costs substantially. Therefore, many scholars hope to reduce the computational complexity of the transformer through sampling or window-sliding strategies. Li et al. [7] designed a multi-scale transformer combined with a residual pool connection to reduce the computational complexity. Liu et al. [8] proposed a hierarchical transformer that uses sliding windows to limit self-attention calculations to non-overlapping windows to improve computational efficiency.

In recent years, there has been a growing trend toward leveraging the complementary strengths of CNNs and transformers by cascading them or establishing dual-branch pathways for integration. For example, Peng et al. [9] achieved image recognition and detection by designing feature coupling units to fuse local features and global representations. Wu et al. [10] introduced FAT-Net, a feature-adaptive transformer network with a dual-encoder architecture tailored for skin disease segmentation. The methods mentioned above apply the same operations to all features of the input data. However, different frequency features are inclined to convey distinct types of information. Therefore, it is crucial to consider how to express specific information with different frequency features. Fourier transformation can convert signals in the time domain into signals in the frequency domain, thus facilitating the separation of frequency features. Huang et al. [11] recognized retinal images by exchanging low-frequency information in the spectrum images of images from different domains using Fourier transformation. Wu et al. [12] designed a hybrid domain feature learning module based on the Fast Fourier Convolution Pyramid to classify medical image datasets.

Inspired by the aforementioned work, this paper introduces a multi-modality frequency feature customized learning (MFCL) method to identify the VSD, which combines the spectral analysis characteristics of the Fourier transform and the complementary advantages of convolution and transformer. The following are the contributions of this paper: (1) This paper constructs an MFCL method from the perspective of frequency decomposition and multi-modality fusion to improve the VSD identification accuracy. (2) Leveraging the cross-pooling fusion Transformer module (CPFT) and the cross-convolution fusion module (CCF), this paper separately learns different modalities' low-frequency global features and high-frequency local detail features. (3) This paper constructed a new multi-modality dataset (5CH) for achieving VSD identification and validated the efficacy of MFCL.

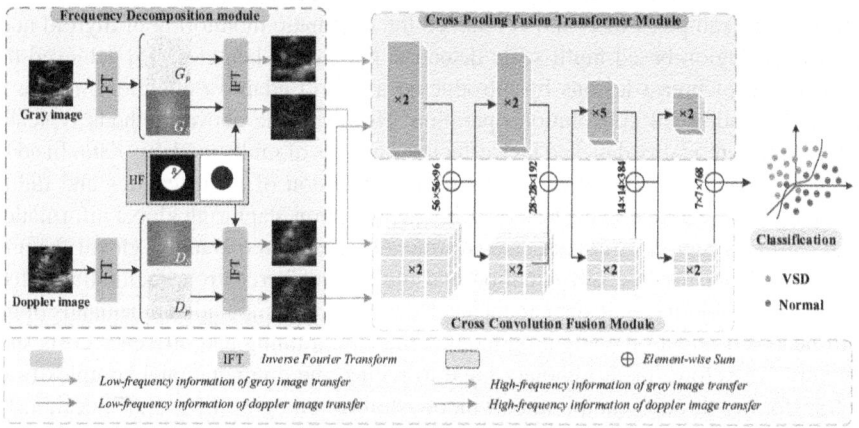

Fig. 2. The framework of MFCL. R represents the measure of low-frequency pass-through. A larger R indicates that more low-frequency information is retained in the low-frequency filtering. (G_S, D_S) represents spectrogram. (G_P, D_P) represents phase map.

2 Methodology

Figure 2 shows the overall framework of the proposed method MFCL. Due to the involvement of multimodal ultrasound data in this paper, it starts with the enhancement of multimodal features. First, this paper constructs a frequency decomposition (FD) module based on the Fourier transform to extract high-frequency (G_h, D_h) features and low-frequency (G_l, D_l) features corresponding to an original Gray image $\mathcal{G}$ and a Doppler image D. These features are used subsequently for learning anatomical structure edge characteristics and color Doppler flow information. Subsequently, considering that low-frequency components often reflect the global information from the original data and high-frequency components enhance local detailed features, this paper uses the CPFT branch to enhance the learning of low-frequency features and the CCF branch to integrate high-frequency features. These branches serve as fundamental units in constructing a parallel network structure. Finally, dual-branch features are combined to achieve the identification task of VSD.

For FD module, the radius $R_D = (H_{in} + W_{in})/64$, $R_G = (H_{in} + W_{in})/32$ of the filters, $H_{in} = W_{in} = 224$. For CPFT branch and CCF branch, each branch consists of four stages taking $F_l \in \mathbb{R}^{H \times W \times C}$ as the input of CPFT branch, taking $F_h \in \mathbb{R}^{H \times W \times C}$ as the input of CCF branch. For each stage, $H = W = [224, 56, 28, 14]$, $C = [6, 96, 192, 384]$ [6, 96, 192, 384]. For stage 1, $F_l = CAT(G_l, D_l), F_h = CAT(G_h, D_h)$. The input $F_l = F_h$ for stages 2–4 is the output of the previous stage.

2.1 Frequency Decomposition Module

Compared to performing the same operation on all features to learn local or global information, this paper uses Fourier transform and hybrid filters as the basic units to build an FD module to extract low-frequency global features and high-frequency local features (See Fig. 2 on the left for details). This paper first performs the Fourier transform on the input $\mathcal{G}$ and D, and obtains the spectrogram (G_S, D_S) and phase map (G_p, D_p) corresponding to different modalities. This paper then performs a hybrid filtering operation on the spectrograms of different modalities, in which low-pass filtering (f_l^G, f_l^D) is used to extract the low-frequency components corresponding to the original data, and high-pass filtering (f_h^G, f_h^D) is used to extract the high-frequency components of the original data. Finally, different frequency characteristics and phase images are used as the input of the inverse Fourier transform to obtain the high-frequency information (G_h, D_h) and low-frequency information (G_l, D_l) corresponding to the original data. The specific implementation definition is as follows:

$$D_S, D_p = FT(D) \tag{1}$$

$$\int_l^D, \int_h^D = HF(R_D) \tag{2}$$

$$D_h = IFT((D_S \times f_h^D), D_p) \tag{3}$$

$$D_l = IFT((D_s \times f_l^D), D_p) \tag{4}$$

$$G_S, G_p = FT(G) \quad (5)$$

$$\int_l^G, \int_h^G = HF(R_G) \quad (6)$$

$$G_h = IFT((G_s \times f_h^G), G_p) \quad (7)$$

$$G_l = IFFT((G_s \times f_l^G), G_p) \quad (8)$$

where $FT(\cdot)$ is fourier transform, $IFT(\cdot)$ is inverse fourier transform, $HF(\cdot)$ is circular hybrid filter, R_D, R_G are the radius of the circular hybrid filter.

2.2 Cross-Pooling Fusion Transformer Module

To reduce the computational burden of the transformer and enhance the interactive learning of multi-modality low-frequency features, this paper constructs a CPFT module.

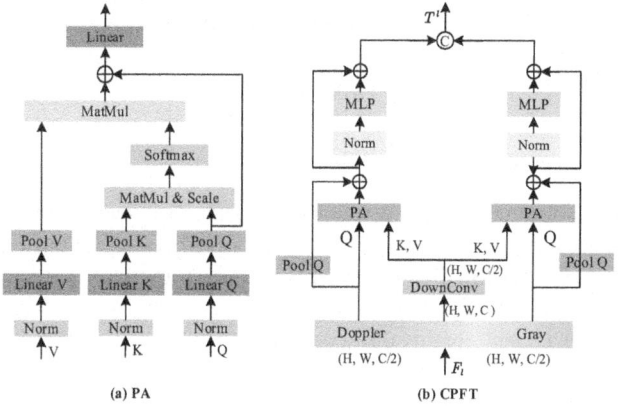

Fig. 3. (a)The architecture of PA module. (b)The architecture of CPFT module. H, W, C represent the height, width and number of channels of the input features.

This paper applies pooling attention (PA) in CPFT, which is in Fig. 3 (a). PA uses pooling operations to replace the linear transformation in the original transformer to reduce the amount of calculation and increase the information flow by adding residual pooling connections of the query vectors. The specific implementation definition is as follows:

$$Q' = P_Q(QW_Q), K' = P_K(KW_K), V' = P_V(VW_V) \quad (9)$$

$$PA(Q', K', V') = \text{Softmax}\left(Q'K'/\sqrt{D}\right)V' + Q' \quad (10)$$

where P_Q, P_K, P_V represent pooling operation. Softmax($\cdot$) denotes the softmax function along the spatial dimension. $Q, K, V \in \mathbb{R}^{N \times D}$ are query, key, value (N is the sequence length, D is the embedding feature dimension). $W_Q, W_K, W_V \in \mathbb{R}^{D \times D}$ are parameters that can be learned in the network. The length N of $Q', K', V' \in \mathbb{R}^{\tilde{N} \times D}$ can be reduced by P_Q, P_K, P_V.

In this module, features F_l of two modalities are taken as query vectors D_q, G_q, key vectors D_k, G_k, value vectors D_v, G_v are generated in a convolution manner, enabling direct interaction between different modalities. As illustrated in Fig. 3(b), the implementation definition is as follows:

$$D_q, G_q = Split(F_l) \tag{11}$$

$$D_k = D_v = G_k = G_v = DeConv(F_l) \tag{12}$$

$$T_D^l = PA(D_q, D_k, D_v) + P_Q(D_q) \tag{13}$$

$$\hat{T}_D^l = mlp\left(norm\left(T_D^l\right)\right) + T_D^l \tag{14}$$

$$T_G^l = PA(G_q, G_k, G_v) + P_Q(G_q) \tag{15}$$

$$\hat{T}_G^l = mlp\left(norm\left(T_G^l\right)\right) + T_G^l \tag{16}$$

$$T^l = CAT(\hat{T}_D^l, \hat{T}_G^l) \tag{17}$$

where $Split(\cdot)$ is split into two parts along channel, $CAT(\cdot)$ is a cascade operation, $norm(\cdot)$ is a layer normalization operation, $mlp(\cdot)$ is multilayer perceptron in vit [6].

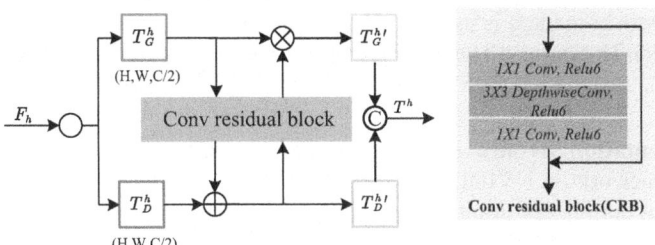

Fig. 4. The architecture of the CCF module.

2.3 Cross Convolution Fusion Module

CCF module takes advantage of convolution to extract local detailed features and takes multi-modality high-frequency features $F_h \in \mathbb{R}^{H \times W \times C}$ as input, see Fig. 4 for details. It first uses the convolution residual block (CRB) to fuse the cardiac structural features of the ultrasound image into the Doppler blood flow features to enhance the multi-modality high-frequency features. The high-frequency Doppler features $\left(T_D^{h'}\right)$ that combine structural features and blood flow information are then back-propagated to the grayscale features to enhance the low-frequency features of echocardiography $\left(T_G^{h'}\right)$. Finally, $T_D^{h'}$ and $T_G^{h'}$ are connected through cat operation to obtain the fused bimodal information. The specific implementation definition is as follows:

$$T_G^h, T_D^h = Split(F_h) \tag{18}$$

$$T_D^{h'} = CRB(T_G^h) + T_D^h \tag{19}$$

$$T_G^{h'} = T_G^h \odot \exp\left(CRB\left(T_D^{h'}\right)\right) \tag{20}$$

$$T^h = CAT(T_G^h, T_D^h) \tag{21}$$

where • represents the Hadamard product, $CRB(\cdot)$ is conv operation.

3 Experiments and Results

3.1 Experimental Setup

Dataset. This paper uses a multi-modality five-chamber section dataset (5CH) of the pediatric heart as analysis data, which are Gray images and Doppler images of patients aged 1–12 years collected from Shenzhen Children's Hospital. The 5CH dataset includes video sequences of 443 patients, which are converted into image frames for analysis. Specifically, the paper uses a total of 8141 image frames for training, consisting of 4769 normal image frames and 3372 VSD image frames. Additionally, 2015 image frames are reversed for testing, with 1226 normal image frames and 789 VSD image frames. In data preprocessing, the paper crops the image and reduces it to 224 × 224 pixels. The five-fold crossover method is used for training learning in the training set.

Evaluation Indicators. The paper selects four indicators including Accuracy (Acc), F1-score(F1), Sensitivity (Sen), and Specificity (Spe) to analyze the classification performance.

Implementation Details. All experiments are implemented by configuring the PyTorch framework on NVIDIA GTX 1080Ti GPU with 11 GB of memory. ADAM is used as the optimizer during the training process. The initial learning rate is set to 1e-4, the momentum is set to 0.99, and the training epoch is 25. At the same time, focal loss is selected as the loss function.

Comparison Methods. This paper selects eight open-source classification models with similar model parameters for comparative methods, which include 3 CNN algorithms (MobileNetV2 [13], Shufflenet [14], Efficientnet [15]), 4 Transformer algorithms (Vit [6], Mvit-v2 [7], Swin-T [8], P2T [16]), 1 algorithm that combines CNN and transformer (Conformer [9]). This paper concatenates the Gray image and Doppler image in the channel dimension to achieve modal fusion and uses the fused features as the input of the contrast methods. To ensure the fairness of the experiments, this paper shares the same operating environment and hyperparameters and uses the same training, validation, and test sets based on previous literature.

3.2 Classification Results of Different Algorithms

To evaluate the classification performance of the proposed algorithm, the receiver operating characteristic (ROC) curves of different algorithms are illustrated in Fig. 5(b), with the gray-green curve representing our method. Our method achieves the highest area under the curve (AUC) of 0.94, outperforming all other comparative methods. Furthermore, Fig. 5(a) presents the histograms of various performance metrics for the different methods. It is clear that the proposed method consistently surpasses other algorithms across all evaluated metrics. The visualization of Grad-CAM is shown in Fig. 6. It demonstrates that our method can more accurately pinpoint regions in the image that are relevant to the category.

To observe the distribution of objective indicators more intuitively, the experimental results are shown in Table 1. Compared with the classification results of using CNN or Transformer alone, the multi-branch structure, which combines the advantages of CNN and Transformer, has better feature representation capabilities. The classification accuracy of our algorithm is approximately 3.72% higher than the Efficientnet network (81.69% vs. 85.41%) and 3.91% higher than the Mvit-v2 network (81.50% vs. 85.41%). In the classification framework that combines CNN and Transformer, the classification accuracy of our network is 0.9% higher than that of the Conformer network (84.61% vs. 85.51%), and our algorithm is 6.02% higher than the Conformer network in the Sensitivity indicator (78.72% vs. 73.70%). Overall, our proposed method achieves the best performance in the VSD identification task.

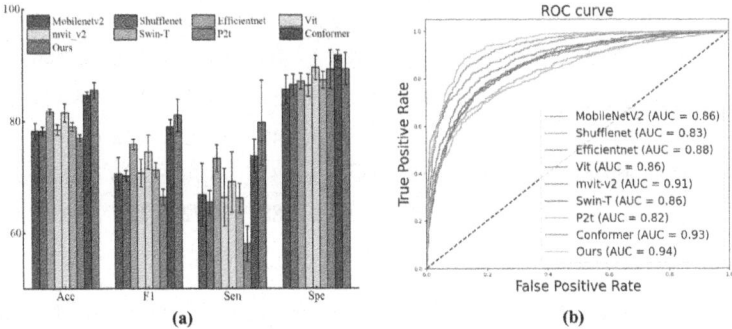

Fig. 5. (a) The histograms of evaluation indicators for the different methods. (b) The ROC curves for the comparative methods.

3.3 Ablation Experiment

As shown in Table 2, we evaluate the impact of each component FD, CPFT, and CCF on the proposed algorithm. Using both the CPFT module and the CCF modules, Acc and Sen reached 84.67% and 77.31%. After adding the FD module, Acc and Sen increased by 0.84% and 2.41% respectively. The above combination achieves an Acc of 85.51% and a Sen of 79.72%. Additionally, we investigated the capabilities of the CPFT and

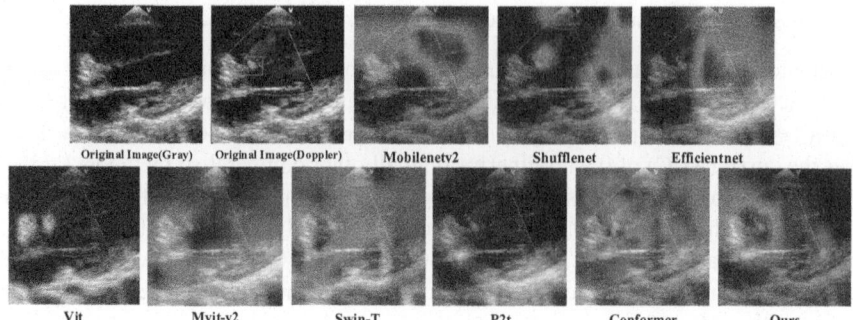

Fig. 6. Grad-CAM highlights the discriminative regions for identifying VSD and Normal cases. Red regions correspond to high scores for class. The red box in the original image marks the observation location of VSD.

Table 1. Identification performance of different methods.

Category	Method	Acc	F1	Sen	Spe
CNN	MobileNetV2 [13]	78.23 ± 1.44	70.52 ± 2.91	66.77 ± 5.58	85.61 ± 2.51
	Shufflenet [14]	78.22 ± 0.76	70.18 ± 0.93	65.45 ± 2.08	86.44 ± 1.92
	Efficientnet [15]	81.69 ± 0.47	75.81 ± 0.89	73.31 ± 2.38	87.09 ± 1.42
Transformer	Vit [6]	78.49 ± 0.90	70.65 ± 2.47	66.33 ± 5.10	86.32 ± 1.99
	Mvit-v2 [7]	81.50 ± 1.61	74.43 ± 3.08	69.07 ± 5.39	89.49 ± 2.14
	Swin-T [8]	79.03 ± 0.75	71.18 ± 1.31	66.21 ± 2.60	87.28 ± 1.52
	P2t [16]	76.97 ± 0.65	66.38 ± 1.45	58.05 ± 3.12	89.15 ± 3.45
CNN + Transformer	Conformer [9]	84.61 ± 0.59	78.96 ± 1.31	73.70 ± 2.96	**91.68 ± 0.93**
	Ours	**85.51 ± 1.37**	**81.03 ± 2.88**	**79.72 ± 7.57**	89.23 ± 2.90

CCF modules in learning high-frequency and low-frequency features, as illustrated in Table 3. The results indicate that the CPFT module excels in extracting low-frequency features, whereas the CCF module demonstrates superior performance in high-frequency feature extraction. The result aligns with our expectations regarding the respective roles of transformer and conv operation in feature extraction.

The results of ablation experiments using Gray images alone, Doppler images alone, and both images simultaneously for classification tasks are shown in Table 4. The results show that better performance can be achieved by using data from both modalities simultaneously. In addition, it was observed that the classification results using gray images alone were poor, which we believe is related to the small gap of VSD that is difficult to distinguish.

Table 2. Structural ablation experimental analysis

FD	CPFT	CCF	Acc	F1	Sen	Spe
	✓		81.50 ± 1.61	74.43 ± 3.08	81.01 ± 2.57	69.07 ± 5.39
		✓	83.58 ± 0.34	78.48 ± 0.99	80.64 ± 1.37	76.52 ± 3.04
	✓	✓	84.67 ± 0.21	79.79 ± 0.04	82.45 ± 1.34	77.31 ± 1.25
✓	✓	✓	**85.51 ± 1.37**	**81.03 ± 2.88**	**82.93 ± 2.93**	**79.72 ± 7.57**

Table 3. Input feature ablation experimental analysis (H represents high-frequency features, L represents low-frequency features)

CPFT	CCF	Acc	F1	Sen	Spe
H	L	84.53 ± 0.76	80.54 ± 0.97	81.78 ± 2.98	86.30 ± 2.24
L	H	**85.51 ± 1.37**	**81.03 ± 2.88**	79.72 ± 7.57	**89.23 ± 2.90**

Table 4. Modality ablation experimental analysis

Gray	Doppler	Acc	F1	Sen	Spe
✓		55.73 ± 2.43	45.58 ± 4.05	44.10 ± 2.13	47.82 ± 9.08
	✓	84.34 ± 0.18	79.99 ± 1.45	80.12 ± 3.46	**80.16 ± 6.36**
✓	✓	**85.51 ± 1.37**	**81.03 ± 2.88**	**82.93 ± 2.93**	79.72 ± 7.57

4 Discussion

In this paper, we initially explore the potential of using filtering to address the challenges of dual-modality fusion. However, certain limitations still deserve further attention. In the FD module, we have chosen specific filter sizes $R_G = (H_{in} + W_{in})/32$ for Gray images and $R_D = (H_{in} + W_{in})/64$ for Doppler images, as illustrated in Fig. 7. It is evident that as R decreases, the Doppler flow information contained in D_h gradually increases, while the anatomical structure information in G_h also increases. Additionally, the global information contained in D_l and G_l progressively increases. Although reasonable, this approach may not be optimal, as different combinations of filter sizes could potentially yield better separation of information. These limitations are the motivation for our future research.

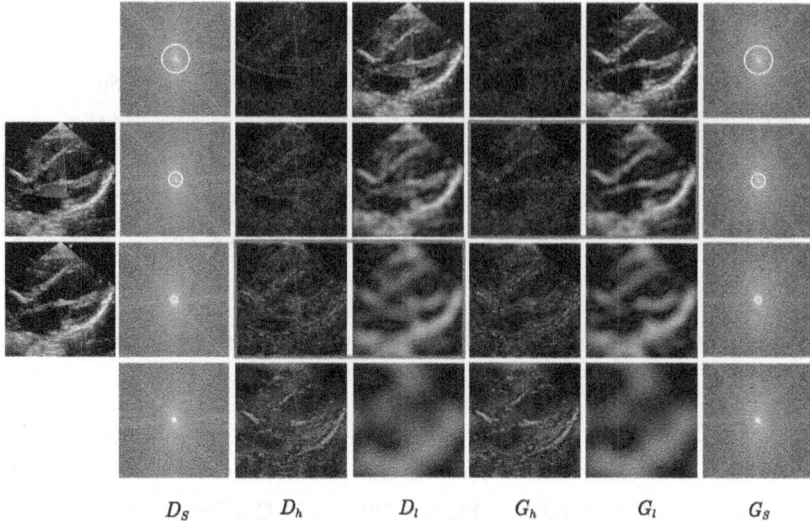

Fig. 7. Comparison of the filtering effects of two modalities under different filters. In each column, from top to bottom, the radii of filters are 1/16, 1/32, 1/64, 1/128 of $(H_{in} + W_{in})$. The white circle represents the size of the filter. The red boxes represent the results obtained from the original images after applying specific filters selected in this paper.

5 Conclusion

This paper proposes a novel MFCL for the identification of VSD. The proposed algorithm extracts different frequency features through the FD module and then realizes the fusion of multi-modality global information through the CPFT module. It combines anatomical structure detailed features with blood flow information using the CCF module. The experimental results verified the effectiveness of MFCL in identifying VSD.

Acknowledgments. This work was supported by the National Natural Science Foundation of Guangdong Province (No.2022A1515110704), Postdoctoral Science Foundation of China (2023M732358), National Natural Science Foundation of China(62301329, 62071309, 62371312).

References

1. Hoffman, J.I., et al.: The incidence of congenital heart disease. J. Am. Coll. Cardiol. **39**(12), 1890–1900 (2002)
2. Mitchell, S., et al.: Congenital heart disease in 56,109 births incidence and natural history. Circulation **43**(3), 323–332 (1971)
3. Liu, S., et al.: Deep learning in medical ultrasound analysis: a review. Engineering **5**(2), 261–275 (2019)
4. Liu, T., et al.: Automated detection and classification of thyroid nodules in ultrasound images using clinical-knowledge-guided convolutional neural networks. Med. Image Anal. **58**, 101555 (2019)

5. Chen, G., et al.: AAU-net: an adaptive attention U-net for breast lesions segmentation in ultra-sound images. IEEE Trans. Med. Imaging **42**(5), 1289–1300 (2022)
6. Dosovitskiy A, et al.: An image is worth 16x16 words: transformers for image recognition at scale. arXiv preprint arXiv:2010.11929 (2020)
7. Li Y, et al.: Mvitv2: Improved multiscale vision transformers for classification and detection. In: Proceedings of the IEEE/CVF Conference on Computer Vision and Pattern Recognition, pp. 4804–4814. New Orleans (2022)
8. Liu Z, et al.: Swin transformer: Hierarchical vision transformer using shifted windows. In: Proceedings of the IEEE/CVF International Conference on Computer Vision, pp. 10012–22 (2021)
9. Peng, Z., et al.: Conformer: Local features coupling global representations for recognition and detection. IEEE Trans. Pattern Anal. Mach. Intell. **45**(8), 9454–9468 (2023)
10. Wu, H., et al.: FAT-Net: Feature adaptive transformers for automated skin lesion segmentation. Med. Image Anal. **76**, 102327 (2022)
11. Huang Y, et al.: Fourier test-time adaptation with multi-level consistency for robust classification. arXiv preprint arXiv:2306.02544 (2023)
12. Han, Q., et al.: EHDFL: Evolutionary hybrid domain feature learning based on windowed fast Fourier convolution pyramid for medical image classification. Comput. Biol. Med. **152**, 106353 (2023)
13. Sandler M, et al.: Mobilenetv2: Inverted residuals and linear bottlenecks. In: Proceedings of the IEEE Conference on Computer Vision and Pattern Recognition, pp. 4510–20 (2018)
14. Zhang X, et al.: Shufflenet: An extremely efficient convolutional neural network for mobile devices. In: Proceedings of the IEEE Conference on Computer Vision and Pattern Recognition, pp. 6848–56 (2018)
15. Koonce B, et al.: EfficientNet. Convolutional Neural Networks with Swift for Tensorflow: Image Recognition and Dataset Categorization, pp. 109–23 (2021). https://doi.org/10.1007/978-1-4842-6168-2
16. Wu, Y.-H., et al.: P2T: Pyramid pooling transformer for scene understanding. IEEE Trans. Pattern Anal. Mach. Intell. **45**(11), 12760–12771 (2022)

Author Index

A
Adeli, Ehsan 198
Ahn, Somin 235
Ang, Gabriella 26
Ardon, Roberto 75
Arias-Vergara, Tomás 147

B
Bai, Wenjia 52
Basaran, Berke Doga 52
Beets-Tan, Regina 101
Bercea, Cosmin I. 113
Bert, Christoph 147
Bian, Chang 184
Bian, Zhangxing 157
Bodalal, Zuhir 101
Boellaard, Thierry N. 101
Bucho, Teresa M. T. 101

C
Cabezas, Mariano 136
Cagol, Alessandro 38
Calamante, Fernando 136
Chaptoukaev, Hava 170
Charachon, Martin 75
Chen, Rui 124
Chen, Weiling 248
Chen, Xunyi 248
Cho, Daehyun 235
Colinco, Alexa Gail 157
Cootes, Tim 184
Cuadra, Meritxell Bach 38

D
d'Angremont, Emile 3
Davoudi, Neda 223
Demler, Olga 223
Denner, Stefan 64
Dewey, Blake E. 157
Dickmann, Jannis 147
Disch, Nico Albert 15

F
Fan, Shumin 248
Farshad, Azade 198
Felsner, Lina 113
Feng, Anqi 157
Fergie, Martin 184
Fu, Xiaoyong 124

G
Galati, Francesco 170
Gordaliza, Pedro M. 38
Granziera, Cristina 38
Gutman, Boris A. 3

H
He, Rosemary 26
Hofmann, Christian 147
Huang, Yuqing 223
Hudelot, Céline 75

I
Isensee, Fabian 64

J
Ji, Zizhen 124
Jin, Feifei 248

K
Kelly, Brendan S. 88
Khan, Adnan 211
Killeen, Ronan P 88
Kim, Su Hwan 113
Kim, Young Ho 235
Kirchhoff, Yannick 64
Kleesiek, Jens 15, 64
Kovacs, Balint 64

L
Lawlor, Aonghus 88
Lee, Jiah 136

Lei, Baiying 248
Li, Jun 113
Li, Sheng 124
Lorenzi, Marco 3
Lüpke, Sven 198
Lv, Jinglei 136

M
Maggi, Pietro 38
Maier, Andreas 147
Maier-Hein, Klaus 15, 64
Marcianó, Vincenzo 170
Mathur, Prateek 88
Matthews, Paul M. 52
Menze, Bjoern 223
Molchanova, Nataliia 38
Müller, Philip 113

N
Navab, Nassir 198
Nguyen-Kim, Thi D. L. 101

O
Oh, Jaeryung 235

P
Peretzke, Robin 15
Phillips, Beth 184
Prince, Jerry L. 157

Q
Qiu, Pinyu 124

R
Rokuss, Maximilian R. 64
Roy, Saikat 15, 64
Rueckert, Daniel 113

S
Schnabel, Julia A. 113
Schwarz, Annette 147
Shaaban, Mai A. 211
Stiefelhagen, Rainer 15

Sun, Yifei 136
Szkitsak, Juliane 147

T
Tan, Jun 124
Taveira, Mateus 101
Trebeschi, Stefano 101
Tward, Daniel 26

U
Ulrich, Constantin 15, 64

V
Viani, Alessandro 3
Vollmuth, Philipp 64

W
Wald, Tassilo 64
Wallraven, Christian 235
Wang, Chenyu 136
Wang, Tianfu 248
Wiestler, Benedikt 113
Wittmann, Bastian 223
Wynen, Maxence 38

X
Xiang, Zhuo 248

Y
Yang, Peng 248
Yaqub, Mohammad 211
Yassine, Walid 75
Yeganeh, Yousef 198

Z
Zenk, Maximilian 64
Zhang, Wei 136
Zhang, Xinru 52
Zhang, Yu 248
Zhao, Cheng 248
Zhou, Luyao 248
Zhuo, Jiachen 157
Zimmerer, David 15
Zuluaga, Maria A. 170

The manufacturer's authorised representative in the EU is Springer Nature Customer Service Centre GmbH, Europaplatz 3, 69115 Heidelberg, Germany. If you have any concerns regarding our products, please contact ProductSafety@springernature.com

Printed and bound by CPI Group (UK) Ltd, Croydon, CR0 4YY

25/03/2026

02078191-0012